THE EXTINCT SCENE

MODERNIST LATITUDES

MODERNIST LATITUDES

JESSICA BERMAN AND PAUL SAINT-AMOUR, EDITORS

Modernist Latitudes aims to capture the energy and ferment of modernist studies by continuing to open up the range of forms, locations, temporalities, and theoretical approaches encompassed by the field. The series celebrates the growing latitude ("scope for freedom of action or thought") that this broadening affords scholars of modernism, whether they are investigating little-known works or revisiting canonical ones. Modernist Latitudes will pay particular attention to the texts and contexts of those latitudes (Africa, Latin America, Australia, Asia, Southern Europe, and even the rural United States) that have long been misrecognized as ancillary to the canonical modernisms of the global North.

Barry McCrea, *In the Company of Strangers: Family and Narrative in Dickens, Conan Doyle, Joyce, and Proust*, 2011

Jessica Berman, *Modernist Commitments: Ethics, Politics, and Transnational Modernism*, 2011

Jennifer Scappettone, *Killing the Moonlight: Modernism in Venice*, 2014

Nico Israel, *Spirals: The Whirled Image in Twentieth-Century Literature and Art*, 2015

Carrie J. Noland, *Voices of Negritude in Modernist Print: Aesthetic Subjectivity, Diaspora, and the Lyric Regime*, 2015

Susan Stanford Friedman, *Planetary Modernisms: Provocations on Modernity Across Time*, 2015

THE EXTINCT SCENE

LATE MODERNISM
AND EVERYDAY LIFE

THOMAS S. DAVIS

COLUMBIA UNIVERSITY PRESS

NEW YORK

Publication subvention grant from the College of Arts and Sciences at the Ohio State University. Portions of this book initially appeared as articles in *Literature Compass, Twentieth Century Literature,* and *Textual Practice.* They are reprinted here with permission. I would also like to thank the editorial boards at those journals for valuing my work and for finding readers that asked hard questions. Sian White and Pamela Thurschwell were kind enough to include me in their special issue of *Textual Practice* on Elizabeth Bowen.

Auden, W. H. "Spain 1937," copyright © 1940 and copyright renewed 1968 by W. H. Auden; from *Selected Poems* by W. H. Auden, edited by Edward Mendelson. Used by permission of Vintage Books, an imprint of the Knopf Doubleday Publishing Group, a division of Random House LLC. All rights reserved.

Auden, W. H. "Musée des Beaux Arts," copyright © 1940 and renewed 1968 by W. H. Auden; from *Selected Poems* by W. H. Auden. Used by permission of Random House, an imprint and division of Random House LLC. All rights reserved.

H. D. (Hilda Doolittle) from *Trilogy* copyright ©1945 by Oxford University Press; Copyright renewed 1973 by Norman Holmes Pearson. Reprinted by permission of New Directions Publishing Corp and Pollinger Limited.

MacNeice, Louis. *Collected Poems.* Ed. Peter McDonald. London: Faber and Faber, 2007. Reprinted with permission of David Higham and Associates.

Auden, W. H. "Musée des Beaux Arts," "Spain 1937," "The Voyage," "Hong Kong," "In Time of War." Copyright ©1937, 1939, 1940 by W. H. Auden, renewed. Reprinted by permission of Curtis Brown, Ltd.

Columbia University Press
Publishers Since 1893
New York   Chichester, West Sussex
cup.columbia.edu
Copyright © 2016 Columbia University Press
All rights reserved

Library of Congress Cataloging-in-Publication Data
Davis, Thomas S. (Thomas Saverance)
The extinct scene : late modernism and everyday life / Thomas S. Davis.
    pages   cm. — (Modernist latitudes)
Includes bibliographical references and index.
ISBN 978-0-231-16942-4 (cloth : acid-free paper) — ISBN 978-0-231-53788-9 (electronic)
1. English literature—20th century—History and criticism.   2. Modernism (Literature)—Great Britain.   3. Literature and society—England—History—20th century.   I. Title.
PR478.M6D38 2016
820.9'112—dc23

                                                         2015005493

COVER DESIGNER: Archie Ferguson
COVER IMAGE: © Henry Moore, *War: Possible Subjects* (1940–41). Reproduced by permission of the Henry Moore foundation.

FOR MAYA AND GAEL

CONTENTS

ACKNOWLEDGMENTS

MOST FIRST SCHOLARLY books and the questions that animate them take shape in graduate school. This one began elsewhere, notably in an underground punk and hardcore scene in the mid to late 1990s where DIY music, leftist politics, queer and feminist thought, creative activism, and living-as-art intermingled freely. From that community I learned about the power of art and music to emancipate marginalized individuals, to generate collective action, and to transform everyday life. It was also there that I first heard the name Guy Debord. I quickly became convinced that art could reveal things about everyday life and possibly help us conceptualize the political and social pressures that shape what and how we think. I carried that conviction into graduate school and turned it into something of a question, one perhaps bearing the traces of age, skepticism, and disappointment: If art bears any relationship to everyday life, what is it? How does that relationship morph over time? I don't know that I found a perfect answer, but this book was one way to think through that and to do so by living with a handful of artists that I loved and came to love.

Of course, questions don't emerge or develop in solitude. I was fortunate to have colleagues and mentors that truly shaped my intellectual development and political commitments. Maud Ellmann, Luke Gibbons, and Barbara Green not only increased my interest in modernism, they demonstrated the importance of methodology, of asking fruitful questions and thinking at once historically and theoretically. I learned an enormous amount simply by observing them and listening to them. Kevin Hart cultivated my interest in philosophies of everyday life, making Maurice Blanchot a permanent—one might say infinite—part of my life. He provided wonderful guidance throughout the development of this project and managed to describe philosophical debates with unparalleled clarity. Jerry Bruns took a semester and read Walter Benjamin, Martin Heidegger, and Theodor Adorno with me; much of what I think about art goes back to those weekly conversations. Conversations with Marlene Daut Zaka, Juan Sanchez, Nathan Hensley, and Jay Miller were all important, and they became my most trusted interlocutors and remain dear friends. Nathan has likely read more of this manuscript than anyone else, and our conversations about it over the years have made it all the better.

My intellectual home at Ohio State University has provided an incredibly nurturing environment. Several colleagues read and commented on drafts, offered advice in research and professional matters, or simply engaged me in conversations that helped this project in ways they probably do not realize. I can but name them here (and I am sure this list is incomplete): Chad Allen, Jonathan Buehl, David Brewer, Molly Farrell, Jill Galvan, Aman Garcha, David Herman, Pranav Jani, Koritha Mitchell, Steve Kern and the Modernism Working Group, Ethan Knapp, Leslie Lockett, Sandra MacPherson, Brian McHale, Debra Moddelmog, Sean O'Sullivan, Jim Phelan, Joe Ponce, Jesse Schotter, Antony Shuttleworth, and Robyn Warhol. Friends and colleagues in modernist studies have been more than generous with their time and advice. Amy Clukey, Jed Esty, James Gifford, Janice Ho, Aaron Jaffe, Marina MacKay, Allan Hepburn, Jesse Matz, Liesl Olson, Peter Kalliney, Nicole Rizzuto, Stephen Ross, Aarthi Vadde, and Tim Wientzen either read chapters, discussed ideas and problems with me that are central to this book, or simply offered encouragement at times when it was needed most. As this project came to a close, Chris Holmes, Jennifer Spitzer, and Aarthi Vadde gave me the opportunity to share some of these ideas at the Global Modernisms Symposium in Ithaca, New York. Paul Saint-Amour and Jessica Berman have demonstrated confidence in this project all along and offered more kindness and encouragement than I had any reason to expect. Philip Leventhal has provided expert editorial advice (and admirable patience!) along the way, often helping me navigate and weather some of the complexities of book production. I thank, too, the anonymous readers that Paul, Jessica, and Philip selected. Their commentary and criticism was extraordinarily incisive and helpful.

Librarians played a crucial role in the assemblage of my archive. The staff at the Mass Observation archive at the University of Sussex helped me sort through an unimaginably large set of materials. The librarians and archivists at the Imperial War Museum, Tate Britain, the British Film Institute, the Harold Washington Library in Chicago, the Newberry Library, and the University of Rochester Special Collections were all attentive, provided guidance, and helped me unearth new materials. Kate Hutchens and the staff at Special Collections at the University of Michigan provided last-minute assistance with some material from *Picture Post*. I am also grateful to Trey Conatser and Amy Spears at the Digital Media Project at OSU for their help. My ability to travel and conduct research in these libraries was greatly assisted by a faculty grant from the Mershon Center for International Security Studies.

Many of my arguments and assumptions were challenged, revised, and clarified during conversations with very bright undergraduate and graduate students. I will always be grateful to the students in my undergraduate seminars on late modernism in 2010 and 2014 and to all of the graduate students who participated in my seminars at Ohio State.

My family has supported even the craziest of my endeavors for so long that I grew accustomed to relying on them when I began this project in graduate school. Josie, Tommy, and Amy have all of my love and gratitude. Drew Katchen has been a lifelong interlocutor and friend, swapping colored vinyl and books of poems with me long before we knew how enduring the words of others would be in our lives. Maya Chavez has contributed to the writing of this book in innumerable ways, but it is her biting wit and boundless love that have made everyday life far from routine. Our son Gael was born as I wrapped up work on this book, and his smiles and cries have enchanted our lives in ways we never thought possible.

THE EXTINCT SCENE

INTRODUCTION

LATE MODERNISM AND THE OUTWARD TURN

IN THE PREFACE to her volume of short fiction from the Second World War, Elizabeth Bowen apologizes for not giving "'straight' pictures of the British wartime scene."[1] Her readers will find no harrowing portrayals of air raids and no heroism from the civilians of the so-called People's War; instead Bowen recreates the "war climate" of a besieged city where the routines, habits, and affective dimensions of everyday life are turned inside out. In Bowen's war city, the simple acts of buying flowers and reading acquire the most extraordinary significance while "a bomb on your house was as inexpedient, but not more abnormal, than a cold in your head."[2] In her 1941 story "In the Square" Bowen tracks these changes in everyday life and openly wonders if they are ciphers for something else. In the story's opening scene, Rupert, recently returned to wartime London, steps out of a taxi and into a windswept, vacant city square. Shuttered and glassless windows stare out from Blitz-damaged buildings. The square is newly awash in late sunlight, "able to enter brilliantly at a point where three of the houses had been bombed away."[3] Bowen's narrator dubs this urban dead zone "the extinct scene" (609): empty, depopulated, eerily still. For Rupert, this place is still familiar. He remembers it as the setting for dinner parties "on many summer evenings before" (609). Despite its ruinous appearance, "the square's acoustics had altered very little" (609). When Rupert ventures inside to see Magdela, an old friend, his attention turns to other familiar things: furniture, the ringing telephone, smells of cooking from the basement, and the arrangement of rooms. And yet these things have all been slightly altered—the chairs and sofas are newly worn; a sheltering family lives in the basement; the drawing room, once "the room of a hostess" (610), has "no aspect at all" (610). Bowen's extinct scene, then, is not just an evacuated, ravaged war zone; it is the place where we glimpse an uneasy coexistence of familiarity and disorientation, of everydayness and history. Those places, memories, things, and habits that ground experience and knowledge become unsettled and draw attention like a magnetic field. In their sustained attention to those disruptions of everyday life, Bowen's stories ask what the unsettled surfaces of the everyday might tell us about less visible historical transformations. This is exactly why the story concludes with Magdela's question to Rupert: "Do you think we shall see great change?" (615). The question is not if "great change" will occur, but if—and how—we shall see it.

Bowen's extinct scene typifies a broader set of questions about everyday life that cuts across late modernism. How do these agitations at the level of everyday life correspond to "great change"—that is, the large scale of war, systemic change, and historical events? And what form of attention to the everyday is required to establish that correspondence? This book unfolds the relationship between late modernism's outward turn—the form of attention it gives to the temporalities, spaces, surface appearances, textures, and rhythms of everyday life—and the disorder in the world-system that pushed the locus of global power from Britain to America.[4] More specifically, I argue that late modernism's outward turn figures everyday life as a scene where world-systemic distress attains legibility. In works as varied as Elizabeth Bowen's wartime stories and Vic Reid's anticolonial fiction, late modernist texts look to the everyday to explain a historical transformation in the structure of the world-system.

This book developed out of an initial curiosity about the organization Mass-Observation and the unimaginably large archive of everyday life they assembled in the 1930s and 1940s.[5] Why would an oddball collective of surrealists, documentary filmmakers, poets, and anthropologists feel so compelled to scrutinize everyday life during periods of national and international distress? Was it possible—and even desirable—to create some form of cooperation between avant-garde aesthetic practices and sociological inquiry? I was rather surprised to find the same constellation of everyday life, historical crisis, and aesthetic experimentation taking shape in other zones of late modernist cultural production. That early curiosity evolved into the research questions that animate this study: why would writers in a historical period plagued by extraordinary crises divert their attention away from those crises and focus instead on the everyday? What could it mean that this preoccupation with the everyday surfaced in the late work of older modernists, former surrealists, cinematic neophytes, and colonial novelists? Indeed, some of the most direct confrontations with everyday life emerged from places as different as the editing rooms of the nascent documentary film movement and the confines of the Bloomsbury Group. John Grierson, godfather and brash proponent of documentary film, conceived his own cinema of everyday life in explicit opposition to the high modernism of the 1920s: "Documentary represent[s] a reaction from the art world of the early and middle 1920s—Bloomsbury, Left Bank, T. S. Eliot, Clive Bell, and all—by people with every reason to know it well. Likewise, if it was a return to 'reality,' it was a return not unconnected with Clydeside Movement, ILP's, the Great Depression, not to mention our Lord Keynes, the London School of Economics, Political and Economic Planning and such."[6]

By 1932 Virginia Woolf declared a similar move away from the thickly interiorized narration of her earlier fiction: "There's a good deal of gold," she writes, "—more than I'd thought—in externality."[7] Perhaps Stephen Spender captured the mood best when he claimed in 1935 that the economic and political convulsions of the era should "turn the reader's and writer's attention outwards from himself to the world."[8] In its efforts to track the various manifestations of the outward turn, this book aims to produce a version of late modernism elastic enough to encompass figures as dissimilar as Woolf and Grierson but focused enough to pull into view the reciprocal relationship between aesthetics and world-systemic change during this transitional period.

It should be said from the outset that I make no grand claim that these writers and artists were the first to see everyday life as artistic material, nor do I believe that modernism, in any of its phases, is better equipped to mediate everyday experience than realism, romanticism, naturalism, or anything else.[9] If literary history has gained anything from the study of modernism, it should be a suspicion of claims for modernism's absolute novelty. I suggest that the depth, scale, and particularity of late modernism's encounter with everyday life becomes apparent only by way of a dialectical inquiry into the interrelationships between late modernism's use of various genres—documentary cinema, the historical novel, auto-ethnography, travel writing, the gothic, vernacular fiction—and the accumulating pressures attending the breakup of the British world-system. My argument turns on two interrelated propositions. First, I claim that late modernism's outward turn constitutes a dialectical twist in a long trajectory of modernist aesthetics, one that significantly affects the mediating powers of modernist forms, genres, and techniques; second, I argue that late modernism figures everyday life as the scene where structural changes in the world-system attain legibility. The remainder of this introduction will elaborate both of these propositions and show how late modernism's descriptions of everyday life serve as mediated expressions of world-systemic disorder and its far-reaching consequences.

MODERNISM AND THE SCENE OF EVERYDAY LIFE

The very notion of late modernism as aesthetically and historically unique is still relatively new.[10] This project joins the field carved out most recently by Tyrus Miller, Jed Esty, Marina MacKay, Robert Genter, and many others, all of whom link late modernism's aesthetic distinctiveness to specific historical pressures. While my project follows their lead in this respect, it tells a different story about late modernist aesthetics and historicity. I want to start, then, with a two-part question: how is the outward turn specifically a late modernist form of attention, and how did late modernists themselves understand their aesthetic practice as distinct from their predecessors? To begin answering these questions, we should first note that everyday life is a central, abiding concern of the most iconic works of high modernism. James Joyce's *Ulysses* (1922) marshals a stunning array of narrative techniques to capture a single day in the life of the rather unremarkable Leopold Bloom; another single-day novel, Woolf's *Mrs. Dalloway* (1925), interweaves complex observations on sexual and psychic life with the rather mundane tasks required to host an evening party. And, amidst the dense thicket of literary and theological allusions in T. S. Eliot's *The Waste Land* (1922), demotic speech buzzes in public houses and hushed interiors while taxis hum on the streets and a typist listens to a gramophone. This is to say nothing of the avant-gardes of the teens and twenties—futurists, surrealists, Russian futurists—who expended a great deal of energy trying to transform everyday life into something radically new. In fact, we might say that modernism is the name we give to art that treats everyday life as a problem and not a given.

Still, recognizing the importance of the everyday to modernist aesthetics raises more questions than it answers. Why does attention to everyday life require formal complexity? How does the aesthetic treatment of everyday life vary over space and time? What would be political about such aesthetic treatment? Recent work in modernist studies by Liesl Olson, Bryony Randall, and Juan A. Suárez reframes the typical features of modernist writing—dilated, contracted, and multiple temporalities, fragmented *and* encyclopedic forms, anaesthetizing repetition, weak plots—as the result of a specific form of attention to everyday life.[11] In Suárez's words, modernism "was a way of doing something" with the materials of everyday life and "in this process, it exposed and critiqued the limitations of everyday life while it simultaneously sought to escape them."[12] Olson's *Modernism and the Ordinary* formulates an altogether different, and one might say less critical, version of modernism's rapprochement with the everyday. Rather than transforming or defamiliarizing everyday life, modernism, Olson argues, shows us how "the ordinary indeed may endure in and of itself, as a 'final good.'"[13] In this argument, the construction of modernism as the art of epiphany, shock, or rupture altogether misses the role played by a persistent ordinariness.[14] The formal innovations so celebrated in the works of high modernists such as Joyce, Woolf, and Gertrude Stein result from a struggle to represent everyday life without transforming it into something extraordinary or transcendent.

The first distinction I want to mark here is that late modernism's engagement with the everyday cannot be explained as either the defamiliarization or the preservation of the ordinary. This means my account moves away from the set of conceptual dyads that govern existing studies of modernism and everyday life: ordinary and extraordinary, familiar and unfamiliar, mundane and ecstatic.[15] I suggest that late modernism requires us to leverage that internal dialectic onto the larger terrain of world-systemic disorder where the very concept of everyday life, however riven with contradictions, acquires specificity and coherence within an articulated network of political, economic, and social life. Less bewitched by the comfort of routine or the ecstasy of the unfamiliar, the late modernist texts that I examine describe the particulars of everyday life and arrange those particulars in a way that expresses some feature of world-systemic disorder. In short, late modernism's encounter with everyday life is not primarily aesthetic or ethical; it is simultaneously aesthetic *and* political.

John Grierson's early writings on documentary crystallize the volatile realignment of aesthetics, politics, and everyday life after the 1920s. In his efforts to develop a documentary aesthetic, Grierson subjected what would become infamously known as the inward turn to a scathing critique. However, he also understood documentary as spearheading another wave of aesthetic innovation. In August of 1930 he pondered over the fate and future of modernism in his young, troubled decade:

> It may be—and what I understand of aesthetic bids me believe—that in making art in our new world we are called upon to build in new forms altogether. Fantasy will not do, nor the dribblings of personal sentiment or personal story. The building of our new forms has been going on, of course, for a long time in poetry and the novel and architecture, and even within such limitations of medium as one finds in painting and sculpture. We have all been abstracting our arts away from the personal, trying to articulate this wider world of duties and loyalties in which education and invention and democracy have made us citizens.[16]

Grierson's call for "new forms" harmonizes with Ezra Pound's "make it new," replaying the most recognizable of all modernist doctrines. His antipathy to the personal is but a thinly veiled critique of the experiments with psychic interiority and subjective experience underwriting some, but not all, of the most significant high modernist achievements—Marcel Proust's *Remembrance of Things Past*, Virginia Woolf's *Mrs. Dalloway*, James Joyce's *Ulysses*, D. H. Lawrence's *Women in Love*. Christopher Isherwood also pointed to the political and economic realities of the 1930s as the moment when Virginia Woolf, Bloomsbury, and the modernism it represented lost some of its luster: "After he and Stephen [Spender] had been to see *Kameradschaft*, Pabst's film about the coal miners, in 1931, Christopher told Stephen that, when the tunnel caved in and the miners were trapped, he had thought: 'That makes Virginia Woolf look pretty silly.' Stephen replied that he had been thinking something similar, though not specifically about Virginia."[17] In Grierson's and Isherwood's diagnoses, the modern aesthetic practices of their predecessors now appear newly aged, cloistered from the political and economic storms surging around them.

The salient point here is that these writers, artists, and filmmakers already understood the bloc of figures later institutionalized as high modernist as an identifiable, if not entirely coherent, set of cultural producers. Though Edmund Wilson did not employ the "m" word, which Vincent Sherry tells us Wilson found offensive, *Axel's Castle* did much in 1931 to consolidate a self-consciously modernist aesthetic.[18] The figures that head Wilson's chapters would not look out of place in a university seminar on modernism today: W. B. Yeats, Paul Valéry, Marcel Proust, James Joyce, Gertrude Stein, and, of course, Arthur Rimbaud. But if a version of a modernist aesthetic was recognizable as early as 1931, this meant artists could now work both with and against it. Yet, as the coming chapters will bear out, a wholesale abandonment of modernist techniques was never on the agenda. On his BBC broadcast series "The Poet and the Public," Humphrey Jennings would offer T. S. Eliot's *The Waste Land* as a model poem for bridging the gap between poetic work and public life; in a similarly unlikely venue, Cecil Day-Lewis would defend modernism and Eliot's poem in the pages of the *Left Review* against hardline calls for social realism.[19] Mass-Observation plundered surrealism in order to develop new forms of social research while Jennings marshaled surrealist techniques in his wartime propaganda films. Modernist experimentation as exemplified by Eliot, Joyce, and Woolf might have served as a foil for Grierson, Isherwood, George Lamming, and even late Woolf, but it was also open for conscious manipulation and renovation.

Whatever techniques or ideas late modernists borrowed from their predecessors, it is certainly true that their efforts to render everyday life look markedly different than anything by Proust, Joyce, or Woolf in the teens and twenties. To demonstrate a characteristically late modernist form of attention to everyday life, I turn to Henry Green's obscure novel *Party Going*. At the level of genre, Green's daybook would seem to fit neatly with other modernist masterpieces such as *Ulysses* or *Mrs. Dalloway*. Yet Green's novel generates another form of attention to everyday life, one specifically aimed at transforming quotidian experience into signs of the economic and political crises of the late 1930s.

Michael North sees *Party Going* as "a throwback to an earlier decade."[20] And, from one angle, Green's novel does seems more at home with the daybooks of the 1920s than with the literary production of the 1930s. While his novels rarely assume pride of place next to Woolf, Joyce, and Lawrence, his contemporaries thought him on par with these decorated authors.[21] For my purposes, *Party Going* emblematizes two distinct and interrelated features of late modernism's treatment of everyday life: first, the novel renovates familiar modernist techniques in order to interrogate daily life as a pressure point for class antagonisms and to express the decade's war anxiety, or what Paul Saint-Amour memorably dubs "pre-traumatic stress syndrome."[22] Like other modernist daybooks, Green's novel weaves in and out of the lives of multiple characters, oscillating between a third person omniscient point of view and free indirect discourse; it creates moments of narrative simultaneity through cross-cutting and spatial form. Second, Green's novel de-emphasizes interiority and subjective experience, choosing instead to scrutinize the everyday as a sign of historical transformation. By tracking these two features in more detail, we can underscore the type of reading late modernist texts require.

Party Going follows a group of well-to-do, mostly young Londoners taking a holiday at the expense of Max Adey, a handsome rake about town. Their plans are stalled when a thick, slow-moving fog settles over London, halting all trains and disrupting the movement of the city. Green's leisured youths spend most of their time in a hotel above the train station as it fills with Londoners anxious for the city to resume its normal operations. Green's characters kill their empty time with cocktails, gossip, and idle talk. Unlike *Mrs. Dalloway* or *Ulysses*, Green's daybook does not chronicle a day in the life of a bustling modern metropole. By contrast, Green's London is a suspended city. This urban stasis is recapitulated in the virtual plotlessness of *Party Going*. Nothing much happens and when the trains resume after four hours, nothing much is resolved. We might see the novel, then, as a chronicle of a minor interruption in the structures, rhythms, and habits of everyday life. Yet, for Green, even a minor disturbance in the everyday is enough to make the social and economic structures of daily life appear.

Green organizes the narrative of *Party Going* spatially. For much of the novel, Max and his party sit comfortably in a hotel room overlooking the train station and "that swarm of people" below.[23] The novel translates class difference into spatial separation, but, as Marina MacKay notes, Green's narrative "shifts backwards and forwards between the hotel and the station floor with an air of neutrality."[24] In addition to the narration's movement between these two spaces, Green's novel is equally concerned with the pressure placed on the very structural divisions between the wealthy party goers above and the restive masses below. This brief suspension instigates a period of disorder, which Green expresses in terms of breached boundaries, heightened vulnerability, and a nightmarish anxiety that an entire social and economic system may falter. Green articulates these fears through the trope of infection. The novel opens with a cryptic but ominous scene that leads to the story's first infection. A pigeon, blinded by the fog, flies into a balustrade and drops dead in front of Miss Fellowes. She fetches the dead bird and washes it in the train station restroom and quickly grows weak. When she encounters Angela Crevy and Robin Adams in the train station, she passes her dead pigeon, now cleaned and swaddled in paper, to Robin and asks him to dispose of it. "She felt better at once, it began to go off and relief came over her in a glow following out of her weakness" (387). She soon retrieves her "parcel" from the wastepaper basket and falls into the illness that will grip her throughout the novel. Miss Fellowes succumbs to fearful fever dreams:

> Miss Fellowes, in her room, felt she was on a shore wedged between two rocks, soft and hard. Out beyond a grey sea with, above, a darker sky, she would notice small clouds where sea joined sky and these clouds coming far away together into a darker mass would rush across from that horizon towards where she was held down. As this cumulus advanced the sea below would rise, most menacing and capped with foam, and as it came nearer she could hear the shrieking wind in throbbing through her ears . . . it was so menacing she thought each time the pressure was such her eyes would be forced out of her head to let her blood out. (423)

This instance concludes with the storm receding and "a sweet tide" (423) washing over a relieved and relaxed Miss Fellowes. But the stock imagery—accumulation of amassed clouds, an unstoppable force, physical vulnerability—allegorizes the encroaching threats to the relative security of both the upper classes and, more broadly, a British population who had long enjoyed the geographical protection afforded to an island state with the world's most powerful navy.

The trope of infection reappears throughout the novel to figure the fraying lines between classes. Julia Wray leans out of her upstairs hotel window and gazes onto the crowds below, but their spatial distance offers little protection from the infectious nature of the crowd.[25] Noises and tobacco smoke from below rise up, creeping into Julia and Max's ears and throats. "Also whatever there is in crowds had reached into her, for these thousands below were now working up a kind of boisterous good humour" (467). At first blush, Green suggests some sort of transmission of joy from the crowds "into" Julia. Yet the novel switches from Julia's free indirect discourse to an omniscient narrator who assures us that what has "reached into" Julia is far more insidious: "What she could not tell was that those who were singing were Welshmen up for a match, and what they sang in Welsh was of the rape of a Druid's silly daughter under one of Snowdon's wilder mountains" (467). Julia's misrecognitions continue: "Also she felt encouraged and felt safe because they could not by any chance get up from below; she had seen those doors bolted, and through being above them by reason of Max having bought their room and by having money, she saw in what lay below her an example of her own way of living because they were underneath and kept there" (468). Her space of security inverts into one of entrapment. The steel doors protecting the hotel from the masses limit the mobility of those inside, putting the hotel into "a state of siege" (451). Like the accumulating clouds in Miss Fellowes's fever dream, the sheer density of the masses precipitates destruction and disorder.

Party Going deploys recognizably modernist techniques—free indirect discourse, fragmented narration, spatial form—to diagnose economic, social, and political anxieties of the 1930s. Unlike other famous modernist daybooks that employ similar narrative techniques, Green's novel cavalierly dismisses the inner complexity of character. On more than one occasion, he underscores the triviality and sheer depthlessness of his characters' inner lives. *Party Going* moves outward to the scene of everyday life, registering a social order mortally wounded by the economic pressures of the 1930s and the coming war. In this winding, unremarkable story about a mass of people waiting for the trains to move, Green's narrative techniques sap characters of their robust subjectivities and create a scene of everyday life that lays bare the structure, function, and anxieties of an entire city.

As Green, Isherwood, Mass-Observation, and others discovered, modernist aesthetics would not easily map onto the historical realities of the post-1920s world. Those historical realities seep into Green's text, infecting it at every level. In this way, *Party Going* stands in here for the aesthetic conflicts that arise in all of the following chapters. For Green and the other late modernists that populate these pages, the everyday carries the traces of past historical events, internalizes the antagonisms of the present, and sometimes serves as a mute indication of possible futures. As late modernist works demonstrate directly or indirectly, the accumulating world-systemic distress of the decades after the roaring twenties migrated into the aesthetic theories and formal structures of modernism, changing their role, appearance, and mediating power.

By turning their focus outward, these texts renovate established modernist techniques, often dispensing with certain features and ideas, replicating others, and putting still others to uses for which they were not quite intended. In late modernism, we see radical avant-garde techniques marshaled for state-sponsored film and liberal norms; high modernists retreat from aesthetic practices that defined their earlier careers and cemented them as icons; the cosmopolitan allure of travel gets distorted by layered networks of financial and political might that maintain geopolitical order; texts from a wartime capital convert the city from a vibrant center of intellectual activity into a mass grave; and, finally, the "revolution of the word" slides down from the airy world of abstract art into a tool for articulating unauthorized forms of political belonging. Late modernism designates the moment when modernism no longer recognizes itself.

While much of the work I investigate cuts its figure against earlier forms of modernism, late modernism should not be misconstrued as either a retreat from modernist aesthetics *tout court* or a return to realism. To be sure, Woolf's enchantment with "externality" and her fascination with Ivan Turgenev and Leo Tolstoy in the 1930s, like Mass-Observation's outspoken commitment to the actualities of daily life, might sound like a return to realism. However flexibly defined, realism has typically been considered the proper style for registering the seemingly insignificant details of daily life and making ordinary people and experiences the central subject matter of literature.[26] Arguably, no one inventoried the materials of daily life with more care and attentiveness than Honoré de Balzac.[27] Yet, as the coming chapters will show, writers and filmmakers constantly negotiated the conflict between an art attuned to the gritty realities of social and political life and the viability of aesthetic experimentation. This tension drives a good deal of midcentury cultural production, including documentary film, anglophone Caribbean vernacular fiction, and wartime art. We might say that late modernism's fascination with the everyday discloses an uneasy relationship between the epistemological claims of realism and the aesthetic resources of modernism.

In order to account for this uneasy relationship, we might begin by questioning the conventional wisdom that positions modernism and realism as dialectical opposites. At first blush, this critical commonplace has much to do with stylistic categories serving as periodizing terms. As literary history tells us, certain stylistic features emerge, peak, and decline over a period of years: romanticism gives way to realism, which then develops into naturalism. At the summit of these nineteenth-century literary innovations stands modernism, canceling out its predecessors and offering something "new" and "radical." A twice-told tale, to be sure, but this story forgets as much as it preserves for cultural memory. The problem of accounting for the prolonged existence of styles and techniques after their purported demise remains the embarrassment of literary history's fidelity to periodization.[28] Although modernist studies has admirably flexed the temporal and spatial dimensions of modernism to include more variegated aesthetic practices, modernism and realism have lost none of their descriptive and evaluative force; campaigns for an expanded or more inclusive modernism rarely question the power "modernism" or "realism" wield as markers of value.[29]

How might we think of the aesthetic techniques "modernism" and "realism" designated separately from the periods they denote? These questions in part drive Fredric Jameson's arguments in *A Singular Modernity*. While acknowledging the ineluctability of periodization, Jameson also criticizes periodizing gestures and, along the way, undercuts the pat narrative of modernism's supersession of realism: "Modernism is an aesthetic category and realism is an epistemological one; the truth claim of the latter is irreconcilable with the formal dynamic of the former. The attempt to combine the two into a single master narrative must therefore necessarily fail."[30] Splitting the difference between modernism and realism into aesthetics and epistemology certainly renders useless any "single master narrative" of literary history.[31] As Jameson knows well, aesthetics and epistemology may be derived from "two unrelated systems," but the fate of art in any given era is tied to the types of relationships it tries to stage between these two.[32] Aesthetic theory since Immanuel Kant has attempted to refigure the relation of art to both pure (epistemology) and practical reason (ethics and politics). One may uncover a different form of relation between art and knowledge across modern aesthetic theory—the Jena romantics' literary absolute, Georg Hegel's supersession of art by philosophy, and Friedrich Nietzsche's positioning of art against knowledge are but a small sample. Marxist aesthetics itself is caught in these very dynamics, particularly those key debates on modernism and realism. For everything else that sets them apart, Georg Lukács's broadsides against modernism and Theodor Adorno's unflinching defense of it both address the question of art's relationship to knowledge, whether it functions as a way to cast class structures into relief or as a pointed critique of instrumental rationality. The problem modernism *and* realism pose is precisely *how* art relates to knowledge.[33]

While it has become almost routine to pit realism and modernism against one another, some scholars of nineteenth- and twentieth-century literature have recognized several points of overlap and continuity. If realism's initial discovery was, in the words of Peter Brooks, that it "found and dramatized the exceptional within the ordinary," then it isn't so much of a leap to see "the realist vision is alive in Woolf," even if Woolf flips that vision predominantly, but not entirely, from the external world into the "quivering subjectivities" populating her novels from the 1920s.[34] Like Brooks, Laurie Langbauer's study of realism and everyday life ends with Virginia Woolf and Dorothy Richardson; similarly, Ruth Yeazell's *Art of the Everyday: Dutch Painting and the Realist Novel* meanders through French and English realists before concluding with Marcel Proust, "this last of the realists."[35] The point is not to put periodizing or stylistic categories on trial or to assume righteously that fluid boundaries and pluralized modernisms and realisms are inherently better. Instead we might note that for Langbauer, Brooks, and Yeazell, querying the relationship of aesthetics to everyday life brings these odd convergences into focus and, as a result, contests the most dearly held conventions of literary history. In one way, these works of literary criticism demonstrate the very problem that puzzles philosophers of everyday life such as Henri Lefebvre, Walter Benjamin, Michel de Certeau, Maurice Blanchot, and others: the everyday proves to be both generative and corrosive to those critical, theoretical, and aesthetic projects that attend to it. But more than that, we might also say that conflating styles and periods proves to be, at best, provisionally useful and, at worst, historically flat. In certain historical moments, one style appears dominant, the other recessive; and, as is the case with late modernism, styles often coexist, producing the sort of texts that fit their historical moment, but prove disobedient to stadial narratives of literary history. The way to make sense of late modernism, then, is to plot it more firmly within its historical moment and to ask how it marshals aesthetics to think that moment.

"A SINGLE INTEGRATED SCENE": LATE MODERNISM AS GEOPOLITICAL DESCRIPTION

The most convincing and influential versions of late modernism describe it as part of British imperial decline or as a response to the pressures of the Second World War. In my account, late modernist texts mediate what Immanuel Wallerstein would call the "terminal transition" of a highly networked, interconnected British world-system.[36] To be clear, I am not swapping one context for another, nor am I contesting the claims made by Esty, MacKay, and others, all of which greatly inform this book. Unlike other theories of conceiving the world that tend to foreground cultural flows, ethical encounters, or multiple versions of something dubbed "modernity," world-systems analysis prioritizes the interplay of force and capital accumulation that link different states, geographical areas, and international actors. It is true that many world-systems analysts have spent little time poring over the particulars of cultural activity (much less literary history) or demonstrating how such macro-level thinking might be applicable to humanistic inquiry. This negligence is partially to blame for the reluctance, and even suspicion, voiced by many humanities scholars.[37] Yet, as Richard E. Lee has recently noted, the picture of the world we get from world-systems analysis does not by necessity marginalize culture. A world-system, he argues, is composed of "three analytically distinct but functionally, and existentially, inseparable structural arenas . . . : the axial division of labor, the interstate system, and the structures of knowledge. They define a singular "world."[38] Structures of knowledge, call it the cultural sphere, may not garner as much attention as the other two arenas in the works of the aforementioned thinkers, but culture *is* an integral part of the world.[39] For my purposes, plotting aesthetic activity within the capitalist world-system opens the way not only for relating artworks to geopolitical realities but also for theorizing how artworks generate a valuable, if not singular, mode of conceptualizing those geopolitical realities.

How exactly do we draw the relationship between late modernism's outward turn and the world-system? This is, above all, a question of scale. In many ways, it isn't an entirely new question as it recalls old, abiding problems of relating the general to the particular, history to art objects, and macro-level analysis of world processes and events to the micro-level interpretive work of close reading. Recent work by Franco Moretti, Pascale Casanova, and Nirvana Tanoukhi has clearly demonstrated that there are multiple ways to calibrate the relation between the world-system and the literary.[40] For my purposes, I want to demonstrate that late modernists render legible their moment of systemic disorder by attending to the particulars of everyday life and hoping, in the end, that the arrangement of those particulars might yield some tangible knowledge about a crumbling world-system. So, in this regard, the question of scale asks how literary descriptions of daily life broaden out to geopolitical description.

Late modernist efforts to think the world-system at the moment of its undoing will be one of the narrative threads running through all of the chapters. For now, though, we can glimpse the difficulty of thinking and describing geopolitical disorder in Christopher Isherwood and W. H. Auden's *Journey to a War*, their account of the Sino-Japanese war. The duo sit in a foreign concession on the heavily guarded river island of Shameen; British and American gunboats patrol the outer shores and armed men ensure that terrified, immiserated Chinese civilians won't stampede the protected area in the event of a Japanese air raid. But bombs do fall beyond the secured enclosure of the concession, and Isherwood nervously scans the interior of their room:

> My eyes moved over this charming room, taking in the tea-cups, the dish of scones, the book-case with Chesterton's essays and Kipling's poems, the framed photograph of an Oxford college. My brain tried to relate these images to the sounds outside; the whine of the power-diving bomber, the distant thump of the explosions. Understand, I told myself, that these noises, these objects are part of a single, integrated scene. Wake up! It's all quite real. And, at that moment I really did wake up. At that moment, suddenly, I arrived in China.[41]

Isherwood assembles for us the parts of this single integrated scene—a piece of territory reserved for foreign imperial powers, a brutal war occurring just beyond its boundaries, and the cultural objects and literary texts that fall into his vision as his body registers the thud of detonating bombs. Even if he cannot discern how these pieces all fit into a geopolitical totality, Isherwood knows they are part of a highly networked system. This moment from Isherwood's text becomes a central question for my own project: how do we coordinate the complexities of a highly interconnected world with individual art objects? And, moreover, how do we understand the aesthetic techniques that attempted to relate everyday activities like taking tea with global war and imperial rivalry? In what ways might the aesthetic developments of late modernism be tied to these efforts to construct the "single integrated scene"?

As Isherwood's war diary illustrates, late modernists themselves understand that a vast interdependent network of states, colonies, and outposts constitutes a geopolitical totality even if such a totality remains impossible to comprehend or describe fully. They are also acutely aware that this system has entered a phase of heightened disorder. John Darwin points to 1929 as the year when "the British system was caught up in the world's economic and geopolitical earthquake. . . . By the mid-1930s the British system seemed plunged (to some observers at least) in a terminal crisis."[42] For Darwin, this terminal crisis resulted from the erosion of three specific conditions the British world-system required to maintain any semblance of order: "a 'passive' East Asia, a European balance of power, and a strong but unaggressive United States. If those conditions broke down, the imperial archipelago, strung across the world, would soon start to look fragile."[43] The late modernists I take up in the coming chapters are openly preoccupied with these and other phenomena that upended the British world-system: the Sino-Japanese war, the expansionist policies of fascist states and a civil war in Spain that destabilized the continental equilibrium Britain so needed, and transformations in sovereignty and political belonging wrought by decolonization and mass migration after the Second World War. In order to take full measure of this period of systemic disorder, the geographical coordinates of this study include two states competing to control the balance of power in Europe (Britain and Germany), semiperipheral states (Spain and, less directly, Ireland), and peripheral states (Jamaica and China). Although I maintain throughout that late modernist texts attempt to describe systemic disorder as it unfolds, their description of it and its consequences varies. For example, we will see in chapter 4 that the end of a system of order generates profound anxiety in the war stories of Elizabeth Bowen; yet, as

I show in chapter 5, disorder signals a possibility for greater political autonomy for Jamaica in Vic Reid's optimistically titled novel *New Day*.

These works and others like them engage in descriptive acts as a means to conceptualize their historical moment as it occurs, which they by and large understand to be transitional (although their idea of what that transition portends varies).[44] In the chapters that follow, I foreground multiple instances of late modernist description that move us from the particulars of quotidian experience to broader levels of world-systemic change: Isherwood's probing, panoramic look at the architecture outside of his Berlin window gives shape to Weimar's decline and the rise of a totalitarian state; Vic Reid's description of the violence wrought on the Jamaican population during the Morant Bay rebellion reimagines the history of colonial revolt; George Orwell's scrutiny of the daily doings in a war zone counteract the grand allegory of good versus evil that framed the Spanish Civil War for so many international observers and participants. These writers, then, do not engage in description as some sort of value neutral practice; nor are they invested in re-enchanting or preserving the everyday for its own sake. Late modernism's geopolitical description attempts to arrange concrete particulars so that they yield something tangible about world-systemic disorder. In certain instances, the oscillation between these two levels takes the more familiar shape of allegory. Vic Reid's *New Day*, for example, functions as a national allegory, presenting Jamaica's movement toward independence through the eyes and speech of the colonized. In other moments, and this is the core argument of chapter 3, attention to everyday life dismantles allegory or makes allegorization impossible. In both instances, however, these texts attempt to think of the relation between everyday life and world-systemic change. In this way, late modernism emerges as an aesthetic response generated by world-systemic transition but also as a response that conceptualizes that transition and its consequences.

AGAINST AUTONOMY, WITHOUT COMMITMENT: LATE MODERNISM AND POLITICAL FORMALISM

These brief forays into Christopher Isherwood, John Grierson, and Henry Green should immediately clarify why we can no longer sort literature from the thirties onward into separate camps labeled "modernist" or "realist." Those stylistic divisions have also segregated literature from this period into the heavily policed zones of aesthetic autonomy or committed literature. Yet, when we historicize late modernism within the world-system, aesthetic autonomy looks more and more tenuous; similarly, if politics and literature converge only in committed works, there is little space to think of literary form "doing" politics, as Jacques Rancière would say. Jessica Berman rightly observes that the split between aesthetic autonomy and political commitment forecloses any investigation of the political work of modernist form or the formal operations of those texts marked as "political" literature.[45] Like Berman, a number of scholars have recently located the political work of modernist form beyond the boundaries of autonomy and commitment. John Marx's *Geopolitics and the Anglophone Novel, 1890–2011* reads form in modernist and contemporary fiction as modeling and critiquing modes of liberal governance; Matthew Hart's *Nations of Nothing but Poetry* explains how the melding of vernacular and avant-garde aesthetics functions as "the gateway to a negative dialectical politics of autonomy and interrelatedness that was alone adequate to the unevenly transnational character of the modern world"[46]; and Jed Esty's *Unseasonable Youth: Modernism, Colonialism, and the Fiction of Development* shows the way the modernist bildungsroman tropes uneven global development into its very form.[47] All of these studies ground modernism historically but do not presume that historical and political pressures arrive in literary texts or artworks in any direct, easily discernible way. The political formalism I advance in my reading follows from the lessons of these scholars and, more directly, from Theodor W. Adorno's dictum from *Aesthetic Theory*: "The unsolved antagonisms of reality return in artworks as immanent problems of form."[48] In short, I suggest late modernism's politics of form has little to do with either autonomy or commitment and far more to do with the formal mediation of those antagonisms.[49]

Statements like the one from Adorno often serve as inflexible aesthetic maxims. Rather than graft one of these maxims onto a set of aesthetic phenomena, I want instead to derive a methodological procedure from Adorno. In *Aesthetic Theory* and elsewhere, he asserts that art's relationship to society cannot be explained by direct references to this or that historical phenomenon, through a vast array of sociological information, or by marshaling biographical data. We have to consider another way in which those "unsolved antagonisms" arrive in aesthetic form:

Society is not . . . directly, tangibly, and . . . "realistically" continued in its works of art. It does not become directly visible in them; else there would be no difference between art and empirical existence, no such line as even the ideologues of dialectical materialism must eventually draw when they refer art and culture to special departments of their administration. True, even the most sublime esthetic qualities have a social positional value; their historic side is a social one at the same time. Yet society's entrance into them is not immediate; it often occurs only in rather hidden formal constituents. These have a dialectics of their own, which then, of course, reflects the real one.[50]

What Adorno calls society is not "directly visible" in art, nor is its penetration into artworks "immediate." Instead, historical and social antagonisms appear in aesthetic form in indirect, highly mediated ways. For Adorno, formal complexity does not detach art from its historical conditions of possibility. No work of art, not even those hermetic works of Samuel Beckett and Franz Kafka that Adorno so prized, ever attains pure autonomy or pure separation. The internal dialectics of an artwork disclose for us the contradictions of its historical moment. We might say that Adorno's analysis thaws the frozen dichotomy of immanence (formalism) and transcendence (historicism), putting this static binary opposition into motion. Because this formalist account is dialectical, it preempts the causal structure of certain types of historicism. The task is not to rebuild a "context" and illuminate the historical truth of an artwork or to declare its replication of or resistance to ideology. The late modernists I examine register a structural transformation in the world-system as it unfolds. The context we as critics may erect retrospectively is not available to them; their historical experience and our historical perspectives may not always align, and we would do well to suspend any impulse to fashion direct causal explanations for aesthetic developments.[51]

This is what I take Adorno to mean when he states that the aesthetic dialectic "reflects the real one" of an historical process. Reflection, again, is nothing direct. The contradictions and movements within a work of art encrypt and disclose an historical process in its moment of unfolding. If we read for form in this way, then form emerges as "the enabling condition and the product of reading. . . . It becomes both theory's/ideology's/history's shadow and the force that permits the text to emerge as ideology's or theory's interlocutor, rather than as its example."[52] As a rehabilitated category of analysis, and as one that does not necessitate the negation of history or the political, form encrypts the multidirectional, multi-layered workings of a world-system.

The politically inflected analysis we can derive from Adorno formulates a dialectical relation between art and history. History does not determine art's meaning or content, nor is art sealed off from the outside world. This type of relationality recalls the structure of Karl Marx's analysis of the commodity.[53] As readers of *Capital* will recall, the commodity bifurcates into use–value and exchange–value, ultimately disclosing the idea of value as "socially necessary labor time."[54] No single component causes the other, and no component can be discussed without the others; the ensemble exists in a highly mobile, generative relationship. This is the model for thinking form historically and critically. As I try to show throughout this book, formalism of this sort neither elevates artworks outside of the material and social world nor does it come at the expense of historical and archival work (quite the contrary). Conceived in this way, a critical formalism does not imply that artworks transcend their historical circumstances nor does it value only those works that, through some tour de force reading, appear to replicate or rebuke ideological forces. In other words, my approach to aesthetic objects prioritizes the relationship of form and politics but in a way that circumvents what Rita Felski has rightly identified as the formulaic readings grounded in a hermeneutics of suspicion. In this regard, political formalism—or any political reading, for that matter—needs to avoid the burdens and, indeed, dead ends of suspicious reading: the nearly reflexive attribution of ideological resistance to aesthetic techniques; the distrustful, sometimes disdainful approach to texts that elevates the critic's heroic reading above the assumed political naiveté of authors and texts; and, ultimately, "the threat of banality" such reading bears with it.[55]

In opposition to the narrow political formalism that Felski rightly criticizes, others such as Nathan Hensley and James Hansen have called for another critical disposition, which Hansen describes as a "politically and historically inflected formalism . . . capable of doubting its own truth-claims without giving up on the object's *Warheit-Gehalt* (truth-content) wholesale."[56] Sensitive to both the dangers and potentialities that Felski and Hansen outline, this book's assemblage of historical, archival, and formal methods demonstrates two things: the past is not a static master code, and the artwork should not be cast solely as a privileged site of resistance or transgression.[57] As part of an expanded constellation of materials, artworks come to reveal as much about those historical and archival sources we use to explain them as that material discloses about the art object. In this way, formal analysis is dialectical analysis. Artworks operate within a widened historical and social field. With such a dynamic conception of form, the text, in Eleanor Rooney's memorable words, "bites back."[58]

The chapters that follow provide an historical and formal account of late modernism's figurations of everyday life. I have tried to see the period and all of its aesthetic vicissitudes beyond the conventional ways to frame British literature in the post-1920s era, whether it be the Auden Generation, the fading of high modernism, or the literature of the Second World War. My sense is that everyday life surfaces as the foremost preoccupation in multiple areas of late modernist activity, whether it be in the late work of Virginia Woolf, the British surrealists, documentary film, or the fictions of Caribbean migrants arriving on English shores after the Second World War. The forthcoming chapters are roughly chronological, but they are arranged around particular genres that have long been judged and defined by how closely they attend to everyday life. Each chapter pairs a genre with a specific facet of world-systemic disorder. Briefly, these pairings are documentary and the British state's management of national and international affairs; the historical novel and the unraveling of the progressive philosophies of history that underwrote the British world-system; the war travel book and the rise of a new geopolitical realism; the war gothic and enhanced state security; and, finally, vernacular fictions and historic transformations in political belonging after the Second World War. Operating within a genre is "an interpretive choice," one that directs our attention and frames what we see and how we see it.[59] Yet, as signifying systems embedded in historical processes, genres are never immutable. Wai Chee Dimock sees genres as "provisional set[s] that will always be bent and pulled and stretched by many subsets."[60] The "bending and pulling" of genres in the coming chapters results from both the urgency of examining everyday life within a hemorrhaging world-system and the strain such examination places on aesthetic practices.

The first chapter focuses closely on the aesthetic theories and practices of the British documentary film movement and Mass-Observation. These two groups exemplify one way that late modernists repurposed avant-garde techniques to investigate everyday life. I argue that both groups create versions of everyday life that extol and maintain the norms and values of British liberalism during the troubled years of the 1930s. In films such as Basil Wright's *Song of Ceylon* and Humphrey Jennings's *Listen to Britain*, montage and asynchronic sound produce images of everyday life that normalize the imperial and domestic policies of the British state. Similarly, Mass-Observation's published works draw on the aesthetic energies of surrealism to measure (and extend) the reach of political power into everyday life. Because Grierson's definition of documentary as "the creative treatment of actuality" will reverberate throughout all of the chapters, I devote considerable time to his early, lesser known publications on vorticism and modern painting for the *Chicago Evening Post* as well as his various writings on cinema for *Sight & Sound* and *Cinema Quarterly*. I pair the British documentary film movement and Mass-Observation not simply because their membership overlapped; even more compelling is the way their projects used techniques culled from surrealism and Soviet cinema to advance the interests of the British state when the state's authority was under duress. In the end, the version of the outward turn we find here is one that strives to preserve the liberal norms of the British world-system when they are most aggressively challenged.

The combination of historical crisis and aesthetic innovation resurfaces in the second chapter, where I take up Virginia Woolf and Christopher Isherwood's versions of the historical novel. Although Woolf and Isherwood represent either side of the high and late modernist generational divide, they similarly disfigure the historical novel, a genre that traditionally reads the movement of history through the daily lives of characters. Woolf's late novel *The Years* jettisons many of the narrative techniques that mark her other novels as decidedly Woolfian and, indeed, as high modernist. And yet Woolf's novel is not simply a resuscitation of a familiar realist genre. At the level of form, we find spotty occurrences of free indirect discourse, fragmented plots, and—what most concerns my analysis—aprogressive temporalities. In her scrupulous presentation of the daily lives of the Pargiter family, Woolf encodes a recursive time whereby past events return in augmented form in the present: childhood traumas and fantasies return in the personal and political lives of the young Pargiter women, past historical violence returns in more destructive forms of war, and, ultimately, the present promises no relief from these cycles. What we ultimately find in Woolf is the appearance of an aprogressive time at the level of everyday life, which achieves its most spectacular articulation in

Woolf's characterization. In Woolf's novel, this conflict between the recursive time of daily life and the linear march of historical time, reflected so clearly in the dated chapters, encodes a crisis of historical consciousness, a creeping disbelief in those philosophies of inevitable historical progress that attended the rise of the British world-system and substantiated it for decades.

Like *The Years*, Isherwood's novel will not be confused with those high modernist experiments he believed were outmoded and shabby by the turn of the 1930s. Often celebrated for its camera-eye narration and close attention to the details of everyday life in Weimar, Germany, Isherwood's *Goodbye to Berlin* employs a range of modernist techniques: spatial form, fragmented narration, and weak plots. The novel's greatest achievement is the way it transforms the minor details of everyday life into tropes of an ailing German republic. The combination of disorientation and familiarity, of historical rupture and everyday life, with which this introduction opens, pulses throughout Isherwood's novel. If *The Years* treats Britain's waning geopolitical power as a historical disaster slowly unfolding, Isherwood's novel tells us how a totalitarian state emerged and contested the balance of power in Europe.

Chapter 3 moves out to Spain and China, two of the global hot zones of the late 1930s. While travel books traditionally recorded daily practices in foreign or "exotic" locales, books such as Orwell's *Homage to Catalonia* and Auden and Isherwood's *Journey to a War* figure the everyday in a war zone as a problem; it is simultaneously upended by and quickly accommodated to the nightmare of total war. Despite their attention to the particulars of quotidian experience, be it the boredom of the trenches or the normalization of air raids in China, these texts are unable to organize those particulars into a narrative totality. This breach between the particularity of experience and a general framework for assembling and narrating that experience mirrors another separation I chart in the sphere of international law and geopolitics: the technologies and practices of warfare have outpaced the legal and conceptual apparatuses for defining and limiting total war. In the dialectical arrest between the particulars of quotidian experience and conceptual knowledge, *Homage to Catalonia* and *Journey to a War* register an emergent form of warfare shifting the balance of power in Europe and Asia.

The fusion of war and daily life abroad arrives in Britain in 1940. The popular People's War myth and a great deal of wartime cultural production show the

British resolutely continuing their daily lives during the worst of the bombing. This fourth chapter examines ways late modernists modulated the gothic in order to render the insecurity pervading everyday life in wartime Britain. In these works, everyday life is a site of perpetual insecurity. Henry Moore's famous sketches of the Tube shelters convert these spaces of safety into mass graves; photographic surveys of bombed London nervously archive the destroyed buildings, monuments, and spaces of everyday life; and, finally, Elizabeth Bowen's short stories express deep fears about the coming redistribution of wealth and power in postwar Britain. Taken collectively, these gothic figurations of daily life in wartime England make legible the insecurity about Britain's present and near future.

These first four chapters suggest that late modernism operates under the dual anxieties of loss and anticipation; it express disenchantment with the philosophical, political, and psychic givens that ground everyday life and ensure its continuity. In the closing chapter, late modernism's outward turn renders the changes in political belonging wrought by the twin phenomena of decolonization and mass migration from the Caribbean to British shores. By focusing on the seemingly negligible dimensions of everyday existence, Vic Reid, Samuel Selvon, and Colin MacInnes produce vernacular fictions that juxtapose the ideas of political belonging emerging in political discourse, the mass media, and the courts with the everyday lives of marginalized populations. Whether written from the Caribbean or within the postimperial metropole, these novels suggest that figural procedures have material effects. Their use of vernacular does not ask us merely to see from another perspective but to see how perspectives are produced and delimited.

My epilogue cycles back to the concerns of description and periodization. This book contends that, on one hand, the outward turn is generated during the late stages of the British world-system; on the other hand, late modernist attention to everyday life makes systemic disorder legible. In the closing pages I look at W. G. Sebald's *Austerlitz* and consider the possible afterlife of the outward turn, of the prolonged existence of a technique after its period of emergence and relevance would seem to have closed. I follow Sebald's wandering amnesiac Austerlitz as he extracts the material of history from the spaces and objects of everyday life. The labyrinthine, hypotactic prose of Sebald's novel mediates the winding, nearly endless process of retrieving Austerlitz's all but extinguished past. In its close attention to the sedimentation of history in architecture, photographs, postcards, and other ephemera, the novel's descriptive techniques bear forth Walter Benjamin's imperative to read history against the grain, to recover the vanquished from the debris of a violent historical process. This is, after all, why Austerlitz reminds us "we also have appointments to keep in the past."[61] Yet the infinite regress of Austerlitz's archive of everyday objects suggests that remembering is an endless, maybe impossible task. *Austerlitz*'s descriptions of everyday life transform quotidian experience into signs of history. Yet Austerlitz's quest indicates that such signs may be illegible and, perhaps, that we have arrived too late to read them.

1

THE LAST SNAPSHOT OF
THE BRITISH INTELLIGENTSIA

DOCUMENTARY, MASS-OBSERVATION,
AND THE FATE OF THE LIBERAL AVANT-GARDE

NEAR THE END of the July 1936 edition of *World Film News*, one of the key publications of the documentary film movement, the journal listed its supporters (figure 1.1). The names read like a who's who of modernism and the avant-garde: S. M. Eisenstein, T. S. Eliot, André Gide, Fritz Lang, Henry Moore, László Moholy-Nagy, and G. W. Pabst all find their way into this rather distinguished cast. Directly above this list are two advertisements: one from the Imperial Institute Cinema announcing films to be shown in July and another plugging the "Double Surrealist Number" of the little magazine *Contemporary Poetry and Prose*, a special issue that coincided with the London International Surrealist Exhibition at the New Burlington Galleries. At first glance, this trio appears to make for odd company. But this assemblage is instructive. The journal wears its modernist and avant-garde credentials on its sleeve and finds little conflict with something as vulgar as state-sponsored films lauding the virtues of empire. This conjuncture of radical aesthetics and the political status quo captures much of what is initially counterintuitive about late modernism's documentary culture but also singular in its approach to everyday life. Like the other late modernists this book examines, the documentary film units pioneered by John Grierson and the avant-garde sociological outfit Mass-Observation understood their approach to everyday life in aesthetic and political terms. The documentary film units hoped to create narratives of everyday life that would advance the interests of the British state by normalizing its policies and activities. Mass-Observation also aimed to

IMPERIAL INSTITUTE CINEMA

PROGRAMME FOR JULY

Empire programmes of Life, Scenery and Industry, for schools and all those interested in the countries of the British Commonwealth of Nations

DAILY: 10.15 and 11.35 a.m., 2.15 and 3.35 p.m. (Sundays 2.30 to 6 p.m.)

28th June to 4th July—Gold—South African Fruit Harvest.

7th to 11th July—Australia—Heart of Australia—Fruit Canning—Dried Fruit (Story of the Sultana)—Making Butter. Monsoon Island (Ceylon)—Air Post (G.P.O.).

12th to 18th July—How Gas is Made—South Africa—Dance of the Harvest (Rice)—Negombo Coast (Native Fishermen, Ceylon)—Under the City (G.P.O.).

19th to 25th July—O'er Hill and Dale—The Other Half of the World—King Log—Villages of Lanka (Ceylon)—Radio Interference (G.P.O. & B.B.C.).

26th July to 1st August—Industrial Britain—Loco-motives—Alert To-day, Alive To-morrow (Road Safety Film)—Canberra, Australia's Federal Capital—Conquest of the Prickly Pear—John Atkins Saves Up (P.O. Savings Bank).

SOUTH KENSINGTON · LONDON S.W.7

KENSINGTON 3264

CONTEMPORARY POETRY AND PROSE No 2 *is a*

DOUBLE SURREALIST NUMBER

ELUARD, PERET, BRETON, MESENS, DALI, HUGNET, ROSEY, CHAR, HENRY, BUNUEL, PRASSINOS, JARRY, CROS, GASCOYNE, JENNINGS, ALLOTT contribute.

JUNE 1936. Price one shilling.

The July number will contain poems by Wallace Stevens, E. E. Cummings, Dylan Thomas, Kerker Quinn, Gavin Ewart, also another traditional ballad, a Greenland folk-legend and a story by Isaac Babel.

Edited by Roger Roughton, at 1 Parton Street, London, W.C. 1.

Yearly subscription (including double numbers) 7/- ; (in the U.S.A. $1.75, in France Fr. 30).

Also out now:

CONTEMPORARY POETRY AND PROSE EDITIONS, Number One: Poems by] Benjamin Peret, selected and translated by Humphrey Jennings and David Gascoyne, with a note by Paul Eluard and an illustration by Pablo Picasso. Price two shillings.

W.F.N. enjoys the support and goodwill of the following :

Sidney Bernstein. James Bridie. Sir William Crawford. A. J. Cummings. J. H. Duveen. S. M. Eisenstein. T. S. Eliot. André Gide. Jean Giono. Mary Hamilton. Wilson Harris (editor of *The Spectator*). Julian Huxley. Alex King. Fritz Lang. Charles Laughton. Low. Ken Nyman (Chairman, London and Home Counties Branch, C.E.A.). Carl Mayer. E. McKnight Kauffer. Darius Milhaud. Henry Moore. Moholy Nagy. G. W. Pabst. Erich Pommer. S. G. Rayment (editor of *The Kine Weekly*). Flora Robson. Victor Saville. Josef Von Sternberg. Szigeti. Herbert Thompson (editor of the *Film Weekly*). H. G. Wells. Charles Wright.

We hope you have enjoyed reading the first number of WORLD FILM NEWS in its new form. The Film Guide, published in this issue, is going to be a regular feature; in the near future, we shall expand it, and include more towns, and we shall also widen its scope by including shows at film societies, and other clubs and organisations. This guide gives the booking dates and places of the *Best* Continental, Documentary and other Specialised, which we think are of particular interest to W.F.N. readers. Another regular feature is the REVIEW OF REVIEWS.

Another section we want to draw your special attention to is what we've so far called "Public Relations"; under this heading come Documentaries, Advertising, Propaganda, and Publicity, and Educational Films. You will notice this section increase in successive issues, because

it's a subject that's becoming increasingly important.

There's a regular section on COLOUR, and a regular section on MUSIC IN FILMS in each issue. There's regular news from the studios at home and abroad; there's a regular page for the amateur cinematographer. There's regular news from the Film Societies. (*W.F.N. is the official organ of the Federation of Film Societies*).

This issue contains a special RADIO AND TELEVISION SUPPLEMENT—if you've read *films, and the men who make them.* If these subjects interest you, why not post a cheque or postal order right away for a year's subscription to:—

WORLD FILM NEWS is a magazine about *films, and the men who make them*. If these subjects interest you, why not post a cheque or postal order right away for a year's subscription to:—

WORLD FILM NEWS, (Publishing Dept.), 217-218 Temple Chambers, Temple Avenue, E.C.4

Owned and Controlled by Cinema Contact Ltd., 9 Oxford Street, London, W.1. Printed by The Shenval Press Ltd., 58 Bloomsbury Street, London W.C.

FIGURE 1.1 *WORLD FILM NEWS*, JULY 1936.

align the desires, hopes, and fears of the population with the political institutions of the British state. Unlike any other late modernist phenomenon, this version of the outward turn was defined by an uneasy coexistence of radical aesthetics and a reformist politics that promoted liberal norms and values.

Little else had the aesthetic novelty and the political charge of documentary in the 1930s. Grierson first used the word "documentary" in a 1926 *New York Sun* review of Robert Flaherty's *Moana*.[1] In this instance, "documentary" was more or less a direct translation of the French *documentaire*, which typically refers to expedition films.[2] Later in the 1920s and throughout the 1930s Grierson would theorize documentary in a more pointed, precise way. He eventually called documentary "the creative treatment of actuality," a phrase he tosses out parenthetically and with little elaboration in a 1933 piece in *Cinema Quarterly*.[3] Although it now serves as a textbook definition in film studies, it is not entirely clear how widely known Grierson's phrase was to other writers outside of his circle. However, the impulse to turn toward actuality, to find in the everyday signs and measures of contemporary problems, was a shared one. J. B. Priestley's *English Journey* (1934) gave a panoramic view of English life during the slump. Photographer Bill Brandt's photo-essay *The English at Home* (1936) and George Orwell's *Road to Wigan Pier* (1937) also tried to convey the intensifying economic desperation and inequality threatening any sense of a shared national cultural identity.

In 1937 *Fact* published a special issue calling for a "literary equivalent of the documentary film," citing Orwell's book (at the least the first half of it) as an example of literature attuned to "the factors of change and the rumour of the real world."[4] W. H. Auden, E. M. Forster, and Benjamin Britten would all contribute to documentary films.[5] With the exception of Brandt, a surrealist-influenced photographer with a keen eye for paradox and coincidence, the majority of these documentary efforts aim for accurate representation, fitting more within traditions of reportage or autoethnography than anything remotely modernist, experimental, or avant-garde. I focus on the film units pioneered by Grierson and the writings of Mass-Observation precisely because their projects develop out of and modify modernist and avant-garde techniques.

Recent reappraisals of documentary and its aesthetic lineages try to correct the misperceptions of documentary as some sort of regressive realism. Tyrus Miller and Bill Nichols both highlight the affinities between documentary and the European avant-garde. Miller finds formal homologies between the late modernist prose poem in Britain and documentary; if we follow Miller's logic, pitting modernism against documentary conceals a great deal of literary and cinematic activity that developed from this conjuncture. Like Miller, Nichols suggests that critics and historians too easily "perpetuate a false division between the avant-garde and documentary that obscures their necessary proximity."[6] Nichols argues that documentary becomes possible only when it combines "three preexisting elements—photographic realism, narrative structure, and modernist fragmentation—along with a new emphasis on the rhetoric of social persuasion.[7] Both approaches restore the role of avant-garde aesthetics to the history of documentary. And yet the political valences of this relationship have been improperly contextualized. Nichols, for example, misreads the relationship of politics and aesthetics underwriting Grierson's theories and practices. Grierson's theories of documentary do not approximate "neoconservative political theory" nor do they resemble "more virulent forms of totalitarianism."[8] And, lastly, Grierson would be rather surprised to hear of his "affinity with the aesthetics of the Bloomsbury group."[9]

Miller, Nichols, and others have been right to assert the modernist or avant-garde pedigrees of both the documentary film movement and Mass-Observation. What we now need to understand are the many ways the aesthetic was theorized, recoded, and put at the service of securing liberal norms. In other words, we should now ask how documentary prescribes a new social function for innovative art.[10] The social function of art underwrites many avant-garde and modernist declarations and, to be sure, the philosophical debates that followed. We can roughly categorize art's social function in three ways: emancipation, separation, and reconciliation.[11] Avant-garde manifestoes from the futurists to the situationists ascribe an emancipatory function to art. The works of these avant-gardistes are profoundly nonmimetic; in place of identifiable representations of everyday life, they produced cryptic images of worlds and lives that had yet to be realized. The artwork offers a utopic promise of another world where art and the everyday would be so revolutionized that neither would be recognizable. Emancipation, then, means collapsing art's separation from everyday life but on terms established by the avant-gardes. In other sectors of modernist and avant-garde culture, the separation of art and daily life is vigorously maintained, even policed. This type of separation animates Stéphane Mallarmé and symbolist poetry, T. S. Eliot's poetry through the 1920s, and, if one follows Theodor Adorno's unsparing defense of modernism as separation, Samuel Beckett and Franz Kafka. Art's apartness, what Adorno calls its asociality, is the condition of possibility for any critique of society. Like Eliot's *The Waste Land*, the work of art can diagnose the malaise of modernity and model solutions, but, formally, it will bear "the scars of damage and disruption."[12] In a dialectical way, "only by virtue of separation from empirical reality, which sanctions art to model the relation of the whole and the part according to the work's own need, does the artwork achieve a heightened order of existence."[13] Aesthetic separation, then, names artworks in which appearance negatively designates the poverty of everyday life; what appears in art, what is pleasurable and enticing, can never be realized.

Jacques Rancière sees these two roles as the definitive antipodes of modernism: "a contrast is thereby formed between a type of art that makes politics by eliminating itself as art and a type of art that is political on the proviso that it retains its purity, avoiding all forms of political intervention."[14] But there is a third role, one I call reconciliation, which designates the documentary's liberal avant-garde project. In these works, appearance neither hearkens the yet-to-come nor is it a dark reminder of impoverished reality. Appearance is a reconfiguration of what is—it makes visible what has already been realized but reframes it, allowing us to see anew the practices of everyday life. Reconciliatory art deprives the aesthetic of its adversarial position. To borrow Rancière's terms, reconciliation promotes consensus, not dissensus.[15] Although his argument proceeds in a slightly different context, his remarks on the changed meanings of the avant-garde are more than apropos. In his estimation, art that shifts from dissensus to consensus makes art "responsible for the functions of archiving and bearing witness to a common world. This gathering, then, is part of an attitude to art that is stamped by the categories of consensus: restore lost meaning to a common world or repair the cracks in the social bond."[16] Establish consensus, merge the advances and potentiality of art with the social and political order, and remake art's social function into one of compatibility, not antagonism: this is what drives the documentary aesthetic. As I argue throughout the rest of this chapter, this is how we should understand the adaptation of Soviet cinema techniques in Grierson's film units as well as the rehabilitation and deployment of surrealism in Mass-Observation.

To begin looking at the documentary's reformatting of the avant-garde, I turn to Walter Benjamin's remarkable 1929 essay "Surrealism: The Last Snapshot of the European Intelligentsia." Benjamin asks how the radical potentiality of the avant-garde might be recovered and mobilized to spur change in everyday life. Quite simply, he asks what social function might be ascribed to a form of art that is antagonistic and, in some instances, asocial. He opens with an extended metaphor of critical distance and appropriation. "Intellectual currents," he writes, "can generate a sufficient head of water for the critic to install his power station on them. The necessary gradient, in the case of Surrealism, is produced by the difference in intellectual level between France and Germany."[17] This difference affords the German critic a privileged, detached perspective on surrealism that those caught up in its initial flourishing in France could not have had. Those critics, he suggests, squander their time bickering over the origins of the group or they simply are too close to surrealism to see the critical energies it might offer; they "are a little like a gathering of experts at a spring who, after lengthy deliberation, arrive at the conviction that this paltry stream will never drive turbines."[18] The German, however, sits not at the source but in the valley, and this particular position enables a wholly different engagement: "The German observer is not standing at the source of the stream. This is his opportunity. He is in the valley. He can gauge the energies of the movement."[19] Benjamin also believes surrealism in 1929 is at a pivotal moment: it can transform into an anarchic group locked in a struggle for power or petrify into an identifiable art form, a museum piece of sorts. Benjamin's effort is not a reappraisal of surrealism but an interrogation into dormant potentialities that have yet to be actualized. How might surrealism serve as a source for critical thought, as an endless spring for other critical projects? Benjamin sought techniques to awaken class consciousness, to dissolve the phantasmagoria capitalism had cast over modern life; he would eventually, even if mistakenly, uphold film and Brecht's theater as more satisfying models. While the documentary film movement and Mass-Observation do not share Benjamin's political project, they do possess the national and critical distance from the avant-gardes they so admired.

Revolution and radical politics were anything but the endgame for Grierson's documentary film movement or Mass-Observation. From their vantage point, the problem was not so much how to promote a revolution from the left but rather how one might use the avant-garde's unique powers of aesthetic disclosure to affirm and promote a normative British liberalism domestically and internationally during a period of world systemic distress. Grierson's documentary circle and Mass-Observation calculated that distress in a very particular way. In his 1935 book *Documentary Film*, Paul Rotha renders the historical moment as an accumulation of existing and potential economic and political catastrophes:

> But conditions and events are such that we cannot continue in this way of thinking and living for long. With the constant repetition of strikes, assassinations, disasters,

pogroms and every form of economic and political crisis that have crowded the social horizon of recent years, it is true to say that the individual is beginning to take a greater interest generally in public affairs and to enquire more into his relations with society than he has one previously in this so-called age of democracy.[20]

Penning their inaugural pamphlet just two years later, Mass-Observation would also assemble an unnerving inventory: "The bringing of civilization to Abyssinia, the coming of civil war to Spain, the atavism of the new Germany and the revival of racial superstition have forced the issue home to many. We are all in danger of extinction from such outbursts of atavism."[21] For both the documentary film movement and Mass-Observation, these situations presented grave threats to liberal democratic societies; at this historical juncture, the extinction of liberal democracy was a very real possibility. Their answer was to sift through everyday life to find evidence of how the population's wishes and fears, the psychological and affective shape of their daily lives, related to the state and its institutions. Grierson firmly believed that attending to the course of daily life would open the way for more robust political participation and a healthier relationship between the citizens and the state. Documentary cinema, in particular, offered a "new instrument of public influence, which might increase experience and bring the new world of our citizenship into the imagination."[22] Similarly, Mass-Observation set out "to see how, and how far, the individual is linked up with society and its institutions."[23]

These statements of purpose scarcely resemble the aggressive declarations of Marinetti's futurists, the blasting and bombardiering vorticists, or the radical negativity of Dada. The threat to the state and its social institutions comes not from a boisterous, cocksure avant-garde but from inefficient democratic institutions at home and enemies abroad. Securing democracy meant revitalizing those institutions and tightening the social bond between the citizenry and the state. Grierson was well aware that liberalism was on the ropes in much of Western Europe, but he did not believe that contemporary history spelled the end of liberal philosophies of governance. In a 1937 essay Grierson described the challenges to liberalism and set up documentary as a proper response:

Many of us after 1918 (and particularly in the United States) were impressed by the pessimism that had settled on Liberal theory. We noted the conclusion of such men as

Walter Lippmann, that because the citizen, under modern conditions, could not know everything about everything all the time, democratic citizenship was therefore impossible. We set to thinking how a dramatic apprehension of the modern scene might solve the problem, and we turned to the new wide-reaching instruments of radio and cinema as necessary instruments in both the practice of government and the enjoyment of citizenship.[24]

Citizenship and knowledge, governance and communication, the role of the state in the era of mass society: Grierson crystallizes here the concerns that led both documentary film movement and Mass-Observation to put the avant-garde at the service of the liberal state.

JOHN GRIERSON AND THE
THEORY OF DOCUMENTARY

"The creative treatment of actuality": the staying power of Grierson's famous phrase attests more to its allure than its clarity. There are several good histories of documentary, and nearly all of them dutifully recite Grierson's definition.[25] Most, however, don't acknowledge that the concept of documentary evolved over a period of years, often in an antagonistic and dialectical relationship with other types of cinema.[26] The nascent "documentary" cut its teeth against the fantasies and excess of Hollywood, the perceived aestheticism of some modernist and avant-garde films, and the politicized cinema of the Soviet Union. Grierson was documentary's most avid theoretician and its greatest publicist. He published in *Close Up* and *Sight and Sound* and spearheaded *Cinema Quarterly*, *World Film News*, and *Documentary News Letter*; he delivered lectures at universities, film societies and institutes and served as a judge at film festivals.[27] Paul Rotha's books *Documentary Film* (1935) and *Documentary Diary* (1973) helped canonize Grierson's version of what documentary was and how it should operate.[28] In this section I want to examine Grierson's conceptualization of documentary as both aesthetically innovative and a tool for managing domestic and imperial affairs. Two distinct priorities organize Grierson's thoughts on documentary: first, documentary film uniquely wields the power to form the raw material of everyday life into something meaningful; and second, "meaningful" designates the creation of consensus, a refashioning of the national social bond around a set of norms and values. Through Grierson's meditations on modern art and cinema we can recover documentary as both an evolving aesthetic and a political tool.

As late as 1970 Grierson would combat the perceptions of documentary as merely mimetic: "Most people . . . when they think of documentary films think of public reports and social problems and worthwhile education and all that sort of thing. For me it is something more magical. It is a visual art which conveys a sense of beauty about the ordinary world, the world on your doorstep."[29] Coming from someone who received a master's degree in philosophy and literature, these comments should not be altogether surprising. Grierson remained remarkably consistent in his aesthetic philosophy. Some of his early commentaries on modern art from the 1920s offer a glimpse into his passion for modernism, his suspicions about its potential detachment from everyday life, and the beginnings of a theory of art and reception that would guide his conceptualization of documentary some years later.

Grierson's positions on modern art take shape in his writings from the mid-1920s. He received a Rockefeller Research Fellowship in social science and left for Chicago in 1924. Ian Aitken writes that Grierson was no stranger to the modern art scene, and it was in part responsible for his decision to go to Chicago. He read the *Dial* while at university and "had argued that, whilst Russia was the home of political revolutionaries, America was the home of aesthetic revolutionaries."[30] Chicago meant Vachel Lindsay, Carl Sandburg, and Frank Lloyd Wright; it also meant industry, immigration, social flux, and modernity. Grierson's fellowship placed him at the University of Chicago, where he would learn much about mass democracy, media, and communications. Before film grabbed his imagination, he was fascinated with the newspapers. As he investigated the impact of newspapers on the American public, he started contributing to them. In 1925 he published the first of a series of articles in the *Chicago Evening Post's* weekly *Magazine of the Art World*. These essays cover everything from Plato to vorticism, from Henri de Toulouse-Lautrec to B. B. Lollipop. Apart from their apparent subject matter, they serve primarily as meditations on the use and effects of modern art. Grierson's *bête noire* in these articles is Clive Bell, and it is against Bell's idea of significant form that Grierson articulates his version of modern art. Grierson's first piece for the *Chicago Evening Post* lauds painter Rudolph Weisenborn's set design for George Kaiser's play *Gas*. In Grierson's analysis, Weisenborn puts the principles of vorticism to use, capturing the movement and kinetic force of industrial life. Weisenborn, he thinks, represents artists who have moved beyond cubist design and, more importantly, are "a little impatient with Mr. Clive Bell and the 'will o' the wisp, Significant Form,' which he (till lately) has so consistently hunted. They have caught something of the power and energy of modern life and wanted to express it. They have tried to tear away the confusion, see thru the details to the essentials, and make an art a little worthy of turbines and dynamos."[31] The vitality and innovation of the avant-garde clearly has a champion in Grierson but only so long as the modern is not the private property of the cultural elite.

When Grierson makes the case for how one should approach a modern painting, he wrests the knowledge and capacity for judgment away from the specialists and grounds it instead in everyday intuition. Paintings, he argues, are not coded messages awaiting the highly trained individual to decipher them for a befuddled public. Rather than games for the specialist, artworks should be "lived with." We come to know artworks, he argues, through time and "comradeship."[32] Anyone, he believes, can enter into a relation with an artwork in a meaningful way. What obscures art more than anything are those he refers to as the aesthetes: "Mr. Clive Bell knows a lot about art, but he fogged the whole question when he made it so abstract. All that he meant by significant form was just this intimacy the philosophers stated so much more simply. Significant forms are shapes you feel an unaccountable affection for."[33] The "Britannic Esthetes," as he calls them elsewhere, transfer painterly abstraction into equally abstract and meaningless language; they do not explain or assist, but confound and complicate.[34]

Grierson's mockery of Bell and Roger Fry serves two purposes: first, he reduces his antagonists' conceptual vocabulary to modish nonsense; second, and this becomes a key component of his theory of documentary, the aims and effects of modern art can be democratized—anyone with interest in art should be able to enter into a relationship with it without picking through the semispiritual claptrap of highbrow art theory. It is important, though, to recognize the critique of Bell and significant form is not an aggrieved middlebrow assault on the difficulties and pretensions of elite culture. For Grierson, modern art was not nearly as abstract as its pundits and advocates claimed. In what might be his apology for painting, Grierson passionately, almost lyrically, defends the power of modern art:

> For the real power of art is the power of the artists to the renewing of vision and the enlivening of consciousness. One may call that esthetic if one pleases; it scarcely matters. What one knows is that in a knowledge of their work and participation in the secret of their eyes, one passes anew among the ordinary things of one's own life. The sidestreets and the people on the stoops of an evening, the faces of children, the breasts crushed heavily on tenement window sills are signalled in one's consciousness with a new warmth. The hot reds and greys of the sky, the swift angles of light that merge into the steel kaleidoscope of the city become an aureole for the drama of humanity.[35]

If modern art were to live up to its promise of challenging and reorganizing our perceptions of everyday life, it would need a larger, less specialized audience with confidence in its powers of judgment.

Such a discerning citizenry was the subject of much debate and speculation beyond the walls of museums and galleries. Walter Lippmann's *Public Opinion* appeared in 1922 and expressed significant reservations about the viability of democracy in an era of the masses. Lippmann thought democratic governance impossible in populous nations with underdeveloped means of informing and educating its citizenry. We would be foolish, Lippmann claims, to believe liberal democracies can continue to function in mass societies. Grierson absorbed Lippmann's diagnosis but not his prognostications. He recalls his own interaction with Lippmann this way: "I met Lippmann, who is the high priest in public opinion hereabouts, we disagreed a whole lot about it. And I never thought much of Lippmann to begin with."[36] Still, Grierson knew that any theory of democracy built upon the presumption of rational individuals was shaky at best. If the masses were not inherently rational, though, it did not follow that they could not be educated. Moving some distance from Lippmann's antidemocratic theories, Grierson "argue[d] for a distinction between a 'rational' and a 'mature' citizenry."[37] For Grierson, film's sophistication and wide appeal offered the best possible means for a political education of the masses.

Documentary film, as a concept and as a practice, emerges from Grierson's dual investments in modern art and in contemporary political science and sociology. We hear as much when he states that documentary "was a new instrument of public influence, which might increase experience and bring the new world of our citizenship into the imagination."[38] Creating the conditions for that imagined citizenship should act as a counterforce to what Grierson identified in Lippmann and others as "the unnecessary pessimisms of democratic theory."[39] In other words, the propagandistic element of documentary film could educate and influence the masses, sustaining the conditions and consent necessary for the operation of a liberal democratic society. But, as Grierson's investments in modern art make clear, documentary film would need to be as advanced and as technically sophisticated as any other art form if it truly sought to make the population look anew at everyday life.

Grierson derived his approach for an aesthetically sophisticated and politically attuned cinema from a multitude of sources. "What I know of cinema," he writes in a 1929 piece on his own film *Drifters*, "I have learned partly from the Russians, partly from the American westerns, and partly from Flaherty, of *Nanook*. The westerns give you some notion of the energies. The Russians give you the energies and the intimacies both. Flaherty is a poet."[40] Grierson paid endless tribute to Robert Flaherty, and *Nanook of the North* remained a solid point of reference in Grierson's writings. Flaherty ventured out and lived with the natives he put on screen. For Grierson, Flaherty showed that cinema need not rely on the manufactured article or depend entirely on the studio or Hollywood stardom (although critics have shown that Flaherty manufactured quite a bit on location, often putting his subjects in peril). Despite his distaste for Flaherty's "Neo-Rousseauism," he maintains that "Flaherty illustrates better than anyone the first principles of documentary."[41] Flaherty's commitment to the actual and, most importantly, "his distinction between description and drama" served as imperatives for documentary film.[42] If *Nanook* was exemplary in form and intention, its content proved far too romantic for Grierson. These films had nothing of the contemporary world in them. Sergei Eisenstein's *Battleship Potemkin* supplemented Flaherty's oeuvre. Grierson worked with John S. Cohen Jr., the film critic for the *New York Sun*, on the subtitles for the American version of *Potemkin*. He acquired an intimate knowledge of Eisensteinian montage and the political impact of the film. Although Eisenstein's politics were not his, the use of montage for dramatic effect indelibly marked Grierson. When Grierson premiered his own film *Drifters* to the London Film Society in 1929, he put *Battleship Potemkin* on the bill as well, inviting the audience to see the formal compatibility between these two.

From Flaherty comes an emphasis on actuality, raw material, and location; from Eisenstein documentary acquires both a technique to dramatize the actual and a sense of cinema's political power. Both of these touchstones for documentary presented significant risks. If Flaherty veered too far into primitivist fantasy, the Soviets tended to aestheticize their own material. Dziga Vertov's *The Man with the Movie Camera* and *Enthusiasm* dazzled Grierson with their avantgardism; yet *The Man with the Movie Camera* verged on becoming "ridiculous" while *Enthusiasm* "failed because he was like any bourgeois highbrow, too clever by half. . . . He has given us everything of the mechanism and nothing of the people."[43] The ever-important Eisenstein did not escape these dangers either. For Eisenstein, "the style is nearly everything."[44] Whether one agrees with Grierson's judgments of Vertov and Eisenstein or not, it is hard not to hear echoes of his earlier criticisms of Bell, Fry, and Bloomsbury. In Grierson's view, art must capture and reveal something about everyday life. It should neither assume a mimetic function nor drift into a self-contained world of endless experimentation. In a 1930 review of *One Family*, Grierson clearly defended the need for the new in art: "It may be—and what I understand of aesthetics bids me believe—that in making art in our new world we are called upon to build in new forms altogether."[45] The new in art is necessary, but, on its own, it is not enough.

PROJECTING ENGLAND: EMPIRE AND WAR

Grierson's ideas for a socially functional, aesthetically innovative cinema found their proper home in the two government agencies that funded his film units throughout the 1930s: the Empire Marketing Board (EMB, 1926–1933) and the General Post Office (GPO, 1933–1937). Paul Swann's meticulous reconstruction of these institutions demonstrates how absolutely essential they were to the growth of documentary film in Britain. By the time Grierson resigned from the GPO in 1937, documentary film had enough of a footing to continue under the leadership of Brazilian/Italian filmmaker Alberto Cavalcanti and flourish under the umbrella of the Ministry of Information during the Second World War.

While Grierson had little patience for civil servants and byzantine bureaucracies, government agencies provided the proper counterweight to the profit-driven world of popular cinema. Filmmaking was a costly enterprise, and there was no way around the massive amounts of capital needed to make even the most rudimentary film: "There is money for films which will make box-office profits, and there is money for films which will create propaganda results. These only. They are the strict limits within which cinema has had to develop and will continue to develop."[46] By 1935 Grierson thought the turn to "propaganda was inevitable."[47] For a brand of cinema designed to promote the economic interests of the state, government sponsorship would not prove so restrictive. Grierson even cast the EMB as "giving a freedom to its directors never recorded before in cinema."[48] Despite any "ideological limits," the propaganda cinema, with state patronage, presented challenges and opportunities that lead "the director to new forms and rich perspectives."[49] His enthusiasm for the propaganda film knew no bounds. He would even declare "the G.P.O. Film Unit is the only experimental centre in Europe."[50]

It is certainly true that the EMB, the GPO, and the Crown Film Unit produced some commercially successful and formally dynamic films. Most histories of documentary extol *Song of Ceylon*, *Night Mail*, *Listen to Britain*, and *Diary for Timothy* for their lyricism, imagery, and experiments with sound. What documentary filmmakers would come to discover is precisely what Grierson intuited early on: experimental films that avoided high abstraction or overt didacticism had the greatest effect on the public. Grierson's early experiences with the EMB made him acutely aware that film could shape perceptions and advance the board's mission to transform the idea of empire from a relation of domination to one of economic cooperation. This idea that documentary film could, in the words of EMB secretary and GPO public relations officer Sir Stephen Tallents, project a version of England and shape public imagination underwrites the entire early history of documentary, whether guided by Grierson or his successors.[51] I want to turn now to two films whose aesthetically appealing projections of empire and domestic life readily accomplished the goals of the documentary and cemented their place in film history. In each instance, avant-garde film techniques mold scenes of everyday life into lyrical visions that relieve antagonisms and manage public affect.

The most successful venture Grierson presided over during the transition from the EMB to the GPO was Basil Wright's *Song of Ceylon*.[52] Wright's film gained wide acclaim for its inventive, asynchronic sound and its use of montage. In 1935 it won the Prix du Gouvernement at the International Film Festival in Brussels. Although the film was made for the Ceylon Tea Propaganda Board, Wright was given no script or directive. With free rein over the accumulation and arrangement of material, Wright produced a four-act film that showed British interests in Ceylon as benevolent, causing no interruption in what it perceived to be the traditional rhythms of Ceylonese life. The lyricism of *Song of Ceylon* that so enchanted audiences in the 1930s has lost little of its magic. In *A New History of Documentary Film*, Jack C. Ellis and Betsy A. McLane remind us that Wright's film is "one of the accepted masterpieces of documentary."[53] That status hinges on two things: first, it is "so remarkable in being so fully and freely a work of art while doing so little to sell the sponsor's product"[54]; second, the film, whether by Wright's intention or sheer aesthetic force, subverts any vision of imperial benevolence. Because Wright's film is so masterful, it could only ever upend imperial ideology. Ellis and McLane are not alone. Although William Guynn takes issue with the orientalist representation of the natives, he ultimately argues that "*Song of Ceylon* produces a critique of the whole enterprise of National Projection, stigmatizing the British presence as callous and exploitative."[55] To be clear, the relation of aesthetics and politics in these receptions of *Song of Ceylon* are the exact negative of what I am proposing in this chapter. These readings preserve in amber an old liberal idea of the aesthetic: the film replicates unfortunate cultural images of the Other (bad), but because it is a work of art, it always retains the ability to resist participation in the reproduction of imperial ideology (good). In a way that recalls the famous debates over Joseph Conrad's *Heart of Darkness*, these readings suggest that *Song of Ceylon*'s brilliance resides precisely in its ability to lay bare the structural violence of imperial labor.[56] Ontologically, the work of art resists, subverts, or refuses. This is a nice story, but it is not the one that plays out over the four acts of Wright's film.

Wright's tale casts the empire as flexible enough for Western modernity and this timeless Eastern civilization to coexist with little conflict. This version of liberal empire displays openness to, even reverence for, non-Western cultures and religious practices. It suggests that the cultivation and extraction of resources occurs only with the native population's blessing and participation. *Song of Ceylon*'s opening act, "The Buddha," charts a pilgrimage up Sri Pada (Adam's Peak), a holy site that bears the footprint of the Buddha. The camera glides from right to left, capturing images of nature, dissolving one into the other. Eventually we see a massive statue of the Buddha amid the foliage. The trope of harmonious, natural time established here gets developed over the four acts. Throughout this act and the second one, aptly named "The Virgin Island," we see happy natives living in concert with nature and their peaceful religion. The second act takes us from the religious devotion of "The Buddha" to a montage of scenes from daily life. A mother washes her child, and the film cuts to a mother elephant doing the same with her calf. The film switches back to the scene of mother and child, ensuring that we see the symmetry between native and nature. This trope is then put to work in images of labor. The narrator, reading from Robert Knox's seventeenth-century *An Historical Relation of the Island Ceylon*, tells us that the natives are "ingenious" laborers and are entirely self-sufficient. Their labor is aimed solely at reproducing their conditions of survival; there is no profit motive driving their work, and Knox's commentary asserts that "work for hire is a great shame" among the natives.

After two acts we have watched the Ceylonese cultivate their land for survival and comfort, live in accordance with their religion, and move in harmony with nature. The third act of the film, "Voices of Commerce," dramatizes the role of the British in this self-contained island world. Wright's use of asynchronic sound makes this act the most provocative and perplexing; it is also the act that Wright's critics point to as subversive of empire. Roughly summarized, "Voices of Commerce" pairs scenes of natives readying pounds of tea for shipment abroad with beeps and blips of Morse code, fragmented lines from commercial correspondence, stock quotes, and investment information. Critics are right to suggest that the disjuncture of sound and image describes how colonial labor gets converted into finance capital. But one should not mistake description for critique. The apparent conflict of sound and image is not staged to jolt us out of our ignorance of the human cost of imperial economics. Instead Wright stages and resolves this conflict to show how seamlessly the empire operates without disrupting native life.

"Voices of Commerce" opens with the percussive rhythms of a train moving across the land, recalling the drums we hear early on in "The Buddha." A native on an elephant appears as the rhythmic churn of the train slows. The elephant presses against a tree and forces it down; the wheels stop and the crashing of the tree drowns out the sound of the train. Inviting us to perceive some conflict, or at least an encounter, between machine and nature, the film instead introduces the first of several voices announcing the financial gain to be had from Ceylonese resources. As we gaze at the elephant towering over the fallen tree, we hear "new clearings, new roads, new buildings, new communications, new developments of natural resources."[57] At the very least, the first two novelties operate as captions for what we have just seen; the elephant clears the way for new railways and new transport. Sound and image collaborate to produce this moment of cooperation. Ceylon, then, is a land of plenty and a site of admirable cooperation between the empire and the natives. Depictions of labor are signs of participation. This is the same population that only requires the same basic necessities for the comfortable life they have led for epochs (and the fact that a seventeenth-century text supplies the narrative for Wright's film without the slightest hint of irony only reinforces this idea). These natives live in a land of abundance and the cultivation and use of their resources places no burden on their daily life.

The concluding act of *Song of Ceylon* returns to the thematics and imagery of the first two acts. "The Apparel of God" takes us back to scenes of daily life and to the Buddha. The massive steam liners we see in "Voices of Commerce" are gone. Outriggers move across the screen and the Ceylonese continue with their lives as before. As a bookend to the film, "The Apparel of God" suggests that no facet of Ceylonese life has been interrupted and no human labor has been unduly extracted. This is the cooperative liberal empire that the EMB so hoped its film unit would project at home and abroad. That the film bewitched its viewers and continues to enchant critics with its astonishing ability for critique attests to how well it merged aesthetic innovation with liberal norms. If the film manipulates sound to stage a contrast between the modern, capitalist West and the circadian, "primitive" East, it is not done to cast the "British presence as callous and exploitive."[58] The apparent conflict is swiftly resolved in the "Voices of Commerce," and the effects of empire are as minimal as the lingering sounds of Morse code that phase out as we gaze at the mute colossus of the Buddha in the film's final act.

Humphrey Jennings's *Listen to Britain* turns the camera eye onto a nation at war. The war climate altered the mission of the documentary, but it also heightened its stature. Government officials believed that film could inform the population about the war effort and sustain morale on the home front. In a wartime discussion of documentary film with J. B. Holmes and Ian Dalrymple, Jennings articulated the relationship between war and documentary in this way:

> It is well known that one of the most remarkable things that has come to everybody out of the war has been the breakdown of partitions and prejudices, and barriers of one sort and another between individuals. To that extent war conditions have definitely helped us, because it is precisely the breaking down of prejudices and partitions that documentary producers have always aimed at, and it is one of the basic aims and ideas of the documentary.[59]

When Jennings comments that "it is well known" that the exigencies of the war collapsed all sorts of barriers—class, gender, regional—he refers to that sort of People's War ideology the documentary films were specifically charged with producing. James Chapman describes "the ideology of the people's war which emerges from wartime films is one of national unity and social cohesion: class differences have all but disappeared and have been replaced instead by a democratic sense of community and comradeship."[60] Arguably, no film—perhaps no text at all——from the Second World War propagates this normative version of everyday life during the war as lyrically and effectively as *Listen to Britain*.

Often referred to as Jennings's masterpiece, *Listen to Britain* owes much to those European symphony films pioneered by Walter Ruttmann and Alberto Cavalcanti. Ruttmann's *Berlin* and Cavalcanti's *Rien que les heures* magnificently rendered the extraordinary dynamism of an ordinary day in the life of a city. Jennings's film bids us to listen to and to see everyday life under extraordinary conditions as remarkably ordinary. The title screen depicts a violin with a gun barrel extending over its neck. The crossing of these two images previews the film's dialectical form: sounds of war against sounds of music, the rupture of an historical event against the continuity of everyday life, and, more broadly, the barbarism of war against a civilized, cultured population. Its preference for music over any narration produces a disjunction of sound and image, an apparent conflict between what is heard and what is seen. The trick of Jennings's film—and, indeed, its strongest ideological signal—is that such differences cannot only be managed but they can counterintuitively confirm a single idea: war has not dramatically altered the shape of everyday life in Britain. Like *Song of Ceylon*, *Listen to Britain* formally stages a series of conflicts and resolves them dialectically.

Malcolm Smith sorts out two levels of montage in *Listen to Britain* that enable the film to highlight and manage conflict.[61] There is "micro-montage," or the often dizzying arrangements of scenes showcasing subjects from different classes engaged in any number of tasks. The "macro-montage," the sequential ordering of the film into a twenty-four hour period from late afternoon to early afternoon offers some framework for these otherwise jumbled, unrelated episodes. The real connective tissue between these two levels of montage comes from Jennings's manipulation of sound. Sounds often precede the image of their source in the film and continue over to another unrelated image. Jennings's asynchrony first disjoins image and sound and then fuses together disparate scenes of agricultural workers, air raid observers, and factory workers. In the film's signature sequence, an audience of factory workers watches and whistles along to a performance by comedy duo Flanagan and Allen. The final chord of their tune carries over to an image of the National Gallery before blending into the very same chord of a Mozart recital by Dame Myra Hess and the Royal Air Force Central Band. The music travels outside of its source in the canteen and transitions seamlessly to the National Gallery, its new source. The cultural contrast is rather clear: a workers' audience at a low-cultural performance versus a more distinguished audience, one that includes National Gallery and War Artists Advisory Committee director Kenneth Clark and the Queen herself, at a decidedly high cultural event in a proper venue. The effect is rather remarkable; the cultural contrast and the musical harmony are perceived together. Difference articulated quickly becomes difference harmonized.

At one level, then, the film's ideological mission is to thread together disparate scenes of life in Britain, disarming social antagonisms by stressing a shared British culture. At another level, though, *Listen to Britain* goes beyond the typical People's War message of class and cultural unity. It also calibrates the relationship between the continuity of everyday life and the interruptions of war. In Jennings's hands, even a day at war is not all that extraordinary. If we return to the scene at the National Gallery, we find Jennings performing the same dialectical synthesis within a single episode that he executes so masterfully between multiple episodes. Jennings's camera looks downward at a couple eating lunch on the stairs just inside the gallery; the revolving door turns as people go in and out. The camera looks upward from this otherwise ordinary museum scene, offering three shots of what can only be bomb damage to the interior walls and windows of the National Gallery. The film cuts back to the attentive audience at the lunch concert and then offers a close up of the revolving door and the couple eating on the stairs. Damaged or not, the National Gallery continues playing host to national culture and the public still passes in and out of its doors. To be sure, this isn't everyday life outside of war. Rather, the everyday is flexible enough to accommodate any such interruption without being noticeably altered. Concerts continue, but the orchestra are all military men; art exhibitions continue, but, as the sign announces, this is a "War Artists' Exhibition." Observers gaze at paintings, a woman flips through a turnstile of postcards, and museum-goers eat and converse. Everyday life proceeds as ever.

Again, the point is not to erase conflict but to draw it into the film, manage it, and thereby defuse it. It might seem curious that the primary conflicts in this film are cultural and social. German bombers make no appearance, and the violence of the war scarcely figures at all in *Listen to Britain*. Unlike *First Days* (1939) and *London Can Take It!* (1940), *Listen to Britain* was filmed and compiled near the end of the Blitz, but before the turning point at the Battle of El Alamein and before the Beveridge Report spurred widespread discussion of a more hopeful, more equitable postwar Britain. In other words, as Chapman argues, *Listen to Britain* appears at a moment when the war seems sure to be a taxing affair with no end in sight. As a propaganda film in 1942, its mission is not to extol the endurance and quiet resolve of the British under attack from the air; it is to show that everyday life can accommodate and endure all the pressures of wartime. By the conclusion of Jennings's film, our eyes and ears should convince us that German bombing campaigns have neither paralyzed nor altered Britain. If anything, the war strengthens the perception of a shared cultural and social fabric in Britain

MASS-OBSERVATION AND CRISIS POETICS

Up to this point I have argued that late modernist documentary repurposes avant-garde techniques by merging radical aesthetics with liberal reformist politics.

From Grierson's meditations on art in the 1920s to Wright's and Jennings's films, the documentary film movement harnessed the power of avant-garde aesthetics to arrange public perception and to quiet antagonism. For these reasons I've suggested the documentary be categorized as an aesthetic of reconciliation. In other words, the appearances of everyday life on the screen are meant to generate consensus, to reconcile any differences between the workings of the state and the citizens' judgments of the state. Turning now to Mass-Observation, we find another group who mined avant-garde aesthetics for ways to investigate and mold their depictions of everyday life. Like the documentary film producers and directors, some of whom participated in Mass-Observation, this group also saw the creation of consensus as its primary goal. There are, however, important institutional and conceptual distinctions to be made. Although the Ministry of Information would fold Mass-Observation into its operations during the Second World War, Mass-Observation did not begin with any form of state sponsorship. It also required participation from the masses; in Mass-Observation's own words, the idea was not to project a version of everyday life for the masses to receive passively but rather for each citizen to participate in observing the daily life of the nation. Ideally, each participant would be "like Courbet at his easel, Cuvier with his cadaver, and Humboldt with his continent."[62] Individual citizens were the best experts on mass society, and Mass-Observation relied on them to generate the raw material of their narratives. It is within these two areas—generating material and giving it form—that we see Mass-Observation drawing upon and modifying avant-garde aesthetics, especially surrealism.

The pedigree of Mass-Observation's initial membership gives a snapshot of the range of influences animating the group during its first phase of activity. In December 1936 a curious mélange of poets (Charles Madge, William Empson, and Kathleen Raine), documentary filmmakers (Humphrey Jennings and Stuart Legg), and British surrealists (David Gascoyne, Sheila Legg, and Jennings) gathered in a Blackheath apartment to develop a method for decoding the political and social import ciphered within the minutiae of everyday life. Madge announced the existence of Mass-Observation in a letter to the *New Statesman and Nation* on January 2, 1937. That letter was a response to one penned earlier by Sir Geoffrey Pyke, who cited the need for an anthropology of English life, one that might make sense of the social hysteria following King Edward VIII's abdication. Echoing Pyke's desire for a home anthropology, Madge invited volunteers to participate in what would later be described as the "observation of everyone by everyone."[63] Tom Harrisson, an amateur anthropologist who had just returned from a three-year stay in Malekula, published his only poem in the *New Statesman and Nation*. By coincidence alone, it appeared on the same page as Madge's letter. Harrisson had just settled in Bolton with the intention of studying the working classes with the same participant-observer method he used in Malekula. Detecting possible parallels between his project and this emergent group of Mass-Observers, Harrisson contacted Madge, and the two agreed to coordinate their projects under the Mass-Observation banner.

Harrisson, Jennings, and Madge coauthored another letter to the *New Statesman and Nation* on January 30, 1937. Their project was to be the "anthropology of our own people," a populist ethnography that would excavate the myriad life practices throughout England.[64] Harrisson's arrival brought a heavier emphasis on the sociological side of the project. Kathleen Raine recalls these early days of Mass-Observation as a "strange half-poetic half-sociological expression of the prewar years."[65] These two halves would never sit as easily with one another as they did in the documentary film groups. Harrisson's imperious personality, his insistence on the empirical fact, and his distrust of poetry sparked a bitter conflict, precipitating insoluble problems for Mass-Observation's aesthetico-anthropological aspirations. Jennings departed later in 1937 and Madge's turbulent relationship with Harrisson continued until he left in 1940 to work on wartime economics with John Maynard Keynes.[66]

Most interpretations of this first phase of Mass-Observation praise their flirtation with aesthetics and bemoan their eventual merger with the Ministry of Information in 1940.[67] Jed Esty elegantly traces their narrative arc in this way: "Mass-Observation's attempt at a radically democratic and decentralized representational apparatus . . . ended up becoming normative and even statist in its effects. The centralizing effect of Mass-Observation, particularly with the onset of World War II, took the litany of shared Englishness on a short trip from radical intentions to conservative organicism."[68] We might further complicate this story by addressing the many ways in which the group articulated the political dimension of their project.[69] Mass-Observation conceived their group as a response to a wider cultural and political emergency: "the science of ourselves is a crying necessity to-day."[70] In his afterword to *First Year's Work*, Bronislaw Malinowski echoes Mass-Observation's political necessity in equally urgent, if not grandiose, terms: "Mass-Observation, alas!, is inconceivable in any of the totalitarian communities. Yet, in countries where democracy is still at work, Mass-Observation may not only be a useful instrument of scientific research, but it may become an extremely important practical contribution towards the maintenance of human civilization where it still survives."[71] Similar presentiments reverberate across all publications between 1937 and 1940. These writings prop up Mass-Observation as a counterforce to the rise of fascism on the continent and the burgeoning threats to liberal democracy at home. Accordingly, Mass-Observation's narratives of everyday life address those areas where state institutions and the citizenry seem most at odds. In *First Year's Work* they express the aim of their investigations in this way: "In all researches on the older institutions, we are continually impressed by the discrepancy between what is supposed to happen and what does happen, between the law and the fact, the institution and the individual, what people say they do and what they actually do, what leaders think people want and what people do want."[72] The group's raison d'être, their dual investment in narrating the everyday and in avant-garde aesthetics, is aimed at fixing these discrepancies.

Reading Mass-Observation's aesthetics of daily life as part of a project to defend Britain's liberal order at home and abroad means that we reconsider what has long been termed their passage into a "nakedly authoritarian" organization.[73] As I will show, Mass-Observation undergoes no such dramatic transformation. There was never a radically democratic project to become a centralized, near authoritarian state apparatus. The supposed authoritarian turn occurs simultaneously with the passage of the Emergency Powers Act in 1939, the legal measures that effectively suspended democratic procedures in order to preserve democracy for the future. While there are indeed noticeable formal changes between *May the Twelfth* (1937) and the so-called authoritarian *War Begins at Home* (1940), the group's guiding principle remains the same: knowledge of everyday life will close the gap between the leaders and the led and ensure a democratic future. For now, though, it is enough to position Mass-Observation within that wider field of documentary culture that marshaled radical aesthetics for liberal reformist politics.

"SURREALISM FOR THE ENGLISH"

Two public events opened the way for Mass-Observation: the abdication of King Edward VIII and the burning of the Crystal Palace.[74] King Edward VIII's relationship with the twice-divorced American Mrs. Wallis Simpson sparked outrage on legal, religious, and political fronts. In the end, he opted to marry Mrs. Simpson and leave the throne. Although suppressed by heavy censorship, news of the abdication broke, inspiring a public scandal that caused particular shame for British royalty. Not long afterward, the Crystal Palace burned to ash on November 30, 1936, lighting the sky around it and prompting Prime Minister Winston Churchill to declare "the end of an era." Churchill's apocalyptic remarks lend a certain gravity to the event, but, as Valentine Cunningham says, the palace's incineration had less to do with a bygone era; it fits more with the cadence of destructive events signaling a shift in the European balance of power: "When the Crystal Palace went up in flames at the end of November 1936 it was widely taken as an apt emblem for the times: a sort of Reichstag Fire for Britain, mirror image of what was happening to Madrid. It would be looked back on as an accurate augury of many blazing cities to come: Warsaw, Coventry, Plymouth, Dresden."[75] The symbolic charge of the abdication and the Crystal Palace was not lost on Jennings and Madge. Madge's reflections on these originary events from his unpublished autobiographical writings are worth quoting at length:

Humphrey Jennings and I had been noticing the way in which the items on a newspaper page, especially the front page, added up to make a kind of "poem"—or so we interpreted it. There was an affinity between the items at a symbolic level, which must have been due partly to the news editor's assessment of what made front page news on that particular day, partly to the layout men, partly to the current and shifting concerns of the popular readership, partly no doubt to chance or what is called coincidence. Neither Humphrey nor I were inclined toward Jungian ideas of a collective unconscious, but we had read Freud's essay on coincidence, which had led to an interest among certain French surrealists, especially André Breton, in coincidental happenings of various kinds. So when the papers were full of Edward and Mrs. Simpson we saw them as in part an expression of mass wishes and fantasies, and were on the look out for other symbolic news-material that might be related to them. At the end of November the Crystal Palace was burned down, and the flames were visible from 6 Grotes Buildings as a distant glow in the sky: the shock that this seemed to evoke at a symbolic level was perhaps akin to the shock that the abdication crisis brought to our stable monarchy.[76]

For Mass-Observation, surrealist techniques of reading and assemblage capture submerged currents of public affect. Shock and collective response, symbolism and coincidence: knowledge of everyday life yields itself indirectly, almost in spite of the more narrow informational discourse of journalism.

How one accounts for their surrealist inclinations often guides the assessment of the group's politics. Jeremy MacClancey's classic reading of Mass-Observation hails them for pursuing a "postmodern" critique of anthropology *avant la lettre*, evincing the same sensibility popularized later by James Clifford and Clifford Geertz. MacClancey characterizes Mass-Observation as a "democratic surrealism," but his interest in Mass-Observation is coterminous with its surrealist affinities, which he declares over after Jennings leaves the organization in 1937.[77] Ben Highmore plots Mass-Observation in the fault lines between art and science. Although he points to some of the contradictions and discontinuities with any story of Mass-Observation as either an avant-garde project or a hard science, he nonetheless upholds Mass-Observation as an effort in "direct democracy," as a "radically democratic project" because their texts deploy the "destabilizing effects of collage."[78] Despite the differences between the two, MacClancey and Highmore's critical narratives follow a similar plot: radical aesthetics equals radical politics. With this in mind, I want to revisit the influence of surrealism over Mass-Observation and suggest two things: first, the surrealism of Mass-Observation would be scarcely recognizable to their continental counterparts; second, where Breton was looking for those "who would be ready to create the Revolution," Mass-Observation was concerned with securing the principles and institutions of liberal democracy and maintaining order.[79]

Paul Ray and Michel Remy's thickly researched accounts of English surrealism track the proliferation of surrealist activity in journals, visual and literary works, and exhibitions in the 1930s and after.[80] Early Mass-Observers Julian Trevelyan and Humphrey Jennings as well as Hugh Sykes Davies first coalesced around anarchist Jacob Bronowski's journal *Experiment*. They sought to "de-axiomatize literature and the arts," isolating experimentation as the only proper criterion for art.[81] These young writers merged European trends with British writing, trying to create something new, daring, and unlike the high modernism that dominated the postwar years. Eugène Jolas's *transition*, perhaps most famous for its early publications of James Joyce's *Work in Progress*, donated over thirty pages of space to the "Experiment Group" in June 1930, weaving ever tighter the bonds between England and France. A few years later, the first English surrealist poem flowed easily and eloquently from the pen of seventeen-year-old David Gascoyne. "And the Seventh Dream Is the Dream of Isis" appeared in October 1933 in Geoffrey Grigson's *New Verse*, a publication that later became a primary venue for Madge, Jennings, and Mass-Observation's early literary experiments. These were the early tremors, mere signs of another art quake that would generate disgust and fascination in equal proportions to Roger Fry's 1910 Post-Impressionist exhibit. The International Surrealist Exhibition of 1936 at the New Burlington Galleries and the Surrealist Objects and Poems exhibition in 1937 thrust surrealism onto the English public; the former exhibit drew twenty-three thousand people and placed works by lesser known English artists and writers next to their continental counterparts.

If these publications and events suggest that the surrealist phenomenon spread far and wide, it should not lead to the conclusion that surrealism's transmission from the continent to England occurred in any programmatic way.[82] Surrealism's arrival entailed numerous efforts to define and redefine what exactly it meant in its new English home. The word itself doesn't enter into an English dictionary until 1933; that same year, Herbert Read tried to distinguish between "*surréalisme*" and "super-realism," a distinction he attempted to refine again three years later. A greater indication of English surrealism's problems of self-definition comes by way of David Gascoyne's *The First Manifesto of English Surrealism*, which was first published in French translation in *Cahiers d'Art* in 1935. These early problems of definition set the course for a deeply uneven sense of "English surrealism." Remy maps out two contradictory versions of English surrealism: "Read and Davies's approach, which aims at making surrealism "acceptable" and part of English tradition, and Jennings and Madge's approach, which warns people against reducing surrealism to simple formulas and stresses its break with the past."[83] By tracing out this latter course, we can see how Mass-Observation harnessed and eventually modified surrealist energies, ideas, and practices.

Jennings and Madge's gravitation toward surrealism parallels Grierson's interest in vorticism and Soviet cinema: the avant-garde argued that to uncover everyday life you had to look at it otherwise than how it offered itself. Although his own poetry was considerably less influenced by surrealism than were Jennings or Gascoyne, Madge authored reviews and articles on surrealism for *New Verse* as early as 1933 and eventually used the same journal to stage early Mass-Observation experiments. In "Surrealism for the English" (1933) Madge argues that surrealism's potential hinges on time and place. It would be easy to read Madge's article as re-territorializing surrealism, of planting it firmly in English soil. But this isn't exactly what Madge has in mind. Referencing two exhibits of surrealist art at the Mayor Gallery in 1933, Madge underscores the problem posed by the rather late appearance of surrealism in England. "But before exposing ourselves to a ten-years-belated imitation of Paris, there is need of perspective and a remedying of our own ignorance."[84] Madge reminds his readers that surrealism is "dialectical in its nature," and its integration will require English writers to possess a deep "knowledge of their own language and literature."[85] The important point, then, wasn't for surrealist style to be anglicized. Madge knew that any life for surrealism would reside in how its philosophical energies could be applied to the contemporary social and political realities facing Britain in the 1930s. Poaching a quote from the poet Edward Young, Madge specifically prioritizes the philosophical side of surrealism, hoping to prevent it from becoming one more literary or painterly style among others: "We should rather imitate their example in the motives and fundamental methods of their working, than the works themselves."[86] A year later in a review of Georges Hugnet's *Petite anthologies poetique du surrealisme*, Madge advances surrealism "as a science": "One cannot treat surrealist poetry separately from the other activities of the surrealist laboratory."[87]

In many ways, Madge's approach to surrealism coincides with his evolving conception of art as a form of interrogation, one that would capitalize on aesthetic modalities of disclosure that could illuminate daily life. In one of his essays for the fledgling *New Verse* in May 1933 Madge writes "the mind is a poetic instrument and so is poetic despite itself even when it sets out to be scientific, as any text-book proves."[88] Madge's contact with surrealism pushed his thinking further along these lines. In his 1934 essay for *New Verse*, he weighs art and science more carefully, permitting some objectivity to art and questioning the truth claims of pure science: "Surrealism is science by virtue of its capacity for development and discovery and by virtue of the anonymity of its researches. Like science, it is an apparatus which, in human hands, remains fallible—it has its own margin of error, and its own type of superstition."[89] As Breton does in the first *Manifesto of Surrealism*, Mass-Observation disarticulates art from all the tenets of Kantian aesthetics—beauty, individual genius, aesthetic autonomy, and *sensus communis*. By the time Madge pens his review of Gascoyne's *A Short Survey of Surrealism* a year later, he sees the doors closing on the surrealist laboratory: It is "in its academic period—the period of explanation and anthologies."[90] The question is whether Madge escaped the laboratory with any tools or plans adopted for other purposes.

Jennings's encounter with surrealism assumed a greater intensity than Madge's comparatively cool, reasoned examinations. Perhaps the peak of his surrealist activity comes in 1936. Along with André Breton, Herbert Read, and others, Jennings served on the organizing board for the International Surrealist Exhibition. During this year he translated poetry from E. L. T. Messens and Paul Eluard for Roger Roughton's surrealist organ *Contemporary Poetry and Prose*. Like Madge, Jennings interest drifted toward a carefully considered use of surrealist techniques that was sensitive to the demands and problems of contemporary England. In his review of Herbert Read's edited volume *Surrealism*, he laments the translation of surrealism from its auspicious beginnings in Paris to its declawed English version as a revived "romanticism," "aestheticism," or "style." Jennings recalls the Surrealist Exhibition in these brackish lines:

How can one open this book . . . and compare it even for a moment with the passion terror and excitement, dictated by absolute integrity and produced with all the poetry of bare necessity, which emanated from *La Révolution Surréaliste* and *Le Surréalisme au Service du Révolution*, without facing a great wave of nostalgia, and bringing up a nauseating memory of the mixed atmosphere of cultural hysteria and amateur-theatricality which combined to make the Surrealist Exhibition of June so peculiar a "success". . . . Now, a special attachment to certain sides of Surrealism may be defendable, but the elevation of definite "universal truths of romanticism" (pp. 27–28) in place of the "universal truths" of classicism is not only a short-sighted horror, but immediately corrobo-rates really grave doubts already existent about the *use* of Surrealism in this country.[91]

Jennings's optimism for surrealism in England seems exhausted by December 1936, just six months after the International Surrealist Exhibition and, coinciden-tally, the moment of Mass-Observation's genesis.[92] He expresses "nostalgia," not hope, for the possible transmission of the "passion terror and excitement" that prompted his own interest in French surrealism—this nostalgia can only indicate the dwindling of French surrealism's revolutionary promise for the English. For Jennings, it seems, this potentially explosive event misfired, and English surreal-ism now veered toward entertainment.

Mass-Observation historian Nick Hubble observes that when Madge and Jen-nings begin exploring the relations of poetry and science "they had foreseen that their literary and surrealistic activities were becoming increasingly inseparable from a cultural racket—and M[ass]-O[bservation] was their attempt to move beyond that."[93] Interestingly, Tom Jeffrey claims that Mass-Observation's transi-tions away from surrealism to "something much closer to documentary."[94] The important point is not that Mass-Observation evolves from avant-gardism into something more akin to documentary; Jennings, for example, was already work-ing with the GPO Film Unit at least two years before Mass-Observation, indicat-ing that his interests in surrealism, documentary film, and Mass-Observation all overlapped. Rather, we risk misconstruing their method if we don't track precisely how Mass-Observation sublates surrealism into its own methodology. The experi-mental and "scientific" side of surrealism rhymes with Madge and Jennings's inter-est in Mass-Observation's other abundant references to a kind of "realistic" art and literature, which includes Leo Tolstoy, Gustave Courbet, and, oddly, Marcel Duchamp. Still wedded to techniques of defamiliarization and montage, Mass-Observation's aesthetic aims to produce a "collective expression" of the everyday. But what sort of articulation of the masses (the ones being observed and the ones doing the observing) does it enable? In *First Year's Work*, they identify part of their undertaking as bringing to light what typically falls outside our awareness. "The function of Mass-Observation is to get written down the unwritten laws and to make the invisible forces visible. One part of social behaviour is already written down and codified, but this part only concerns Mass-Observation in so far as a knowledge and understanding of it is necessary for the study of the unwritten and the uncodified."[95] For Mass-Observation, the aesthetic discloses whatever exists on the hither side of knowledge and common sense. In more concrete terms, if the unexpressed anxieties and affective responses of the masses to national emergencies can be drawn out into the light of day, they can be organized and managed. Although there are hints of this strategy early on in Mass-Observation, the declaration of war in 1939 makes it the central feature of their work.

METHOD, AFFECT, AND POETICS

An early experiment with narrative and everyday life comes from "Poetic Description and Mass-Observation," a piece Madge and Jennings published in *New Verse*. They define Mass-Observation as "a technique for obtaining objective statements about human behaviour. The primary *use* of these statements is to the other observers: an interchange of observations being the foundation of social consciousness."[96] The kind of *poiesis* they have in mind is one that brings forth of all the concealed material—gestures, thoughts, affects—of daily life that falls beyond the pale of common sense or scientific knowledge. Moreover, the excavation of these minor knowledges should increase social consciousness and cast into relief the most taken for granted of social relations. The piece opens with the juxtaposition of three paragraphs from different literary genres. The first passage is excerpted from a contemporary novel, the second from an historical narrative, and the third, quoted in full below, from a report by an observer:

> Coming home on a Midland red 'Bus from Birmingham (a distance of approx. 6 miles) I was sitting on the front seat, near the large sliding door. There was a cold easterly wind blowing through the door, and after having some cigarette ash blown in my eyes, I touched the Conductor on the sleeve to attract his attention, and said "May we have the door closed, Conductor?" He turned round and leant towards me in a confidential way, and then said in a most insolent manner "Yes, when I'm ready to shut it!" I was too surprised to make any reply. The door remained open until I left the 'bus.[97]

For Madge and Jennings, the observer's account avoids the fictionalizing of experience endemic to the novel and, unlike historical narratives, the observer experiences the events she records. The poetics of her account reside in what she reveals about the social circumstances of this particular event. The observer's report carries the authority of firsthand experience and, so the theory goes, the anonymity focuses the report on the objectivity of the event, rescuing it from subjective distortion. Ostensibly, *what* is revealed comes to the fore, and *to whom* it is revealed recedes into the background. Madge and Jennings resolve the tensions of subjectivity and objectivity in this way: the subjective statements such as "I was too surprised to make any reply" "become objective because the subjectivity of the observer is one of the facts under observation. The process of observing raises him [any observer] from subjectivity to objectivity. What has become unnoticed through familiarity is raised into consciousness again."[98] The affective response to the driver's brazen reproach is itself a fact to be considered. What demands our attention is the structure at play—subordinate/insubordinate, public servant/the general public—and the thoughts and affects that occur within that structure.

Madge and Jennings extended their investigations into public perception with the "Oxford Collective Poem" experiment. Madge wanted the Oxford Collective Poem to pull the observations of twelve student volunteers into an authoritative image of the "social landscape." The students were instructed to gather images "indicated by external rather than internal evidence."[99] Six recurring images were selected, and each participant wrote a pentameter line for each image. All lines were "printed in block capitals to ensure anonymity."[100] Selecting from these lines, the group assembled a single poem that was later submitted to the collective for a final series of anonymous "corrections." For all the emphasis on anonymity and alteration, the experiment failed, but it failed in an instructive way. Madge admits that the palimpsestic text "proved insufficiently radical. . . . The original was still too visible under the corrections."[101] To be sure, the collective's archive of images does register something of the multiplicity of everyday life; still, the poem lacks the connective tissue needed to string together the images into an objective rendering of the social landscape.

These two early exercises give a specific task to the aesthetic: uncover the particularities of everyday experience and show how that experience permeates the collective. In short, construct an objective portrait of the general from the particular. These experiments in collective poetics put into practice, even if in a crude way, the very idea that Madge and Jennings had while reading the newspaper as a poem: there is a shared collective experience of everyday life, but new methods are required to articulate it. At least in these early works, the aesthetic is the primary way to excavate and portray collective experience. These small-scale endeavors preview the relationship of experimental aesthetics and liberal politics in the larger books. Techniques borrowed from the avant-garde will produce new methods for investigating everyday life and offer modes of composition that will weave together all the quotidian stories and experiences into a coherent, dynamic public sphere. This impulse to merge aesthetics and politics hearkens back to Grierson's efforts in the late 1920s to use aesthetic innovation to educate the citizenry and, by extension, breathe new life into moribund democracies. The fate of Mass-Observation's liberal avant-gardism, though, was inevitably shaped by the local and international emergencies of the late 1930s and early 1940s.

THE POETICS OF EMERGENCY:
FROM DOMESTIC SCANDAL TO TOTAL WAR

Mass-Observation declared their first book, *May the Twelfth*, to be an exception to the rule. As a sort of disclaimer, they write that their organization will generally focus on "everyday things rather than special occasions."[102] Malinowski, for one, thought Mass-Observation's studies of the everyday during "special occasions" might have heightened value: "The normal is far more difficult to penetrate than the exceptional, but it is equally important. The close study of such exceptional situations, however, may give the clue to much that is baffling in the uniform and impassive surface of everyday things."[103] Published between 1937 and 1940, Mass-Observation rarely had the chance to consider everyday life apart from abnormal conditions. The abdication crisis, the Munich crisis, and the Second World War loom large over their books. For Mass-Observation, these moments of political emergency prioritize the relationship between the state and the population. If enough information about the everyday lives of the masses could be collected and properly narrated, Mass-Observation could function as a form of mediation.

Their first book follows King George VI's Coronation Day. Mass-Observation approached this day through "three distinct lines of attack."[104] First, observers completed surveys and made lengthy reports on the twelfth day of February, March, and April; these documents record the events that transpire on an ordinary day and provide the backdrop for the "special occasion" of Coronation Day. Second, the group distributed questionnaires and compiled the results from the seventy-seven responses they received. Third, they dispatched a so-called mobile squad of twelve observers who moved out into the London streets, furiously taking notes and relaying their reports to Mass-Observation headquarters via telephone. The observers' backgrounds, social positions, and class covers a relatively broad range: there are reports from a thirteen-year-old schoolboy, a children's nurse, an unemployed East End resident, a schoolmaster, leftists and conservatives, Anglicans and atheists. According to their findings, enthusiasm for the day was not necessarily due to any collective feeling for the new king or for the event itself; many observers simply welcomed it as an interruption to the humdrum of daily life. In this regard, Mass-Observation concluded that "any break-up of the routine of life is satisfactory to most people."[105] The heterogeneous, carnivalesque atmosphere *May the Twelfth* documents is inscribed into its very form: "official" newspaper reports of the day sit alongside speeches of politicians, accounts from lower and middle class citizens, and from the Mass-Observers themselves. There is little by way of narrative in *May the Twelfth*, but its arrangement is hardly haphazard. Jennings, "responsible for the business of presenting results," ensures that readers will find any number of coincidences and connections among the reports.[106]

The book's second chapter, "London on May 12," looks at the unfolding of Coronation Day from multiple perspectives. With asterisks, footnotes, and occasional commentary, the editors highlight references to other paragraphs, inviting the reader to trace a web of indirect connections among the reports. Their references never make the link explicit but merely imply that the careful reader will find a narrative thread between these passages. In one example a mobile observer reports an encounter with a prostitute: "3.15. Cambridge Circus. I am accosted. I say 'You look as if you've done enough for to-night.' Reply: 'None of your sauce, me lad.'*."[107] The asterisk guides the reader to "*cf.* para. 16," where we find another similar encounter: "On way push against somebody, say 'Sorry' and hear 'That's all right, dearie, don't be in a such hurry'. . . . I realize that I am being quite nicely accosted by a prostitute, quiet-voiced, good accent, etc."[108] Folded within this same entry is yet another reference pointing ahead to a report recorded twelve minutes later. A mobile squad member sees "a woman carrying a folding chair" at

London Bridge, at 4:20 a.m. presumably seeking a spot from which to watch the procession. The implication is that this woman may very well have purchased her chair from the "hawkers" selling "boxes, stools, or other devices for standing clear of the kerb" referenced in the 4:08 a.m. report.[109] Jennings models a way of reading social life akin to the way he and Madge perceived the newspaper: everyday life is composed of coincidences, echoes, and juxtapositions and these may very well carry symbolic value.

This chapter also contains a section entitled "Simultaneous accounts of relayed cheering—later sections of return route—rain: 2.40–4.30 p.m." As several readers have remarked, this is the most "literary" and "radical" moment in *May the Twelfth*, placing it alongside "those great modernist day-books like *Ulysses, Mrs. Dalloway, The Waves*, and *Under the Volcano.*"[110] To the delight of modernist critics, this daybook flashes with moments of simultaneity and montage, establishing a loose but dynamic relation among all the fragmentary reports. Jennings provides some direction on what the reader should make of these simultaneous accounts in a lengthy footnote: "Not only do they agree with each other, but they show the same stimuli affecting different parts of the crowd, and the same impulses travelling through it. . . . When it starts to rain, at both Marble Arch and Apsley Gate, people immediately begin to sing—it is the same rain and has the same effect. Singing is regarded as an aid to keeping up the spirits, or a kind of moral support."[111] The same stimuli, same impulses, the same rain, and the same effect: this is "The Oxford Collective Poem" on a far grander scale. A shared, affective response lies encrypted within minor acts and gestures. Textual echoes, montage, and simultaneity all operate as techniques for finding anew in everyday life what often hides in plain sight.

With its wide spectrum of experience and perspectives, the book operates formally as a more perfect, or more representative, democracy; voices from below are placed alongside quotes and speeches from members of Parliament, the royal family, and the clergy. The intent here is clear enough. More voices in a more dynamic public sphere means a more vital and sustainable democracy. By uncovering multiple publics and arranging them in a kind of textual collage, the text averts any kind of closure, a strategy bound to a utopic projection of liberal democracy thriving on some kind of openness without end.[112] But for Harrisson, who did not collaborate with Madge and Jennings on *May the Twelfth*, the book was only "a detailed piece of documentation."[113] That is to say, it was not scientific. It lacked formal synthesis, he said; it lacked interpretation of social phenomena, and it ultimately lacked any coherence. Despite occasions of formal brilliance, searing irony, and low-grade humor, we can concede to Harrisson that the text lingers as so much white noise, but, at least in this text, it is a white noise significant enough to drown out any grand declarations of national unity. To be sure, no other Mass-Observation text bears the formal dexterity of *May the Twelfth*, nor are the utopic yearnings for a seamless identification of the population and the state pitched in the same key. By 1940 Mass-Observation exchanges multiplicity for the single, collective voice of a population adhering to the demands of a functional security state.

Coming on the heels of Neville Chamberlain's appeasement of Hitler, *Britain by Mass-Observation* identifies the widespread public disappointment following the Munich crisis as evidence of Britain's ailing democracy: "This decreasing interest is highly significant as a reflection of the stage our society has reached. It is partly a defence against nervous strain, partly a kind of fatalism, a mistrust of newspaper information. Broadly speaking, it is a symptom of a serious breakdown in the relation between the individual and society."[114] The increasing indifference to international crisis among the population after Munich indicates a growing crisis at home: "the democratic system has broken down in other countries," write Madge and Harrisson, "and may break down in our own, because the 45,000,000 do not feel sufficiently strongly that they are able to speak through Parliament."[115] The rhetoric of crisis moves ever so slightly away from *May the Twelfth*, where the disobedient energies of the everyday were conceived as vital to an open democratic state, provided they are properly managed. Their critique is still aimed at the failure of liberal institutions to reflect the public will, but the solution is not for an expanded public sphere but a seamless identification of the population and the state. Mass-Observation presents itself as a potential mechanism to bind popular will with the state: "If democracy as an ideal can function and survive, this great gap between the intellectual leader and the ordinary man has to be bridged."[116] This all sounds rather consistent with what we have seen in *May the Twelfth*. But how do we square that with the following prognostication: "In the event of war there would be no room for, no safety in, individual liberty. Uniform national service would be imperative."[117] Mass-Observation predicts that war would induce a state of emergency where the basic principles and institutions of governance would be suspended in order to preserve them.

After the passage of the Emergency Powers Act in September 1939, politics became a matter of ensuring, in Chamberlain's words, "the maintenance of the life of the people," of defending the population and using exceptional powers to do so.[118] Suspending democratic procedures to protect the idea of democracy inaugurated a formal problem at the level of governance.[119] W. Ivor Jennings, British lawyer and founder of the University of Ceylon, published an essay entitled "The Rule of Law in Total War" in the *Yale Law Journal* in January 1941 with the expressed intent to reconcile the extensive powers granted to the state with the British Constitution, whose rights and provisions exist only in a suspended way under the new emergency legislation. He searches for limits, implicit and explicit, on the authority the 1939 Emergency Powers Act granted to the state to compel military or industrial service, conduct military tribunals, and appropriate private property for the state. A version of the act passed a year later extended those powers even further and granted the government the capacity to create new legal offenses and punish perceived violations if the security of the nation was thought to be at stake:

> The Act further enacts that Defense Regulations may provide for amending any enactment, for suspending the operation of any such enactment, and for applying any enactment with or without modification. In other words, the suspending power declared illegal by the Bill of Rights is restored. The Act, as originally enacted, was in force for one year only, but it has been extended for another year by the Emergency Powers (Defense) Act, 1940. It may be continued for a further year (and presumably from year to year) by Order in Council made after addresses from both Houses of Parliament, and it may be terminated at any time by Order in Council.[120]

Whatever limitations may be prescribed on the extent of such powers, be they implicit or explicit limitations, there is always the provision that such limitations can be transgressed; this is, after all, the intrinsic force of exceptional powers. Jennings attempts to reinscribe emergency powers within the functional order of parliamentary democracy. He grants that the state must have such powers at its disposal in order to protect the population and prosecute the war, but it is also key that such powers not dissolve or displace the rule of law. He concludes his meditations with these insightful and stirring lines:

> The conclusion must be, therefore, that while the powers which the emergency legislation has vested in the Government are wide enough to infringe altogether the principles which might reasonably be regarded as those of the rule of law, these principles, reasonably interpreted, are in fact carried out in the actual exercise of those powers. In other words, the law which actually touches the individual citizen through the application of the "children" and the "grandchildren" of the Emergency Powers Acts is not arbitrary or despotic. The Emergency Powers Acts themselves would, in a legal sense, permit of arbitrary government; political conditions, through the control of Parliament, forbids abuses in the exercise of the Acts. The continuing flexibility of the British Constitution has made it adaptable to total war. The Government has powers almost as vast as those of any dictator, but parliamentary control prevents those abuses which are associated with dictatorship.[121]

With emergency legislation opening the way for absolutism, Jennings turns to liberal rationality as the limiting force. Even though the "children" and "grandchildren" of the Emergency Powers Act grant absolute sovereign power to the state, parliamentary control—despite having its legislative function potentially transferred to the executive—will nevertheless safeguard the "reasonable" use of these powers and, at the end of the day, the British Constitution will be all the stronger for it. Jennings's dual efforts to highlight the reach of emergency powers and to locate constitutional and political limitations to them alludes to an irresolvable structural crisis: the suspension of democracy for its preservation. This crisis recurs in the form and intent of *War Begins at Home*.

War Begins at Home largely addresses the problem of two disconnected spheres: "Statesmen-Diplomacy-Foreign Affairs-War and Workmen-Pub Talk-Home Affairs-Everyday Life."[122] Several excerpts from interviews and diaries attest to the enormous distance between the two. The state and the population are at odds and, for Mass-Observation, this jeopardizes "the whole structure of society by allowing the mass to get more and more on to a different plane of reaction and feeling."[123] After the mandatory blackout imposed in September, for example, the number of people killed in road accidents increased 100 percent. Angus Calder explains how scores of others stumbled "into canals, fell down steps, plunged through glass roofs and toppled from railway platforms. A Gallup Poll published in January showed that by that stage about one person in five could claim to have sustained some injury as a result of the blackout—not serious, in most cases, but it was painful enough to walk into trees in the dark, fall over a kerb, crash into a pile of sandbags, or merely cannonade of a fat pedestrian."[124] In addition, "a number of suicides were reported to have resulted from listening to BBC news bulletins. Fellow civilians presented a far more compelling danger than the enemy: the number of automobile accidents nearly doubled with the national ban on the use of headlights. Of the nearly 1800 casualties recorded in the first two months of hostilities, the black-out was responsible for over 1100, the German Army for none."[125]

By way of response, *War Begins at Home* critiques state power for its clumsy mismanagement of civilian life. Mass-Observation advances this curative measure: "It is difficult to run a war in which all the civilian population is so concerned unless every part of the administrative machine is focused in one direction, with one idea, with private and public interests fused, military and civil interests fused."[126] *War Begins at Home* aims to refocus "the administrative machine." The anarchic energies of the everyday in *May the Twelfth* all but disappear. Everyday life is figured not as a site of political potentiality but as an impediment to a new paradigm of security. The text details all the micro-practices of daily life—work habits, sleeping schedules, dance, sport—and provides something of a blueprint for a more coordinated, and more totalizing deployment of emergency powers. *War Beings at Home* presents itself as a site of mediation between statesmen/workmen, diplomacy / pub talk, foreign affairs / home affairs, war / everyday life, posing as the motor for a dangerous dialectical synthesis.

War Begins at Home views the mutability of the everyday with suspicion and anxiety. Daily life falls under the microscope to measure the reach of emergency powers, to find where they have misfired, and to propose correctives that will enable a seamless identification between the population and the state. *War Begins at Home* believes its very existence testifies to the perseverance of democracy even after its restructuration by emergency powers legislation: "This book is possible because we live in a democracy."[127] Mass-Observation reminds us that although war "makes everything different . . . the structure of our society is not fundamentally altered."[128] Interestingly enough, all that follows suggests otherwise. The writings on mass conscription, air raid fears, evacuations, and mandatory blackouts represent a social structure fracturing from every angle: "The expectation of enemy aeroplanes had already, before the war started, begun to change the social structure of Britain; the structure of the family, through evacuation; the structure of leisure and sex and shopping through the blackout; the structure of the home, through incendiary bomb and gas preparations; the structure of civil authority, through A.R.P. [air raid precautions]."[129]

At first glance, the frisson between an unaltered society and its changing social structure would appear to be at odds. Indeed, Mass-Observation openly acknowledges "the very fact of a democracy being at war is in itself a confusion."[130] But this narrative contradiction merely replays the legal one that crops up in Jennings's 1941 essay. Augmented executive powers, restricted rights, and tight management of public life must somehow be configured as safeguards, not inversions, of democracy. *War Begins at Home* registers a transforming political logic; as the state's legal structure sheds adherence to democratic procedures, it assumes a form of rule that suspends those procedures.

In many ways, the dichotomy between liberal democracy and totalitarianism underwriting Mass-Observation's political project is not the proper optics for reading this text. These rigid oppositions are precisely what blinds Mass-Observation to the crossing of these two forms of governance in both the deployment of emergency powers and the change in their own political script. From *May the Twelfth* to *War Begins at Home*, Mass-Observation remains preoccupied with the relation of state and population. In the earlier text, Jennings's formal arrangement suggests that the everyday escapes traditional modes of inquiry, and, moreover, parliamentary democracy will best weather crises if it attends to and integrates the multiplicity of everyday experience. *War Begins at Home* emphasizes a similar concern but finds the drift of popular sentiment away from the imperatives of state policy to be threatening. Like Jennings's *Listen to Britain*, Mass-Observation's war work wants to facilitate a process of normalization; it wants to adapt citizens to everyday life under the cold reach of the security state. It would be tempting to read *War Begins at Home* as a retreat from their democratic commitments. If we follow that temptation, the early writings in *New Verse* and *May the Twelfth* sit opposite *War Begins at Home*. Their poetics of everyday life always aimed at greasing the gears of the state and defusing any antagonisms among the population. Rather than positing two versions of Mass-Observation, one radically democratic and avant-garde and the other authoritarian, we might best see their works as two stages in the unfolding of a political logic of security that perceives democratic procedures as unfit for protecting democratic states.

POLITICAL AND AESTHETIC PLOTS

Tracking the "fate" of the avant-garde or any other group implies a plot, one overshadowed by the downward turn of its narrative arc. In this final section, I want to consider some of the implications—theoretical, literary historical, art historical—of this chapter for late modernism's peculiar rapprochement with the avant-garde. Treading in the footprints of some of the twentieth century's most formidable critics of modernism and the avant-garde, I argue that the most radical art experiments of the last century were pulled magnetically toward one of two poles: radical emancipation or melancholic separation. A truly unique facet of the documentary film movement and Mass-Observation consists in their disarticulation of adversarial politics from avant-garde aesthetics. Both groups relax the combative postures of those unhappy avant-gardes that tilted left or right in their critiques of bourgeois liberalism. The governing idea in these projects was to reconcile the population with the state's economic and political imperatives. Documentary film projected versions of everyday life that formally modeled how the viewers should perceive the operations of the state at home and imperial economics abroad; Mass-Observation disclosed the multiple ways in which state policies shaped or interrupted everyday life. In both instances, the idea was to trim the margins for public dissent and to counter disaffection. These peculiar late modernist phenomena bolster the social bond between the population and the state, effectively marshaling avant-garde aesthetics for the maintenance of liberal consensus. At the level of style, the disorientation and shock that should follow juxtaposition, montage, and simultaneity disappears. In the cases examined here, those techniques normalize and habituate.

What has happened in this modulation of avant-garde aesthetics? Why did the bourgeois liberal world, which proved an endless source of seething anger and profound disappointment in the pre– and post–World War I years, suddenly seem compatible with the avant-garde? Part of the answer resides in Grierson's writings from the late 1920s and Madge and Jennings's encounters with surrealism: avant-garde techniques were becoming recognizable, familiar, and moribund. The same aesthetic modes that first appeared on the far horizon of sense perception were no longer abnormal (and this is surely what Walter Benjamin recognized in his 1929 essay on surrealism). Grierson and Mass-Observation were not making it new; instead, their aesthetico-political projects assigned new purposes to existing forms and techniques. This replays what I claim in the introduction as late modernism's tendency toward renovation, not innovation. When the spark of novelty dwindles, and when negativity loses its creative destructive force, forms and techniques attract what they previously rebuke; they enter unforeseen combinations and acquire new political valences.

After a long life of involvement with some of the twentieth century's most storied avant-gardes, Henri Lefebvre composed the third volume of his *Critique of Everyday Life*. He asserts that "the state is now built upon daily life; its base is the everyday."[131] The dialectical relation between state power and the administration of daily life is not a late-twentieth-century novelty and, as this chapter shows, it was already central to Britain's efforts to sustain the reach of its economic power abroad and its political power at home. But Lefebvre also knows that the penetration of daily life by state power does not need to take the shape of an authoritarian regime; liberal ones are equally capable of this sort of population administration. As for the adversarial nature of art, particularly the avant-gardes, these political regimes thrive on what he terms recuperation. Recuperation is a process: "an idea or a project regarded as irredeemably revolutionary or subversive—that is to say, on the point of introducing a discontinuity—is normalized, reintegrated into the existing order, and even revives it."[132] Late modernist documentary marks such a recuperative moment. The world systemic disorder of the 1930s and 1940s warmed the likes of Grierson, Jennings, and Madge to a new social function for art that mitigated the anxieties wrought by global economic turbulence and the fearful spectacle of the fascist war machine. As we move from documentary to the historical novel in the next chapter, we find a similar confrontation between actuality and its creative treatment. In Virginia Woolf's *The Years* and Christopher Isherwood's *Goodbye to Berlin* we can discern a similar documentary impulse as well as the mutation of form and genre under the pressures of crisis and war.

2

THE HISTORICAL NOVEL
AT HISTORY'S END

It seems as if there were no progress in the human race, but only repetition.
—VIRGINIA WOOLF, *THREE GUINEAS*, 1938

IN THE INTRODUCTION I identify two dimensions of late modernism's outward turn to everyday life: it mediates a structural transformation in the world-system and induces a change in the priorities and functions of modernist art and literature. In this chapter I address two late modernist renovations of the historical novel in the 1930s. For a decade laboring under sustained economic decline and increasing war, this genre offered one way to think historically about the present moment.[1] Both Virginia Woolf and Christopher Isherwood, one a dominant figure of the teens and twenties and the other who flourished in the thirties and after, spent the better part of the 1930s trying their hand at the historical novel. For nearly six years, Woolf agonized over the composition and structure of what began as an experimental essay-novel before splitting it into *The Years* and *Three Guineas*. Isherwood's efforts to synthesize his various writings on Berlin into a single novel swallowed up the same amount of time. Neither novel turned out as planned, and both bear an uneasy relationship to the genre of the historical novel. In compliance with the long tradition of historical novels from Sir Walter Scott through expert nineteenth-century practitioners like Honoré de Balzac and Leo Tolstoy, Woolf and Isherwood wanted the everyday lives of their characters to dramatize the definitive tensions of their historical moment. In a letter to Stephen Spender in 1937, Woolf wrote that she hoped *The Years* would "give a picture of society as a whole . . . [and] envelop the whole in a changing temporal atmosphere."[2] If successful, the daily doings of her Pargiters would bear the imprints of English history from the late nineteenth century into the present. Taking Balzac's *Splendeurs et misères des courtisanes* as a model, Isherwood planned a series of deftly interwoven plots and interrelated characters that would fuse into a richly detailed account of everyday life in the Weimar Republic during its twilight years.

Commenters on the historical novel both past and present isolate the crucial relationships between two formal features—characterization and plot—and a progressive philosophy of history.[3] *The Years* and Isherwood's *Goodbye to Berlin* recalculate the construction of character and plot, divesting themselves from the prevailing sense of history as a rational process. This chapter focuses on Woolf's and Isherwood's subtle transgressions of the historical novel's generic parameters. Both novels figure everyday life as a scene where we can witness the emergence of an aprogressive philosophy of history. By tracking the way *The Years* and *Goodbye to Berlin* resemble and depart from the historical novel, we can see how these texts render the protracted decline of a British-centered world-system as a crisis of historical consciousness.

Regardless of political or aesthetic affinities, the sense of the present as a moment of historical crisis pervades the literary and cultural activity of the 1930s. Marxist and left-leaning writers awaited the pivotal event that would usher in a more equitable, egalitarian society. Conservative onlookers such as T. S. Eliot often narrated the crisis in terms of Spenglerian moral decline, a situation his *After Strange Gods* proposes to resolve via a nativist community bonded by blood and soil. The avant-garde sociological group Mass-Observation enumerated the anxious decade's worries this way in their inaugural pamphlet: "The bringing of civilization to Abyssinia, the coming of civil war to Spain, the atavism of the new Germany and the revival of racial superstition have forced the issue home to many. We are all in danger of extinction from such outbursts of atavism."[4] Cultural feeling, political philosophies, and current events coalesced into a collective crisis mentality, or what Valentine Cunningham dubs the decade's "destructive element."[5] The perception of history as nearing a possible end, of careening toward extinction, is not exactly the end of existence as such. As Maurice Blanchot notes, "it is not history that comes to an end with the end of history, but certain principles, questions, and formulations."[6] The anticipated end of history signals the end of history as a rational process that bequeathed to the twentieth century a political system of liberal democracy, a capitalist economy with unprecedented power to produce wealth, and a general sense that humankind was capable of solving its own problems and shaping its future. The threat of extinction is not posed to life itself but to a form of life.

History's presumed end induces a number of formal problems for late modernists. This aesthetic challenge surfaces in a remarkable way in a diary entry from the precocious young surrealist David Gascoyne. When Gascoyne walked up Hampstead Heath on October 13, 1936, he looked down on London but saw two cities—the sleepy, peaceful metropole of the present and the war metropolis of the future:

> Ducks on the ponds, the water flaking into silver, the October sky remote and luminous. As the afternoon bordered on dusk, I climbed to the highest point of the Heath. A fresh wind blowing. Highgate far on its hill beneath slow-tumbling clouds to the left; to the right, below, London spread out under mist and smoke, grey-blue, immense, mysterious. What a heart-shaking spectacle it will be from this height some night soon to come, when the enemy squadrons blackening the sky rain down destroying fire upon those roofs! I turned away.[7]

Gascoyne's undisturbed London is almost Wordsworthian, a slumbering city shrouded in natural beauty where "all that mighty heart is lying still."[8] The poet attentively notes the mist, smoke, and clouds hovering over the city, but it is the city's vulnerability, not its grandeur or mystery, that punctuates his observation. Indeed, the very pacing and syntax of Gascoyne's prose changes as he turns from the idle, enshrouded city to the fiery spectacle. The penultimate sentence mirrors the swift destruction from the air that Gascoyne and many others feared would be London's fate. The very anticipation of disaster forces a shift in aesthetic registers from the beautiful to the sublime, from the harmonious relation of form and content to a point where language loses its representational powers ("I turned away"). Gascoyne's entry indexes in an exemplary way how these historical pressures and dark anticipations compelled, even necessitated, changes in literary form.

How might the mediating powers of the historical novel alter during a decade as troubled as the 1930s? The collective anxieties of what W. H. Auden famously dubbed this "low dishonest decade" did little to hamper interest in the historical novel;[9] in fact, the decade proved to be a fertile one for both the production and theorization of the historical novel. Critics have noted that the genre flourished throughout the decade, particularly in the hands of women writers.[10] Sylvia Townsend Warner, Rose Macaulay, Vera Brittain, and Jack Lindsay all wrote historical novels with an eye toward contemporary events in Europe. Janet Montefiore suggests that the spread of dictatorships across Europe pushed many of these writers to return to "the events of the past in terms of a present need for narratives about surviving defeat."[11] These novels exhibit the crisis mentality of the 1930s, but they still seem to understand history, even as it lurches forward to some infernal future, as a progressive force.

To see how Woolf's and Isherwood's works cut against the novels of their contemporaries in terms of their form and their sense of history, I turn to the most sustained and most cited anatomization of the genre from the 1930s: Georg Lukács's *The Historical Novel*.[12] For Lukács, one of the primary tasks of the historical novel is the "disclosure of all the contradictions of progress."[13] By definition, the genre is predicated on a belief in history as incessant conflict, but such conflict drives historical progress. According to Lukács's typology, the properly historical novel must conceptualize and treat historical events in a particular way; it cannot simply foreground major historical figures, nor should it treat history as the "decorative backdrop" (206) against which characters and plots operate more or less autonomously (this was Flaubert's cardinal sin). Instead the historical novel should disclose the migration of historical antagonisms into the most oblique regions of everyday life. Scott's fiction stands as the vade mecum of the genre precisely because it shows "how important historical changes affect everyday life, the effect of material and psychological changes upon people who react immediately and violently to them, without understanding their causes" (49). For these reasons, Lukács prioritizes two generic features: First, the novel mediates historical events through the everyday lives of its characters; for Lukács, Walter Scott's novels and Tolstoy's *War and Peace* present "the indirect contact between individual lives and historical events" (285). Second, characters should be typical in the sense that their plots and narrative arcs rhyme with those of the general population. Lukács's reading of *War and Peace* shows that it matters little if these characters are plucked from the aristocracy or the lower classes. In any case, their daily lives must represent in miniature the impact of historical events on the nation.

This second priority constitutes Lukács's most rigid categorical distinction, and according to his logic, it should prohibit any incorporation of modernist techniques into the historical novel. Modernism's preference for interiorized—or, in Lukács's parlance, "eccentric"—characters makes any such correspondence impossible, even if the Leopold Blooms and Franz Biberkopfs are closer in class to the masses. In Lukács's argument, modernist introversion categorically fetishizes alienation and social detachment, whereas Tolstoy's counts and princes function more properly as examples of "popular character" (86). These two requirements, the emplotment of historical events in the narrative discourse and the mode of characterization, reproduce the conception of history as a rational process. To analyze the relationship of Woolf's and Isherwood's texts to the genre of the historical novel means we think of genre in a more dynamic way than Lukács allows.

Whatever future developments Lukács imagined when he foresaw the historical novel's certain "renewal in the form of a negation of a negation" (350), it is safe to say that, even at his most charitable, Lukács would never permit anything resembling *The Years* or *Goodbye to Berlin*. For him, historical fiction belongs primarily to the world of realism and, thus, prescinds any integration of modernist techniques. To call *The Years* or *Goodbye to Berlin* late modernist historical novels assumes a convergence of opposing styles. Even though these two particular novels drift far from high modernist stylings, they are hardly blithe resuscitations of realist fiction. Because they enact a recoding of the genre's requirements, we might say that their works participate in the genre of the historical novel without properly belonging to it.[14] Their particular form of participation amounts to what Jacques Derrida calls "contamination";[15] such contamination only becomes apparent when we see the extent to which these novels contest the categorical divide between realism and modernism, a boundary that I have argued late modernism scarcely heeded. When critics refer to Isherwood's camera-eye narration or emphasize the realism of *The Years*, they tacitly acknowledge a change of direction from earlier modernisms but misread both the novelty of this turn and its contaminating effect. The value of addressing *The Years* and *Goodbye to Berlin* as historical fiction is that such a reading treats these texts as contestations and performances of historical knowledge; they conceptualize a philosophy of history at its moment of unraveling.

In order to accommodate the present and to think it historically, *The Years* and *Goodbye to Berlin* aggressively decouple generic traits from their customary effects. To write a historical novel at the end of history, then, means constructing a mode of thinking historically that is independent of, or at least in contradistinction to, those narratives of inevitable progress. In sum, Woolf's and Isherwood's novels are incapable of adapting historical phenomena to narrative structures or interpretive frameworks; instead their focus on the minutiae of daily life reveals phenomena that corrode the historical systems and laws governing the longer tradition of the historical novel.

While the individual sections on Woolf and Isherwood will take up their fulfillment of and departures from the generic protocols of the historical novel, it is worth raising the question of historical distance. How historically removed from the author's time period must the work be to be classified as historical? This is a particularly pointed question for the status of *The Years* and *Goodbye to Berlin* as historical novels. Neither of these works reaches very far back in historical time. Published in 1937, *The Years* begins in 1880, only two years prior to Woolf's birth, and ends in the 1930s; Isherwood's 1939 book covers late Weimar and early Nazi Germany, bracketed between 1930 and 1933. Historical distance has long plagued critical efforts to define historical fiction. As Woolf and Isherwood wrangled with their own historical novels, Hugh Walpole's 1932 meditations on Sir Walter Scott ask very directly how a work becomes historical.[16] Is it the author's distance from the time of his narrative or the reader's distance? He settles somewhat modestly with this definition: "A novel is historical when, in time, its action is antecedent to the period of the novelist who has written it. It is the historical *view* of the author of it that determines its genre, and that moment when there is an attempt at the re-creation of customs, thought and feeling no longer contemporary with the author, the novel is historical."[17]

Walpole raises two determining factors, both of which will become central components of Lukács's more rigorous theorization in the late 1930s: historical time and historical perception. Like Lukács after him, Walpole does not exempt works focused on the near past from inclusion in historical fiction. Walpole cites

William Makepeace Thackeray's *Vanity Fair* as a successful historical novel, although the time period is not entirely antecedent to the author, and Lukács makes a similar argument regarding Balzac's novels of postrevolutionary France.[18] By "historical view," I take Walpole to mean the perception of a moment in time as distinctly historical or "no longer contemporary."[19] My reading of these two late modernist historical novels suggests that the rampant discourse of history's end in the 1930s makes the relative present seem historical in two senses: first, the present appears as the explosive point of a long fuse set years earlier; second, the anticipation of disaster makes the experience of the present the experience of becoming historical. If narrating the present historically remains one of the foremost tasks of historical fiction, Isherwood's and Woolf's works formally degenerate precisely because they cannot imagine their present moment of systemic disorder as anything but the prologue to history's end.

HISTORY, EVENT, CHARACTER: *THE YEARS*

Most readers of Woolf trace the arc of her career from the nascent experiments in characterization and psychic interiority in *Jacob's Room* to their apex in *The Waves*. The works that follow throughout the 1930s constitute the last, tired efforts of exhausted genius. Although the critical fortunes of *Three Guineas* and *Between the Acts* have only improved in recent years, *The Years* remains the stray, ugly duckling of her oeuvre, an unfortunate blemish on an otherwise handsome career. Woolf's own assessment of *The Years* has done little to help its status. In an oft-quoted diary entry, Woolf declared her experiment "a failure" and curiously characterized that failure as "deliberate."[20] For a long time critics have taken her judgment as axiomatic.[21] To be sure, *The Years* resembles neither the svelte, introverted novels that preceded it nor the acclaimed posthumous novel that followed; it lacks the poetic rapture of *To the Lighthouse* and the hypnotic prose of *The Waves*; it displays little of the daring characterization of *Jacob's Room* and *Mrs. Dalloway*. Missing too is the staunch political commitment underwriting her imaginative epistles in *Three Guineas*, *The Years*' counterpart.[22] It falls shy of that amalgamation of the "granite and the rainbow," the concrete and the poetic, that the other novels achieve so gracefully.[23]

A few recent assessments of *The Years* seem less beholden either to Woolf's judgments or to the near reflexive equation of high modernist style with literary value. Karen Levenback, Judy Suh, and Maren Linnet, among others, have all recast *The Years* as central to Woolf's political thinking on war, fascism, and, perhaps more complexly, antisemitism.[24] In these readings, *The Years* exemplifies Woolf's imaginative confrontation with the mounting crises of the 1930s. John Whittier-Ferguson's analysis of *The Years* suggests that this social and political turmoil prompts changes in the "local details of her style," giving us what he memorably dubs her "inventively exhausted prose."[25] My reassessment of *The Years* joins this renewed attention to the tangled aesthetic and political problems of Woolf's novel. As a late modernist historical novel, *The Years* seems primarily concerned with establishing a correspondence between the minutiae of the everyday lives of the Pargiter family and the world-historical processes that underwrite the novel's half-century timespan.

Woolf's concern with everyday life did not begin with this novel, but *The Years* marks an astonishing departure from the signature interiorized, phenomenological explorations of her earlier fictions.[26] The treatment of everyday life in *The Years* bears stronger resemblances to historical novels and family chronicles such as Leo Tolstoy's *War and Peace*, Thomas Mann's *Buddenbrooks*, and John Galsworthy's *Forsyte Saga* than the modernist novels of James Joyce, Marcel Proust, or Joseph Conrad.[27] And yet *The Years* contains many of the signature preoccupations of Woolf's more esteemed works: the construction of character, temporality, the lives of women, and the multidirectional effects of major historical events, to name but a few. Like other late modernist texts, *The Years* figures the everyday as a barometer of historical change. To that end, Woolf's simultaneous adaptation to and disfiguration of the protocols of the historical novel attest to the indirect and lingering effects historical events have at the level of daily life.

My point of departure here is a review of Ivan Turgenev that Woolf published in 1933 when she was fast at work on *The Years*. Despite its pithy statements on the Russian writer's technique, the essay is perhaps most valuable for what it discloses about Woolf's efforts to rethink her approach to everyday life as she wrestled with her historical novel.[28] In a particularly revealing passage from "The Novels of Turgenev," Woolf meditates on Turgenev's method and points to one of the key aesthetic problems of *The Years*: "For he is asking the novelist not only to do many things but some that seem incompatible. He has to observe facts impartially, yet he must also interpret them. Many novelists do the one; many do the other—we have the photograph and the poem. But few combine the fact and the vision; and the rare quality that we find in Turgenev is the result of this double process."[29]

This "double process" animating Turgenev's novels offers one way to fuse sharp, empirical attention to fact and appearance with the poetic or visionary power to see beyond it. Woolf's description of Turgenev's style echoes other formulations of the outward turn, not the least of which is John Grierson's definition of documentary as "the creative treatment of actuality." The conflict Woolf locates in Turgenev resurfaces in *The Years*. In this regard, the terminology Woolf uses in her meditation on Turgenev proves particularly revealing: "photograph," "observe," and—a term that carries several meanings in Woolf's lexicon—"vision." The first two refer to a type of looking, an ideal of impersonal observation that Nancy Armstrong and Peter Brooks ascribe to nineteenth century realism. In *Realist Vision*, Brooks describes realism as "attached to the visual, to looking at things, registering their presence in the world through sight."[30] And what is most often the object of realism's searching eye? The everyday, the unexceptional, and the negligible prose of the world.

"Vision" suggests a more subjective, interiorized form of experience: this is the cornerstone of Woolf's modernism that readers know well from her previous novels. And yet the conjunctive "and" indicates connection with "fact," not opposition to it. In this regard, Brooks's conclusion on the relation between modernism and realism is instructive:

> That seems to me irreducible in the realist project: to register the importance of the things—objects, inhabitations, accessories—amid which people live, believe they can't live without. The realist believes you must do an elementary phenomenology of the world in order to speak of how humans inhabit it, and this phenomenology will necessarily mean description, detailing, an attempt to say what the world is like in a way that makes its constraints recognizable by the reader. Note that Woolf—and also James, and Joyce, and Proust—don't really reject this premise: their work is full of significant things.... What is different in the modernists is most of all the selectivity of consciousness applied to the phenomenal world, and the establishment of a perspective resolutely within consciousness as it deals with the objects of the world.[31]

Things, objects, gestures: the clutter of daily life. These are the obsessions of realism, whether in Honoré de Balzac, Charles Dickens, or Gustave Courbet; they are equally the obsessions, so says Brooks, of Woolf and her modernist contemporaries. When Woolf later reviewed the relation between her fiction and the everyday in "A Sketch of the Past," she evoked the great realists of the nineteenth century and their powers of description:

> Often when I have been writing one of my so-called novels I have been baffled by this same problem; that is, how to describe what I call in my private shorthand—"non-being".... A great part of every day is not lived consciously. One walks, eats, sees things, deals with what has to be done; the broken vacuum cleaner; ordering dinner; writing orders to Mabel; washing; cooking dinner; bookbinding. . . . The real novelists can somehow convey both sorts of being. I think Jane Austen can; and Trollope; perhaps Thackeray and Dickens and Tolstoy. I have never been able to do both. I tried—in *Night and Day*; and in *The Years*.[32]

Woolf's "private shorthand" refers to the routine activities of daily life—cleaning, walking, eating—but finds those activities to be highly significant and extraordinarily difficult to capture. In Woolf's account, *The Years* fell short in its effort to coordinate "being" and "non-being." We might see Woolf's admission of failure as an acknowledgment that *The Years* fails to fulfill the expectations of a realist *or* a modernist novel. If Brooks is right to de-emphasize the supposed stylistic and epochal rupture between realism and modernism, then we might recast the distinction between realism and modernism more modestly as a modal shift, one that, for Woolf at least, has everything to do with the relation of subjective consciousness to the objective world. *The Years* recalibrates the relations between inward consciousness and everyday reality and, more broadly, stands as a prime example of late modernism's treatment of everyday life more as a measure of systemic disorder, not solely as an object of phenomenological investigation.

This becomes most evident by juxtaposition. In *To the Lighthouse*, for example, there is a good deal about objects and everyday things. The novel mediates the everyday world through individual consciousness, detailing the varieties of subjective experience. Neatly separating aesthetics and epistemology, the novel gives us Lily Briscoe and Mr. Ramsay, the artist figure and the philosopher; we have two modes of addressing the world—the poetic and the realistic. Aesthetic experience is redemptive and feminine; analytic, rational knowledge is tyrannical and masculine. Mr. Ramsay's analysis of objects and systems reduces them to base formulas while Lily's observations of tables, trees, and shapes imbue them poetically, multiplying their possible meanings. This stark, antagonistic division loosens considerably by the early 1930s when Woolf begins *The Years* (and the review of Turgenev).[33] The treatment of everyday things has far less to do with hard rationality and "angular essences," or even abstract, poetic qualities.[34] Instead, the dialectic of art and knowledge in *The Years* proceeds by transfiguring "any scrap of everyday life into a sign of history."[35] In a marked departure from the novels that preceded it, *The Years* seems far less interested in the psychic life of individual characters than in the histories they live (perhaps this goes some way toward explaining why *The Years* lacks a main character).

In the "1880" chapter, Woolf's free indirect discourse demonstrates precisely how the novel sees everyday life as a sign of history. She gives us the servant's eyes and catalogs the objects of Abercorn Terrace: "The whole room, with its carved chairs, oil paintings, the two daggers on the mantelpiece, and the handsome sideboard—all the solid objects that Crosby dusted and polished every day—looked at its best in the evening."[36] Crosby's labor gives her an intimate knowledge of the "solid objects" of the Pargiter house, objects that tell the family history and identify the Pargiters with a specific class.[37] But if the text positions these objects as decorations for the Pargiter family, it suggests that they ground an entire world for Crosby. When the family sells Abercorn Terrace in 1913, Woolf focalizes the final inventory of the house and its objects through Eleanor, diagramming the move for her, the upper class resident, as liberatory; by contrast, leaving Abercorn Terrace for Crosby is evidently world-destroying:

> Crosby was crying. The mixture of emotion was positively painful; she [Eleanor] was so glad to be quit of it all, but for Crosby it was the end of everything.
>
> She had known every cupboard, flagstone, chair and table in that large rambling house, not from five or six feet of distance as they had known it; but from her knees, as she scrubbed and polished; she had known every groove, stain, fork, knife, napkin and cupboard. They and their doings had made her entire world. And now she was going off, alone, to a single room at Richmond. (216)

Eleanor and Crosby's opposite reactions to the sale of Abercorn Terrace multiply the perspectives on this slice of daily life, but they do so in order to draw attention to a long and changing history of class divisions. This mode of describing historical processes through the everyday is precisely what animates *The Years* and distinguishes it from Woolf's introverted fictions.

While scenes like this one demonstrate how everyday life carries historical meaning, the most significant world-historical events that occur between 1880 and the 1930s are largely displaced from the center of the narrative. *The Years* trains its eye on the traces such events leave on everyday life and, indeed, detects the ways these past histories from across the globe give form and shape to it in the present: the 1857 Indian Mutiny is never discussed in the narrative, but the finger Abel lost during the rebellion attests to its abiding presence in the family's history; Parnell's death, like the speeches of dictators and the rumblings in the Balkans, comes to us by way of a newspaper headline; King Edward VII's death is announced through the drunken shouts from a pub at the corner of Sara and Maggie's slum apartment.[38] Woolf's two chapters on the First World War are exemplary in this regard. The "1917" and "1918" chapters gradually chart the transformation of total war from an interruption of everyday life to a permanent condition of it.

The "1917" chapter opens innocently enough with Eleanor Pargiter stumbling through blacked-out London, using the dim light of her hand torch and the air raid searchlight overhead to find Renny and Maggie's house. Air raid sirens interrupt the family's dinner and conversation, setting into motion one of the strangest war scenes in literary modernism. Just as Stendahl's Fabrizio never sees the Battle of Waterloo, The Pargiters never properly see the bombing raid. Instead, it is experienced through the impressions it leaves on the domestic, private interiors of daily life. As Eleanor and company descend into the cellar, Nicholas, their Polish friend, charts the location of German bombers by timing the bursts of gunfire on his pocket watch. Eleanor tries to witness the event as well; she gazes up at the ceiling and figures "the Germans must be overhead by now" (291). The crackling of anti-aircraft guns shakes a spider web suspended in the corner of the ceiling, and Eleanor monitors its movement, using it as a metronome to measure the rhythms of the air raid. The event only becomes legible through these faint impressions or, even more suggestively, through the very impossibility of seeing which Woolf represents literally and figuratively with the blacked-out city. *The Years* holds the direct, immediate presentation of events to the side, opting to show instead how they press upon daily life in scarcely detectable ways.

On a general level, Woolf's recreation of the air raid in *The Years* highlights the impact of the war on the noncombatants, something Woolf had done with relative consistency in all of her novels from *Jacob's Room* forward. Levenback convincingly shows that Woolf drew heavily from her own wartime diaries to re-construct the air raid section in "1917," the chapter that was "the most difficult and strenuous section of her novel."[39] Yet Woolf's reconstruction of the 1917 air raid has as much, if not more, to do with postwar air raid anxiety.[40] Woolf's narra-tion of the First World War forecasts the militarization of daily life in a besieged city that would become de rigueur in the 1940s.[41] The memory of those raids—mandatory citywide blackouts, defenseless populations, the conversion of the Tube into a shelter—provide a glimpse of what shape the coming war will take.[42] Perhaps Eleanor, warm with wine, best characterizes the dramatic changes await-ing daily life in the war metropolis: "It was light after dark; talk after silence; the war, perhaps, removing barriers" (284). The barriers between war zone and civil-ian area, combatant and noncombatant, private and public life, would diminish greatly in a war fought through the air.

The "1917" chapter mimes these boundaries and charts their gradual disso-lution. It establishes its own set of distinctions and shows us the moment they become inoperative. Fumbling about in the darkness where the lack of lighting "seemed to muffle sound as well as sight" (279), Eleanor enters Renny and Mag-gie's house and notes with exceptional sensitivity the solidity and distinction of objects. "It looked strange after the streets—the perambulator in the hall; the um-brellas in the stand; the carpet, the pictures: they all seemed intensified" (280). The cataloging and differentiation of these objects draws a firm line between the muffled dark outside and the clear visibility of the inside. Street and home, pub-lic and private, exterior and interior—these are the divisions of everyday life the chapter maps out in its initial pages. They are also the very ones the air raid un-settles. The trembling spider web and the crackling of guns outside draw the war into the warmest, most private interior spaces. After the planes pass and the raid concludes, the motions of daily life seem to continue unabated: "The bugles blew again beneath the window. Then they heard them further down the street; then further away still down the next street. Almost directly the hooting of cars began again, and the rushing of wheels as if the traffic had been released and the usual night life of London had begun again" (295). When Eleanor later that evening waits for the omnibus, she has nearly forgotten the air raid. The omnibus arrives as per usual, and the passengers "looked cadaverous and unreal in the blue light" (300). The daily functions of the city resume quickly, but Eleanor's altered perception registers the aftereffects of the war, morbidly casting everyday life as everyday death.

The curiously brief "1918" chapter reinforces in a less direct way the collapse of the boundaries between everyday life and total war. Crosby walks through London on errands for her new employer, Mrs. Burt. The siren sounds to a "dull explosion" (304) and Crosby only mutters "them guns again" (304); through Woolf's narration, everyday routines and war appear intertwined in the metropolis. Another explosion elicits a momentary pause in the daily doings in the city:

> A man on a ladder who was painting the windows of one of the houses paused with his brush in his hand and looked around. A woman who was walking along carrying a loaf of bread that stuck half out of its papers wrapping stopped too. They both waited as if for something to happen. A topple of smoke drifted over and flopped down from the chimneys. The guns boomed again. The man on the ladder said something to the woman on the pavement. She nodded her head. Then he dipped his brush in the pot and went on painting. The woman walked on. Crosby pulled herself together and tottered across the road into the High Street. The guns went on booming and the sirens wailed. The war was over—so somebody told her as she took her place at the counter of the grocer's shop. The guns went on booming and the sirens wailed. (304–5)

The incessant noises of war give pause to otherwise ordinary actions: a servant running errands, a man painting, and a woman returning from a store. Though they wait for something to happen, it never does. In the midst of this nothing happening, Woolf threads together a formidable scene where war no longer figures as an interruption of everyday life but a constitutive part of it.

The figuration of the First World War as anything less than a decisive historical and formal break sets *The Years* apart from so many other modernist texts that inscribe the rupture of the First World War into their verbal textures, temporal arrangements, and narrative structures, including, most conspicuously, the "Time Passes" section of *To the Lighthouse*. Viewed from the vantage point of the "present day" of the 1930s, the First World War does not appear as an aberration in the movement of history. Here, the war engenders a new world in which, as Carl Schmitt claimed, total war is "an ever present possibility . . . is the leading presupposition which determines in a characteristic way human action and thinking."[43] This marks a significant change of scale: Woolf's retrospective view of the First World War figures it as exemplary, not interruptive, of the historical process as such. The philosophy of history that unfolds over the course of Woolf's narrative treats conflicts and antagonisms in a notably nondialectical manner: on the one hand, they are the generative, mobilizing force of history; on the other hand, such destruction and violence forecloses any possibility of historical progress. While we might see Woolf's coordination of the historical event with everyday life as perfectly compatible with Lukács's version of the historical novel, this reconfigured philosophy of history generates characters and plots that could not be less compatible. The extensive catalog of historical conflicts in *The Years*—imperial, national, economic, sexual—showcases the formative and ultimately deleterious effects they have on those who live through them and, often, those who live after them.

FLOWERS, STONES, AND LIBERTY: HOW DELIA AND ROSE DREAM

By sliding the focus toward characterization, I want to foreground the peculiar way *The Years'* broken historical dialectic manifests itself most explicitly in the lives of the Pargiter women. The "1880" chapter introduces us to the Pargiter household, which is run primarily by the younger women; an ailing mother withers away upstairs, and erstwhile patriarch Abel Pargiter relies on his daughters to maintain the daily operations of his estate. Preoccupied as it is with introducing the complex dynamics of the Pargiter family, the "1880" chapter is also concerned with dreams and fantasies: Delia's Parnell daydreams, Rose's imaginative adventure games, Kitty's erotic fantasies, and Edward's fantasies of Kitty. It is Delia's and Rose's early daydreams and fantasies, and their extension into their adult lives, that most clearly echo the history they inherit. Daughters of a former imperial soldier, Delia and Rose's dreams are coded in explicitly imperial terms: Delia conjures up visions of Irish Home Rule icon Charles Parnell while Rose fancies herself as a soldier from Pargiter's Horse. As time passes and these two characters mature, their daydreams become integral parts of their waking lives. Delia eventually marries an Irishman, and Rose's childhood war games translate into actual militant activity with the suffragettes. If *The Years* turns a skeptical eye toward historical development, character development reveals a similar skepticism toward the agency of everyday individuals. As we see with Delia and Rose, Woolf's characters do not progress but live out and repeat their family histories with disastrous consequences.

Daydreams, like their unconscious counterparts, transfer latent content into a manifest form; as psychoanalysts have argued, daydreams may be more conscious and consciously directed, but they too are phantasmatic.[44] While it would be tempting to read Delia's attraction to Parnell, the antagonist for Irish Home Rule, as a sublimated reaction against her father, Woolf structures Delia's fantasy in a way that avoids such symmetry. The opening chapter positions Delia's adoration for her father against her hatred of her mother. When Abel Pargiter takes his place at the dinner table, he transforms from bygone imperialist and adventurer into storyteller and patriarch, further twining the Pargiter family's imperial past with its present. Delia especially falls under the enchantment of Abel's exotic tales. "Delia liked listening to her father's stories about India. They were crisp, and at the same time romantic. They conveyed an atmosphere of officers dining together in mess jackets on a very hot night with a huge silver trophy in the middle of the table" (36). Unmoored from their specific context, these stories of empire take on a more contemporary form in Delia's fantasies. Delia imagines herself at the side of Charles Parnell, effectively translating his desire for Irish Home Rule into her own dreams of personal independence.[45] "Somewhere there's beauty, Delia thought, somewhere there's freedom, and somewhere, she thought, *he* is—wearing his white flower. . . . But a stick grated in the hall. 'It's Papa!' Milly exclaimed warningly" (12). The white flower becomes a metonym for Parnell and his contestation of British rule; it is bound in Delia's daydream sequence with "beauty" and "freedom," all of which exist "somewhere" beyond the confines of Abercorn Terrace.

Delia's yearning for greater autonomy negatively reflects her deep enmity for mother. At her mother's bedside, Delia lapses into her private dream world and names Parnell for the first time. Delia "longed for her [mother] to die" (22), but, unable to stave off creeping guilt, she attempts to excavate a simple memory of affection for her. When Delia recalls such a memory, it dissolves and gives way to "the other scene" (22): "The man in the frock coat with the white flower in his button-hole. But she had sworn not to think of that till bedtime" (22). She skirts across other memories to keep "the other scene" at bay, but it manifests itself fully and sweeps Delia away with it. Setting the scene just right with the "hall; banks of palms; a floor beneath them crowded with people's heads" (22), Delia envisions Parnell at her side. "'I am speaking in the cause of Liberty,' she began, throwing out her hands, 'in the cause of Justice. . . . ' They were standing side by side" (23). The "other scene" appears twice more at her mother's funeral, and Delia again struggles to suppress it.

Why do these daydreams manifest so powerfully at these specific moments? For Delia, it is not her father, whom she admires and looks upon lovingly, but her mother who constrains her, representing antiquated but no less constraining late Victorian feminine roles. When the elder Rose Pargiter's health slides for the final time, Delia presumes it is another false alarm. "'But it's all for nothing,' Delia said silently, looking at her father. She felt that they must both check their rising excitement. 'Nothing's going to happen—nothing whatever,' she said, looking at him" (45–46). But something does happen, and her mother's death provides Delia the opportunity to achieve her dreams of justice and liberty: "She was possessed by a sense of something everlasting; of life mixing with death, of death becoming life . . . life came closer and closer" (87). For Delia, this much anticipated death extends her horizon of possibilities beyond the domestic confines of the late Victorian household. As we learn from later chapters, Delia flees Abercorn Terrace after her mother's passing, seeking the more egalitarian, open world of her fantasies. Even in those chapters where Delia does not appear, she remains connected to the family's history through Parnell and Ireland; Eleanor and Abel immediately think of her when Parnell's death is announced in "1891" and Rose reports to Maggie in "1910" that Delia "married an Irishman" (168) as Maggie "took a blue flower and placed it beside a white flower" (168), again pairing the metonym for Parnell with Delia.

In the "Present Day" chapter, we see Delia some fifty years older. Her daydreams and political aspirations have merged completely with her daily life, right down to her mannerisms and gestures. She greets Peggy with "her imitation Irish flattery" (362) and assists North while "assuming the manner of a harum-scarum Irish hostess" (365). *The Years* pairs Delia's acquired "Irishness" with a marriage that simultaneously completes Delia's past yearnings and undermines them. Delia's daydreams of liberty, justice, and "the Cause" find their ironic fulfillment in her husband, Patrick, an older Irishman who repeatedly laments Ireland's new freedom and longs instead for the old empire: "It seems to me," says Patrick of the Irish Free State, "that our new freedom is a good deal worse than our old slavery" (399). Delia's political fervor leads to neither justice nor liberty. Lisa Weihman characterizes Delia's marriage as a continuation of the very injustices she fled the Pargiter house to combat. Delia "inadvertently, comically, champions the forces of English colonial imperialism in spite of her declared politics when she marries a wealthy Anglo-Irish landlord."[46]

The novel treats her as something of a caricature, undermining whatever lofty ideals fueled her antagonism toward late Victorian domesticity and Abercorn Terrace: "Thinking to marry a wild rebel, she had married the most King respecting, Empire-admitting of country gentleman" (398). Delia's artificial Irish mannerisms and her marriage are cast as aberrations by the novel; her daydreams have become her waking life, and she is none the better for it. Seeking a way out of the domestic life of Abercorn Terrace, Delia's adversarial daydreams find their moment of realization and undoing in a marriage to an Irishman mourning the loss of empire, decrying the gains of suffrage for women, and wishing for the return of the very time and life Delia so longed to escape.

This type of characterization replays in miniature the recursive historicism of *The Years*. Social and political antagonisms drive the movement of history, but they only reproduce those very tensions in other forms. The fate of Woolf's characters detail inescapable, anticlimactic conflicts, which suggest two points that are the precise opposite of Delia's youthful yearnings: first, history unfolds independently of the will and desires of historical subjects; second, the liberal narrative of history as progress surrenders its place to a vision of history where tensions are amplified, not sublated. While we might anatomize *The Years'* disquieting philosophy of history as symptomatic of "the destructive element" in literature of the

1930s, we would be remiss in not accounting for the aggressive depoliticization that attends the novel's historical consciousness. The subplots of two other prominent women characters resemble Delia's but metonymically stand in for the struggle for women's rights in the Edwardian years (Rose) and the material gains of those struggles for women in postwar England (Peggy). What should operate as a story of a victorious struggle transforms into one of futility. Rose is identifiably the most political character in the novel. She joins and leads a militant wing of the suffrage movement. Through the conversations of other family members, we learn that Rose throws a brick through a shop window during a suffrage march, is imprisoned and force-fed, and, like many other suffrage activists, works for the British war state during the First World War. Christine Froula traces Rose's development in the novel in terms of progress: "As Rose grows up, unconscious guilt, shame, rage, and fear fuel her distinguished career as a militant suffragette."[47] And yet the novel makes it difficult to see anything heroic or progressive in Rose's trajectory from childhood guilt and shame to activism. What first appears to be a narrative of political awakening inverts into one of psychopathology.[48]

Retracing Rose's characterization from her childhood to her later life in the 1930s presents a pattern of development similar to Delia's. With Rose, Woolf ultimately conjoins political action with pathology. What we might call Rose's primal scene occurs during one of her evening adventures that take her on missions beyond Abercorn Terrace. Unable to leave the house without her brother or any other male escort, Rose absconds to visit Mrs. Lamley's shop. Her "mission" is dressed with all the details of military espionage, linking the very structure of her fantasies, like Delia, to her father's stories: she is on a "desperate mission to a besieged garrison," delivering a "secret message" in "enemy country." She imagines herself as a secret agent, as "Pargiter of Pargiter's Horse" (27). Rose runs past a man leaning against a pillar box and "shoots" him, but here the real breaks through the thick web of fantasy. The man reaches out for Rose, nearly grabbing her: "The game was over. She was herself again, a little girl who had disobeyed her sister" (28). As she leaves the shop, she tries again to conjure the fantasy "but the story no longer worked" (29). The man by the pillar box returns and exposes himself to Rose. The scene makes a ghastly return in Rose's nightmares, but, having disobeyed Eleanor, Rose cannot explain what happened without admitting her own guilt. There is more, however, behind Rose's militancy than this single traumatic event. In the "1908" chapter we learn that Rose took the blame for a young boy who broke a microscope in elementary school. Afterward she cut her wrist with a butter knife in the bathroom: "And I dashed into the bathroom and cut this gash"—she held out her wrist. Eleanor looked at it. There was a thin white scar just above the wrist joint" (158). Far more than another instance of trauma and repetition, this scene acquires more significance through the narrative sequencing of these events and their recollection.

Rose joins Eleanor and Martin after giving a speech in Northumberland on women's suffrage. "A stone had been thrown at her; she put her hand to her chin. But she had enjoyed it" (157). The narrative juxtaposes this scene with Rose's childhood stories, coding Rose's political life as an unfortunate, even masochistic repetition of earlier traumas.

Like the cyclical historical plots to which Delia and Rose are held captive, *The Years* features Rose's political maturation as an indirect effect of psychic damage; those previous personal experiences are not sublated into collective politics. Politics is discounted as mere effect. The link of past violence to future acts of violence assumes its only collective dimension in an exchange between Rose and Martin in the "Present Day" chapter. Like many of the suffragettes, Rose assisted the British war effort after 1914, recruiting men for the war and performing industrial work, among other things. Rose obtains a "decoration" (359), a red ribbon, for her work for the state during wartime.[49] Martin mirthlessly acknowledges a seeming contradiction between Rose's prewar political antagonism to the state and her reward for trading revolutionary politics for cooperation with the state in its most violent and murderous war of the young twentieth century: "'She smashed his window,' Martin jeered at her, 'and then she helped him to smash other people's windows'" (420). In the narrative logic of *The Years*, historical violence begets more historical violence, and, turning the liberal narrative of history inside out, antagonisms return in augmented form.

Where Rose's and Delia's characters demonstrate the ironic fulfillment of youthful wishes in their later lives, Peggy Pargiter turns away from the future altogether, pining for a more secure, romanticized version of the late nineteenth century. Peggy has reaped the rewards of Rose and the militant suffragettes; she works as a doctor in London and has earned all the praise and esteem of her male colleagues. Despite her expanded social and economic horizons, Peggy desires the life of the elder Pargiters from the 1880s, particularly Eleanor. Peggy interrogates Eleanor about "that past of the 'eighties," which seems "so interesting; so safe" (333). To Peggy, Eleanor represents the last generation of "believers" (331): "It was as if she still believed with passion—she, old Eleanor—in the things that man had destroyed. A wonderful generation, she thought" (331). Peggy wants to excavate this past, to bind all that is lost from that world to her own present. "Where does she begin, and where do I end?" (334), Peggy asks herself. She arrives at no conclusions, but the insistence on demarcating beginnings and endings, of establishing the past's relation to the present, signals Peggy's desire to apply some narrative structure to history. Peggy, of course, gets very little from Eleanor. Eleanor offers only a few scattered musings that are constantly interrupted. Eleanor mostly wants to hear about Peggy, to comment on contemporary dress and fashion, and dissolve herself into the trivialities of the present.[50] Of course, the past for Eleanor is neither safe nor beautiful nor peaceful; it is full of family conflicts, missed opportunities, and, to be sure, memories of war. When Eleanor recounts her first sighting of an airplane, she turns and fumbles with her papers. Peggy misreads her behavior as a sign of old age, but Eleanor's story recalls the war she experienced but never saw: "She had seen the sky; and that sky was laid with pictures—she had seen it so often; any one of which might come uppermost when she looked at it. Now, because she had been talking to North, it brought back the war" (329).

The memory of war sheds any longing for the past for Eleanor; Eleanor wishes only to be "happy in this world" (388), this immediate present full of young people clad in pretty dresses who say interesting things. For Peggy, though, "this world" is on the verge of apocalypse:

> There was a lull—a silence. Far away she heard the sounds of the London night; a horn hooted; a siren wailed on the river. The far-away sounds, the suggestion they brought in of other worlds, different to this world, of people toiling, grinding, in the heart of darkness, in the depths of night, made her say over Eleanor's words, Happy in this world, happy with living people. But how can one be "happy," she asked herself, in a world bursting with misery? On every placard at every street corner was Death; or worse— tyranny; brutality; torture; the fall of civilization; the end of freedom. We here, she thought, are only sheltering under a leaf, which will be destroyed. (388)

Peggy's litany of miseries names all the fears attending the nightmare of another global war, but it also maps two different versions of "this world." Eleanor's "this world" is the immediate present, a place full of youth, beauty, and possibility. For Peggy, "this world" verges on a collision with "other worlds" where the horrors of historical violence threaten to tear asunder the comforts and complacencies of everyday life in Britain. Woolf employs two narrative voices in this passage, the narrator's and Peggy's, to align the historical process that precedes Peggy's lifetime with her own present. The narrator's voice imports colonial atrocities into the present with its unmistakable reference to Conrad's novel; further, the very language grafts the past war onto the present moment: the "siren wailed" is a repetition from the "1917" (288, 289) and "1918" chapters (304). The lulls and silences too are repetitions from the lulls and silences in conversation during the air raids. The dual voices also underscore a contradiction as they place Peggy's disenchantment with the present against those past histories that have made her life possible. Peggy represents the material realization of the struggles and dreams of the suffragettes; she is their protagonist of the future. And yet her fear of the world's extinction induces nostalgia for the very world her predecessors worked so ardently to undo. When Peggy does venture to put into words her fleeting vision of the "state of being" (390), she ultimately fails; "there was the vision still but she had not grasped it. She had broken off only a little fragment of what she meant to say. . . . Yet there it hung before her, the thing she had seen, the thing she had not said. But as she fell back with a jerk against the wall, she felt relieved of some oppression. . . . Now she could rest" (391). Peggy's vision and exhaustion significantly recalls Lily Briscoe's final effort in *To the Lighthouse*. Yet Lily completes her painting; her vision becomes material in due time. For Peggy, the vision fails, leaving only exhaustion. Neither words nor art offer redemptive potential.

Unable to recover the 'eighties, to redeem them and restore the continuum of history, Peggy's vision for a new world falters. Peggy's yearnings are the novel's own: despite the desire for history as unimpeded progress, the novel can only demonstrate the impossibility of ever realizing that desire. The novel closes with the same impossible hope. Unlike the other chapters in the novel, the lengthy closing one has no date for its title; it is simply an undefined "Present Day." Is this the culmination of historical time or its dissolution? Will this present moment mitigate, if not resolve, the antagonisms of the past? The closing scene gives us some clue. Eleanor and Delia stare out of the window, repeating a similar moment from "1880." In the earlier chapter, Delia twice gazes out of the window at a hansom cab, waiting and wishing for her mother's death. The novel gestures toward a parallel between the arrival of the hansom cab and the passing of Mrs. Pargiter but then quickly disrupts it. The arrival of the cab does not coincide with any death, and it does not usher in the arrival of "justice and liberty" for Delia. If the final scene repeats these early ones, it maintains the disjoined parallel of the cab's arrival and the arrival of a new world. Eleanor watches the taxi pass and excitedly says "There. . . . There!" (434). She turns to Morris with hands outstretched and asks "And now?" (434–35). Eleanor's memory of the past returns; her gesture toward Morris symbolizes a desire to bring the family's past in line with their present. Eleanor's question and gesture go unanswered. The only form of response the novel gives is the hackneyed line that resembles the beginning of every other chapter: "the sun had risen, and the sky above the houses wore an air of extraordinary beauty, simplicity and peace" (435). Things repeat and the everyday goes on.

Reading to the Bloomsbury memoir club on September 9, 1938, John Maynard Keynes sketched this portrait of his generation's understanding of the world and what it meant to be an historical agent in that world:

> We were among the last of the Utopians, or meliorists as they are sometimes called, who believe in a continuing moral progress by virtue of which the human race already consists of reliable, rational, decent people, influenced by truth and objective standards. . . .
> It was not only that intellectually we were pre-Freudian, but we had lost something which our predecessors had without replacing it.[51]

By 1938 the increasingly metastatic movement of war threatened to engulf much of the globe, and hope and optimism were certainly in short supply. September would not pass before Chamberlain would wrongly prophesy that the Munich Agreement signified peace in our time. Of course, much of this could not have been a total surprise to Keynes; he foresaw this situation from its very origins in Versailles in *The Economic Consequences of the Peace*. The sheer gravity of Keynes's statement is astounding nonetheless. The liberal project of enlightened modernity was incapable of addressing the economic and political problems of the postwar world. Woolf heard Keynes read from this memoir and judged it "profound & impressive."[52] What Keynes states so candidly, and indeed regrettably, remained a perpetual question in Woolf's novel. To echo Keynes, something has been lost and there is nothing to replace it. Through its deployment and disfiguration of the historical novel, *The Years* encodes the waning of a world-system and its concomitant ideologies of history and progress. Like Keynes's memoir, *The Years* is a pained eulogy for the narrative of historical progress and the promise of human emancipation. It is this bleak note that resounds through the novel's generic dissolution and the unanswered questions, empty hands, and exhausted, unspoken visions for other futures that linger beyond its end.

Bleak though this may be, Woolf's examination of everyday life as the scene where historical processes attain legibility is ultimately neither an endorsement of quietism nor a mere resignation. The novel models a way of investigating and interpreting everyday life. Throughout *The Years* we see the tendency to catalog, describe, detail, or index everything that appears extraneous to the story. But what this novel tells us is that nothing is extraneous; all signs, regardless of how minor they are to the characters or how quickly they are passed over in the narrative, have something to tell us. When Martin Pargiter flips through a newspaper story about the political frailty of the Balkans in 1913, it may indeed seem like a stray detail at the moment of reading. Such unrest, however, is the most obvious foreshadowing of the First World War. Is this how Woolf hoped her contemporary readers would receive Eleanor's outbursts about dictators she sees in the newspaper in the "Present Day" chapter? What about North, recently returned from Africa, noting offhand that "somebody had chalked a circle on the wall with a jagged line in it" (310), clearly referring to Oswald Mosley's fascist insignia? In one way we might say that the novel has a pedagogical value. It trains its contemporary readers to look, observe, see, and read everything with the same intensity before the event of war as one would do in retrospect. *The Years* establishes these relationships between historical events and the minutiae of everyday life to assert to its readers that long historical processes proceed ahead with or without the knowledge of those who ultimately have to live with the consequences.

LOST NOVEL, LOST REPUBLIC

Like *The Years*, Isherwood's most well-known novel, *Goodbye to Berlin*, prioritizes everyday life as the scene where historical change manifests itself most vividly.

Unlike *The Years*, *Goodbye to Berlin* is retrospective, not anticipatory. Where *The Years* generates a recursive model of historical time and awaits a coming catastrophe, Isherwood and the Berlin demimondaine have witnessed their catastrophe with Hitler's ascension to power. The novel took Isherwood the better part of the 1930s to finish, allowing him to write and revise as Germany upset the geopolitical equilibrium in Europe. On Isherwood's own account, his novel was "written with a good deal of political hindsight," despite being almost contemporary with the events it records.[53] *Goodbye to Berlin* covers a short but feverish period of German history. Isherwood's novel follows characters through those grim years, from autumn 1930 to the winter of 1933, when Berlin was "almost already on the brink of civil war." [54] During the time frame of the novel, Weimar Germany existed in a near continual state of emergency to keep what Isherwood called "the Berlin brew,"—an unsavory mix of "unemployment, malnutrition, stock-market panic, hatred of the Versailles Treaty"—from boiling over into widespread unrest.[55] When the American stock markets collapsed in October 1929, President Paul von Hindenburg appointed conservative Heinrich Brüning as chancellor to ameliorate the worsening economic situation.[56] Brüning's deflationary policies did little to halt the sharp decline of the German economy. As unpopular and ineffective as his efforts were, Brüning kept power for two years and "essentially ruled by decree under Article 48 of the Weimar Constitution," giving him the unfettered authority to rule as a presidential dictator.[57] Wielding extraordinary executive power, Brüning still had to negotiate with the Reichstag; individual freedoms and parliamentary oversight remained, at least hypothetically. On September 20, 1930, the Nazis increased their seats in the Reichstag from 12 to 107, attaining majority party status for the first time and becoming a major counterrevolutionary force. By the time Isherwood's final Berlin Diary closes in 1933, Hindenburg and his conservative allies have legally appointed Hitler as chancellor, giving a stark answer to any lingering questions over the Weimar Republic's capabilities to avert political and economic disaster. The Nazi Party dissolved the republic, putting an end to the democratic experiment that the post-1918 revolutions brought into being.[58]

Weimar's crisis of sovereignty during these troubled years marks an irreparable historical break, distributing accounts of German history into periods before and after the republic's dissolution. *Goodbye to Berlin*'s primary task is to give form to the process by which the Weimar Republic became historical or, in Walpole's words, became "no longer contemporary" in a relatively compressed period of time.[59] While most of my analysis will focus on the way *Goodbye to Berlin* describes this process of becoming historical, it is worth noting that the book we have is not the one Isherwood planned to write. The initial drafting of his Berlin fictions occurred in mid-August of 1932. Individual parts of *Goodbye to Berlin* first saw the light of day in a few issues of John Lehmann's *New Writing* between 1936 and 1938; Woolf's Hogarth Press issued "Sally Bowles" as a novella in 1937.[60] Appearing as a single novel in 1939, *Goodbye to Berlin* added the "Berlin Diary (Winter 1932–33)" to the previously published portions. Initially these individual sections were intended to be components of a much larger design. Each plot and each character were to find their place within a wide panorama of everyday life in Berlin, giving his readers "one huge tightly constructed melodramatic novel, in the manner of Balzac."[61] With Balzac's *Splendeurs et misères des courtisanes* as the primary model, Isherwood's novel would have abided by the same generic protocols that Lukács celebrates. In Lukács's preferred form of the novel, "every phenomenon shows the polyphony of many components, the intertwinement of the individual and the social, of the physical and the psychical, of private interest and public affairs."[62] If configured properly, Isherwood's colorful and expansive cast would have accomplished just that: each character and plot would unveil a dynamic social totality where each piece provided insight to another. Ideally, holding all of the elements together and slotting them into a rather capacious plot would give form to the chaos that plagued Weimar Berlin in its twilight years and would ultimately establish the historical logic underwriting its demise.

In place of a fully orchestrated city novel in the vein of Balzac, Isherwood's unmanageable archive of daily life yielded only "an absurd jumble of subplots and coincidences," "a cat's cradle of strings and wires and connections and plots."[63] Isherwood solved these compositional challenges by simply dispensing with the intricacies of plot and focusing his energies on the "loosely connected sketches" that make up *Goodbye to Berlin*.[64] Oddly, Isherwood's pivotal decision to jettison plot has received scant attention. If the novel consciously abandons the organizational structure of plot, its very arrangement teases readers with a chronological framework: the first story is "A Berlin Diary (Autumn 1930)," and the final one is its perfect companion, "A Berlin Diary (Winter 1932–33)." David Garrett Izzo states that the "stories are staged chronologically from "Autumn 1930" to "Winter

1932–33."[65] However, a closer look betrays a more complicated and far less orderly timeline. The two Berlin diaries that bookend the collection are fairly clear in their dates; the others, however, stretch forward and backward into this period of time. "Sally Bowles" occurs between October 1930 and the summer of 1931; "On Ruegen Island (Summer 1931)," the story that follows, occurs in that same time frame and is briefly referenced in "Sally Bowles"; "The Nowaks" begins in winter 1931, but the following story, "The Landauers," reverts back to October 1930, placing it within the same window of time of "Sally Bowles." Without the connective tissues of plot, these episodes are organized, in Isherwood's words, as a series of "portraits" or "sketches" in opposition to "form" or "a unified novel."[66] To be clear, what is important is not whether the book resembles a collection of short stories or a proper novel; rather, *Goodbye to Berlin* mediates the historical antagonisms of the Weimar Republic through its fragmentary and elliptical narration, which Isherwood himself would later describe as the "little broken bits of something" where "the gaps are not worth filling in."[67]

Isherwood's narrative strategy bears many traits of modernist prose, and, like the works of Joyce, Proust, and Stein, *Goodbye to Berlin* marshals these strategies to interrogate the most oblique details of everyday life. Yet Isherwood's most popular work is remembered not for its proximity to the avatars of high modernist prose nor for its emphasis on dense subjective experience; rather, it draws interest primarily for its heralded camera-eye narration. The opening passages of *Goodbye to Berlin* contain Isherwood's most quoted and debated line: "I am a camera with its shutter open, quite passive, recording, not thinking."[68] Isherwood scholars and biographers alike have wrangled over the implied preference for subjective or objective narration, the novel's place within the documentary tradition of the 1930s, and Isherwood's precise intention.[69] One need not venture far from the text to confirm that the camera eye was never intended to provide objective, detached representation. That very paragraph concludes with an admission of editorial intervention or, in this case, authorial construction: "Someday, all this will have to be developed, carefully printed, fixed" (1). In this way, *Goodbye to Berlin* bears strong affinities with the documentary aesthetic of the 1930s, which understood documentary as a combination of description, editing, and narration. While it would be reductive to read *Goodbye to Berlin* solely as a documentary novel, it shares the documentarist's conscious decision to assemble fragments of everyday life as a way to give narrative form to the historical present.

Isherwood's signature line indicates a mode of attention that transforms the apparently negligible details of the everyday into something revelatory. The opening sequence surveys a Berlin street scene:

> From my window, the deep solemn massive street. Cellarshops where the lamps burn all day, under the shadow of top-heavy balconied facades, dirty plaster frontages embossed with scrollwork and heraldic devices. The whole district is like this: street leading into street of houses like shabby monumental safes crammed with the tarnished valuables and second-hand furniture of a bankrupt middle-class. (1)

So compiled, these details convey the slum-like conditions of Fraulein Schroeder's neighborhood. However, the comparison of the houses as safes for "second-hand furniture of a bankrupt middle-class" suggests these quotidian details are not mere background details; they are material signs of Weimar's economic and political troubles. The narrative proceeds by marshaling details of space and interior to diagram the economic despair that would soon fuel right-wing political violence. Fraulein Schroeder tells Christopher of the good days before the war, when she still took vacations and would only take lodgers from higher classes and professions. As she points to stains and ink marks on the rugs and walls that reference her less professional and lower class lodgers, she describes in miniature Germany's deteriorating economic security after 1918. The dilapidated lodgings of the prewar, pre-inflation middle class are contrasted with the luxurious and incongruously decorated abode of the Bernsteins, filled as it is with "modernist lamps" (14) and "nineteenth-century landscapes in massive gold frames" (15). The objects of everyday life—furniture, decorations, paintings—rises from the background to the foreground to delineate Weimar's combustible economic situation, asking us to decipher the historical fortunes concealed within insignificant details.

The juxtapositions contained within the opening chapter get elevated to a larger formal principle in the novel. The exchange of plot for portraiture ultimately privileges contrapuntal character sketches or what we might call spatial form. What is at stake in this exchange? Why would spatial form more adequately mediate the crisis of sovereignty in Weimar Germany? The classic and still provocative work on space and modernist form remains Joseph Frank's *The Idea of Spatial Form*. Frank asserts that spatial form has become dominant in modern poetry and in the plastic arts. Few would gainsay that proposition. His more strik-ing claim is that narrative literature, despite its reliance upon time, plot develop-ment, and sequence, inclines toward spatial form (at least the novel since Gustave Flaubert). The passing of time and the occurrence of events do not govern the modern novel. Moreover, such an approach will do little to help us understand the more recalcitrant works of modernist fiction. Frank insists that Joyce, Proust, and Djuna Barnes demand to be "re-read" so that all the juxtaposed fragments can be grasped as a totality in a single moment; all the disconnected parts of modern-ist fiction only gather coherence by their relations in space at a given moment in time. For Frank, this narrative form has its analog in cross-cutting techniques in film where the succession of individual scenes are in fact happening simultane-ously in the story but not in the narrative discourse. So what we have instead of temporal development is "reflexive reference" whereby certain images, symbols, or scenes refer back and forth to one another in order, creating a complex of scenes that must be perceived in an instant. This exchange of narrative time for spatial form entails the evacuation of history from art. "The dimension of histori-cal depth," he writes "has vanished from the content of the major works of mod-ern literature."[70] Isherwood's book, though, shows that Frank's thesis is equally ca-pable of producing the opposite result. Spatial form in *Goodbye to Berlin* registers dramatic historical change. In other words, spatial form serves as a way to think through a historical process outside of Lukács's progressive temporality.

There is perhaps no better manifestation of the narrative force of Isherwood's spatial form than the two juxtaposed stories of two German families, "The Nowaks" and "The Landauers." As mentioned earlier, these two stories do not move forward chronologically: "The Nowaks" takes place in the winter of 1931, and "The Landauers" moves us back into the previous year before extending for-ward to 1933. Nevertheless, the juxtaposition of these two stories foregrounds ex-traordinarily powerful distinctions. The Nowaks are a German family struggling mightily under economic hardship. Herr Nowak, evincing somewhat liberal and cosmopolitan sympathies, was a former soldier in the First World War. His son, Lothar, a Nazi, works and donates his earnings to the family. At first sight, Frau Nowak is dressed in a "mangy old black coat" (101). The apartment is cramped, and Isherwood and Frau Nowak can barely stand in the "tiny kitchen" (101) at the same time. Roving from the kitchen to the living room, Isherwood's descriptions emphasize the lack of space and the decrepit rooms: "The living-room had a sloping ceiling stained with old patches of damp. It contained a big table, six chairs, a sideboard and two large double-beds. The place was so full of furniture that you had to squeeze your way into it sideways" (101). These dreary surroundings directly correspond to Frau Nowak's weakening state. She is eventually admitted to the sanitorium. Once removed from the claustrophobic, squalid lodgings in the Wassertorstrasse, Frau Nowak's physical and mental condition greatly improves. Accompanying Otto to visit Frau Nowak at the sanitorium, Isherwood is struck with her initial appearance: "She looked years younger. Her plump, oval, innocent face, lively and a trifle crafty, with its small peasant eyes, was like the face of a young girl. Her cheeks were brightly dabbed with colour. She smiled as though she could never stop" (133). To be sure, Isherwood's depiction of the strange sanitorium makes it clear that Frau Nowak's condition—her decline in the Wassertorstrasse and rejuvenation in the sanitorium—is related primarily to space, but the sanitorium is hardly described as a place for recovery or relaxation. "The smell of the warm, clean, antiseptic building entered my nostrils like a breath of fear" (133). Reprising the role of the camera, Isherwood's narration trades sensation and judgment for description of the sanitorium:

> Everything which happened to me to-day was curiously without impact: my senses were muffled, insulated, functioning as if in a vivid dream. . . . My eyes could explore every corner of their world: the temperature-charts, the fire extinguisher, the leather screen by the door. Dressed daily in their best clothes, their clean hand no longer pricked by the needle or roughened from scrubbing, they lay out on the terrace, listening to the wireless, forbidden to talk (134–35).

The solution to the pressures of impoverished life appears here as total management and administration of daily life itself, presaging the murderous statecraft that will emerge in Weimar's wake.

The Landauers, a successful Jewish family who own one of Germany's largest department stores, live in a sumptuous modern home filled with art and manned by servants. Isherwood meets Natalia Landauer, one of his pupils, in a large sitting room "cheerful, pre-War in taste, a little overfurnished" (140). The Landauer family's home, Bernhard Landauer's modern flat and county cottage, and, of course, the Landauer department store stand in stark contrast to the ramshackle lodgings of the Wassertorstrasse. The markings, then, are clear: poor, suffering Germans and wealthy, well-placed Jews. Because they are arranged in a reversed temporal order, the two stories do not exactly chart the growing anti-Semitism in Germany. Divested of an overarching chronology, their spatial proximity works instead to examine, in the words of Samuel Hynes, "how a civilized democracy with a liberal tradition could choose fascism."[71] Nazism, it seems, brews and steeps in the slums; while non-Jewish German families struggle economically, wealthy Jewish families like the Landauers become targets for Nazi propaganda and German anxiety. This is perhaps why Isherwood opens "The Landauers" with a Nazi protest in the Leipzigerstrasse. The Nazis "manhandled some dark-haired, large-nosed pedestrians and smashed the windows of all the Jewish shops" (139). Fraulein Mayr, the anti-Semite with whom Isherwood lodged at Fraulein Schroeder's flat, "was delighted" (139) at the violence. Her vitriol gives expression to the seething anti-Semitism in Berlin in the fall of 1930; coming as it does after "The Nowaks" story, one cannot help but link her anger with the declining economic status of formerly middle-class German families. Fraulein Mayr's rant names the Landauers specifically: "This town is sick with Jews. Turn over any stone, and a couple of them will crawl out. They're poisoning the very water we drink! They're strangling us, they're probing us, they're sucking our life-blood. Look at all the big department stores: Wertheim, K.D.W., Landauers'. Who owns them? Filthy thieving Jews!" (140). The novel's citation of these and other instances of anti-Semitic feeling acquires further meaning next to "The Nowaks." In the arrangement of these two chapters, the economic disparities underpinning far right populism are situated next to Isherwood's depiction of increasing anti-Semitism in everyday German life.

By abandoning chronology and the organizational structure of plot, *Goodbye to Berlin*'s spatial narrative measures Germany's crisis of sovereignty as a historical rupture and a rupture in historical thinking. Yet my argument suggests that the novel's contestation of historical time, or certain models of historical time, is not ahistorical. It does not signal repressed historicity, or what Jameson identifies in the spatial forms of fiction after high modernism as "a nostalgia for nostalgia, for the grand older extinct questions of origin and telos."[72] *Goodbye to Berlin*'s spatial turn comes from neither nostalgia nor repressed trauma but from a sense that historical events have depleted the representational powers of those narrative forms underwritten by developmental time schemes so prized by Lukács and other theorists and practitioners of the historical novel. For Isherwood, the aesthetic task is still very much to capture the event-sequence that precipitated the downfall of Weimar and the ascent of the Nazi state. Spatial form, then, emerges not as an absolute counter to historical time but as a negation of historical fiction's attachment to progressive and developmental temporalities. Read negatively, the very form of *Goodbye to Berlin* internalizes Weimar's crisis of sovereignty as a crisis of historical thinking.

We should recall here that the formal mechanisms of Isherwood's fiction attest to the unique status attributed to Weimar Germany by historians and political theorists alike. The fascination with the troubled republic still follows from what most historians see as its descent into barbarism, its regression from a democratic state into an authoritarian regime. Not least of the problems manifested in Weimar's collapse was the example of a democratic state morphing into an authoritarian regime in compliance with Weimar's constitution. In a perversion of G. W. F. Hegel's system, the unfolding of history produces a state that is anything but "the embodiment of rational freedom."[73] In this way, Isherwood's retreat from historical plots to spatial form signals the momentous rupture that Weimar's sovereign crisis poses to those forms of historical thinking undergirded by progressive and developmental temporalities. More recent efforts in political theory like Giorgio Agamben's *Homo Sacer* and *State of Exception* employ spatial figures to explain Weimar's end. With Weimar as his privileged case, Agamben's theorization of sovereignty employs a vast array of spatial terms and metaphors: words like "localization," "threshold," "borders," "inside/outside," "zone" and the etymological origin of exception, *ex-capere* or "taken outside," ground his discussion of sovereignty and its foundational crises. These spatial rhetorics and concepts bring to light a paradigm of government and its operation throughout history; history, though, supplies examples for Agamben, but not causal or explanatory logic for a case like Weimar Germany.

In both literary historical and philosophical discourse, Weimar's collapse registers as a proper event, one both corrosive to and generative of conceptual structures, whether aesthetic or epistemological. Yet even as *Goodbye to Berlin's* form contests progressive versions of historical time, it generates another type of temporality. The juxtaposed sketches and contrapuntal form that make up *Good-bye to Berlin* has led Alan Wilde to liken reading the novel to "turning the pages of a photograph album."[74] A photograph extracts a moment in time out of the movement of history, but, as Roland Barthes's incisive commentary on photography makes clear, the photograph induces truly singular temporal experiences. The photograph is a "fugitive testimony" that "possesses an evidential force."[75] Every photograph testifies to the existence of whatever it captures, showing us a past (this existed at this moment in time) without future (it no longer exists in this way) that is somewhat perversely repeated endlessly in the present. This strange temporality is what Barthes refers to as "this-has-been": the photograph manages to repeat the past without ever promising any future. This is the pathos of the photograph and, indeed, its melancholic temporality; the photograph, Barthes tells us, possesses "that rather terrible thing . . . the return of the dead."[76] Perhaps nothing exemplifies Barthes's theory of photography's pathos better than his reaction to the photograph of young Lewis Payne. This particular photograph captures the young man sitting in his cell and awaiting the death penalty for an attempted assassination of Secretary of State W. H. Seward, Barthes describes the temporal experience of the photograph in this way: "The photograph is handsome, as is the boy: that is the *studium*. But the *punctum* is: *he is going to die*. I read at the same time: *This will be* and *this has been*; I observe with horror an anterior future of which death is the stake. . . . Whether or not the subject is already dead, every photograph is this catastrophe."[77]

Isherwood's spatial fictions induce this type of anterior futurity, inviting us to find in these past portraits a future awaiting its disclosure. The lives of Isherwood's characters are tied directly to the health and survival of the liberal republic; as it dies, so too do his characters deteriorate. As *Goodbye to Berlin* follows its characters across the threshold to Nazi Germany, political life and biological life become inseparable. Christopher's visit to Ruegen Island offers an early indication of Nazism's diagnosis of political difference as a medical condition. A Nazi doctor tells Christopher that he cannot be communist because "there isn't any such thing as communism. It's just an hallucination. A mental disease" (86–87). The doctor will later confide to Christopher that his young English friend Peter's head displays all the characteristics of a criminal, and he should be placed in a labor camp. When the Nazis strengthen their numbers in the Reichstag, Isherwood's characters decompose. After an eight-month absence, Christopher visits Bernhard and finds a frail, aged man: "I thought I had never seen Bernhard looking so ill. His face was pale and drawn; the weariness did not lift from it even when he smiled. There were deep sallow half-moons under his eyes. His hair seemed thinner. He might have added ten years to his age" (178). Bernhard's aggressive deterioration has nothing to do with illness; it is purely biopolitical. Nazi threats to his life and business have increased in frequency and ferocity. Bernhard will only leave Germany after the Reichstag fire, and Isherwood never locates him again. It is only in May of 1933 in Prague that Isherwood overhears a conversation that gives him the "last news of the Landauer family" (183). Two men discuss the newspaper report that Bernhard Landauer has died of heart failure. The ensuing conversation suggests that Bernhard's death was not exactly a medical condition: "'If you ask me,' said the fat man, 'anyone's heart's liable to fail, if it gets a bullet in it'" (184). The other possible fate for Bernhard is equally stark. The fat man later refers to the camps: "They get them in there, make them sign things. . . . Then their hearts fail" (185). Bobby, former cabaret bartender and one time lodger at Fraulein Schroeder's charming hovel, suffers a similar deterioration. Isherwood finds Bobby unemployed in the winter of 1932–33. "People like Bobby *are* their jobs—take the job away and they partially cease to exist" (188). Again, Isherwood's emphasis falls more on biological life; within a year Bobby's "hair is thinner, his clothes are shabbier, his cheekiness has become defiant and rather pathetic" (188). Both Bobby's and Bernhard's biological well-being hinges on their political status as either citizens or existential enemies.

Careful not to portray Bobby and Bernhard as isolated instances, Isherwood extends biological decay into a collective metaphor for Berlin itself. For the purposes of contrast, recall briefly the first camera-eye shot of the city in "A Berlin Diary (Autumn 1930)." Buildings and houses suffer from a poor economy; they are "monumental safes crammed with the tarnished valuables and second-hand furniture of a bankrupt middle class" (1). Yet that setting recedes to the background and we hear young men whistling to girls and see electric signs over seedy hotel rooms rented by the hour. Shifting from description to a rare moment of introspection, the narrator bemoans his own status as a lonesome foreigner. Berlin is still a lively place with its cabarets, romantic trysts, and bustling nightlife; the narrator's foremost problem is a personal one. In the final diary, Berlin has passed from the waiting room of history to its deathbed: "Berlin is a skeleton which aches in the cold; it is my own skeleton aching. I feel in my bones the sharp ache of the frost in the girders of the overhead railway, in the ironwork of balconies, in bridges, tramlines, lamp-standards, latrines. The iron throbs and shrinks, the stone and the bricks ache dully, the plaster is numb" (186). Isherwood's first sentence metaphorizes the city as a skeleton but then modifies that comparison. The figural language narrows and makes the condition of the city and its inhabitant interchangeable. Christopher's body feels the "sharp ache" of the city's infrastructure, and, likewise, the material of that infrastructure suffers physical pain. City and inhabitant share the same grim condition, and as one era of history dies, the people it sustained no longer have a place.

Using the German word "Die Verlorenen," Isherwood wanted the title of his planned novel to convey the double sense of "The Astray and the Doomed."[78] *The Lost* would refer to the "people whom established society rejects in horror";[79] it also indexes the only possible futures for the character types of the Berlin demimonde. Isherwood's colorful cast—prostitutes, crooks, a coy bachelorette, German Jews—exist with relative ease on the outskirts of German society during the Weimar years but will be the target of fascist enmity and state violence soon thereafter. In his effort to escape, Bernhard is recovered and murdered; Isherwood tells us that "the dives," the sort of place Fritz Wendel, Christopher, and Sally frequented, were suddenly of "great interest" (192) to the police. The establishments are routinely raided and "the names of their clients are written down" (192). The fringes and outskirts of Weimar society are drawn within the full reach of the Third Reich: the regime keeps the city under surveillance and finds those people who will no longer be lost to the Third Reich. And yet unlike most of Isherwood's Berliners, Natalia Landauer and Sally Bowles demonstrate another way of being lost. Natalia relocates to Paris and returns briefly during the August 1931 referendum on the Brüning government. Set against the tense background of the republic's potential demise, Isherwood notes that Natalia's laugh had become more delightful and "her eyes were sparkling" (175): "She has escaped—none too soon, perhaps. However often the decision may be delayed, all these people are ultimately doomed. This evening is a dress-rehearsal of a disaster. It is like the last night of an epoch" (177). Similarly, but perhaps in a more radical way, Sally Bowles demonstrates the proper way to be lost. Sally's English nationality would not endear her to the Nazis, and her open sexuality that was nourished in the Weimar cabaret scene would not have been permitted after 1933. Sally disappears and remains lost, even to the narrator.[80]

At the close of "Sally Bowles" Isherwood writes that he has lost touch with her for nearly six years and inscribes a note to her at the conclusion of the story: "So now I am writing to her. When you read this, Sally—if you ever do—please accept it as a tribute, the sincerest I can pay, to yourself and to our friendship. And send me another post-card" (76). Sally's absolute disappearance moves her far from the scrupulous registries of the Third Reich and perhaps even farther away from the narrator's own ability to sketch out the final turn in the narrative arcs of his characters. Whether they end in departures, mysterious disappearances, or presumed executions, the political valence of these characters' fates is quite clear: there is no future for these people in a totalitarian state.

Isherwood's disconnected plots, spatial narration, and the ultimately failed attempt to weave the individual components into a narrative totality signals the disarticulation of a genre from the philosophy of history that has long buttressed it. Detached from humanist, Hegelian, or Marxist conceptions of historical progress, *Goodbye to Berlin* captures a dying republic that itself stands for the end of a kind of historical thinking. Like so many other late modernist works, this reprogrammed historical novel also serves as a political allegory; *Goodbye to Berlin*'s descriptions and snapshots of daily life transfer the political problem of the failed state into the form of a failed novel. Isherwood's fragmented historical novel tells us that the grand narratives of history have no purchase on Weimar's sovereign crisis and, in many ways, may themselves have become historical and no longer contemporary. In place of their explanatory power, Isherwood offers the particularities of everyday life where thoughts, gestures, places, and biological life itself give visibility to historical shifts that are otherwise invisible.

BECOMING HISTORICAL, BECOMING NORMAL

As Woolf and Isherwood's novels graze the surface of the daily lives of the Pargiters and Berliners, they diagram two aprogressive philosophies of history: Woolf's novel models a recursive historicism whereby the historical violence of the past returns in amplified form; Isherwood's disintegrated novel treats Germany's crisis of sovereignty as an epochal break. And yet if Woolf and Isherwood respond to a perceived historical crisis in significantly different ways, their narratives conclude in strikingly similar fashion. The final scene in *The Years*, as we have seen, punctuates the novel's recursive form by repeating an earlier scene. Yet the final lines of the novel, hearkening to the very style in which every chapter begins, reminds us that the everyday goes on: "The sun had risen, and the sky above the houses wore an air of extraordinary beauty, simplicity and peace" (435). The closing chapter, "A Berlin Diary (Winter 1932–33)," compiles a series of vignettes of daily life in Berlin during the republic's final days. From his conversations with pupils and former landladies, an observation of a wrestling match, and the escalation of street violence against Jews, Isherwood details the transfer of power to the Nazis and the population's gradual adaptation to Nazi rule. The muted violence of the previous chapters overwhelms the final one, setting up the counterpoint to the novel's introductory, camera-eye narration:

> I catch sight of my face in the mirror of a shop, and am shocked to see that I am smiling. You can't help smiling in such beautiful weather. The trams are going up and down the Kleiststrasse, just as usual. They, and the people on the pavement, and the teacosy dome of the Nollendorfplatz station have an air of curious familiarity, of striking resemblance to something one remembers as normal and pleasant in the past—like a very good photograph.
>
> No. Even now I can't altogether believe that any of this has really happened.... (207)

Nazi rule, increased paranoia, and routine violence run against the "usual," the air of "curious familiarity," and what "one remembers as normal." That everyday life appears to continue as normal after and amid such a catastrophe is enough to turn the camera eye inward, leaving the novel to end with the narrator's pure bewilderment. The focus on everyday life as a barometer of historical change reveals how historical crises become normalized. In the late modernist historical novel, everyday life is where crisis becomes routine and emergencies become normal.

3
LATE MODERNISM'S GEOPOLITICAL IMAGINATION

EVERYDAY LIFE IN THE GLOBAL HOT ZONES

Meanwhile our daily round had to continue.
W. H. AUDEN AND CHRISTOPHER ISHERWOOD, *JOURNEY TO A WAR*

Meanwhile the daily—more particularly nightly—round, the common task.
GEORGE ORWELL, *HOMAGE TO CATALONIA*

PART OF THE argument I have advanced thus far is that late modernism's outward turn to everyday life doesn't simply reflect historical events or reproduce ideological tempers; rather, it functions as a mediated expression of world-systemic disorder. The documentary film movement and Mass-Observation detected at the level of everyday life a fraying compact between the citizenry and the British state during a protracted period of economic and political crisis. *Listen to Britain*, *Song of Ceylon*, *May the Twelfth*, and *War Begins at Home* produced narratives of daily life that tried to normalize the political and economic activity of the state and, by extension, secure the relationship between the population and the state. In the last chapter we saw two historical novels focus on everyday life and gradually undo the progressive philosophy of history that had long underwritten both the genre of the historical novel and attended the expansion and function of the British world-system. This chapter follows late modernism's outward turn into the hot zones of Spain and China, two areas that were crucial to the maintenance of the world-system. Both George Orwell's *Homage to Catalonia* and W. H. Auden and Christopher Isherwood's *Journey to a War* depict versions of everyday life traumatized by and yet quickly habituated to total war. But these texts are more than mere records of war. They showcase the corrosive power of war on the very concepts, discourses, and narrative systems that historically defined it and contained it. These texts derive material from the everyday that does not fit with the available discursive and conceptual models for understanding modern war. The forms of warfare these writers experience do not discriminate between combatant and noncombatant, civilian area and war zone. In their account, it is sui generis; the shape and power of war appears when it distorts the generic contours of the travel book. This is exactly where their engagement with everyday life becomes so illuminating. In the broken circuit between the particular experiences of daily life at war and their transformation into conceptual knowledge, these texts register the emergence, or partial appearance, of a new geopolitical realism, one that challenges the British world-system's balance of power, the legal institutions that sustain it, and the conceptual apparatus that legitimates it.

Before moving further ahead it is worth noting that these two travel books appear readymade for the recent global turn in modernist studies.[1] *Homage to Catalonia* features a multinational constituency of volunteers fighting for the Spanish Republic, offering a compelling model of solidarity exceeding national, linguistic, and even class affiliations. Auden and Isherwood's venture to the Sino-Japanese war moves British literature into another contact zone where anglophone modernism has vexed and underexplored cultural and political relationships.[2] And while recent work in modernist studies has favored cosmopolitanism, transnationalism, and the global, I want to retain the geopolitical as the proper category for addressing *Homage to Catalonia* and *Journey to a War*.[3] Unlike certain strains of cosmopolitan, transnational, or global approaches to literary and cultural study, geopolitics foregrounds problems of world order, territoriality, and enmity. In many ways the "political" in geopolitical has been anathema to the intercultural aspirations of global modernism.[4] Melba Cuddy-Keane's "Modernism, Geopolitics, Globalization" imagines a modernism cognizant of the multiplicity and cultural complexity of a globalizing world.[5] Methodologically, however, this requires the separation of the geopolitical from the global, the political from the cultural, and the economic from the social. Globalization emerges primarily as a process of cultural exchange where identities become more fluid and recognition of difference proceeds in a less aggressive way. Geopolitics, concerned as it is with territory, power politics, and the spatial ordering of the world, provides a far narrower horizon for thinking of such amiable cultural exchange. Yet this latter category helps us understand the formal and generic moves of both *Homage to Catalonia* and *Journey to a War*.

This chapter builds on recent work by Christopher GoGwilt, Laura Winkiel, Laura Doyle, and others that prioritizes the geopolitical over the cultural and ethical orientations of other methodologies.[6] While the genre of the travel book would seem to be an ideal location to negotiate cultural differences and, in the words of Cuddy-Keane, to "delineate the transformative possibilities arising when the self is resituated out in the world of global flows," the wars in Spain and China mutate the travel book's generic code and politicize all human experience and relations.[7] *Homage to Catalonia* and *Journey to a War* indirectly document the implosion of two of the three conditions John Darwin outlines as central to the maintenance of British hegemony after 1919: a stable balance of power in Europe, a "passive" Asia, and a powerful but not aggressive America. The influx of German and Italian arms, fighters, and military advisors to Spain expanded the geography of Fascist power in Europe and offered a coastal post for future challenges to British sea power; the Japanese assault on China threatened British financial interests and territorial possessions within the mainland and along the coast. It was from Shanghai that the British Royal Navy policed the sea-lanes of maritime trade in and around Asia. Pairing *Homage to Catalonia* and *Journey to a War* makes sense at the historical level because they are both situated in contested zones that were important to the British world-system. At the literary level, both books short-circuit the generic operations of the travel book as they account for the forms of warfare altering the distribution of power in the world-system.

In his foundational study of modernist travel writing *Abroad*, Paul Fussell suggests that the hybridization of war and travel initiates the "decadent stage in the course of the between-the-wars travel book."[8] Fussell specifically tags *Homage to Catalonia* and *Journey to a War* as exemplars of this late stage because, formally, they "unravel" or "dissolve."[9] Despite what one might think of Fussell's value judgment of these books, he is certainly right that travel writing from a war zone exhibits a range of generic changes and interpretive problems.[10] Between the covers of books like Orwell's *Homage to Catalonia* and Auden and Isherwood's *Journey to a War*, a curious reader would find formerly romantic frontiers transformed into frontlines, bustling cities turned into refugee camps, and a broad spectrum of cultural differences subordinated to a far narrower sense of political alignment. What Orwell witnessed in Spain and what Auden and Isherwood scarcely grasped in China was a shift in the post-1919 world order from collective security modeled on international law to a more aggressive, technologically enhanced geopolitical realism. The so-called unraveling of *Homage to Catalonia* and *Journey to a War*, then, is better understood as the textual mediation of these shocks to the British world-system. In their formal maneuvers and rhetorical contradictions, in the broken circuit between the everyday experience of a war zone and the impoverished conceptual frameworks that could not sort that experience, *Homage to Catalonia* and *Journey to a War* make this event in geopolitics appear.

In the following pages, I plot *Homage to Catalonia* and *Journey to a War*'s treatment of everyday life at war alongside the overlapping spheres of legal, cultural, and geopolitical thought that sought, and failed, to keep pace with the evolving practices of warfare. I examine a number of legal and cultural efforts in the interwar years that understood the reconceptualization of war and the security of the world-system as intertwined projects. From this limited sample set of texts, we glimpse both the urgency of the problem and the diminished power of those cultural, legal, and historical narratives to address it. It is within this context of an emergent yet illegible shift in world order that these travel narratives'—and, more broadly, late modernism's—geopolitical imagination takes shape.

WAR OUT OF FORM

To begin unfolding these overlapping problems of genre, war, and geopolitics in the mid-to-late 1930s, I turn first to Carl Schmitt's provocative magnum opus *Nomos of the Earth*.[11] Schmitt's narrative charts the rise and fall of a geopolitical system organized around sovereign European states. For Schmitt, this so-called golden era stretched from the Treaty of Westphalia to the outbreak of the First World War in 1914. In this story, European stability rests on three interlocked notions shared by all sovereign states: the political legitimacy of war, the conceptualization of the enemy as a legitimate and just opponent, and a stable spatial order. For Schmitt, the major achievement of the interstate system was its "rationalization and humanization of war."[12] "The transformation of creedal, international civil war in the 16th and 17th centuries into 'war in form,' i.e., into state war circumscribed by European international law, was nothing short of a miracle."[13] In theory, wars attain form when they begin, operate, and close within a system of rights mutually recognized by sovereign states. Formal declarations precede these wars, and treaties conclude them. Like a duel (Schmitt's preferred analogy), bracketed war is war conducted according to a set of rules. Yet Schmitt's idea of "war in form" acquires meaning only when positioned against colonial wars, which were in Schmitt's terms "wars of annihilation."[14] Where interstate European wars largely abided by international law and recognized enemies as sovereign states, these conflicts marshaled theology or morality to justify their acts. As a consequence, enemies were inhuman and subjected to boundless violence. What Schmitt feared, and what this chapter will address at length, are the consequences for world order and the geopolitical imaginary when war loses form and the war-making practices Europeans had long reserved for policing the colonies— bombardment, scorched earth, collective punishment—become a normative feature of warfare within Europe and against European interests abroad.

This is, of course, part of Hannah Arendt's argument in *The Origins of Totalitarianism*. In her account, the techniques of totalitarianism and European genocide gestated abroad during the long history of colonial rule. The statistical evidence historians have accumulated for this claim is staggering. In *History of Bombing*, Sven Lindqvist notes that the rocket, so lacking in precision, was considered an improper weapon for interstate European wars but was deployed by the British against native populations:

They were reserved for savages and barbarians—in Algeria in 1816, Burma in 1825, Ashante in 1826, Sierra Leone in1831, Afghanistan in 1837–42, China in 1839–42 and 1856–60, against Shimonoseki in 1864, in Central America in 1867, Abyssinia in 1868, against the Zulus of South Africa in 1879, against the Nagas on the Afghani border in 1880, against Alexandria in 1882, and against rebellious subjects in Sudan, Zanzibar, and East and West Africa in 1864.[15]

Machine guns were infamously used to mow down over ten thousand Sudanese at the Battle of Omdurman in 1898. Lindqvist solemnly remarks that in this battle "it was possible to anticipate Verdun and Sedan."[16] Enzo Traverso's *The Origins of Nazi Violence* relays the frequency with which European colonial violence served as a reference point for the ways in which Germany conceptualized its geopolitical expansion:

> In conversations with Marin Bormann in 1941–42, Hitler frequently compared the German war on the eastern front to the colonial wars. The Slavic world had to be conquered and colonized so as to turn it into a sort of "Germanic India," and its population had to be put down using methods of destruction comparable to those employed by the English in their empire and the Americans against the Indian tribes.[17]

Hitler remarked that Germany should "follow the example of the English, who, with 250,000 men in all, of whom 50,000 were soldiers, rule over 400 million Indians."[18] In this way we might say that the only thing truly novel about the horrors of total war were where they happened and to whom they happened.

War, enmity, and the spatial order of the earth: for Schmitt, geopolitical order depended not only on the intellectual labor of European jurists and statesmen but also on these spaces beyond the frontiers of Europe where the atrocities of asymmetrical warfare were the norm, not the exception. On one hand, Europeans could, and did, freely employ methods and tactics in non-European spaces that would have been viewed as heinous and illegitimate within Europe. On the other hand, this lawless zone, this constitutive outside, preserved the peace within and between European states. As Peter Hallward has observed, in Schmitt's theory of geopolitical stability, "it is as rulers of the world, lords over non-Europe, that Europe's powers temper their own quarrels."[19] For Schmitt, though, the existence of unregulated war beyond the horizons of Europe is not just a pressure valve, a measure that allows for limitless violence elsewhere in order to constrain it at home. The very conceptualization of war and the smooth functioning of a geopolitical order require these spatial divisions. Thus, symmetrical warfare within Europe attains legibility against the asymmetrical violence exercised in the Americas, Africa, and Asia. Dividing the world into these zones secures the concepts of war and enmity and, by extension, enables European stability.

The threat of formless, lawless war was exacerbated by technological advancements in weaponry at the turn of the century. Prior to the First World War, the Hague conferences in 1899 and 1907 attempted to keep pace with the rapid developments in modern warfare. In August of 1898 the Russian tsar Nicholas II called the major powers together to discuss methods for settling future disputes between states and to codify new rules for governing interstate war. In four conventions and three declarations, the members of the Hague Conference sought to outline the customs of land and sea warfare, to prohibit the "launching of projectiles and explosives from balloons, or by other methods of similar nature," and "to abstain from the use of bullets which expand or flatten easily in the human body."[20] The conference met again in 1907, but there was very little consensus on a number of issues—the status of private property on the open sea, the use of military force to collect debts, the creation of an international court—and it was expected that another conference would be held in 1914. The war these meetings hoped to prevent in turn prevented any future meetings.

By focusing on the evolving means of warfare on land, sea, and air, The Hague conferences attempted to keep war in form. Yet the cruel stasis of the trenches, the Zeppelin bombings of civilian areas, and the deployment of chemical weapons in the First World War exemplify the speed with which the war-making capabilities of modern states outpaced the development of international law. As early as 1920 the American political scientist James Wilford Garner argued that the First World War exposed the breach between the highly advanced nature of war and the conceptual torpor of international law:

> It was inevitable that the recent war, embracing as it did so large a number of the States of the world, conducted to a great extent by new instrumentalities and according to new methods and carried on under conditions widely different in many respects from those of previous wars, should not only have revealed many imperfections in the existing rules of governing the conduct of war, but that the whole system of international law itself should have been rudely shaken to its very foundations. . . . In the first place, the war demonstrated in a striking manner that many of the rules which had been agreed upon by the body of States for the conduct of war were inadequate, illogical, or inapplicable to the somewhat peculiar and novel conditions under which they had to be applied during the late war.[21]

Garner's language is striking, pitting as it does the novelty of war against the inertia of international law: "new instrumentalities," "new methods," and "novel conditions" of war render international law "inadequate, illogical, or inapplicable." Formless war, in Garner's words, dismantled "the whole system of international law." The reconstruction of that system was the center of much debate in the early years of the First World War. Politicians, jurists, and intellectuals imagined and debated alternative systems and institutions of international law. Leonard Woolf was directly involved with plans for such an international body as early as 1915.[22] In *International Government*, he declared with confidence that "the alternative to law is war."[23] Law required advances as rigorous as those of modern warfare. His book made a lasting impression on the British Foreign Office and, per his own account, it was "used extensively by the government committee which produced the British proposals for a League of Nations laid before the Peace Conference, and also by the British delegation to the Versailles Conference."[24]

Despite the establishment of the League of Nations, Schmitt would look back on the years following the First World War as a lengthy interregnum in world order.[25] From its inception until its dissolution after the Second World War, the league tried to restore peace as the norm of international affairs. Appended to the Versailles Treaty in 1919, the League of Nations Covenant delineated its duties, its mode of operation, and its mechanisms for circumventing war.[26] While the league proved somewhat capable of adjudicating minor territorial disputes between lesser European powers in the 1920s, the strength of its declarations did little to stifle the ambitions of more powerful states.[27] One can track the events precipitating the Second World War by indexing the failures of the league to minimize military conflict: the Manchurian Incident (1931), Italy's invasion of Abyssinia (1935), Hitler's remilitarization of the Rhineland (1936), the Spanish Civil War (1936–1939), the Sino-Japanese War (1937), the Anschluss (1938), and the annexation of the Sudetenland (1938). Withdrawals from the league by Japan, Italy, and Germany also severely weakened the force and legitimacy of the institution's decisions. Hitler ended Germany's participation in the disarmament conference on October 4, 1933, and withdrew altogether from the League of Nations by the month's end. Suddenly the league's hope of achieving collective security among all member states seemed a weak proposition.

The league's tactical failures stem in part from a profoundly stunted ability to reconceptualize war and determine its role in geopolitical affairs. In many ways, the league came into being in advance of the psychological, cultural, and political orientation it needed to reestablish peace as the normative condition of global affairs. To its credit, the league-sponsored efforts beyond law and politics to cultivate what Akira Iriye calls "cultural internationalism."[28] Reconceptualizing war—its technological augmentations, the contour of its legality, its relationship to human nature, determining its cultural and historical origins—was among the foremost priorities of such league-sponsored projects and committees. With the blessings of British and French government officials, Henri Bergson created the International Committee on Intellectual Cooperation (ICIC) in 1922. It sought to "form a general mentality among the peoples of the world more appropriate to co-operation than the nationalistic mentality of the past."[29] The committee did not lack the star power or intellectual heft needed for such a task: along with Bergson, Paul Valéry and Madame Marie Curie were central to its initiatives; Sigmund Freud, Albert Einstein, Rabindranath Tagore, Aldous Huxley, and H. G. Wells also contributed to its efforts. Gilbert Murray, a classicist at Oxford and Bergson's successor as committee chairman, published a series of open letters, or "conversations," between leading intellectuals.[30] These publications addressed collective security, broadcasting and media, the future of letters, translation, music, the relations between East and West, and the conditions of intellectual life in different nations.[31] These various interventions sought to keep pace with the development of war by exhuming its cultural origins, revisiting European history, and positing alternative forms of cooperation that might mitigate political violence. Outside of the official sponsorship of the League, intellectuals, writers, and artists participated in public debates on war and world order. I want to turn attention to two such endeavors, the first published under the auspices of the ICIC and the other published independently: Einstein and Freud's *Why War?* and *A Challenge to Death*, a collection on war, international government, and peace featuring Rebecca West, Storm Jameson, Vera Brittain, and J. B. Priestley, among others. Both efforts reveal the shrinking conceptual horizons for grasping and potentially bracketing the emergent role of war in making and unmaking geopolitical realities.

The most enduring contribution of the "Open Letters" series is Einstein and Freud's *Why War?* Published in 1933, this exchange between two of the world's foremost intellectuals begins with Einstein's question: "Is there any way of delivering mankind from the menace of war?"[32] Einstein's and Freud's responses cut in two directions: they endorse the idea of a supranational sovereign body, and they examine what Einstein calls "the dark places of human will and feeling" (12) driving modern war. Einstein endorses a more robust, authoritative international governing body that will require the "unconditional surrender by every nation, in certain measure, of its liberty of action, its sovereignty" (15). Should states agree to embolden an international sovereign body, Einstein still worries that, in the end, the human's "innate lust for hatred and destruction" (18) will stymie any advances toward international security. Freud, too, underscores the absolute necessity for an international body possessing the authority to mediate interstate disputes and to maintain international order. Echoing his arguments from *Civilization and Its Discontents* (1930), Freud diagnoses the "destructive instinct" (44–45) within the human as the unavoidable cause of war.[33] Freud argues that such drives can be diverted and potentially altered by the ongoing evolution of culture. "The psychic changes which accompany this process of cultural change are striking, and not to be gainsaid. They consist in the progressive rejection of instinctive ends and a scaling down of instinctive reactions. Sensations which delighted our forefathers have become neutral or unbearable to us" (55). As an heir to and custodian of the Enlightenment push toward progress, Freud invests his hopes in the telos of culture: "Meanwhile we may rest on the assurance that whatever makes for cultural development is working also against war" (57). In Einstein's rough formulation and Freud's more elaborate one, the available forms of sovereignty, whether it be the nation-state model or the as yet unfulfilled promises of the League of Nations, cannot maintain peace; war, in this estimation, is not merely a matter of jurisprudence or political maneuvering but something innately human. Freud's best hope is for cultural evolution to extirpate the drives, instincts, and even pleasures underlying all acts of violence.

When Einstein and Freud penned their letters in 1932, they may have anticipated a longer interval of time for culture to displace humanity's death drive. It is safe to speculate that their exchange would have assumed a different tone after Hitler's appointment to chancellor in January 1933. When Philip Noel-Baker, a former member of Parliament and fervent supporter of the league, Storm Jameson, and Lord Robert Cecil enjoined writers such as Rebecca West, Vera Brittain, and J. B. Priestley to examine the interplay of war, international law, and Europe's threadbare peace, the outlook on world affairs had grown dark. Viscount Cecil's foreword to *A Challenge to Death* urgently frames the book as "the outcome of a vivid realisation by its authors of the menace to peace which has grown up so alarmingly in recent months."[34] Like Einstein and Freud, the authors in this volume explore alternative arrangements of state power and international law. Rebecca West's "The Necessity and Grandeur of the International Ideal" advocates a form of international governance capable of limiting the aggressive ambitions of individual states. Yet, like Einstein and Freud, West's diagnosis and imagined solutions trail the development and employment of contemporary warfare. She ultimately argues for an international body with the means and authority to use force to keep global peace. She acknowledges a widespread reluctance among nations to cede power to an international body. This attachment to nationalism, she suggests, is not necessarily incompatible with a new internationalism. In fact, West extols the affective force of nationalism, praising the "visceral pull" and the "feeling for his country" that an Englishman should feel as intensely and intimately as he does for his family.[35] Rather than opposites, she says, the two are "counterbalances which can keep nations in equilibrium."[36] Her essay then weaves internationalism into the historical and cultural fabrics of European nations. Bearing a remarkable resemblance to the rhetorical maneuverings of T. S. Eliot's "Tradition and the Individual Talent," West inserts the international ideal into English and European tradition. "The test of real and valuable nationalism," she writes, "is to avail oneself of the tradition of one's country; and it happens that internationalism is one of the most ancient and firmly established elements in our tradition."[37]

West's periodization of the international ideal stretches back to the Roman Empire and traverses the "great international body called Christendom" under Charlemagne, the collapse of the Church, and concludes with "the pressure of present-day events."[38] Her analysis swaps the psychological framework of Einstein's and Freud's letters for a theological one. In Hegelian fashion, West reads the advances and shortcomings of each period, showing how each failure enabled the next progression. She begins with Augustine's reflections on the Roman Empire. Augustine's key insight was to acknowledge the positive and negative effects of imperial rule. On one hand, an empire can secure its people; the consequence, though, is that imperial citizens live under an "imposed peace" that was, in the last instance, aggressive and violent.[39] Thinking beyond these limitations, Augustine "looked around for a system that would tolerate the nationalist spirit and maintain the peace necessary for its development."[40] Augustine's vision was a society of small states, which West sees as a rudimentary predecessor to the League of Nations. Such a society would ameliorate the "standardising influence" Augustine disdained in the Roman Empire and preserve the national identities, even destinies, of individual states.[41] Charlemagne's Holy Roman Empire carries the international ideal to its next stage of development. West commends Charlemagne for rebuilding Europe into a sort of "commonwealth comprising the whole body of Christian people in the world, regardless of their speech and race."[42] From Christendom and Charlemagne's Holy Roman Empire, she extracts a pluralist vision where one common principle unites the society of states without impinging upon the "sacred processes" of national destiny.[43] Still, even if West's dream of a new world order is indeed modern and secular, her vocabulary—sacrality, destiny, spirit—and the periodization of the international imports theological concepts of sovereignty, justice, and war into the contemporary scene.[44] This is perhaps most evident in her reflections on enmity and the resuscitation of the just war doctrine.

The First World War figures as the primal scene for West's theory of a modernized just war doctrine. 1914 inaugurates a nightmarish fusion of human creativity, technology, and killing. "As the great war went along," she writes, " . . . it was multiplying the existing forms of death and pain with an obscene creative genius which made life worse than the most melancholic lunatic's dream about it."[45] Exceeding the scale of the war and the horrors it introduced was the sobering fact that "no one was going to be able to stop the war, that in spite of the armistice and all the treaties there was going to be no return to the normal constructive life which man hopes to live in peace-time."[46] West's sense that the war endures long after the armistice echoes in a more forceful way J. M. Keynes's early criticisms of the Treaty of Versailles and perhaps foresees the interwar years as, in the words of Alan Hodge and Robert Graves, "the long weekend." What is striking, though, is her belief that the war utterly changed what is considered normal at the macro-level of world order and the micro-level of everyday life. She refers to the impossibility of reassuming a "normal constructive life" in the postwar years.[47] For West, Europe still suffers collective war trauma: "Since the war Europe has displayed all the characteristics of a person shattered by a traumatic experience: capricious, distracted, given to violence towards the self and others, careless of their environment, and incapable of carrying on a normal constructive life."[48] West anthropomorphizes Europe, figuring its political actions and policies as the behaviors of a suffering person who requires the care and control of another. In West's logic, an international organization with a monopoly on force would rationalize interstate behavior and deprive it of its capacities and opportunities for violence.

But how would it be possible to justify the use of force even for the preservation of peace and order? What would prevent an international body from reverting to the bellicose and irrational actions of nation-states? West again turns to theology. She grounds the proper relation of war and law in the just war tradition. If war adheres to specific conditions—formal declaration, just cause, right intention—it can properly serve as a securitizing and punitive force; it maintains world order while also exacting proper punishment on a "Power for threatening the security of the future."[49] Because this form of war appeals to extrajuridical moral and ethical norms "to avoid evil and pursue good," it will, by extension, be rational, measured, and "waged moderately."[50] This is the most problematic turn in West's argument: the use of force acquires legitimacy not from legal precepts but from extrajuridical norms. The definitions of the enemy and the rules of war pass from the field of agonistic political confrontation to the higher domain of incontestable ethical norms. We recall here Schmitt's claim that the passage from, indeed the progress of, medieval to modern law rests on the exchange of *justa causa* (just cause) for *justus hostis* (just enemy); that is, war's legitimacy resides in the equal status of sovereign states before the law and the mutual recognition of both parties as enemies with rights. Whether or not one buys Schmitt's claim that territorial order and faith in the *jus publicum Europaeum* ultimately constitutes the humanization of war, West's appeal to theological justifications of war is, at best, regressive. The invocation of just war recalls the types of wars waged prior to the Treaty of Westphalia, in the colonies over hundreds of years, and, indeed, in the trenches on the Western Front. What West's imagined international order casts into relief is a limited conceptual horizon; to look ahead West reaches deep into the past, reanimating political formations (empire) and theological doctrines (just war) whose histories contain far more destruction than order.

Routed through psychology, cultural evolution, or theology, these cultural efforts all suggest that one cannot mitigate the destructive character of war without reconceptualizing war itself. Yet, Einstein's, Freud's, and West's glimpses back at history afford little insight into what Garner and Schmitt perceived as the disequilibrium between the development and practice of war and structures of world order. Freud diagnoses war as a problem of human instinct and psychic drives; West diagnoses it as a problem of ethics and international norms. Neither Freud nor West ponders war's novel, and Schmitt would say lost, form and its active role in reshaping geopolitical order. Where Garner and Schmitt acknowledged the transformation of war as an urgent problem for political thought and world order, Einstein, Freud, and West understand war as static, as something to be reigned in through the progressive march of culture or European tradition.

To be clear, the shortcomings I underscore here should not be seen as faults or blind spots of these particular individuals. Because they are among the most formidable intellectuals of their era, they best represent the limits of grand discursive and conceptual schemas. For all of their ambition and erudition, these conceptual exercises lack the material experience of everyday life in the global hot zones. For Orwell, Auden, and Isherwood, material experience is all there is. In *Homage to Catalonia* and *Journey to a War*, everyday life is the scene where the brute realities of formless war and world-systemic disorder appear.

NECESSARY MURDER: WAR ALLEGORY, ENMITY, AND *HOMAGE TO CATALONIA*

Truth on this side of the Pyrenees is error on the other.
PASCAL

Orwell's *Homage to Catalonia* is often heralded for its commitment to the hard, ugly truths of Spain's war.[51] Before leaving Spain, Orwell knew he would write about the war in order to contest "the most appalling lies" circulating in the English press.[52] He wanted to recast Spain as a struggle between "revolution and counter-revolution; between the workers who are vainly trying to hold on to a little of what they won in 1936, and the Liberal-Communist bloc who are so successfully taking it away from them."[53] This version of events contrasted mightily with widespread partisan narratives of the war as a clash of democracy versus fascism, civilization versus barbarism. The unpopularity of Orwell's ideas, especially his comments on the fighting within the Republican ranks and the Communists' suppression of the Partido Obrero de Unificación Marxista? (POUM, or Workers' Party of Marxist Unification) and more radical factions, prompted the *New Statesman* to reject his articles. Victor Gollancz, who had recently published *The Road to Wigan Pier* for the Left Book Club, expressed disinterest in anything Orwell might write about Spain (and against the Communist line). But if *Homage to Catalonia*'s descriptions of everyday life assert the Spanish Civil War's messy complexities and unseasonable truths, it also discovers dimensions of war that it can neither conceptualize nor communicate. In what follows, I map out the narrative maneuvers by which *Homage to Catalonia* negates the allegorical structure of the Spanish Civil War. By virtue of the success of this critique, Orwell's narrative produces an unresolved burden that has thus far evaded critical attention: the text's struggles with the concept of enmity and, more specifically, the process by which this new, formless war converts human beings into inhuman enemies.

The Spanish Civil War ascended to high allegory on the international scene with dizzying speed. Most historians now agree that the local dimensions of the Spanish Civil War were lost on even the most passionate of international participants.[54] More often than not, the international volunteers were not so concerned with the lengthy, complicated history of Spanish politics: the abiding problems of land and agricultural reform, regional versus national unity, and the notorious oppression wrought on the peasants by the Catholic Church were foremost on the minds of the Spanish fighters. By contrast, those who crossed the Pyrenees to join the war imagined themselves as participants in a global struggle against fascism. On the year anniversary of the rebellion against the elected Republican government, former minister and diplomat Salvador de Madariaga wrote of the translation of the Spanish war into a front in a wider European struggle: "By a tragic coincidence this war, essentially Spanish, has 'caught on' abroad. Lured by somewhat shallow parallelisms, men, institutions, and even Governments outside Spain have been adding fuel to the fire which is consuming our unhappy country. Spain is thus suffering vicariously the latent civil war which Europe is—so far—keeping in check."[55] The war in Spain would be decided not by the justness of one cause over the other, but by "the predominance of foreign weapons."[56] Madariaga casts Spain's troubles as a proxy war for an international civil war or what at the time remained a "latent civil war" in Europe.[57]

Looking back on the Spanish Civil War, Hannah Arendt underscored the disturbing novelty of the war's transformation from a domestic affair to an international, ideological one.

> Almost as frightening as these new dangers arising from the old trouble spots of Europe was the entirely new kind of behavior of all European nationals in "ideological" struggles. Not only were people expelled from country and citizenship, but more and more persons of all countries, including the Western democracies, volunteered to fight in civil wars abroad (something which up to then only a few idealists or adventurers had done) even when this meant cutting themselves off from their national communities. This was the lesson of the Spanish Civil War and one of the reasons why the governments were so frightened by the International Brigade.[58]

Paired by ideological conviction rather than any national feeling, the international volunteers were fighting not for territorial integrity but for what many saw as the survival of civilization itself, the preservation of high ideals like democracy and freedom over fascism and barbarism. Spain's war quickly transcended its local particularities; for many international volunteers, this national civil war was primarily, and perhaps only ever, a screen on which the "latent" antagonisms festering within Europe would manifest themselves.

Many authors who cast their lot with the Republican cause further entrenched this allegory of the war.[59] Auden famously declared Spain as the place where "the menacing shapes of our fever / Are precise and alive," while Louis MacNeice wrote that "Spain would soon denote / Our grief, our aspirations; / Not knowing that our blunt / Ideals would find their whetstone, that our spirit / Would find its frontier on the Spanish front."[60] Nancy Cunard and *The Left Review* published the infamous "Authors Take Sides on the Civil War" questionnaire. Cunard insisted "it is impossible for any longer to take no side."[61] She collected responses from the likes of Samuel Beckett, Evelyn Waugh, T. S. Eliot, W. H. Auden, Cecil Day-Lewis, and Geoffrey Grigson, among others. Some, like Waugh, Eliot, Graham Greene, and Orwell, took exception to the stark terms of the questionnaire; Orwell thought its partisan simplicity was "bloody rubbish."[62] But most of the respondents expressed support for the Republic and happily advanced Cunard's either/or version of the Spanish war. Like Auden and MacNeice, Day-Lewis perceived the war as part of a potentially larger global conflict but still found it reducible to a metaphysical "battle between light and darkness, of which only a blind man could be unaware."[63] The allegorization of the war buried its local and political complexities and recoded it as an epochal ethical struggle. This is perhaps stated nowhere more baldly than in a line Stephen Spender poaches from Keats on Peterloo: "No contest between Whig and Tory—but between Right and Wrong."[64]

The purity of this distinction between light/darkness, good/evil, and right/ wrong structures one of the more renowned and controversial poems about the Spanish Civil War—"Spain, 1937" by W. H. Auden. Orwell thought Auden's poem was "one of the few decent things that have been written about the Spanish war," but one line of Auden's poem made Orwell bristle.[65] That line is "the conscious acceptance of guilt in the necessary murder."[66] Auden's poem ties the necessity of the enemy's murder to the world-historical significance of the Spanish Civil War. The reiteration of "yesterday," "to-day," and "tomorrow" throughout the poem casts this war as one of historical necessity.[67] Auden's historical sketch indexes multiple scientific, technological, and cultural developments, but it explicitly ties European development to imperial and territorial expansion:

> *Yesterday the installation of dynamos and turbines,*
> *The construction of railways in the colonial desert;*
> *Yesterday the classic lecture*
> *On the origin of Mankind. But to-day the struggle*[68]

In the historical and temporal logic of Auden's poem, technical advances and colonialism go hand in hand; philosophical and cultural knowledges also develop in tandem with imperial expansion. While we might perceive a glimmer of Walter Benjamin's dialectic of civilization and barbarism moving in Auden's poem, Auden attributes the unfolding of history, at least in part, to individual will and choice.

Crude though Auden's historical framing may be at first sight, it is complicated by the competing voices in the poem. The voice intoning "yesterday," "to-day," and "tomorrow" throughout the poem gives way to a host of other voices: a poet, a scientist, Spain's laboring poor, and, finally, Spain itself. These voices have potential roles to play in the movement of history and they have choices to make. The poem frames that choice as both individual *and* historical. In the appeal to a historical force that might right the wrongs of the present, the voice of history answers "O, no, I am not the mover: "I am whatever you do."[69] History alone is not an oppressive force nor will it set right past wrongs. A just future, one the poem's final stanzas imagine as full of love, play, poetry, and democracy, depends on how individuals respond to "the struggle" in Spain. In the poem's logic, the present may be the inevitable result of a historical process, but human history is made by humans and can be altered. In the grand scheme of history, the Spanish Civil War figures as the pivotal event, the possibility to reroute the historical process away from violence and domination and into a utopic future. Never named in the poem, the Fascists in Spain have but a ghostly presence as enemies not only for the Republicans but also for the future of humanity itself; they are existential enemies and their murder is necessary. It is an individual's choice to accept the burden of killing the enemy, but it is also an act of necessity if one yearns for the emancipated future in poem's final stanzas.

Orwell never got past the necessary murder:

> But notice the phrase "necessary murder." It could only be written by a person to whom murder is at most a *word*. Personally I would not speak so lightly of murder. It so happens that I have seen the bodies of numbers of murdered men—I don't mean killed in battle, I mean murdered. Therefore I have some conception of what murder means— the terror, the hatred, the howling relatives, the post-mortems, the blood, the smells. To me, murder is something to be avoided. So it is to any ordinary person. The Hitlers and Stalins find murder necessary, but they don't advertise their callousness, and they don't speak of it as murder; it is "liquidation," "elimination" or some other soothing phrase. Mr. Auden's brand of amoralism is only possible if you are the kind of person who is always somewhere else when the trigger is pulled.[70]

To be fair, Auden did not look back on this particular line with fondness. He would later edit it, changing "necessary murder" to "the fact of murder."[71] Orwell assails the seemingly flippant use of "murder" by a poet who was absent from the actual fighting. For Orwell, there is a moral weight attached to different types of killing. He explicitly distinguishes murder from killing in war; murder is what dictators do and pass it under another name. But what is killing on the battlefield? What moral valence does it possess that other forms of killing lack? Orwell does not say, but he leaves us to assume that only a detached, amoral poet would ever dare to flatten the distinctions between the moral acts of warfare and the hideous crimes of totalitarian dictators.

What I want to suggest is that Orwell wants to maintain that distinction, to keep space between moral and immoral forms of enmity; and yet, at least in Spain, that form of enmity where killing the other is necessary and morally justified emerges from the allegorization of the war that Orwell decries. This is the central dilemma of *Homage to Catalonia*. On one hand, Orwell narrates the everyday details of war to dismantle the war allegory, to dispel war's abstraction into good versus evil; on the other hand, those very metaphysical abstractions categorize the Fascist as the avatar of radical evil, justifying his killing. Yet, in Orwell's narrative, the Fascist appears as a strikingly—and for him, disturbingly—full-blooded, ordinary human being. My analysis of *Homage to Catalonia* will track these two movements, paying particular attention to the way language and narrative form make this contradiction apparent and, ultimately, fail to resolve it.

To preview where this section will end, *Homage to Catalonia* is very much a kind of political *bildung*, charting Orwell's maturation from a naïve partisan to an enlightened, if unwilling, participant in all the political complexities of the Spanish war. He notes that the resistance to the nationalist rebellion in July 1936 sent shockwaves throughout anti-Fascist Europe. In Spain one saw "democracy standing up to Fascism."[72] Orwell records his initial attraction to the reductive, allegorical version of the war he later came to detest. His first days in Barcelona gave him a glimpse of a socialist utopia. The now famous passages on the worker's state in Barcelona inventory the shift in language used for personal address (from *señor* and *usted* to comrade and thou) the emphasis on social equality, and the mass collectivization of businesses. Initially lured by this utopic city, Orwell acknowledges that "there was much in it that I did not understand, in some ways I did not even like it, but I recognized it immediately as a state of affairs worth fighting for" (5). Romanticized portraits of revolutionary Spain and the heroism and camaraderie of the volunteers are everywhere in the literature of the Spanish Civil War. Orwell's book traffics in some of this imagery, but it also pairs these moments of political enchantment with more sobering and skeptical retrospection. After this portrait of revolutionary Barcelona, for example, he writes that he "believed that things were as they appeared, that this was really a workers' State and that the entire bourgeoisie had either fled, been killed, or voluntarily come over to the workers' side; I did not realize that great numbers of well-to-do bourgeois were simply lying low and disguising themselves as proletarians for the time being" (5); the living socialist utopia of Barcelona is figured retrospectively as "a mixture of hope and camouflage" (113). Despite its utopian atmosphere, revolutionary Barcelona has a "gaunt untidy look" (6–7); "the streets at night were dimly lit for fear of air-raids, the shops were mostly shabby and half-empty" (7). In a similar way, the fall of Malaga in February 1937 and the rumors that some form of betrayal had aided the Fascists gave him his "first vague doubt about this war in which, hitherto, the rights and wrongs had seemed so beautifully simple" (45).[73] The suppression of the POUM, the random imprisonment of anarchists and "Trotskyists" by those loyal to Stalin, and the internecine political struggles introduced several shades of grey into the war for Orwell.

Orwell's attention quickly shifts from the high metaphysical registers of good and evil to the brute materialities of everyday life during war. In his descriptions of Spanish cities and towns, Orwell notes both the disruption of everyday life by war as well as its rapid normalization. Even the utopian atmosphere of revolutionary Barcelona bears the traces of everyday war. Barcelona has a "gaunt untidy look" (6–7); "the streets at night were dimly lit for fear of air-raids, the shops were mostly shabby and half-empty" (7). Orwell records the markings of war on smaller towns like Barbastro and Alcubierre. An old bullfighting poster reminds Orwell that this Spanish cultural mainstay has been suspended. The filth and squalor of Alcubierre, according to Orwell, are not solely the result of war but, as he observes, "the constant come-and-go of troops had reduced the village to a state of unspeakable filth" (16). At Montflorite, Orwell sees the countryside itself as a hybrid of the "usual" with the exceptional circumstances of war: "Montflorite was the usual huddle of mud and stone houses, with narrow tortuous alleys that had been churned by lorries till they looked like the craters of the moon. The church had been badly knocked about but was used as a military store" (77); a possible convent, La Granja, is turned into a "store and cook-house" (78). Huesca, only five miles away, was traditionally the trading point and central marketplace for these villagers, but the war had suspended the weekly trips to Huesca with "an impenetrable barrier of barbed wire and machine-guns had lain between" (79). In this catalogue of war torn cities and towns, disrupted routines and physical deterioration, Orwell traces the long reach of war into all areas of daily life.

On his arrival at the front, Orwell is dismayed that his "idea of trench warfare" (21) does not match up with the dailiness of Spanish warfare. The images of trench warfare that Orwell undoubtedly inherited from the generation preceding his were nowhere to be found. "War, to me," he writes, "meant projectiles and skipping shards of steel" (18). The great tragedies and heroism of war did not apply. When he recalls his attack on a Fascist redoubt, Orwell turns a scene of bayonet combat into a comic episode of a half-naked enemy fleeing an inept soldier. In the words of his superior Georges Kopp, Orwell's version of the war is partially "a comic opera with an occasional death" (32). Orwell gradually comes to understand daily life in the trenches as banal and "uneventful as a city clerk's, and almost as regular" (24). "In trench warfare five things are important: firewood, food, tobacco, candles and the enemy. In winter on the Zaragoza front they were important in that order, with the enemy a bad last.... Up here, in the hills of Zaragoza, it was simply the mingled boredom and discomfort of stationary warfare" (23–24). Orwell's depictions of life at the front often revert to the empty time of war: "nothing happened" (72), "not much was happening" (85), "nothing was happening" (102), "not much happening at the front" (183).

With its emphasis on the eventless, grey everydayness of the war, *Homage to Catalonia* foregoes both heroic and tragic narratives of the war one finds in Ernest Hemingway, André Malraux, and John Cornford. The desuetude of Spanish towns, half-naked enemies, and the endless boredom at the front all contribute to Orwell's leveling critique of the allegory of the Spanish Civil War.[74] Yet, despite Orwell's efforts to demythologize the war, to render it in a low comic mode or accentuate the eventlessness of it, he curiously maintained his belief that "this war was different from ordinary, imperialistic wars" (65); in the final analysis, he seems reluctant to cede the justness of the war. And this is where the dialectic begins to break down: is it possible to dispel the allegories of the Spanish Civil War and still retain the ethical justifications for killing the enemy? What relation of enmity is left when the war allegory is dismantled?

The opening page of *Homage to Catalonia* previews for us what will be a sustained preoccupation with enmity. In the allegorical world of good versus evil, the Fascist enemy is inhuman and his extermination binds all anti-Fascists in what

Orwell figures as an indescribable intimacy. Orwell's first encounter in Barcelona is with an Italian militiaman who inspires these very feelings: "Something in his face deeply moved me. It was the face of a man who would commit murder and throw away his life for a friend—the kind of face you would expect in an Anarchist, though as likely as not he was a Communist. . . . It was as though his spirit and mine had momentarily succeeded in bridging the gulf of language and tradition and meeting in utter intimacy" (4).

In the fight against fascism, Orwell suggests, all human relations intensify into a narrow political relation of friend and enemy; "utter intimacy" names the willingness to kill or to die for any other person fighting the enemy in Spain. What has happened in this extraordinary, libidinally charged scene where the human relation is defined through death? What sort of enemy, so horrific, so inhuman, could inspire such immediate intimacy among those who seek his death?[75] We have already heard from historians and critics who maintain that the relation of enmity fueling the war machines of Europe was novel only in its appearance on European soil.[76] Less than human, these enemies could be—and were—subjected to limitless violence. In *Homage to Catalonia*, Orwell demonstrates how formless war dehumanize all enemies and, perhaps more interestingly, he struggles against that dehumanization.

Orwell first encounters Fascists who have deserted their units: "these deserters were the first 'real' Fascists I had ever seen. It struck me that they were indistinguishable from ourselves, except that they wore khaki overalls" (17). Many of those on the opposite side of the line were, Orwell surmises, "wretched conscripts who had been doing their military service at the time when war broke out" (17). Hardly the demonic, inhuman creatures Orwell came to kill, these enemies are "indistinguishable" from those trying to kill them. In "Looking Back on the Spanish War," Orwell conjures up a similar scene where the Fascist passes from enemy to human. Orwell and another soldier lie in an open field between the trenches within sniping distance of a parapet. A Republican airplane flies overhead and "at this moment a man, presumably carrying a message to an officer, jumped out of the trench and ran along the top of the parapet in full view. He was half-dressed and was holding up his trousers with both hands as he ran. I refrained from shooting at him. . . . I had come here to shoot at 'Fascists'; but a man who is holding up his trousers isn't a 'Fascist,' he is a visible fellow creature, similar to yourself, and you don't feel like shooting at him."[77] In both passages, Orwell's scare quotes set off the idea of the Fascist from the embodied human: the "wretched conscript" or the "fellow creature" scurrying along the top of a parapet half-dressed scarcely figure as the inhuman manifestation of radical evil.

When Orwell recalls the latter incident in his 1942 essay, he contends that it does not prove "anything in particular."[78] And yet his preoccupation with these incidents in *Homage to Catalonia* and his later essays suggests that they upset the relation of enmity that drove Orwell over the Pyrenees and inspired him to kill Fascists. The unease with the humanized enemy, the disquiet that follows the unexpected embodiment and ordinariness of the enemy, seeps into the narration of combat. This is not how critics have traditionally understood the few scenes of war in *Homage to Catalonia*. Valentine Cunningham, for example, plots Orwell's text back into the allegorical structure of good and evil that I claim Orwell disables through his attention to everyday life:

> The one effective bit of killing he allows himself to have committed is narrated as a decent, soldierly scrap. It's arranged, in fact, as a microcosm of The Just War, an illustration of the necessity of killing Fascists lest they kill you. . . . So when he finally succeeds in potting an enemy with a grenade ("Ah! No doubt about it that time"), his deliberate act of violence seems only the most justifiable gesture of self-defence, a perfectly proper personal translation of the general need to defend oneself against Fascism.[79]

Orwell's narration of that very battle scene is far more ambiguous than Cunningham assumes. By the time we reach that scene, Orwell has already alerted his readers to his blatant lack of military skills: he is not going to make a very good solider. At Monte Oscuro, Orwell reports that he fired several shots but he is "reasonably certain" (41) that his shots never connected; later, when firing at a Fascist position, he admits he is a "very poor shot with a rifle" and it is "unlikely" that he hit anyone (184). In the scene Cunningham analyzes, there are two instances where Orwell suggests that he may have injured or killed an enemy. In one incident he acknowledges harming an enemy, but only indirectly: "I knelt beside Benjamin, pulled the pin out of my third bomb and flung it. Ah! No doubt about it that time. The bomb crashed inside the parapet, at the corner, just by the machine gun nest. The Fascist fire seemed to have slackened very suddenly" (91). There are no bodies, no direct confirmation of any harm. Orwell renders it as a matter of perception: the Fascist guns "very suddenly" (91) cease and this alone is the only evidence that Orwell's bomb has killed anyone at all. In the second incident he throws a bomb into a trench and hears "a diabolical outcry of screams and groans. We had got one of them, anyway; I don't know whether he was killed, but certainly he was badly hurt. Poor wretch, poor wretch! I felt a vague sorrow as I heard him screaming" (97). The narrative displaces the emphasis from the actuality of killing to Orwell's well-cultivated powers of sympathy (who, after all, could be expected to feel sympathy for the very Fascists one traveled hundreds of miles to kill?). The act of killing becomes an occasion for showcasing the narrator's humanity. As we have seen, the humanization of the Fascists, their ordinariness and embodiment, introduces the unresolved burden of *Homage to Catalonia*. Where Orwell earlier relied on retrospective narration to chart his disillusionment with the black-and-white version of the war, here he employs a set of narrative evasions to skirt the certainty of killing and shift the narrative away from the "necessary murder" to the narrator's enlarged sense of humanity.

Of course, Orwell never stopped believing in the justness of the Republican fight against Franco. He did, however, retain severe doubts about the management and execution of the war, its allegorization by the left, and, ultimately, its demonization of human beings, be they Fascist or otherwise. The wound he suffered at the front lines ended his brief career as an international volunteer. Upon his discharge, he passed from a warring soldier into "a human being again, and also a little like a tourist" (203). The political *bildung*, then, charts Orwell's maturation from a naïve, politicized soldier to an educated, morally enlightened human being. His disenchantment with political commitment spurs a re-enchantment with universal humanism. "Curiously enough," he writes, "the whole experience has left me with not less but more belief in the decency of human beings" (230). Curious indeed. From this concluding insight, Orwell's *bildung* encodes a development from the black-and-white allegory of the Spanish Civil War to a generally warm feeling about humanity, from an investment in particular and historically urgent political causes to a belief in an ahistorical and universal humanism. The point, though, is not that we judge *Homage to Catalonia* as a successful or unsuccessful story of development; instead, we might read this concluding turn not as a transcendence of ideology, as an individual's newfound realization about "the decency of human beings," but approach it negatively as a sign of radical disappointment. Orwell's aggressive dismantling of the war allegory and this corresponding retreat into what Wendy Brown would call "moralizing politics" or "anti-politics" is very much a double symptom. It plays out the broken dialectic between the experiences of everyday life and conceptual knowledge; everyday experience in wartime Spain dismantled all the rational and political concepts Orwell possessed upon his arrival. If his realization of the complexities and contradiction of the war rendered those concepts and ideas impotent, his book closes with no other political commitments to replace what he lost. In this way the retreat from politics to an empty, shopworn universal humanism conveys the impossibility of imagining political alternatives. The attention to everyday life at war in *Homage to Catalonia* leaves the genre of the travel book and Orwell's political commitment in ruins.[80]

SEGMENTED SOVEREIGNTY: AUDEN AND ISHERWOOD'S *JOURNEY TO A WAR*

War's being global meant it ran off the edge of maps; it was uncontainable. What was being done, for instance, against the Japanese was heard of but never grasped in London. There were too many theatres of war.
ELIZABETH BOWEN (1949)

how everything turns away / Quite leisurely from the disaster.
W. H. AUDEN (1938)

The rich literary history associated with the Spanish Civil War is indeed a phenomenon without parallel in the 1930s. Nancy Cunard's hardline stance against neutrality may seem harsh in retrospect, but it relays the passionate attachments to the events in Spain. The same certainly cannot be said for European writers and the Sino-Japanese war. When Random House and Faber commissioned Auden and Isherwood to write a travel book on the Far East in 1937, the two looked toward the most recent outbreak of hostilities between Japan and China. Unlike Spain, Auden believed China would attract far less fanfare. He told Isherwood with China "we'll have a war all of our very own."[81] Where Orwell set out with clear commitments to the Spanish Republic, Auden and Isherwood simply wanted to understand the Sino-Japanese war as "neutral observers," a form of self-identification that crops up on more than one occasion in *Journey to a War*. Auden would later draw the distinction between Spain and China in cultural terms. "China was utterly different. Spain was a culture one knew. One could understand what was happening, what things meant. But China was impossible to know."[82] Many readers of *Journey to a War* interpret China's inscrutability as a manifestation of Auden and Isherwood's own blinkered Eurocentrism.[83] To that end, Douglas Kerr characterizes Isherwood's prose as a "narrative of disorientations" that "never achieves that stable orientation that would enable him to experience and write about China with any authority."[84] But China's unknowability extended beyond the field of culture. Auden and Isherwood would come to perceive its inscrutability in terms of the shifting geopolitical order of the 1930s.

We can start with Isherwood's diary entry from Hankow on March 12, 1938, where the war in China seems entirely distant from the latest developments in Europe:

> As we walked home the whole weight of the news from Austria descended upon us, crushing out everything else. By this evening a European war may have broken out. And here we are, eight thousand miles away. Shall we change our plans? Shall we go back? What does China matter to us in comparison with this? Bad news of this sort has a curious psychological effect: all the guns and bombs of the Japanese seem suddenly as harmless as gnats. If we are killed on the Yellow River front our deaths will be as provincial and meaningless as a motor-bus accident in Burton-on-Trent.[85]

There are many ways to interpret Isherwood's comments. His attitude to China passes over from the self-declared naiveté with which he opens the book to a dismissive Eurocentrism; the history of China and Japan's power struggles, the daily suffering of the Chinese population, and the cruelty of Japanese militarism all take a backseat to a geopolitical reality he more readily comprehends. This "curious psychological effect," the problem of connecting the Sino-Japanese war in with the events in Europe, replays the spatial and territorial politics of Hankow. Historically, Hankow was segmented into Russian, British, French, German, and Japanese concessions. By the time Isherwood and Auden arrive, only the French and Japanese still maintain their own concessions, but the legacies of imperial history are the first things they encounter: "Stark and blank along the northern shore, the buildings of the old treaty port present their European facades to the winter river. . . . There are consulates, warehouses, offices, and banks; British and American drug-stores, cinemas, churches, clubs; there is a good lending library, a Y.M.C.A., a red-light street of cafés—Mary's, the Navy Bar, The Last Chance" (49). This is the scene of Auden and Isherwood's disorientation. The deep imperial histories, the territorial segmentation of Chinese cities and towns, the Japanese bombs that spare the European administered areas of China, and the movement of war throughout Europe all form a geopolitical and historical totality that Auden and Isherwood intuit but cannot conceptualize.

These problems of quotidian fragments and world-systemic totality, of everyday experience and geopolitical disorder, return in the form and arrangement of *Journey to a War*. Auden and Isherwood's text is an ungainly hybrid: it opens with a sequence of poems by Auden charting the intrepid duo's passage from England to China; Isherwood's daily reports, which he pieced together from his and Auden's travel diaries, constitute the bulky middle portion of the book; the travel diary is followed by Auden's photographs, the sonnet sequence "In a Time of War," and a verse commentary.[86] Some of these materials were published before the book was finally compiled, and "In a Time of War" attracts critical interest as a standalone poem.[87] As Marsha Bryant, Samuel Hynes, and Tim Youngs tell us, one of the first dilemmas for any analysis of *Journey to a War* is to figure out how these parts fit together. Auden and Isherwood's itinerary gives us one way to locate firmly these abstract questions of war and form in a more material context. Their journey takes them from Hong Kong, an entrepôt under formal control of the British Empire since the nineteenth century, to Shanghai and the International Settlement. Along the way they visit cities and villages living under the constant threat of Japanese bombers. Their lived experience of the political and spatial subdivisions of China recodes this moment of geopolitical disorder as a breach between the particular experiences of everyday life in the war zone and the organizational and categorizing force of conceptual knowledge.

Auden's six poems in the "London to Hongkong" announce the book's larger concern with the yawning gap between everyday experience and the impoverished concepts available for making sense of it. This poem sequence tracks their journey from England through various ports of call en route to China. The two poems that bookend this sequence, "The Voyage" and "Hongkong," figure the journey in terms of an unsettled relationship between sense and knowledge, materiality and conceptuality. The first poem, "The Voyage," strips travel of its romantic overtones and speculates instead on the relationship of material experience and conceptual abstractions. The first two stanzas present questions that gradually separate abstract ideals such as "the Juster Life" and "the Good Place" (17) from immediate sense experience:

> When the mountains swim away with slow calm strokes
> And the gulls
> Abandon their vow? Does it still promise the Juster Life?
>
> And, alone with his heart at last, does the traveller find
> In the vaguer touch of the wind and the fickle flash of the
> sea
> Proofs that somewhere there exists, really, the Good
> Place,
> As certain as those the children find in stones and holes? (17)

The material of sense experience drifts out of the scene: the mountains fade from sight, the cry of the gulls becomes inaudible, and the abstract ideas move to the fore. In the second stanza, the speaker questions whether actual sense experience, the solitary traveler's experience of "the vaguer touch of the wind and the fickle flash of the sea," can be converted into "the Good Place." The poet then likens the development of abstract ideals from sense experience to the boundless imaginations of children. The "Juster Life" and "the Good Place" are flights of fancy, conjurings that do not derive from actual experience.

To these opening questions the poem answers decisively:

> No, he discovers nothing: he does not want to arrive.
> The journey is false; the false journey really an illness
> On the false island where the heart cannot act and will
> not suffer:

He condones the fever; he is weaker than he thought; his
weakness is real. (17)

The process of abstraction, of formulating notions of the "Good Place" and the "Juster Life," is figured as delusion and "real" weakness. The final stanza returns the traveler to material experience, but it does not yield universal ideals. He watches "the real dolphins" and "a real island" and "the trance is broken" (17). These sights plunge him deep into personal memory, to "the hours, the places where he was well" (17). The most one can hope for from the journey, it seems, is to extract something of individual value from everyday experience; the formulation of grand ethical ideals from the everyday leads to the errors of childish fancy.

When the pair dock in Hong Kong, they find neither the "Good Place" nor the "Juster Life." Instead, they discover a city full of British and Western officials engaged in familiar rituals and customs. Hong Kong, long a British possession, is by all appearances a colonial Western society untouched by the political strife tearing apart the country; for Auden and Isherwood, this conflict between appearance and reality induces a dream-like state that forestalls their expected arrival:

> One's first entry into a war-stricken country as a neutral observer is bound to be dream-like, unreal. And, indeed, this whole enormous voyage, from January London to tropical February Hongkong had had the quality—now boring, now extraordinary and beautiful—of a dream. At Hongkong, we had said to each other, we shall wake up, everything will come true. But we hadn't woken; only the dream had changed. The new dream was more confused than the old, less soothing, even slightly apprehensive. It was all about dinner-parties at very long tables, and meetings with grotesquely famous newspaper characters—the British Ambassador, the Governor, Sir Victor Sassoon. (28)

Having arrived in China, Auden and Isherwood encounter a city bearing few signs of the Sino-Japanese war. The political tension Auden and Isherwood stumble upon here is not the one between the Chinese and the Japanese but the underlying tensions of an occupied city. "Hongkong," the poem that concludes the "London to Hongkong" sequence and pairs with these first pages of Isherwood's travel diary, conveys the same broken relationship between appearance and reality, the everyday and the universal.[88] With muted disdain, Auden observes a smoothly functioning city. He casts the operations of this city, though, as a dramatic spectacle, highlighting their artifice: those running the city are "the leading characters" who "know the manners of the modern city" (23); they know their parts, they fit their roles. "Only the servants are unexpected; / Their silence has a fresh dramatic use" (23). "Off-stage, a war / Thuds like the slamming of a distant door" (23). How does one determine the relationship between the vibrant urban life circulating within the confines of Hong Kong and the deathscapes just beyond it? Auden writes that "we cannot postulate a General Will; For what we are, we have ourselves to blame" (23). Again, there is no more of a General Will than there is a Juster Life or a Good Place. And, again, Auden's disenchantment with the abstract leads him back to the individual, a problem to which we will return later. For now, though, I want to shift to Auden and Isherwood's movement offstage to find the war.

Auden and Isherwood leave Hong Kong for Canton, where Isherwood believes the real China—that is, the China at war with Japan—awaits them. They leave behind "the dinner-tables, the American movies, the statue of Queen Victoria on the guarded British island, steaming west into dangerous, unpredictable war-time China" (28–29). When Isherwood arrives in Canton, he experiences firsthand an air raid that rattles his nerves. Yet, like Orwell's time on the front in Spain, he and Auden discover how quickly the war yields to routine, boredom, and triviality. On March 25, a raid opens the day in Su-Chow, and Isherwood records it with the same disinterest as he would any other routine event. A day later a "big raid on the station and the centre of town" (102) causes little alarm; Auden and Isherwood hear the bombs, but were too "deeply engrossed in the treasures of Dr. MacFadyen's library" (103) to pay them any attention. By April 20 the air raids are now "not only a danger but a positive nuisance" (152). And by April 29, their last day in Hankow, Auden and Isherwood's cool temperament prevails and the air raids are pure spectacle: "Soon after lunch the sirens began to blare. We put on our smoked glasses and lay down flat on our backs on the Consulate lawn—it is the best way of watching an air-battle if you don't want a stiff neck. Machine-guns and anti-aircraft guns were hammering all around us, but the sky was so brilliant that we seldom caught a glimpse of the planes unless the sun happened to flash on their turning wings" (172). The detachment of spectatorship, the expert advice of how one might avoid a "stiff neck" while watching aerial combat, point to the swift habituation to war, even by two foreigners who remain bewildered through much of their journey and, weeks earlier, shook with fear at the sound of bombs. What Auden and Isherwood find at the end of this incident pierces this warm covering of habit and routine.

The spectacle of the air raid gives way to a gruesome scene of mangled bodies. Auden and Isherwood find "five civilian victims" next to an evacuated and unused arsenal. They are "terribly mutilated and very dirty"; their flesh has been "tattooed" with the gravel and dirt from the explosion (174). All the bodies appear lifeless, but Isherwood jots down these chilling notes from the scene: "As we stood beside one old woman, whose brains were soaking obscenely through a little towel, I saw the blood-caked mouth open and shut, and the hand beneath the sack-covering clench and unclench" (175). Isherwood concludes this gruesome scene with a report that seems out of all proportion to the sight of the dead civilians: "We heard later that five hundred civilians had been killed in the raid and thirty planes destroyed—nine Chinese and twenty-one Japs. Several other Japanese planes had been seriously damaged and were not expected to be able to reach their base. That night Hankow celebrated its greatest aerial victory" (175). A transition, then, from the macabre details of individual corpses to the affectless, actuarial logic of war. *Journey to a War* again presents a set of oppositions, here between the visceral details of the war dead and the mathematics of victory and defeat, which are somehow interlinked but outflank conceptual knowledge.

When the duo arrives in Shanghai, their final destination, the multilayered geopolitical realities of the Sino-Japanese war press against them from all sides. Alexander M. Bain sees Isherwood's Shanghai diary as the moment when the Sino-Japanese war appears less as a global contest against fascism and more as a particular moment of world-systemic disorder. "By framing Shanghai as the epicenter of a multinational economic disaster, *Journey* proposes that the root of the city's crisis is not a fascist aggression that everyone can agree to deplore. Rather, Shanghai is Europe's fault."[89] Isherwood reports from various sectors of Shanghai: an ambassador's garden party at a private villa, a meeting with Japanese bankers and businessmen, the cluttered refugee camps, and a hospital where crippled soldiers learn new trades while ignoring the wispy promises of salvation from a evangelical Christians. Recalling the collage-like format of the final chapter of Isherwood's

Goodbye to Berlin, the Shanghai diary assembles all of these fragments with little sense of continuity or interconnection. Europeans soak in the luscious nightlife within the British-controlled International Settlement; the Japanese army holds its outposts around the International Settlement; Chinese refugees flood into the settlement for security from Japanese military advances. Wen-hsin Yeh describes wartime Shanghai as a splintered city with a brittle security maintained in the European zones and all-out war beyond them. Suzhou Creek, along the northern edge of the International Settlement, provided the line of demarcation:

> North of the creek the explosions of aircraft, machine guns, rifles, and hand grenades reverberated in the air in a sky darkened by the smoke arising from crumbling structures and smoldering buildings. South of the creek, from the roofs, balconies and windows of multiple-storeyed modern buildings—the International Hotel, the China Hotel, the Nine Heavens pub—crowds of men and women looked down into the war zone with the aid of binoculars.[90]

Isherwood called the International Settlement and the French Concession "an oasis" (240), but it might be more of a mirage: "on one side are streets and houses, swarming with life; on the other is a cratered and barren moon-landscape, intersected by empty, clean-swept roads" (240). Perhaps the most suggestive juxtaposition comes during Auden and Isherwood's lunch with the Japanese "distinguished personages" (243). The Japanese explain that there is no bitterness in their war with the Chinese; they are merely trying to protect them from "the red menace" (245). "'And from Western trade competition,' we might have added," Isherwood writes (245). Isherwood's retort isn't needed. "For, at this moment, through the dining-room window which overlooked the river, the gun-turrets of H.M.S. *Birmingham* slid quietly into view, moving upstream. In this city the visual statements of power-politics are more brutal than any words" (245). In a single scene, Isherwood's reportage triangulates the business calculations of the Japanese, a projection of military force to protect Britain's economic and geostrategic interests, and the all-but-invisible Chinese, whose immiseration will come at the hands of one external power or another.

The Shanghai diary closes with three paragraphs that parse everyday life in Shanghai into the harsh realities of the impoverished Chinese and the pleasures

of European privilege. Isherwood structures the first paragraph around two re-
frains: "in this city" draws attention to the grim realities of Chinese life; the second refrain, "in our world," announces the differences of that privileged European
world—lavish parties, "the hot baths and cocktails, the singsong girls and the
Ambassador's cook" (252)—and Auden and Isherwood's belonging to it. These
divisions—the particular realities of the Sino-Japanese war and the broader moment in geopolitical disorder they illustrate—repeat throughout *Journey to a War*
and, indeed, structure much of the diary. In this final moment, Isherwood draws
no closer to synthesizing these oppositions, but he "awakens" to the fact that his
experiences have exceeded comprehension: "And the well-meaning tourist, the
liberal and humanitarian intellectual, can only wring his hands over all this and
exclaim: 'Oh dear, things are so awful here—so complicated. One doesn't know
where to start'" (253). Like Auden's disenchanted traveler from the opening poem
sequence, Isherwood's particular experiences result in a form of disorientation
that, I have suggested, mediates geopolitical disorder.

I've suggested that various components of *Journey to a War* are interrelated
but do not yield a conceptual whole. Many of the poems from the opening sequence and the photo-commentary pair with instances from Isherwood's diary
to heighten the particularity of the Sino-Japanese War. Taken together, these
parts draw into a single matrix the unfamiliarity and the ordinariness of war,
its suspension and remaking of the everyday. However, the latter portion of the
book, "In Time of War" and the verse commentary, shifts attention away from
the particularity of the Sino-Japanese War to the universal experience of war writ
large. Much like "Spain," "In Time of War" begins with an historical narrative,
full of prelapsarian scenes. As history progresses forward, war, cruelty, and disaster attend the most significant events. Painted in broad strokes, Auden's universal
history includes his experiences from China, but its integration robs the Sino-
Japanese War of all the specific detail given to it by the rest of the book. Both
"In Time of War" and the verse commentary view this particular war as one moment in a larger, more general war. Even that general war is no longer a political
war with specific historical causes; as the verse commentary has it, it is a war, perhaps a test, of moral fortitude.

The concluding voice, the last word, as it were, is "the voice of Man" (300)
calling out for "at last a human justice" (301). Like West and Orwell before them,

Auden and Isherwood begin with the inscrutable particularities of a political situation and lapse back into the general, ethical values that are, at bottom, not universal or general at all, but liberal values. Such recourse to seeming depoliticized and timeless virtues operates as a reproach to violence and political power, but, like Orwell's closing visions in *Homage to Catalonia*, they are also melancholic signals of disappointment. In their surgical attention to the everyday at war, these texts from abroad are witnesses to both a world-systemic transformation in the present *and* a future with no perceivable political alternatives.

FORECASTS OF WAR: BRUEGHEL IN BELGIUM, PICASSO IN LONDON

Auden and Isherwood returned home from China in July. Auden quickly left for Belgium, where he would compose perhaps the last bit of verse written under the influence of the Sino-Japanese War. Written in Brussels in December 1938, Auden's "Musée des Beaux Arts" is, on the surface, an ekphrastic poem about Pieter Brueghel's *The Fall of Icarus*. Alexander Nemerov rightly contends that we historicize Auden's poem and read it as a meditation on not only suffering and art but the suffering Auden witnessed in China from which so much of the Western world turned away.[91] Auden's poetic rendering of Brueghel notes how easy it is to miss the disastrous event: "the sun shone / As it had on the white legs disappearing into the green / Water."[92] Auden then shifts attention from the aesthetic appeal of this scene to the indifference of the event it records. "And the expensive delicate ship that must have seen / Something amazing, a boy falling out of the sky, / Had somewhere to get to and sailed calmly on."[93] Daily life for the shipman continues uninterrupted despite Icarus's fall and, earlier, the ploughman too ignores Icarus's death because "for him it was not an important failure."[94] In Auden's rendering, Brueghel's painting pairs an event of historical importance with the uncaring, indifferent world of commerce and labor. The shipman and the ploughman may turn away, but the painting makes us look at the disaster and, perhaps, suggests that the real disaster lies in the failure of these two characters to witness an historical event, to articulate a clear relationship between history and daily life. The demand to recast our attention that Auden finds in Brueghel's painting is the very one carried by *Journey to a War* and *Homage to Catalonia*. As forecasts of a future war, these works ask their readers to look at these wars abroad, to train their eyes on what is happening beyond England's borders, and to bear witness even if they are incapable of understanding.

Auden and Orwell attempted to bear witness and to educate domestic audiences in Britain when they returned from the global hot zones. Auden hit the lecture circuit at the end of September, discussing his experience of the war and the looming threat of fascism. At the end of that very month, on September 30, 1938, Neville Chamberlain returned from his final meeting with Adolf Hitler and Édouard Daladier. Waving a piece of paper in the air, Chamberlain declared the Munich Agreement to be "peace in our time." The illusion of peace would not last very long. The press soon learned the shocking details of the agreement; Chamberlain and Daladier mortgaged the Czechs to appease the Germans. To many onlookers, the Munich Crisis seemed to have emboldened Hitler and advanced the coming war. As the tide of English sentiment drifted from relief to shame, Picasso's *Guernica* made a much less heralded arrival in London on the same day. The organizers and patrons of the exhibit at the New Burlington Galleries—Roland Penrose, Herbert Read, E. L. T. Messens, Virginia Woolf, E. M. Forster, Victor Gollancz—hoped to remind the British public of the brutal war that England, France, and the United States' policy of nonintervention were not only ignoring but enabling.[95] The London exhibit ran from October 4–29, and the drawings and sketches for *Guernica* toured through other galleries that were not large enough to contain Picasso's massive canvas.[96] These three arrivals in England—Germany via Chamberlain's announcement; Spain in an indirect way through *Guernica*; China via Auden—forecast how the geopolitical disturbances of the 1930s would gradually encroach upon England, putting an end to one phase of the world-system. Auden, Isherwood, and Orwell knew the wars abroad were coming to English shores. And as their travel books demonstrate, formless war permeates all facets of daily life and corrodes the very conceptual frameworks and forms of attention long used to narrate and make sense of political turmoil; both *Homage to Catalonia* and *Journey to a War* testify to that split. And what form of attention would be required to render everyday life in Britain when war did arrive? Would war and everyday life fuse as they did in Spain and China? How would everyday life continue during a protracted air war? What political dispensations would collapse or emerge in the rubble of a besieged metropole? And what function would be left to art in such a state of emergency? The next chapter attempts to answer these questions.

4

WAR GOTHIC

Various years in general beat in the one which is just being counted and prevails.
ERNST BLOCH, *HERITAGE OF OUR TIMES*

Then, in the light of exploding bombs and flares and fires, we read that signpost:
To the Real Democracy: the People's Way.
J. B. PRIESTLEY, *OUT OF THE PEOPLE*

LOUIS MACNEICE'S *Autumn Journal* records that nervous season in 1938 when the Munich Crisis nearly pushed England from several years of war anxiety into a full-fledged war state. MacNeice's long poem opens at summer's end and transitions gradually from the warm indifference of pastoral life to the "pregnant air" of a city living under the duress of encroaching war.[1] In his opening lines, MacNeice invites us to see what escapes the attention of his late summer idlers:

> *Close and slow, summer is ending in Hampshire,*
> *Ebbing away down ramps of shaven lawn where close-*
> *Clipped yew*
> *Insulates the lives of retired generals and admirals*
> *And the spyglasses hung in the hall and the prayer-*
> *books ready in the pew*

And August going out to the tin trumpets of nasturtiums
And the sunflowers' Salvation Army blare of brass
And the spinster sitting in a deck-chair picking up stitches
Not raising her eyes to the noise of the 'planes that pass
Northward from Lee-on-Solent.[2]

Safely enclosed and hemmed in, MacNeice's retirees and spinsters go about their daily doings. Although MacNeice's spinster does not raise her eyes to the planes overhead, the poem directs the gaze of readers skyward and, in turn, troubles this peaceful seaside portrait with the sense of England's vulnerability to attack from the air. The ease with which planes pass over the tight enclosures of the coastal town indicates the lost security of an island state whose unquestioned naval power had long granted it immunity from foreign incursions.[3]

The cantos that follow trace the movements of all eyes skyward as England turns its parks into trenches, distributes gas masks to its citizens, and prepares its population for war. Yet MacNeice also notes that this overt display of defensive power induces less visible transformations in the population, which he describes as "the heavy panic that cramps the lungs and presses the collar down the spine."[4] MacNeice intuits a potential disequilibrium between heightened security measures and a diminished sense of security among the population. And yet that palpable sense of vulnerability pervading every facet of daily life in *Autumn Journal* nearly vanishes when the bombings began in earnest in September 1940. All of the psychological pressure of the looming war gave way to a consolidation of national will; a weakening, if not full elimination, of class and social barriers; and a phlegmatic population determined, in the words of Vera Brittain, to "continue our daily occupations, though we know that what we are doing cannot possibly be our best."[5]

Or so the story goes. The creation of what we now call the People's War narrative relied greatly on the coordination of state resources with literary, painterly, and cinematic talents.[6] The Ministry of Information, the Crown Film Unit, the War Artists Advisory Committee (WAAC), and a host of artists, writers, and government workers collectively generated a version of everyday life specifically aimed at presenting the British population as unflappable, determined to endure the German onslaught. Films such as *London Can Take It!* and the GPO Film

Unit's *The First Days* show British citizens going about their typical business by day and turning into homeland defenders by night.[7] A post-raid scene from *London Can Take It!* ensures viewers that a London morning goes on uninhibited by rubble in the street from the overnight war. In Patrick Deer's words, Jennings's film "stages the spectacle of London under attack, but essentially in tact."[8] These films suggested that if the English could continue to deliver mail, go to the cinema, and sleep through air raids, the physical damage wrought by the Luftwaffe had ultimately failed to leave an imprint on the city's collective psyche. The habits, routines, and stubborn persistence of daily life signified a population whose continued existence was a contestation of German militarism.

This chapter excavates another version of everyday life during the war, one that derives much of its expressive power from the gothic.[9] The texts I examine here redeploy gothic images, narrative structures, and modes of characterization to foreground the vulnerability and insecurity that disappears between MacNeice's *Autumn Journal* and the onset of the war a year later. By tracking the employment of the gothic in works as varied as Henry Moore's Tube sketches, Elizabeth Bowen's short fiction, and photographic surveys of bombed London, we recover a narrative of insecurity that extends from individual and collective fears of injury to the future of England's status as a world power. In the works I take up here, secure sites like bomb shelters become mass graves; war legislation that regulates and remakes daily routines threatens to desubjectify individual citizens; and the war populism promoted by the British state threatens to dismantle boundaries between the liberal individual and the collective, between propertied wealthy classes and their less fortunate counterparts. In short, late modernism's war gothic figures everyday life as a scene of dispossession, identity loss, and perpetual insecurity.

GOTHIC AFFINITIES

There is a general consensus among scholars that the gothic gives form to inchoate threats pulsing just beneath the placid surface of daily life. A loose, baggy genre, the gothic acquires some coherence insofar as it depicts what John Paul Riquelme calls "dark modernity"; repressed impulses, forbidden desires, and social antagonisms are all grist for the mill.[10] From its early appearances in the late eighteenth century, gothic literature developed characters and narrative forms in contrast to emergent liberal philosophies of history and the rational, autonomous subjects such philosophies required.[11] The gothic draws the excluded and the exceptional—the poor, the colonized, the dispossessed—back into the field of representation, isolating those forms of political antagonism that exist invisibly, or at best marginally, in other literary forms (like the realist novel). With their preference for vampiric or spectral characters, gothic texts destabilize "boundaries between psyche and reality, opening up an indeterminate zone in which the differences between fantasy and actuality were no longer secure."[12] At the level of plot, the gothic tale "tends to delay narrative development through digressions, interruptions, infolded tales, interpolated poems, etc., which move the narrative backwards as well as forwards."[13] With all of its peculiar formal involutions, the gothic generates many of its effects by short-circuiting the cultural, political, and philosophical protocols governing a particular historical era; suspended plots, labyrinthine narratives, and unnerving characters all encode some type of social or political friction. A text like Bram Stoker's *Dracula* might be said to allegorize the problems of colonial Ireland or stand as an exemplary counternarrative to Victorian ideals of the liberal individual.[14] Different though these interpretations and their contexts may be, the formal qualities of Stoker's novel give perceptible shape to existing tensions.

Elastic as the gothic is, it should not be mistaken as a transhistorical, stable genre. Gothic features accrue power only in relation to their historical situation. The restaging of its familiar tropes, protocols, and narrative techniques in a different historical theater proceeds from a particular dialectic of genre and history. In Fredric Jameson's theory of genre, the "emergent, strong form of a genre is essentially a socio-symbolic message, or in other terms, that form is immanently and intrinsically an ideology in its own right."[15] When the genre reappears in another historical moment, sometimes in combination with other genres, its ideological DNA survives in some mutated form. Still, even with considerable modifications, it would seem that the horrors of the young twentieth century's total wars would render the gothic powerless. What repressed, monstrous thing would not already be apparent in a corpse-filled no man's land or in a smoldering, bombed cityscape? As I will show in the following, gothic images, narrative structures, and characters not only survive, they proliferate across visual and literary culture during the Second World War.

What happens when the gothic is transported into wartime England? What changes does the gothic undergo when it is incorporated into war writing? On one hand, the figural language of the gothic is marshaled to describe and depict the visible destruction and terror of everyday life during war, thereby losing its ability to make legible historical, social, or psychic pressures that have yet to attain the level of visibility; if this is the case, the war gothic appears less as realism's antithesis and more as a language and image bank for describing the realities of war. On the other hand, the seemingly perfect alignment of the gothic with everyday life might not erase the gothic's expressive power; rather, war induces a dialectical change in the figural work of the gothic.

Late modernist writers and visual artists have precedents for this uneasy synthesis of the gothic and modern war. First World War poets and modernists writing in the teens and twenties already staged a confrontation between the grisly reality of total war and the gothic.[16] These writers marshaled a host of tropes and images to depict the mangled, disfigured bodies of soldiers at the front and to capture the collective psychological terror that lingered long after the Armistice. In her reading of Erich Remarque's *All Quiet on the Western Front*, Margot Norris argues that the novel generates a "necrological poetics" that combines the graphic realism of trench warfare with fragmentary narration.[17] What results is a harrowing document of the First World War as well as a reassertion that the totality of that experience can never be fully grasped. Norris shows, too, that for all the gruesome detail in Remarque's novel, corpses often appear animate, contesting the boundary between life and death: "Many have their bellies swollen up like balloons. They hiss, belch, and make movements. The gases in them make noises."[18] On her reading, the corpse slides from morbid literality to something more figural. Allyson Booth suggests as much when she declares that the war inaugurated a figural shift in the gothic, one that supplanted immaterial ghosts with the materiality of the corpse. In the writings of "modernist precursors, the past often insinuated itself into the present in the form of ghosts (as in Henrik Ibsen's *Ghosts*, 1881; or Henry James, "The Jolly Corner," 1909). . . . Later modernists often embodied the persistence of the past within corpses."[19] Like the traditional gothic figures, the corpse reintroduces the disavowed and the excluded, bringing the dead into the space of the living.[20]

Wilfred Owen's "Dulce et decorum est" remains one of the century's most powerful war poems precisely because it merges realist description with gothic figures.[21] In this nightmarish account a gassed soldier's death endlessly haunts the speaker. Thick description fills the first two stanzas but falls away the moment a soldier dies. More specifically, description dissolves into ellipsis in the middle of the second stanza. The poem then shifts from "we" to "I," and death recurs without end in the speaker's present. Demarcating the boundary between the brute powers of description and their limitations, the final stanza of Owen's poem is pitched in the conditional. No account however descriptive will convey the horror of witnessing a soldier's death, nor will it put an end to the psychic recurrence of the horrors of war. The dead soldier's corpse, then, slides from material reality to psychic wound, from the description of an actually existing body to something ghastly and figural. When corpses return later in key modernist works like T. S. Eliot's *The Waste Land* and D. H. Lawrence's *Women in Love*, they too signify past traumas that persist into the present and, more broadly, attest to an historical event that attains legibility through gothic tropes and figures.

While the gothic does not surface explicitly as an analytical category for either Norris or Booth, their investigations highlight a potential contradiction that emerges at the intersection of twentieth-century war writing and the gothic: fusing the gothic with total war disables the tight opposition between the gothic and realism, potentially depriving the gothic of its power to make the invisible visible; and yet, as Owen's and Remarque's writing clearly illustrates, the images, narrative techniques, and figures that populate the war gothic mark out the epistemological limits of realist description. Hardly aporetic, these are two components of a dialectical procedure where gothic features are modulated and deployed in an unlikely context. If the gothic in the First World War brought out the dead bodies that no one wanted to see, the texts I analyze in the following narrate the perpetual insecurity that the British state wanted no one to acknowledge.

INSECURE LIFE (1): SHELTER AND LIVE BURIAL

The conspicuous absence of the injured and the dead counts as one of the more noticeable changes in Second World War texts. This phenomenon was not entirely lost on commenters at the time. Reviewing the "British War Artists Exhibition" for *Horizon*, Lillian Browse commends the formal accomplishments of the artists in the exhibit but sees little evidence of war at all in this so-called war art: "But if it is meant to depict War with all its horrors and tragedies, then it fails, for apart from the strange appearance of the barrage balloons, the sandbags in the streets and the khaki uniforms, nobody would guess that anything was amiss."[22] More specifically, the exhibition omits the "the bitterness, brutality and tragedy that this war has brought."[23] Prefacing an exhibition of British war art shown a year later at the Museum of Modern Art in New York, Herbert Read defended the absence of human casualties from the photographs and canvases. If the artworks "strike the American visitor as tame or subdued, as too quiet and harmonious for the adequate representation of war," that should be interpreted as a signal that the hallmark restraint of English aesthetics has not been transformed by the experience of war.[24] It is, as he says, "the exact expression of our conception of liberty."[25] Although Browse's and Read's judgments of war art diverge significantly, their descriptions of these two exhibitions underline the absence of horror and tragedy from British art in the Second World War.

In many ways, Henry Moore's sketches of the London Underground reinscribe the "horrors and tragedies" that Browse found missing from other canvases. Focusing on the war's most famous of bomb shelters, Moore's series of drawings transform the Tube from a place of protection and refuge into a potential mass grave. This claim may seem counterintuitive given that several of his sketches were used by the Ministry of Information and the WAAC in state-sponsored art exhibitions portraying the steely resolve of the population.[26] Sir Kenneth Clark, head of the WAAC and director of the National Gallery, knew precisely what social function Moore's sketches and other artworks should perform:

What Clark desired for the State, in his capacity as Chairman of the WAAC and a high official of the Ministry of Information (MOI), was a record of sheltering Londoners that would speak to a set of political and social anxieties in that time of crisis. For Clark's role at the MOI was to envisage and draft propaganda that attempted to bolster civilian morale in the face of the German invasion threat in the summer and autumn of 1940. Nationally, any perceptions of a fragile condition of morale amongst British subjects had to be managed: abroad, Britain's positive representation, especially in America, was at stake.[27]

It's not hard to imagine that Clark would be rather taken with the visual power of Moore's sketches. It is rather curious, though, that Clark thought they could be instrumentalized in the way he desired.

In one of the documents Clark sent to the WAAC, he includes a brief description of one of Moore's drawings, *Shelter Scene: Two Seated Figures*, that underscores its value as propaganda: "A fine imaginative conception symbolising the determination of British women who heroically stood up to the attacks by the German night bombers on the civilian population."[28] Perhaps predictably, the public response to Moore's work did not always hit the same heroic tones as Clark's. A Mass-Observer visited a Tate Gallery exhibition of war art and recorded the reactions to three of Moore's drawings: "Three young women stand in front of three Henry Moore's in some astonishment. At first they giggle then one says: 'Horrible!' and moves on to the next picture with a shudder. Another one says: 'They are rather. But I like that one a bit. The colour's nice. And I like the frame.' They move on studying the catalogue."[29]

Moore's sketches elicit multiple reactions: amusement, repulsion, and pleasure. What is important, though, is that these contradictory reactions indicate that Moore's drawings do not consolidate perception at all. Their eerie affective power does not seem to translate into any sort of propagandistic message. Moore's shelter scenes must have seemed even stranger next to canvases depicting the calm, healthy faces of soldiers or the smooth workings of a war factory. Lacking life and motion, Moore's figures hover somewhere between life and death, stuck in these dreary underworlds. As we will see, Moore's spatial arrangements literally and figuratively bury his subjects alive beneath a destroyed city. These huddled, often faceless masses blend into one another and into the surrounding structures, collapsing any distinction between individuals and, at times, between the human and the inhuman. In other drawings, these Tube dwellers morph into mummified figures. The very form of Moore's sketches makes insecurity appear in these scenes of secure shelter life.

According to stories Moore told in his day, the sketches initially took shape in the early days of the Blitz. On September 11, 1940, Moore and his wife returned home to Hampstead on the Northern Line of the Tube after an evening dinner. As the train stopped at various stations, Moore saw firsthand the masses gathered on the Tube platforms. He completed the first sketch, *Women and Children in the Tube* (figure 4.1), the following day. So began one of the most definitive art projects of the Second World War and, indeed, of Moore's career. On his account, Moore never drew his subjects while in the shelter. Instead, he frequented London, absorbing details of everyday life in the underground shelters and taking visual notes of the inhabitants: "I went up to London for two days each week, spending the nights in the Underground, watching the people, and coming up at dawn. Then I would go back to Much Hadham and spend two days making sketches in the tear-off pad. The rest of the week I would be working on drawings to show to the War Artists Committee."[30]

It was only after making the initial sketches that Moore somewhat reluctantly agreed to sell them on a contract basis to Clark. This origin story appears now to be more myth than fact. Julian Andrews points out some inconsistencies regarding Moore's frequent visits to London and the exact timeline of the sketches.[31] To complicate matters even more, David Alan Mellor recently discovered photos in *Picture Post* that strongly indicate Moore copied his images directly from these photographs. If Mellor is right (and his evidence is indeed convincing), Moore's first sketch was hardly the product of an immediate outpouring of aesthetic genius. Because Moore's earliest drawings originate from images of three mothers holding small children in the October 12, 1940, edition of *Picture Post* (figure 4.2), *Women and Children in the Tube* (figure 4.1) could not have been finished directly after his September experience.[32]

How we adjudicate the origin stories of the sketchbooks may very well alter our view of Moore's creative process, and for some it may also affect the aesthetic value of the sketches themselves. But Mellor's discovery suggests something far more provocative: Moore's sketches begin as an active disfiguration of these photographic and documentary representations, the very ones which were marshaled in *Picture Post* to produce a narrative of shelter life that complied with the state friendly People's War mythos. In its October 26, 1940, edition, *Picture Post* produced a visual typology of the shelterers. The bottom of a two-page photographic spread outlines "their qualities: patience, cheerfulness, resignation, friendship, even gaiety" (figure 4.3).

Although it is clear that Moore's sketches do not replicate the ideology of the *Picture Post* editorials, his work does not simply generate a counternarrative. Rather, the gothic work of Moore's sketches showcases the corrosive effects of

FIGURE 4.1 HENRY MOORE, *WOMEN AND CHILDREN IN THE TUBE*, 1940.

Reproduced by permission of the Henry Moore Foundation.

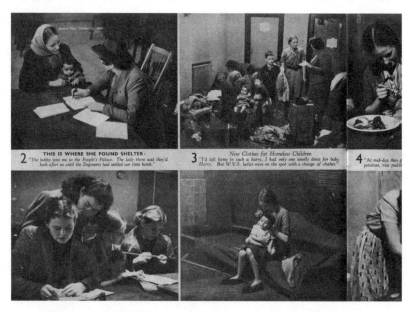

FIGURE 4.2 "BOMBED OUT," *PICTURE POST*, OCTOBER 12, 1940, 10.

FIGURE 4.3 "SHELTER LIFE," *PICTURE POST*, OCTOBER 26, 1940, 10–11.

war on the very narratives and concepts that produce knowledge of everyday life. This helps us understand the gravity of those images grafted from *Picture Post* into *Women and Children in the Tube*. When Moore transfers the mothers and children from the *Picture Post* photos into his sepulchral Tube shelter, he puts them at the front of a crowd of figures losing solidity and line before dissolving into barely perceptible outlines; these dim figures at the far right end of the sketch retain just enough shape to alert us to the formal breakdown of ground and figure, of human subject and the surrounding walls. By recasting these particular photographic images, *Women and Children in the Tube* enacts the erasure of oppositions, transferring a scene of vulnerable citizens in a nominally secure space to some grim, precarious underworld. Those crisp images of life in the shelter morph into an image of diminished life where living beings are scarcely distinguishable from each other and their surroundings.

In a letter to Arthur Sales from October 1940, the very period in which Moore was at work on the sketches and these images from *Picture Post* first appeared, Moore gives his version of what Elizabeth Bowen called the "lucid abnormality" of everyday life in a wartime city:[33]

> The unreality of it all, I think, is because of the complete contrast of everyday normal life, side by side with sudden destruction and danger. In the daytime in London, I can't believe any bombs can fall—the streets seem just as full as ever, with people on buses and in the shops, going along just as usual, until you come across a slice of a house reduced to a mess of plaster, laths and broken glass . . . and of that one's just a spectator, it's like being at the cinema.
>
> The night-time in London is like another world—the noise is terrific and everything seems to be going on immediately over one's own little spot—and the unreality is that of exaggeration like in a nightmare.[34]

Moore's terms divide everyday experience into two opposing categories: there is the perspective of the spectator, observing the cinema-like quality of "everyday normal life" during the day and the amplified terror, the "nightmare," of London under attack after sunset. At first blush Moore's temporal rubric allocates contrasting forms of experience to daytime and nighttime: in this way normal and abnormal, relative peace and unbridled violence, detached observer and unwilling participant acquire descriptive and conceptual authority. His elaborations, though, show us that day and night do not capture two opposed facets of daily life in the war metropolis. Hardly normal, daytime life weaves its own strange aura, setting one off as a type of "spectator" at a cinema; life is not lived as per usual and, clearly, the position of citizen as spectator indicates the heightened strangeness of the most mundane, normal activities. The relentless terror of the raids transforms night into "another world." Daytime life is a cinematic spectacle and night life is a nightmare: both figurations turn on a similar type of unreality and their firm opposition loosens. Remarkably, if inadvertently, Moore's bad opposites don't parse war experience so much as they dramatize the corrosive effect of total war on the very capability to conceptualize experience. In Moore's firsthand accounts and in his individual sketches, war distorts categories and warps boundaries.

This affinity for thinking in oppositions and pushing them into a zone of indistinction underwrites Moore's early studies for the shelter sketches like *Eighteen Ideas for War Drawings* (1940) and *War: Possible Subjects* (1940–1941) (figure 4.4). The provisional frames in *Eighteen Ideas for War Drawings* visualize multiple situations, naming some of them directly "contrast of opposites" while others explore oppositions of night and day and nature and machine. Below the infernal cityscape of *War: Possible Subjects*, Moore indexes a number of ideas that will guide his sketches, and he further expands on the "contrast of opposites": "Blanketed figure in bombed street. Sectional line drawings of draped reeling figures. Contrast of peaceful, normal, with sudden devastation (burning cows). Figure pinned under debris. Night and day contrast." The motif of the burning cows repeats in both of these studies. This particular image lays out the contrast of peaceful, pastoral life with the violence of mechanized warfare. It is only when the oppositions are upended that artworks capture the destructive force of war and, by extension, acquire the ghostly, unnerving quality that emanates from Moore's sketches.

Moore's technique of exposing and subsequently collapsing oppositions generates its most macabre effects in those sketches where the deep shelter of the Tubes mutates into its opposite—a mass grave. Fear of live burial in the shelters wasn't baseless fantasy. In one week in October 1940, three Tube shelters and those within them suffered gravely from the air raids. Damages to Trafalgar Station on October 7 and to Bounds Green a day later buried twenty-six shelterers beneath

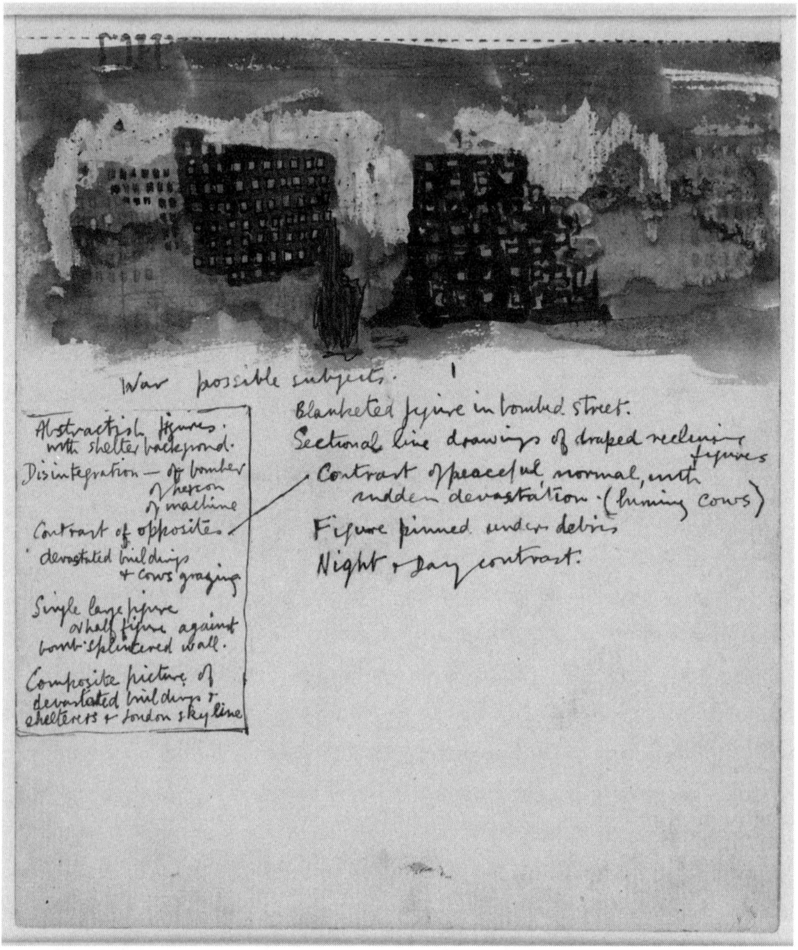

FIGURE 4.4 HENRY MOORE, *WAR: POSSIBLE SUBJECTS*, 1940–41.

Reproduced by permission of the Henry Moore Foundation.

debris and injured another eighty-five.[35] Tube historian John Gregg recounts the worst of these incidents:

> But the greatest tragedy to visit the Tube dwellers in 1940 came at Balham station on
> 14th October, when a very heavy bomb fell in Balham High Road, about 200 feet
> north of Chestnut Grove at a point immediately over the Board's northbound station

tunnel. The cover of ground over the top of the tunnel where the bomb fell was about 30 feet and in a position where a cross passage connects the two station tunnels. As a result, a crater was formed some 60 feet in diameter occupying the full width of the High Road. Into this a bus fell, providing for photographers one of the most enduring and dramatic images of the Blitz as well as a shield against onlookers viewing the ghastly scene below. The explosion, which a policeman on duty at the time recalls "lifting me off the ground," caused a deluge of ballast and sludge to enter the platforms where over six hundred shelterers were gathered, burying sixty-four of them as well as four station staff.[36]

More structurally sound and purportedly safer than any other type of shelter the state doled out, the perceived security of the Tube shelters has its dialectical counterpart in the threat of live burial.

A longstanding gothic trope, live burial names the vanishing lines between life and death, surface and depth, and interior and exterior.[37] The contrast between protected slumber and live burial appears weakly in one of Moore's drawings from 1940–1941 (figure 4.5). The top portion of the drawing features two couples rendered monochromatically, sleeping soundly with no indication of violence or any impending threat. Below them Moore creates an altogether different scene: awash in pink, a figure's head and body peer through a pile of rubble. Faint outlines of buildings in the background assure us that this potential death scene has not taken place in any of the shelters. A similar motif recurs in another sketch, *Landscape with Wrecked Omnibus* (figure 4.6), from the same time period that may reference directly the Balham station disaster and the numerous photos of that bus crashed into the gigantic bomb crater. At the top of Moore's page, a bus teeters over on the left hand side; on the right, wild lines combine with green, yellow, white, and pink colors and shapes to lend this sketch its chaotic atmosphere. An open crater swells below the bus and just beneath we see shelterers in a subterranean space. Unlike many of Moore's sketches, this image stares back. A semicircle of near featureless bodies encloses a mother and child, one of Moore's preferred pairings; those black dots for eyes pierce the viewer, arresting our gaze long enough to ponder the destructive scene above and the calm one below.

In *Blitzed Buildings and Sleeping Woman Holding Child* (figure 4.7), Moore employs a similar color and spatial scheme but to a slightly different end. The

FIGURE 4.5 HENRY MOORE, *TWO SLEEPING FIGURES AND FIGURE PINNED UNDER DEBRIS*, 1940–1941.

Reproduced by permission of the Henry Moore Foundation.

devastated buildings outside occupy the top portion of the drawing while the mother and child sleep unperturbed in some place beneath the earth. A border roughly in the shape of a right angle extends from the left side of the page and divides the slumbering humans from the destruction above. The colossal size of the sleepers exceeds that of the ravaged cityscape above, amplifying their invulnerability. But, again, the seams between these contrasts of opposites are imperfect.

One bit of debris on the far left side perforates the line separating city and shelter, demolition and protection. The spatial logic of the drawing intimates that these deep sleepers are on the verge of being buried alive beneath an avalanche of wreckage. Sleeping through the bombing, one of the favorite images of so much war propaganda, does not signify British resolve or stoicism; these victims remain helpless, frozen in the repose of disaster.

FIGURE 4.6 HENRY MOORE, *WRECKED OMNIBUS AND FIGURES IN UNDERGROUND SHELTER*, 1940–1941.

Reproduced by permission of the Henry Moore Foundation.

FIGURE 4.7 HENRY MOORE, *BLITZED BUILDINGS AND SLEEPING WOMAN HOLDING CHILD*, 1940–1941.

Reproduced by permission of the Henry Moore Foundation.

Some of Moore's early reviewers homed in on these inert, seemingly lifeless husks. One commenter in *Spectator* claims Moore's "drawings look as if he has been excavating in early tombs."[38] Clark himself picked up on Moore's archaeological imagination, likening some of Moore's figures to the remains of Pompeii. The Pompeii reference holds added significance given that the war writings of both Graham Greene and H. D. turned to that disaster as a point of reference;

Rose Macaulay's postwar work also makes similar references. H. D. may very well be right when she states "Pompeii has nothing to teach us."[39] An apocalyptic natural disaster from the ancient world rhymes imperfectly with the technological, manmade destruction of modern warfare. Correspondence need not mean that the two events are interchangeable; it does, however, gesture toward one mode of understanding the pressures of the Second World War. Pompeii can only signify extinction, a civilization's twilight. What still fascinates us about the Pompeii casts is that they seize human beings in their final death throes. While Moore's sketches exude their own terrifying qualities, the depicted subjects remain passive and seem rather unaware of their own precarious situation. *Group of Shelterers, Study for Shelter Drawing,* and *Shadowy Shelter* display human forms crisscrossed with thick white and yellow lines that operate as a sort of x-ray. Here we have living, sleeping beings appearing simultaneously as their own skeletal remains. In the same way Moore converts underground protection into live burial, here we see life crossing over into death, and the present destruction surely recalls that extinguished population from an ancient empire.

Moore's sketches, then, do not depict war as a life-or-death scenario but one in which the lines between life and death become less identifiable. In his gothic depictions, the representative figure of the bombed city is not the ordinary individual who trades in work clothes for the garb of the People's Army. If the narrative of Moore's work, and much of what I will outline below, turns on imminent threat and perpetual insecurity, the protagonists are the living dead. In the broader context of British war art, Moore's "official" work retains its anomalous status because, however dutifully framed or captioned, his sketches do not fit any narrative of the People's War. By making death appear where life should be secure, Moore's gothic allows us to see and feel the imminent danger that his subjects do not recognize and, perhaps, the fears his patrons did not want recognized.

INSECURE LIFE (2): INJURY AND RUINS

Among British literature and art from the Second World War, Moore's sketches are rare in their depictions of vulnerable and hurt bodies. Mark Rawlinson rightly states that the majority of writing and art from the Second World War is about "buildings, not bodies."[40] He concludes that fascination with architectural damage, what he calls "the spectacle of metropolitan ruin," highlights the invisibility of bodies; it eclipses casualties and injuries. Yet Rawlinson's conclusion misses the figurative work of urban wreckage. The damaged city supplied late modernism with "a surreal landscape in which repressed fears and dark emotions erupted through the fissures in everyday life."[41] Commenting on their aesthetic appeal, Bill Brandt remembered how "the bombed ruins made strangely shaped silhouettes."[42] They decorate the landscape of Elizabeth Bowen's short stories, figure heavily in the poetry of David Gascoyne and the New Apocalypse poets, and they become central in Graham Sutherland's paintings and in the photographic work of Cecil Beaton and Brandt. While the allure or, more suggestively, the aura of the ruin appears ubiquitous and inescapable, we should ask how it might signify more than "the disappearance of the hurt body."[43]

As a favored set piece of gothic fiction and painting, ruins have traditionally indicated the indifferent march of time; they are physical evidence of an earlier epoch's passage into history, of the insignificance of its monumental and architectural feats. A ruin denotes the afterlife of what should be extinct. In this way ruins serve as mute memories of an historical period or, sometimes, of a social and political order that has outlived its moment. This is nowhere more apparent than in the works of the nineteenth century's most renowned painter of gothic landscapes, Caspar David Friedrich. Friedrich's canvases are littered with ruins of abbeys, monasteries, and other buildings that time seems to have all but forgotten. In *Monastery Graveyard in the Snow*, an 1819 work that seems to recast the mood and tone of *The Abbey in the Oakwood* from a decade earlier, the fragmented remnants of an old monastery sit between the contorted limbs of lifeless trees. Couples in black cloaks walk among the snowy ruins, leaving the viewer to wonder if these figures are themselves the last of some extinct form of life represented by the time-ravaged monastery. Many of the hallmarks of gothic fiction—Edgar Allan Poe's "Fall of the House of Usher," Bram Stoker's *Dracula*, and Joseph Sheridan Le Fanu's *Uncle Silas* to name only a few—foreground decrepit buildings and link their structural decay with their degenerate inhabitants. Their bare existence, like Usher's mansion or Friedrich's grand cathedrals, simultaneously refers to the monumentality of past greatness and a precarious present that no longer requires or recognizes that monumentality. In all of these works, architectural ruins and the fate of their inhabitants becomes indistinguishable.

Elizabeth Bowen's 1940 story "Oh, Madam . . ." intertwines architectural damage with the lives of urban residents. On the surface, "Oh Madam . . ." is a conversation between a live-in servant and the owner of a home that has suffered severely from the previous night's raid. In this story, though, we only hear the servant's rambling, perhaps panicked monologue. We receive a partial inventory of damages from the servant: "our beautiful fanlight gone," "the windows gone," and "the ceiling in there gone."[44] Walking through the debris, the owner indicates that she will shutter the house and, presumably, ride out the rest of the war far away from the city. Yet, like much of the house, the owner too is gone. She never appears or speaks in the text. Her presence, if it can be so called that, is designated textually by a recurrent ellipsis that often marks where "Madam" would speak or react. The only quotation marks that properly announce dialogue are embedded within the stories the servant tells her phantom interlocutor; there is nothing at the level of syntax or narrative discourse to confirm Madam's actual embodied presence. She exists only through the ellipsis, which interrupts and detours the servant's endless speech: "You won't take *anything*, madam? . . . You'll need your fur coat, excuse me, madam, you will. There's the draught right through the house. You don't want to catch cold, not on top of everything. . . . No, it's useless; you *can't* move that dining-room door. . . . But the house has been wonderful, madam, really—you really have cause to be proud of it."[45]

Madam's syntactic marker should not be read merely as an indication of speech that is withheld from the reader. Ellipsis signifies absence, a missing piece (or person), and we might take its significance here rather literally. Are we to infer that Madam isn't there? Is the discourse actually interior monologue? Is our speaker a traumatized servant who perhaps is rambling to no one at all? Bowen's story leaves these questions open, but it deftly triangulates the ruined house, the missing Madam, and literary form. On the very page, the story appears pockmarked and fragmented by the scattered ellipses, transferring the damage of the house to the actual text.

We would be remiss, then, to read the preoccupation with ruins as the negation of injury, whether injury be physical or psychic. Where Bowen's story associates the diminished existence of a house with the near eclipse of the owner in the narrative discourse, other works like H. D.'s *The Walls Do Not Fall* and Moore's sketches attach physiological characteristics to the architectural structures of the metropolis. In these works, the city appears as a living being, and the ruins and architectural damages are figured as wounds and injuries. Two of Moore's

FIGURE 4.8 HENRY MOORE, *HALF-LENGTH STANDING WOMAN IN FRONT OF WALL*, 1940–1941.

Reproduced by permission of the Henry Moore Foundation.

wartime sketches of the Tilbury Warehouse shelter align architectural and physical injury, blurring the line between the two. In *Half-Length Woman Standing in Front of Wall* (figure 4.8), Moore's exhausted figure reclines against a wall bearing the traces of bomb damage; pink, flesh-colored bricks surround the woman's head, and her face and body take on the bluish-grey tones of the wall behind her, further entwining human and architectural vulnerability. If this juxtaposition of

FIGURE 4.9 HENRY MOORE, *HEAD MADE UP OF DEVASTATED HOUSE*, 1940–1941.

Reproduced by permission of the Henry Moore Foundation.

building and person invites us to consider the frail, defenseless body, *Head Made up of Devastated House* (figure 4.9) merges architectural and bodily injury into one figure. The "bomb scar" from the first image returns on the visage of Moore's cryptic figure; other structural remains—the yellow brick wall, a fallen girder— appear in place of a human face. Lacking distinction between ruined buildings and wounded bodies, Moore's image construes "casualty" simultaneously in both registers.

This very indistinction forms the grand conceit of the opening section of H. D.'s *The Walls Do Not Fall,* where she tropes human remains into a half-destroyed building:

> *the bone-frame was made for*
> *no such shock knit within terror,*
> *yet the skeleton stood up to it:*
> *the flesh? It was melted away,*
> *the heart burnt out, dead ember,*
> *tendons, muscles shattered, outer husk dismembered,*
> *yet the frame held:*
> *we passed the flame: we wonder*
> *what saved us? what for?*[46]

"Bone-frame," "skeleton," "flesh," "heart burnt out," "tendons, muscles shattered": H. D.'s lexical compilation equates ruins with bodily injury. In another way, though, the onlookers in the poem may very well be projecting onto the charred building their own horrific fantasies of dying in an air raid. Skeletal architectural remains showcase the sheer force of the bombs to the onlookers and mirror to them their own vulnerability.

What has taken place in this displacement of injury from human bodies to architectural and urban structures? The figural charge of ruined cityscapes in late modernist war works echoes a specific type of tropology in military theories of air war, an intellectual and speculative industry that flourished in the late teens and twenties. In writings by renowned military figures such as Basil Liddell Hart, J. F. C. Fuller, and Maj. Gen. F. H. Sykes, among others, cities get recast from peaceful urban spaces into war spaces, and they rely on a host of biological and vitalistic metaphors to accomplish this figural transformation. Hart recodes areas of central importance and the pathways of commerce and traffic as a circulatory system: "Every industrial nation has its vitals . . . a fourth [district] so highly centralized that its capital is the real as well as the nominal heart of its life . . . and in all the regular flow of transport along its arteries is a vital requirement."[47] Fuller more completely and systematically anatomizes the city and its defenses from the perspective of an airplane bomber pilot: "Once this supreme point of vantage is gained, the next tactical operation will be to deliver an aerial attack on the landed forces, not only on their bodies—their men, horses and guns, but on their brains—their command headquarters; on their nerves—their system of communications; on their internal organs—their bases, supply depots, chemical and engineering works and workshops."[48] The "point of vantage" refocuses military strategy from the endless game of attrition that characterized the Western Front to Hart's more calculated objective of "dislocating their normal life to such a degree that they [the enemy country] will prefer the lesser evil of surrendering their policy, and by convincing them that any return to 'normalcy'—to use President Harding's term—is hopeless unless they do so surrender."[49] While many of those heralding the strategic benefits of air war would later disavow their utility, the idea that, in Spender's words, "the background to this war, corresponding to the Western Front in the last war, is the bombed city" meant that horrific death would be reserved not only for soldiers but for the collective population of a target city.[50]

To target buildings, streets, parks, and ports is to strike at the collective life of a city and a state, not just its individual citizens. Architectural ruin signals ruination on a larger social scale. This is precisely what Georges Bataille had in mind when he defined architecture as "the expression of the very being of societies, in the same way that human physiognomy is the expression of the being of individuals. . . . Such that if you attack architecture . . . you are in some ways attacking man."[51] In this way the type of injury figured by the ruin also extends outward from individual human casualties to the forms of social order and historical memory embodied in cityscapes. One of Henri Lefebvre's central claims in *The Production of Space* is that the very spatial arrangements of cities produces and guards social and political order while also inscribing that order on the psyches and imaginations of a city's inhabitants. Lefebvre grasps the operations of social space through a tripartite dialectic of spatial practice, representations of space, and representational spaces. Without reducing the complexity of his individual terms and the dynamic relations between them, we can define spatial practice as an association between everyday life and the spaces—home, workplace, networks of travel—that make up a familiar world; Lefebvre calls representations of space the "dominant space in any society" articulated through the codification and rationalization of space via urban planners, engineers, and so on; representational spaces gather up the imaginative, aesthetic, and symbolic charges invested in space.[52] In Lefebvre's rubric, this is the component of social space that "need obey no rules of consistency or cohesiveness."[53] Lefebvre's account suggests that social space emerges from a dialectical relationship of the routines and habits of everyday life, the planned organization of the city and its spatial arrangement, and the imaginative, affective associations attached to various parts of a city. We might retain Lefebvre's dialectical model but shift it from the production of social space to the production of war space. In the bombed city, the systematic destruction of private and public space, monuments, infrastructure, and architecture maintains the relationships between spatial practice, representations of space, and representational spaces. The widespread fascination with ruins outlined earlier casts into relief the interrelations between the disruption of everyday life, damaged buildings and city streets, and the heightened, uncanny affective responses. The production of war space preserves Lefebvre's spatial dialectic to capture the figuration of urban destruction as a collective injury.

Published in May 1941, *History Under Fire*, Cecil Beaton and James Pope-Hennessey's collaborative work on the first wave of air raids, aimed to "convey the early horror of the ruins."[54] In this version of the war gothic, a ruin points to both the material architectural damage and the assault on national histories archived in the buildings, neighborhoods, monuments, and urban spaces of the bombed city. Material destruction, then, never signifies only at the material level; as we have already seen, it becomes imbricated with bodily and physical injury. Here national history finds itself enumerated among the potential casualties of war.

The fifty-two photographs in *History Under Fire* contain no images of and no references to human casualties. As a visual record of decimated squares, churches, and shattered sculptures (including an image of an empty pedestal that once held Milton's statue), Beaton's stunning photographs register the scale and speed of London's ruination. Like Moore's and H. D.'s works, Pope-Hennessy's descriptions of destroyed Georgian houses that accompany Beaton's photographs employ their own biological poetics:

> Some of the finest of the houses *seem* like people who have given up hope: they have shrivelled into a handful of colourless lath and plaster . . . the rubbish *seems* to bear less relationship to a building than the most shrivelled skeleton to a full fleshed human

being. These familiar and symmetrical house fronts are revolting when they have been bombed. The brickwork *is* leprous. (102; emphasis added)

The houses "seem" like psychically broken, hopeless people; the rubbish "seems" as anonymous, lifeless, and diminished as a "shrivelled skeleton." Moving from a relation of semblance to something more properly metaphoric, the brickwork, bearing the discolorations of smoke and fire, "is" diseased and, presumably, has suffered irreversible damage. As historic buildings and private property, these Georgian houses extend the attacks from material objects to the histories and ideological investments they represent.

On one hand, passages like these locate *History Under Fire* within a larger trend of displacing injury from bodies to buildings; on the other, such images and textual commentary foreground English history, a history physically and monumentally embodied in London, as the primary casualty. Pope-Hennessey's running commentary seems intended to counter the dangers of historical erasure. After the preface, the reader uncovers a table of contents and, on the adjacent page, two juxtaposed images of London firefighters, the first from George I's reign and the second, depicting a fireman dousing a burning building during the Blitz, from George IV's besieged London. These images present in miniature the vocation of the book, which is to plot the present destruction of London within a longer cycle of British history. Pope-Hennessy's table of contents arranges Beaton's images of blitzed London into three historical periods: "The Attack on Medieval and Renaissance London"; "The Attack on Wren's London"; and lastly "The Attack on Hanoverian London." The epochal tone of the book's arrangement initiates its effort to counter what Pope-Hennessey identifies as the German strategy to "erase the dignified and treasured memory of a national past" (v). Each section pairs images of the war-scarred city with Pope-Hennessey's annotations and anecdotes, many of which seek to present the histories that threaten to disappear with their architectural markers.

Surveying St. Giles' Cripplegate, Pope-Hennessy admits that it was "never a very exciting church," but "it is chiefly for its associations that we must regret its demolition" (24). Those associations are immense. On the page adjacent to Pope-Hennessey's running commentary is a photograph of an empty pedestal where a statue of John Milton, who is buried at St. Giles', once stood. Pope-Hennessey inventories the other notable figures buried there: Elizabethan explorer Sir Martin Frobisher, sixteenth-century martyrologist John Foxe, and historian and mapmaker John Speed are all discussed. Their inclusion should be understood as an effort at national historical preservation. Turning attention to the Middle Temple Hall, we are reminded of its "international importance" as the place of the first production of Shakespeare's *Twelfth Night* (33). More than mere cataloguing, though, Pope-Hennessey supplements these moments of grave importance with wistful, imaginative recreations of that opening night:

> The end of the hall lighted by torches and candles, the gold-thread clothes and the trim spangles of the actors, the hollow music of viols from the minstrels' gallery, the intricate shadows cast by the carvings on the screen.... An attuned but drunken audience is watching this early incarnation of those deathless creatures Olivia, Orsino, Viola in her boy's clothes, Malvolio in his yellow garters, Maria, Aguecheeh, and Sir Toby Belch. (33)

He goes on to quote lines of dialogue and a song, all as a way to write down and preserve the national imagination once carried by these collapsed buildings.

Touring the other "periods" of London's history produces much of the same: the parish of St. Stephen Coleman Street is recalled for its historic connection to the Great Plague and for the documents of plague burials it once housed; the wreckage to the attic of Dr. Johnson's house in Hanoverian London receives some attention as we are reminded that this is where he put together his dictionary of the English language (this reminder is followed by more lively, imaginative scenes of Dr. Johnson talking with Boswell, writing Mrs. Thale, and confronting his own death with dignity). St. Paul's Cathedral is dubbed "the embodiment of English history for the last two centuries," and the damage to its east end is duly noted (82). Pope-Hennessy knows well that St. Paul's Cathedral bears the burden of a much longer historical memory. Folded within Beaton's image is another infernal scene—the Great Fire of London 1666 in which St. Paul's did not fare so well. Pope-Hennessy conjoins the two historical moments but then suppresses their relationship. On the one hand, we are told that Beaton's photographs "may prove as documentarily important as Hollar's engravings of the area devastated by the Fire of London in 1666" (vi). On the other hand, Pope-Hennessy suggests that the scale of destruction renders the parallel between the two events a "wholly false comparison" (3). Whereas bombs incinerate single buildings or small areas of the city, "the Fire of 1666 burned London medievalism to ashes in five days" (3). Although the Great Fire and the Blitz share a similar status as historical events, Pope-Hennessy counters the notion that the German bombers have erased the deep histories embedded in the cityscape itself.[55] When Pope-Hennessy ends his tour of damage done to London's architecture and history, he assures his reader of the city's enduring history: "The brunt of the *Blitzkrieg* has been borne by houses and streets that are not, from the historical angle, of great significance. It is a narrow, perhaps even an inhuman, viewpoint—but seen from it the bombers' attack upon our London past has failed."[56] On the surface, this appears to undermine the archival project of the book; why strive to preserve what is not threatened? Yet it completes the ideological work of the book: the accumulation of national history in the spaces, buildings, and monuments in London has endured the swift and sustained attacks of the German fleet.

Freighted and cathected with the nightmarish fears and anxieties of a nation, the ruins appear in one light as the objectification of a melancholic philosophy of history. And yet the suspension and potential dismantling of a social order also spurred utopian dreams. On a lengthy stroll through wartime London, Herbert Read surveyed the damages around St. Paul's Cathedral, the offices of the *Times*, and the Bank of England and made this very link: "But the ruins, I reflected, were not merely so much rubble and twisted steel. The endless and intricate structures of a civilization were falling down."[57] Many thought that the war would inadvertently lead to social revolution, one so violent that George Orwell declared in autumn of 1940 that "the London gutters will run with blood."[58] In his 1941 report on the efficiency of social services during the Blitz, Ritchie Calder concluded that the material destruction of the war effectively closed one phase of English history and, with it, an entire political structure: "An epoch went crashing down in the angry brown dust of crumbling property. The ruins of the Victorian town houses in the West End and the slums of the East End were apocalyptic; they were symbolic of the catastrophic End of an Age."[59] But these symbolic ruins were also forecasts of the world to come: "In the perspective of history, the Lesson of London may be that "Black Saturday," September 7, 1940, was as significant in its own way as Bastille Day, July 14, 1789."[60] Divining social revolution from the smoldering

ROADS OF THE FUTURE

■ "They shall beat their swords into ploughshares and their spears into pruning hooks." And out of the factories where bombers and fighters are now made will stream motor cars by the hundred thousand.

As our present system of roads is admitted to be inadequate, even for current requirements, it is certain that one of the very first items on the agenda for reconstruction will be the building of new and better roads to accommodate the increased traffic that must be expected in the future.

A network of great highways will be constructed to link up our important cities and towns with the capital. The purpose of these trunk roads will be to speed a nation on

wheels directly to its objective in the minimum of time with the maximum of safety but with due regard to the separate needs of different types of road user. It is not inconceivable that the petrol-driven car will be superseded by one controlled by radio. Aerials along the roadsides would provide the motive power with varying wavelengths for different destinations. Thus, if the first part of a journey is along radio road A.1, the car is tuned to the wavelength of that road, and if the ultimate

Pears

destination is along the A.3 road, then the car is retuned to the new wavelength when branching off from A.1.

Our post-war main roads will connect us with distant friends and relations; they will open up new ways of enjoying our leisure; they will lead us to better health through recreation and to a keener appreciation of our fellow countrymen through more frequent and more widespread travel.

The roads of the future will give much happiness and a wider outlook to every man, woman and child, while upon these broad highways the whole life of the nation will expand. The roads of the future lead straight into the dawn of a New Age.

FIGURE 4.10 "ROADS OF THE FUTURE," *LISTENER*, OCTOBER 23, 1941, 550.

THE TOWN OF THE FUTURE

■ There can be no doubt that our future towns will be as different from those we knew before the war as a radiogram is different from our first crystal set. And just as our admiration for the elegance and the greater efficiency of the modern does not in any way impair our affection for the old-fashioned, so we need have no regrets when we come to live in the town of the future.

Towns and cities damaged by the war are already considering their rebuilding plans. Residential districts, we are told, will be designed on the garden city principle of villas or semi-detached houses each with its own garden; or ten-storey blocks of flats surrounded by communal lawns, flower walks and rose arbours. It is gratifying to note that experts are planning for a 'green and pleasant land' with plenty of space, light and fresh air. In the past, towns and cities have straggled and sprawled, capturing parts of the countryside with the same inevitable disappointment as the caging of a wild bird. The town of the future will be erect and compact, with the trees, the grass and the flowers of the country-side brought to its front doors. Schools and playgrounds for the children will be included as an integral part of the communal plan. These will be so positioned that children will not have to cross main roads on their way to school. The Shopping Centre, in view of its supreme importance to housewives, will

Pears

receive very special attention. Architects, remembering the British climate, will develop the arcade principle for greater all-the-year-round convenience, specially appreciated on wet shopping days.

Ancient buildings will be restored and records and relics of a glorious past preserved. The town of the future will retain its cherished character, its unique individuality and its historical associations, yet it will sparkle and shine in its new pride.

New buildings, new services, new homes, rising up from the ruins of the old, will make for happier family life in Britain after the war. The better environment will invite us to make the most of our longer leisure and will encourage us to seek new interests within the pleasant, comfortable and healthy precincts of our new homes.

FIGURE 4.11 "THE TOWN OF THE FUTURE," *LISTENER*, OCTOBER 2, 1941, 454.

ruins, Calder's prophecy of a new democracy fit with a wave of utopian thinking that the rose out of the ashes of bombed England. A series of advertisements, for instance, from Pears toilet soap appearing in the *Listener* in 1941 addressed England's future reconstruction one part at a time. As announced in their "Roads of the Future" (figure 4.10) and "Towns of the Future" (figure 4.11), improved travel, more democratic and modern town planning, and faster, more sensible roadways will all form part of this utopic world.

Whether it is radio-controlled automobiles, visions of heightened travel and a deeply connected nation, or the building of arcades and communal neighborhoods, these futural visions all promise "much happiness" in the postwar world. A flurry of reports in the early years of the war attempted to make policy out of these utopic impulses. The Barlow Report of 1940 strove to equalize regional prosperity and growth while the Uthwatt Report in 1941 provided a plan for rebuilding bombed areas that would control speculation and profiteering by landowners.[61] The most widely read and debated of all these reports was the Beveridge Report (1942), which outlined the fundamentals of the future welfare state. In the first year of publication, 256,000 copies were sold to the public, and another 369,000 abridged versions found their way into eager hands. Public enthusiasm for these overtures of state planning and a more egalitarian democratic society led the *Daily Mirror* to declare the Beveridge Report as a "symbol of the new Britain."[62] As time wore on and as people gazed at the ruins, they dreamed of reconstruction in terms of dramatic social change. In the words of J. B. Priestley, England was being "bombed and burned into democracy."[63] The nightmare of the present heralded dreams of the near future.

INSECURE LIFE (3): UTOPIA, EXTINCTION, AND HISTORICAL RECURRENCE

So much talk of the future, so much planning for the world to come: the creative destruction envisioned by Priestley's ever popular BBC talks, corporate advertisements, and policy debates imagined the war as an epochal rupture clearing the way for a reinvigorated, more democratic postwar England. Such hopeful intimations of the world to come locate the war as one stage in a grand historical process, in some way reconstituting the very philosophy of history we saw come undone in Woolf's *The Years*. And yet, in a dialectical twist, the postwar world was as much a screen for barren futures as for more fecund utopias. Vera Brittain gazed at the "brutal changes in London's familiar face" and saw little more than sheer destruction: "These sinister phantoms of a vanished prosperity share no common quality with the planned demolitions of peacetime; they are ghosts raised by the haphazard onslaughts of modern war."[64] Brittain's ghosts signal a ruptured history, an abrupt halt to "prosperity." These "sinister phantoms" are witnesses to destruction without the promise of creation, the pure force of an unbridled negativity. Sharing little of *History Under Fire*'s pathos or affirmation, Brittain's remarks point to the vulnerability of centuries of English prosperity regardless of the war's outcome.

As a debt-riddled empire with devastated towns and cities, Britain's prolonged slide from atop the world-system would only be accelerated by the recovery and rebuilding efforts of the postwar period.[65] Brittain's worrisome meditations on the world to come has a more thoughtful, expanded counterpart in the Blitz fictions of Elizabeth Bowen, perhaps the Second World War's most accomplished writer of short fiction. Bowen's wartime short story collection *The Demon Lover and Other Stories* maps nineteenth-century gothic fiction's anxieties over class, inheritance, and property onto those utopic dreams of a more egalitarian and democratic postwar England.

Reading *The Demon Lover and Other Stories* usually means participating in one of two modes of historicization: either the immediate historical context of the Second World War governs interpretation or Bowen's stories are slotted within a longer tradition of Anglo-Irish gothic fiction that restores the Irish historical context to these stories.[66] Critics who privilege the former over the latter interpret the discontinuous, fragmentary nature of Bowen's stories as direct reflections of wartime distress.[67] For those working primarily in Irish studies, Bowen is something of an ascendancy modernist, to use Vera Kreilkamp's designation.[68] Bowen's fictions, regardless of geographical location, bear the traces of Irish history within their very textual patterns and formal structures.[69] Kreilkamp suggests that the gothic motifs in Bowen not only derive from the most renowned nineteenth-century practitioners—Charles Maturin, Joseph Sheridan Le Fanu, Bram Stoker—but, moreover, that the genre itself encodes a kind of terror particular to the ruling Anglo-Irish: "irregular lines of legitimacy and inheritance; miscegenation; victimized young women; animated ancestral portraits; sudden outbursts of violence; and, always, the imprisoning mythologies of the past."[70] These features indirectly express the protracted erosion of a system of property rights, wealth distribution, and inheritance that legitimated and ensured the ruling power of the Anglo-Irish. Because this particular strain of the gothic is "engaged in a reformation of the past, rather than as any revolutionary assault on a contemporary establishment," it hardly displays any of the subversive or politically antagonistic traits often assigned to the gothic.[71] And yet if this gothic, plagued and defined by a particular type of ascendancy guilt, seems to fit Bowen's biography and her "Irish" writing, it is not at all clear why it fits wartime England.

Rather than privilege one mode of historicization over the other, I suggest that bringing these two ways of reading in closer proximity allows us to see how the Anglo-Irish gothic mediates the Second World War. On my reading, Bowen's stories align the attendant political anxieties of the Anglo-Irish past with the yearnings for a more democratic, postwar British future. To read Bowen in this way, then, means that a genre initially suited for a dying settler colonial class is uniquely, if counterintuitively, appropriate for a bombed imperial metropole. In other words, Bowen's stories anticipate a historical recurrence of Anglo-Ireland's fate in postwar Britain. This recursive logic appears rather poetically in her remarks on dispossession in the October 1945 preface to the American edition of *The Demon Lover and Other Stories*. Bowen's descriptions of the wartime pressures that permeate her short stories construe the war as a process of dispossession, both of property and subjectivity. Bowen claims that the abnormality of wartime collapsed the distinction between author and citizen: "Arguably, writers are always slightly abnormal people. . . . In war, this feeling of slight differentiation was suspended."[72] "Writer" here should serve as a designation of apartness, of separation from the ordinary citizens and the masses in peacetime; the war permits no such separation. The very stories composing this volume, she says, were not her inventions, but rather that of "the overcharged subconsciousness of everybody. . . . It is because the general subconsciousness saturates these stories that they have an authority nothing to do with me."[73] This zone of indistinction between writer and ordinary, or "normal," citizen expands to encompass the entire population:

"sometimes I hardly knew where I stopped and everyone else began."[74] If "general subconsciousness" and permeable lines between the self and others suggests a new collectivity, a nascent mass less restricted by class, it is not something Bowen figures as emancipatory, and certainly not utopic. Rather, in Bowen's estimation it is an aftereffect of the physical devastation of property: "The violent destruction of solid things, the explosion of the illusion that prestige, power and permanence attach to bulk and weight, left all of us, equally, heady and disembodied. Walls went down; and we felt, if not knew, each other."[75] Bowen conjoins the loss of property and "solid things" with subjective erasure. Reading, writing, dreaming, and scavenging for lost objects all serve the same purpose in Bowen's preface: they restore "the communicative touch of personal life" and rescue the "I" that loses its material and immaterial boundaries in wartime.[76]

Equating subjectivity and its security with property ownership and guarded class divisions exposes how much Bowen's comprehension of daily life in the Second World War is rooted in her own experience and understanding of Anglo-Ireland's twilight years. The particular mode in which the British fought the Second World War—the flattening of class levels, the mobilization of all sectors of the population, the empowerment of the working classes—cast into sharp relief the inequitable distribution of property, wealth, and power in contemporary England, conditions that mirrored the asymmetrical economic and social relations of Anglo-Ireland during its troubled tenure and protracted demise. Bowen's war gothic, then, mediates between two historical moments, ultimately giving the events of the narrative present what Reinhart Koselleck terms "structural expressiveness within the framework of long periods."[77] Quite simply, the Anglo-Irish historical memory embedded in these stories offers a completed narrative of class decline that Bowen finds appropriate for, or approximate to, wartime and postwar England.

The titular story of *The Demon Lover and Other Stories* models the recursive temporality that I claim is so central to Bowen's version of the war gothic. The story opens with Mrs. Drover's return to her London home to fetch some remaining possessions and to assess the damage done by air raids. The opening scene paints Mrs. Drover's war-torn neighborhood in decidedly gothic tones: a "steamy, showery day" gives way to clouds "already piling up ink-dark, broken chimneys and parapets stood out."[78] The only witness to the ominous scene accompanying Mrs. Drover's arrival is a sole cat weaving "itself in and out of railings" (80). Against these staple materials of a gothic setting, the known and the familiar turn inside out, introducing a series of uncanny effects: "In her once familiar street, as in any unused channel, an unfamiliar queerness has silted up" (80). Mrs. Drover's house is a relic, a reminder of a life once lived, of a life interrupted and suspended by the war. This unhomely place bears "traces of her long former habit of life": smoke stains on the mantelpiece, traces of furniture moved away for storage, and "the bruise in the wallpaper" (80). This quick inventory of descriptions and plot devices—an abandoned house, a lone woman, encroaching night, the uncanny inversion of familiar places and things, an expertly paced sense of accumulated suspense—might suggest that all these recognizable gothic traits are easily transposed onto a metropolitan city under siege. "The Demon Lover," however, marshals the gothic for its particular ability to detect the afterlife of the past within the present moment.

The historical past first intrudes by way of a letter: it is without a postmark, has no return address, and, as far as Mrs. Drover can determine, it should never have found its way inside her house. Mystery and suspense are redoubled with Bowen's Radcliffe-like description of encroaching night: "the sun had gone in; as the clouds sharpened and lowered, the trees and rank lawns seemed already to smoke with dark. Her reluctance to look again at the letter came from the fact that she felt intruded upon—and by someone contemptuous of her ways. However, in the tenseness preceding the fall of rain she read it" (81). The letter, as we soon discover, is from Mrs. Drover's missing fiancé who disappeared in August 1916 while fighting in the First World War.

> Dear Kathleen,
>
> You will not have forgotten that to-day is our anniversary, and the day we said. The years have gone by at once slowly and fast. In view of the fact that nothing has changed, I shall rely upon you to keep your promise. I was sorry to see you leave London, but was satisfied that you would be back on time. You may expect me, therefore, at the hour arranged.
>
> Until then . . .
>
> K. (82)

She reacts to the letter with pure shock: "her lips, beneath the remains of lipstick, beginning to go white" (82). This is the shock of an impossible but nonetheless unavoidable return. On the literal level, an errant lover keeps his appointment; on the heavily freighted figural level, the first line of the letter, cast as it is in the future perfect, suggests that a potential, dormant event from the past has reached its moment of unfolding. The lover's promised arrival in the present marks the return of total war and shades the Second World War as a moment of repetition: the violence of the First World War returns in a more horrific, ghastly form in the Second World War.

Yet, if the future perfect tense marks a promise kept even beyond the bounds of life and death, the letter also induces a temporal break, a pivotal moment of narrative discontinuity that the story mirrors in its form. In narratological terms, the first narrative that carries the story forward in the present concludes with Mrs. Drover's shock, expressed in a series of questions and ultimately terminates with an ellipsis: "'The hour arranged. . . . My God,' she said, 'what hour? How should I . . . ? After twenty-five years. . . .'" (82–83). A textual space separates Mrs. Drover's present from the analepsis that moves the narrative back twenty-five years to August 1916. Here we see Mrs. Drover with K before he departs for his eventual disappearance, if not death, in the First World War. K asks his lover, who is clearly more disturbed than infatuated, to wait for him and, months later, K goes missing and is never found. The narrative accelerates and takes us through Kathleen's life, detailing what transpired in the years after K's disappearance, how she met William Drover, where they settled, how many children they had, and so on. When we catch up with the rattled Mrs. Drover in her vacated house, we find her musing over the letter's arrival and somewhat frantically planning her quick departure from London. This story famously ends with Mrs. Drover climbing in to a taxi only to realize that K is the driver. She screams and the taxi "made off with her into the hinterland of deserted streets" (87). With its conventional gothic scenery, its building of suspense, missed encounters, and the ghostly return of a lost lover, "The Demon Lover" adapts the most identifiable conventions of the gothic to the war city. But even more than this transposition of scenery and content into a war zone, what makes this story so exemplary of the war gothic is its temporal structure. The narrative rupture following the letter internalizes the "break in continuity that is virtually synonymous with the war itself" and the completed analepsis moves backward twenty-five years into the past in order to explain the terror of the letter and the strangeness of its appearance.[79]

What I am suggesting here is that "The Demon Lover" models two things: first, the horror and trauma of the First World War quite literally returns with the letter, establishing a line of continuity between the two wars that is not uncommon in the literature of the 1930s and 1940s; second, its narrative structure poses a break and goes on to chart a line of cause and effect between the past and the present moment, thereby restoring the continuum of history. The past returns to make sense of the present, or, at the very least, to account for what initially seems incomprehensible. Yet it is the conclusion of this story that marks the most salient feature of Bowen's war stories: even with linear time reconstituted and the explanatory power of narrative restored, the futures that await these characters are disastrous.

The narrative pattern similar to the one I've sketched out for "The Demon Lover" repeats throughout Bowen's war stories, and many of her characters find themselves consigned to similarly unwanted fates. Like the blank Henry Russel in "Sunday Afternoon," the psychologically wounded Gavin Doddington in "Ivy Gripped the Steps," the hopeless Clara Detter of "The Inherited Clock," and the abandoned, affectless daughter in "Songs My Father Sang Me," Mrs. Drover's unsettled past leads only to a grievous end. Perhaps more than the ruinous cityscape, menacing specters, and burdensome inheritances, the philosophy of history modeled by the narrative form of these stories—the recurrence and intensification of the past that leads inexorably to disaster—signals the persistence of the fear of civilizational decline and extinction that marked the Anglo-Irish gothic.[80] Neil Corcoran draws a similar conclusion regarding the employment of the gothic in Bowen's war stories and her "Irish" books, *The Last September* and *Bowen's Court*. "Bowen's discovery in *The Demon Lover and Other Stories*," he writes, "is that a mode of writing inherently appropriate to the circumstances of bombed-out London where, exactly, and as these stories again and again insist, people were feeling pushed to the side of their own former lives."[81] Indeed, in Bowen's other wartime book, *Bowen's Court*, she openly considers how the war years might have shaded the recollection and assemblage of her family's long history in Anglo-Ireland.[82] She notes in her afterword that the "urgency of the present . . . seems to communicate itself to one's view of the past. . . . The Past—private just as much as historical—seems to me now to matter more than ever: it acquires meaning; it loses false mystery. In the savage and austere light of a burning world, details leap out with significance."[83] And what are those details? How do the fears and fantasies of an anxious settler colonial class acquire, even transfer, meaning in the ongoing destruction of an imperial metropolis? Bowen gives us a window onto this odd convergence in her narration of the death of Henry Bowen III, the builder of her family's big house, Bowen's Court.

A popular and highly social man, Henry III was, on Bowen's account, not exactly the most learned or culturally discerning of her ancestors. And yet Bowen's reflections on his death, as well as the inheritance he assumed and expected to pass along in perpetuity, tout his livelihood and its legacy against the liberal and cosmopolitan virtues that would come to signify the *absolut moderne*:

> Henry, a pre-eminently social figure, lived in a Philistine, snobbish, limited and on the whole pretty graceless society. But he got somewhere, and lived to die in his drawing-room surrounded by hosts of children and the esteem of what looked like a lasting order. And to what did our fine feelings, our regard for the arts, our intimacies, our inspiring conversations, our wish to be clear of the bonds of sex and class and nationality, our wish to try to be fair to everyone bring us? To 1939.[84]

Property, genealogy, and clear lines of inheritance ensure continuity and ground a "lasting order" for Bowens past and present. It was the final soundings of these Burkean notes that made *The Last September* so poignant; the same concerns resurface in *The Demon Lover and Other Stories*.[85] The "burning world" of England at the dawn of the 1940s and the near-extinction of the Anglo-Irish merge into a constellation where the past is legible in terms of the present moment; in turn, that present is understood, and indeed narrated, as another iteration, even amplification, of an eclipsed era's fraught hopes. The repetition, then, exceeds even the existential malaise that Corcoran identifies; it is equally, if not more so, one of structural recurrence. The two situations are not "like" or "equal" or "similar" to one another at all, but, in Walter Benjamin's terms, the violent end of Anglo-Irish power achieves the "now of a particular recognizability" in war-torn England.[86]

The alignment of one past moment with the present is precisely what is at stake in two stories—"The Happy Autumn Fields" and "Sunday Afternoon"—that imagine the war city through Ireland past and present. "The Happy Autumn Fields" alternates between two narrative sequences, two autumnal moments: one follows a nineteenth-century Anglo-Irish family and another focuses on a young couple in wartime London. While cleaning out her bombed London apartment, Mary uncovers a box of letters and photographs that tells the story of this nineteenth-century family. The material from this scattered archive, particularly as it relates to the two young sisters, Sarah and Henrietta, migrates into Mary's dreams where she watches the family and the sisters' struggles unfold in her deep slumber. The story opens in the middle of one of Mary's dreams. We see an orderly family procession moving across County Cork with Papa at the head and his children and nephew in tow. The harvest has been bountiful and, to his pleasure, his oldest daughter is set to marry. These early images of family order and continuity are reinforced with the arrival of Fitzgeorge, the sure heir to the estate, who later sits atop the procession, figuring his future position as family patriarch and, indeed, ensuring the continuity of the estate into the next generation. Yet these images of continuity and duration are arrayed against tragic anticipations that loom large over this first narrative sequence: rooks, crows whose appearance have long foretold death, hover over the Anglo-Irish family as they march in procession through newly harvested fields; the two young sisters briefly consider visiting the cottage of a dying neighbor whose death will be followed by the slow decay of his property; finally, sitting in the family home, Sarah strangely apprehends that "the seconds were numbered," forecasting not only the imminent death of her suitor, Eugene, but her and her sister's untimely deaths and, to be sure, the end of the Anglo-Irish way of life her father, like Henry Bowen III, expected to endure.[87]

The second narrative follows Mary, who drifts in and out of sleep in her bomb-damaged apartment, ostensibly conjuring the scenes of Sarah and Henrietta in her dreams. Bowen's narration, however, implies that these historical eras are linked by more than Mary's dreams. The first indication that the nineteenth-century tale is not a discrete story comes by way of a pronominal shift. As we watch Sarah and Henrietta bring up the rear of their family procession, we find their childish jokes and games interrupted with the arrival of Sarah's suitor, Eugene. The shy and timid flirtation between the two distresses Henrietta and, in an echo of Philomela, she transforms her pain into song: "At the other side of the horse, Henrietta began to sing. At once her pain, like a scientific ray, passed through the horse and Eugene to penetrate Sarah's heart."[88] The accumulating tension between the sisters culminates in an abrupt shift in the narrative voice from an apparent detached omniscience to "we," insinuating that Mary has joined Sarah and Henrietta: "We surmount the skyline: the family come into our view, we into theirs."[89] The newly minted "we," and in particular the ghostly and as yet unnamed Mary, pleads with Sarah to "stop oh stop Henrietta's heartbreaking singing! Embrace her close again! Speak the only possible word! Say—oh, say what? Oh, the word is lost!"[90] This moment of urgency, of Henrietta's pending emotional injury, ends abruptly but nevertheless carries the narrative forward into the present. Muttering "Henrietta . . . " as she awakens, Mary is pulled from her dream after her hand strikes the corner of a table. As Phyllis Lassner points out, Mary's physical pain is both a manifestation and continuation of Henrietta's; but more than that, this narrative transition suggests a binding link of shared histories and fates between these two eras.[91]

As the story oscillates between 1940s England and 1800s Ireland, Mary intrudes yet again on the scene of Sarah's family. Back in her family's household, Sarah reveals that she cannot remember anything that occurred beyond the moment when the first narrative broke and shifted to Mary's awakening:

> She drew a light little gold chair into the middle of the wreath of carpet, where no one ever sat, and sat down. She said: "But since then I think I have been asleep."
>
> "Charles the First walked and talked half an hour after his head was cut off," said Henrietta mockingly. Sarah in anguish pressed the palms of her hands together upon a shred of geranium leaf.
>
> "How else," she said, "could I have had such a bad dream?"
>
> "That must be the explanation!" said Henrietta.
>
> "A trifle fanciful," said Mamma.[92]

The sequencing of Sarah's memory loss with Mary's first awakening pairs with Sarah's uncustomary behavior of sitting "where no one ever sat," all but erasing the lines between Sarah and Mary. At first glance, it could very well be the case that Mary is dreaming Sarah and animating the entire scene. Yet Sarah's return in the present complicates any such dream thesis. When the story first transitions to the present and Mary awakens, she is quite possibly an embodiment of Sarah:

Frantic at being delayed here, while the moment awaited her in the cornfield, she all but afforded a smile at the grotesquerie of being saddled with Mary's body and lover. Rearing up her head from the bare pillow, she looked, as far as the crossed feet, along the form inside which she found herself trapped: the irrelevant body of Mary, weighted down to the bed, wore a short black modern dress, flaked with plaster.[93]

The dress appears "modern" only through the nineteenth-century gaze of Sarah; the body is foreign and "Mary's" alone. There isn't much on the literal level that accounts for this episode, but its figural effects are manifold. The invasion, or haunting or perhaps even possession, of Mary's body by Sarah shatters the historical distance between the two narratives and marks the return of that past moment within the present. When we learn toward the end of the story that Sarah, Henrietta, and Eugene all died young, we are invited to think how their tragedy might be Mary's and, more broadly, how the fate awaiting the Anglo-Irish might be recurring at the very moment that Mary passes in and out of sleep as her house is rocked by distant bombs.

In this way the ghosts of Anglo-Ireland have become the ghosts of 1940s England. By aligning the autumn of one form of rule with that of another, the figural language of the gothic accrues its explanatory power. Here, the tragic end of the nineteenth-century family and their world parallels London in the present. The "discovery," then, of *The Demon Lover and Other Stories* is that a recharged gothic aligns an already concluded historical drama with another proceeding toward its denouement at a different historical moment.[94] Like the tales of sinister uncles or vampires of the nineteenth-century Anglo-Irish gothic, Bowen's stories function as expressions of property loss, class leveling, and a coming redistribution of wealth and power. The anxieties and fears of inexorable structural change that made the Anglo-Irish gothic "the political unconscious of Anglo-Irish society" repeat in Bowen's stories to mark a decisively mournful orientation toward the postwar world.[95] One early indication of that form comes from a famous and oft-quoted editorial from the *Times* on July 1, 1940. A future postwar democracy should prioritize social organization and economic planning over individualism, collective equality over individual liberty, and a "new order [that] cannot be based on the preservation of privilege, whether the privilege be that of a country, of a class, or of an individual."[96] Property, land, and income redistribution signaled a new social order and, quite possibly, a paradigmatic shift in what it might mean to be a citizen in a new democracy organized around a welfare state. As we have seen up to this point, the disarticulation of property ownership from the value of citizenship permeating political discourse registers itself in Bowen's fictions as ontological crisis. This may very well be why the emotional inertia and psychological ruin of so many of her characters is bound to places that signify recent historical pasts where their lives were less scattered, less damaged. The coastal house in "Ivy Gripped the Steps," the apartment in "In the Square," the villa in "Sunday Afternoon," and Mrs. Drover's foreboding, bombed house in "The Demon Lover" are all what Bowen called "indestructible landmarks in a destructible world," but they are also relics of lost forms of life that, in Declan Kiberd's words, "may survive the death of their contents."[97]

For Bowen, then, the end of the Anglo-Irish way of life was partially the result of a revolutionary push by the Irish rebels. Maud Ellmann describes Bowen's sense that it was "the clash between the past embalmed in the Big House, and the future imagined by the rebels, that cause[d] the present to erupt into flame."[98] The incineration of the Big Houses and the redistribution of land and property accelerated the degeneration of a social order, its manners and values, and the power it both symbolized and ensured. Casting a glance back at her own family, Bowen remembers how "their natures shifted direction . . . when property could no longer be guaranteed."[99] The final story I want to consider briefly, "Sunday Afternoon," is about living without such guarantees. On a visit to old friends in neutral Ireland, Henry Russell is welcomed as a storyteller from the war zone across the sea: he is expected to tell about his experiences but to include "nothing dreadful."[100] Henry's role quickly changes from storyteller to artifact, from subject to object. He acknowledges that his London flat was bombed and all his possessions destroyed. Again, property loss and ontological ruin go hand in hand. Ria Store suggests he is too resigned to such loss and Sir Isaac hints at a deeper change. "'One cannot help look at you,' said Sir Isaac. 'You must forgive our amazement. But there was a time, Henry, when I think we all used to feel that we knew you well.'"[101] Henry only responds that his experience is one among many and that he is "very glad to remain. To exist."[102] Existence without one's possessions, though, is not life in any recognizable sense to an audience shielded from the violence of the war. "I wonder how much of you has been blown to blazes," asks Ria Store, marshaling the language of material destruction to ponder Henry's diminished existence.[103] Dispossessed and propertyless, Henry can no longer be said to live at all; he simply remains.

Bowen's story casts Henry's dispossession and his part in a collective experience of loss as subjective erasure; his is an existence without a form of life. Henry is effectively caught between two generations: the past of Mrs. Vesey and his old Irish friends and the younger Maria who desperately wishes to become part of history and participate in the war. Maria's arrested development in this vestige of Irish aristocracy is familiar enough in Bowen's work, but wartime England offers no options for an alternative future either. Henry tells the upstart youth that her arrival in London will lead her to a fate not unlike his own; she will not find herself the historical agent she imagines: "You may think action is better—but who will care for you when you only act? You will have an identity number, but no identity."[104] Henry declares his desire to return to the life he had among his Irish friends even though such a return is impossible. With a slip of the tongue, he calls Maria Miranda "presumably because she is compelled to leave the magic island and to confront a brave new world of fire and blood."[105] Henry cannot return to the charmed life of neutral Ireland, and Maria faces either perpetual stasis in Ireland or, like Henry, subjective erasure in the war. Henry's nostalgia for the remnants of an all but extinguished past and Maria's desire for an impossible future sketches out an historical trajectory in generational terms: "half-old" Henry is dispossessed and desubjectified, fit neither for the world that made him nor for the one to come; Maria's ebullience will go nowhere in a deteriorated Anglo-Irish world, and she faces reduction in the world of action.[106] For Bowen, Maria and Henry continue without roles in this unfolding historical epoch; their active participation, or the simple desire for active participation, secures nothing for them. Stasis or erasure, closed pasts or impossible futures: "Sunday Afternoon" lays bare the ontological and temporal parameters of obsolete life in the postwar world. Bowen's wartime fictions lament the old economic and social order of imperial Britain that surely will not survive the war, regardless of its outcome. In Bowen's hands, stories of unsettled pasts and ghostly returns are anxious ruminations on the near future, distress signals from the world to come.

LATE MODERNISM'S LIVING DEAD

Two years after the war Bowen spoke of her admiration for H. Rider Haggard's imperial gothic romance novel *She*. Although she was initially swept up by the "soaring unrealism" of Haggard's tale, Bowen "found something reassuring and comforting in the idea that, whatever happened, buildings survived people."[107] "Mysterious Kôr," the last wartime story Bowen authored, clips its title from Haggard's novel. The bombed city is an extinct scene and, like Kôr itself, an imperial ruin. Two lovers, Pepita and Arthur, wander through moon-bleached London, gazing at "cratered" and "brittle" London.[108] Pepita mutters "Mysterious Kôr" to her lover and cites a few lines from Andrew Lang's ode to Haggard.[109] Pepita imagines Kôr as a refuge from the ravages of historical time; its apartness from the bombed cityscapes of 1945 London suggests other possible futures: "This war shows we've by no means come to the end. If you can blow whole places out of existence, you can blow whole places into it."[110] At first sight, Pepita's conjuring of Kôr signals a form of futurity free of the disaster of Bowen's other stories. Yet in Haggard's *She* Kôr is a dead imperial city. In the logic of Bowen's story, Kôr's imperial decline rhymes with contemporary England and offers an image of its postwar, postimperial future. In the final pages of Bowen's story, Pepita sleeps like a "mummy rolled half over" and dreams her way into the timeless preserves of Kôr.[111] She wanders among its empty streets and monuments and looks down on the city from a terrace. Bowen knows well that these consolations exist only in the realms of dream and fantasy. This late war story ends on a note of solemn resignation and, perhaps, imperial nostalgia.

And yet many would awaken to a new postwar world order. What *had* been bombed into existence? The types of insecurity that the war gothic expresses—individual and collective vulnerability, fragile national histories, precarious imperial futures—did not magically disappear after 1945. Air war and the atomic age placed island immunity far in the past for the British Isles; financial strain, decolonization, and the transition to an American-centered world-system ensured that British reconstruction would not merely be an affair of going back to the way things were before the war. In the decades after 1945, nationalist movements in the empire pushed for more autonomy and independence; Caribbean migrants, many of whom fought in the war, arrived on British shores, inaugurating what Jamaican poet Louise Bennett unforgettably called "colonizin' in reverse."[112] Something had indeed been bombed into existence; if a shift in the world-system engendered melancholic loss in Bowen, it offered new political possibilities for former and soon-to-be-former colonies. The next chapter looks into these emergent worlds and the changing textures and anxieties of everyday life initiated by decolonization and migration.

5

"IT IS DE AGE OF COLONIAL CONCERN"

VERNACULAR FICTIONS AND POLITICAL BELONGING

THIS CHAPTER CLIPS its title from a barbershop scene in George Lamming's 1954 novel *The Emigrants*. A West Indian barber in London converses with an African client about decolonization:

> "Tis the war for actual life that matter," he said. He spoke through the smoke of the cigarette which was almost burning into his lips. "The main historical point of dis age is dis." He took his hand from the man's head, and pinched the butt out of his mouth. "It is de age of colonial concern."[1]

From the perspectives of those who had labored in peripheral and semiperipheral zones of the global economy, the age of colonial concern could only have appeared as "the main historical point" in the years following the Second World War. The twin phenomena of decolonization and mass migration from the colonies to Britain triggered new mechanisms of imperial sovereignty at the very moment that, in Giovanni Arrighi's words, "the redistribution of assets from Britain to the United States . . . hastened the change in leadership in systemic processes of capital accumulation."[2] Britain struggled to hold on to some of its geopolitical influence by transforming its empire into a more manageable commonwealth, one that would decrease the financial burden of imperial administration but also retain some international influence in a world splitting into American and Soviet spheres. Yet emerging nation states, regional formations like the ill-fated West Indies Federation, and the commonwealth were not just new techniques to retain or dissolve assets: these organizations all presented different ideas of political belonging.[3] And yet political belonging was far more than an abstract legal or political problem. For those in the colonies and those migrating to British shores, the stakes could not have been higher. Who belonged and what belonging meant was equal to "the war for actual life."

While this final chapter takes up broadly the concerns voiced by Lamming's West Indian barber, I want to suggest that *how* one articulates the "main historical point" is as important as the point itself. In what follows, I address a cluster of novels that rely on invented vernaculars to describe the changing shape of political belonging in the decade and a half after the Second World War. In writers as different as Vic Reid, Samuel Selvon, and Colin MacInnes, experimentation with vernacular affords two things. First, these vernacular fictions, like the late modernist works I have examined throughout the preceding chapters, mediate between everydayness and geopolitical disorder. More specifically, they form a relationship between the figurations of political belonging happening in the spheres of political theory, legislative debate, and the mass media and the everyday lives of marginalized and dispossessed populations. Second, by contrasting stigmatized and local forms of speech with the Standard English of those "higher" spheres, these novels focus attention on the very processes by which belonging is figured. In Vic Reid's *New Day*, Samuel Selvon's *The Lonely Londoners*, and Colin MacInnes's *Absolute Beginners*, those figural processes have very real, very material effects. All of these novels openly stage conflicts between Standard English and multiple vernaculars. These confrontations often come by way of familiar modernist techniques—juxtaposition, interior monologue, stream of consciousness, and code-switching. Their vernaculars figure the lived experiences of colonial and migrant populations as sites where the constraints and possibilities of political belonging come into being.

Before examining how these vernacular fictions configure problems of political belonging, it is worth recalling the longstanding relationship between modernist innovation and vernacular. Studies by Michael North and Joshua Miller attribute the linguistic developments of modernist writing to an encounter with politically charged vernaculars. In North's story of modernist evolution, "vernacular and dialect distortions of the language are a resource to be mined."[4] The experiments of T. S. Eliot, Gertrude Stein, Jean Toomer, and others develop from their conscious attention to the adversarial, nonnormative position of these vernaculars. As Evelyn Nien-Ming Ch'ien and Matthew Hart have shown, this phenomenon extends beyond Anglo-American modernism. Ch'ien's *Weird English* traces a line of flight from "a tradition begun by James Joyce, William Faulkner, Gertrude Stein, Louis Chu, T. S. Eliot, and others" to Irvine Welsh, Derek Walcott, and Lois-Ann Yamanaka.[5] Stressing the political valence of transnational vernacular writing, Hart emphasizes the unavoidable, perhaps irresolvable tensions between the local and the global that pulsate in the poetry of English, American, Scottish, West Indian, and African American writers.[6] Taken together, these accounts not only prioritize the innovative force of vernacular writing but they also suggest to us that modernism has flexible spatial and temporal boundaries.

But there is more to this critical trajectory than its expanding transnational focus. The literary histories of North, Miller, Ch'ien, and Hart disclose a dialectical process underwriting twentieth-century experimental literature: in the early part of the century, high modernism develops out of an attraction to, and appropriation of, the technical and oppositional dimensions of African American vernaculars; as modernism consolidates into an identifiable literary historical object, migrant, postcolonial, and transnational writers self-consciously employ modernist forms while drawing on their own vernacular languages and cultural practices. For these later writers, vernacular functions simultaneously as the expression of lived experience among a group at a particular time and place and also as a seemingly endless resource for aesthetic invention.

Contemporary critics and reviewers typically overlooked the linguistic innovation of Reid's, Selvon's, and MacInnes's novels. Although these novels were roundly praised, they were valued for their objective recording of vernacular speech. In 1949 Zora Neale Hurston reviewed Reid's *New Day* for the weekly book review of the *New York Herald Tribune*. She praised the "commendable objectivity" with which Reid treated Jamaican history: "the author relates things as they actually happened."[7] Reid "flavors his narrative with the colorful idiom of the island," affirming the historical authenticity of his novel.[8] Selvon and MacInnes received similar treatment by British and West Indian readers alike. Their vernacular novels established them as cultural authorities.[9] Ruth Glass's 1960 home ethnography *Newcomers: The West Indians in London* marshaled Selvon's fiction as an authoritative source on West Indian life. As James Procter notes, Selvon's vernacular was "entirely referential for these early critics."[10]

MacInnes emerged as an authority on youth culture and Afro-Caribbean life in Britain around the same time.[11] He penned articles for *Lilliput, Encounter,* and *The Twentieth Century,* among others, hoping to disabuse readers of any anxieties they harbored about these seemingly new groups. MacInnes's cultural authority was reaffirmed by the reception of *Absolute Beginners.* When Stuart Hall reviewed *Absolute Beginners* in *Universities and Left Review* in 1959, he praised the novelist for his recreation of youth vernacular and for his keen observations of the daily lives of teenagers. Most revealing is the fact that the review pairs MacInnes with three other texts about the teenage and youth phenomenon: two memoirs of public education (E. R. Braithwaite's *To Sir, With Love* and Margareta Hamerschlag-Berger's *Journey Into a Fog*) and a sociological pamphlet on youth spending power (Mark Abrams's *The Teenage Consumer*). Grouping MacInnes's novel with three other nonfiction accounts on postwar youth culture signals how much the novel's value resides in its perceived fidelity to actuality. Indeed, Hall begins his discussion of the novel by measuring its language against the realities of everyday youth culture: "The hero of Colin MacInnes' *Absolute Beginners* comes straight at us . . . with a flow and authenticity which marks the book as an excellent and distinguished piece of social documentary. The book asks to be tested against 'life'—and this is no mean accomplishment."[12] Like Reid's and Selvon's novels, the success of *Absolute Beginners* is measured by its fidelity to the speech forms and cultural practices of the populations it treats.

Yet none of these writers set out to be social documentarians or "realist" novelists. In part, they all aimed to draw attention to the way vernaculars shape and portray daily experience. If vernacular was a unique way to present everyday experience, it does not follow that their projects were entirely anthropological. Perhaps the most glaring evidence of this is the simple fact Reid, Selvon, and MacInnes did not employ actually existing vernaculars. Reid and Selvon forged their own literary vernaculars from West Indian speech but consciously transformed those vernaculars. Both Reid and Selvon adjusted the Caribbean vernaculars they knew well. On several occasions, Selvon openly declared that *The Lonely Londoners* uses a "modified version" of a West Indian vernacular, one that no West Indian actually spoke.[13] By his own admission, his "intention was not primarily to be realistic."[14] MacInnes's youthful, proto-mod vernacular was not even modified; it was his own fabrication, as indicated in the pages of "expressions" he kept in a notebook during the writing of *Absolute Beginners*.[15]

Vernacular works that refuse to replicate actual speech are, as Dohra Ahmad puts it, "works of art, not of reportage."[16] The shift from mimetic recording to literary invention also signals a shift in how these texts operate. The "accomplishment" of these novels is not a question of how they reflect or represent the quotidian worlds of marginalized populations. Their vernaculars expose, and perhaps negate, the very figural procedures by which those worlds acquire public visibility. As we will see, this partially explains why they all seem preoccupied with contrasting the figurative power of everyday speech with official discourse emanating from the mass media, imperial administrators, and the state.

How exactly do these works disclose these figural procedures? To read these texts at the most basic level, one must learn the speech patterns and rhythms, the vocabulary and shared expressions that name and define these worlds. And while these fictions participate in the longer dialectical unfolding of modernism that Ch'ien and Hart map out, they do not exhibit the difficulty of Hugh MacDiarmid's or Braithwaite's poetry or the fiction of writers such as Ken Saro-Wiwa or Irvine Welsh. These vernaculars do not so much shock or alienate as they invite readers to become familiar with the way their quotidian worlds are enunciated and constructed. Rather than using vernacular to ethnographically record or aesthetically alienate, the goal of these novels is to familiarize the reader with their story worlds without altogether eliminating the strangeness and difference the vernacular carries with it.

This vernacular aesthetic enacts what George Lamming calls "a way of seeing." In *The Pleasures of Exile* Lamming pits the habitual ways of seeing developed in colonial cultures against the West Indian writer's use of language. "I do believe," he writes, "that what a person thinks is very much determined by the way that person sees."[17] For West Indians, colonialism was both a material fact and the dominant way of seeing. Lamming records with some surprise the reaction of a Trinidadian civil servant gazing at a white English worker as he tugs their ship into the dock:

> In spite of films, in spite of reading Dickens—for he would have had to at the school which trained him for the Civil Service—in spite of all this received information, this

man never really felt, as a possibility and a fact, the existence of the English worker. This sudden bewilderment had sprung from his *idea* of England; and one element in that *idea* was that he was not used to seeing an Englishman working with his hands in the streets of Port-of-Spain. (25–26)

Everyday life in Port-of-Spain presents an idea of England, a particular way of seeing it that trumps even Dickens's famous tales of labor and poverty. In the colony, white Englishmen occupied positions of power, and, for that civil servant, the asymmetry of the colonial relation was normative; it was the background against which other things occurred. Here we have an educated man who, despite knowing from films and novels that white Englishmen labored and suffered, still experiences shock at the very sight of a white man working.

For Lamming, there is considerable urgency in identifying and altering this way of seeing: "for what is at stake is the historic result of our thinking; what is under tragic scrutiny is our traditional way of seeing" (63). Among other things, traditional ways of seeing have shaped the intellectual foundations of the West Indian and are responsible for the population's "reluctance in asking for complete political freedom" (35). Writing accrues special value because it repossesses the language of the colonizer and transforms "the very structure, the very basis of his [the West Indian's] values" (36). Lamming rehabilitates Caliban as the aesthetic and political model for the West Indian writer.[18] There are two points to make about Lamming's return to Caliban. First, the acquisition of "Prospero's weapons" and the refusal to seek permission for their use is an outright declaration of authority. As Frantz Fanon reminds us, to speak a language properly is to wield authority; to speak that language differently may diminish the speaker's authority and, in the case of a Caribbean vernacular, place that speaker's origins and frames of reference elsewhere, beyond the cultural and geographical boundaries of the "home" country.[19] Because vernacular writing is a claim for narrative authority, it is inescapably political. More specifically, such writing claims for itself a zone of experience, a form of everyday life, that standard and authorized versions of English leave unseen. Caliban's use of language, in the words of Mary Lou Emery, is "inseparable from . . . Caliban's acquisition of the power to see."[20] Transformation at the level of language transforms a way of seeing. In Rancière's parlance, vernacular redistributes the sensible and opens the way for the unseen and the unsaid.[21]

The second point of Lamming's return to Caliban is this: he is not just advocating for the inclusion of minority writers who have proved capable of mastering the colonizer's tongue. This is why he states on more than one occasion that he is not concerned with what "the West Indian novel has brought to English writing" but with what it has "contributed to English reading" (44). Instead, Lamming directly implicates the institution of literature in the social struggles of Britain's black citizens and residents. For Lamming, literature and the three novels I take up here compel us to ask how Caliban's manipulation and mastery of language has made legible the damages of a certain way of seeing.

But can novels do more than just critique? That is, can they authorize alternative ways of seeing? Responses to such questions were already taking shape in the writers that Lamming praises (Selvon and Reid among them). But we should also acknowledge the climate in which Lamming poses these questions and seeks answers. If there is a feverish urgency that accompanies these remarks from Lamming, especially those in his "A Way of Seeing" essay, it emanates from the upsurge in racial violence aimed at West Indians at the end of the 1950s. During the Notting Hill riots of 1958, which I will discuss in more detail with MacInnes, Teddy Boys and white gangs openly attacked and terrorized black citizens, businesses, and residences. When recounting his first poetry reading at the Institute of Contemporary Art (ICA), he reminds his readers of the ICA's geographical proximity to Notting Hill. By pairing the sanitized halls of high culture with the scene of racial violence, Lamming implies that the cultivation of a way of seeing in one space might be continuous with that in another.

For Lamming, racial violence engendered its own way of seeing for Britain's black citizens, which he likens to the air raid anxiety of the 1940s:

After the sirens of Notting Hill had given their warning, I experienced a change in my curiosity about English people who were walking towards me. I didn't live in England during the war, but I imagine it is a feeling you might have had in the early stages of the bombing. The planes might not have been in the sky; but the warning had somehow geared your attention to expect something from above. You might look up, quicken your step; or in a moment of exaggerated anticipation, miss your step, increase your speed, or wonder where the nearest air raid shelter might be. All this could happen without any actual warning that the Germans were on their way. Similarly with me after the sirens of Notting Hill. (79)

And if these crippling feelings of racial terror were particularly acute for the black community in England, Lamming argues that "racial antagonism in Great Britain is, after Notting Hill, an atmosphere and a background against which my life and yours are being lived. Our duty is to find ways of changing the root and the perspectives of that background, of dismantling the accumulated myth, both cultural and political, which an inherited and uncritical way of seeing has now reinforced" (66). The task for West Indian writers was to expose this way of seeing and to link it directly with those spheres of cultural life that might appear at first blush to be disconnected.

Lamming makes that very link when he declares "the West Indian who was murdered in Notting Hill is an eternal part of the writing Caliban" (63). He refers here to the other specter of racial violence haunting these meditations on seeing, thinking, and language: Kelso Cochrane. Cochrane was an Antiguan carpenter who was stabbed to death by white youths within a year of the Notting Hill riots of 1958. Lamming's references to knives conjures Cochrane's ghost within the safe space of the ICA. He tells us that even during the row over a poet's attack on T. S. Eliot, there were "no knives" although the atmosphere was reminiscent of Notting Hill (63). At another point Lamming confirms that "knives are too messy for the ICA." (83). These references invite readers to think how the way of seeing that led to Cochrane's murder might echo in the ICA. For Lamming, changing a way of seeing is a duty and West Indian writers have a responsibility to link seemingly disparate cultural and social worlds.

The way of seeing that frames racial paranoia and led to Cochrane's murder is precisely what Lamming enjoins West Indian writers to change through their experimentation with form, speech, perspective, and content. Yet perhaps it is the famous photograph of Cochrane's funeral procession that captures a moment of collective seeing and, indeed, collective bewilderment. A crowd of 1,200 people gathered in the streets and mourned a man they never knew. The procession stretched nearly a quarter of a mile.[22] Edward Pilkington reports that "after the service the crowd remained for a long time by the graveside, wrapped in silence."[23] Cochrane's death punctuated nearly fifteen years of "unprecedented change in the nature of British society."[24] His death illustrated the grim, very real consequences for black immigrants living in a nation where their legal membership did not translate into political belonging. Those mourners lining up on the sides of the street, peering out of windows and doorways, gazed at a postwar world that scarcely resembled the wartime dreams of a more democratic, egalitarian Britain. Was England now home to the same vicious racial antagonisms common in the United States and South Africa? Whether they were mournful, bewildered, or shocked, did this crowd know what it was seeing? What I am suggesting is that these questions of seeing and its material effects underwrite the vernacular fictions of Selvon, Reid, and MacInnes. All scrutinize *and* enact ways of seeing that permeate multiple facets of daily life in the colonies and in the metropole. These writers use vernacular to make visible the figural procedures that shape the very concept of political belonging. In these fictions, everyday life becomes the scene where those damaging figurations divorce the rights, obligations, and privileges of citizenship from actual belonging, leaving one sector of the population exposed to multiple forms of discrete and brute violence.

VERNACULAR HISTORIES: VIC REID'S *NEW DAY*

Lamming praised the fiction of Reid and Selvon for restoring the perspectives and speech of peasants who "simply don't respond and see like middle-class people."[25] Both writers, he claimed, used "the peasant tongue," or the vernacular, to recreate a way of seeing that might enable the urgent conceptual changes that Lamming agitates for in his own writing. In Reid's 1949 *New Day*, indigenous narrators and characters feel the pressures of imperial rule on their daily lives. The broader process of decolonization is mediated through multiple forms of English that compete for narrative authority. The very title of Reid's novel emblematizes the perception that the disorder in the world-system that so troubled the historical novels of Woolf and Isherwood was also an opportunity for greater political autonomy. As Anne Spry Rush writes, "in the 1940s and 1950s it was by no means certain that the bulk of Britain's colonial possessions would soon be independent, nor was it obvious how limited Britain's power in the international arena would become."[26]

Yet there were signs that the balance of power between Britain and the anglophone Caribbean was changing. Jamaica received a new constitution in 1944 that granted universal suffrage and transferred power to its legislature.

Trinidad and other Caribbean nations were not far behind. The acquisition of more political control for the colonies and former colonies also served as a means for the British to maintain imperial authority and influence. The Jamaican constitution, for example, preserved British executive authority, ensuring "that British officials rather than nationalist politicians remained in control."[27] This transitional moment in the world-system, then, was simultaneously an effort by the peoples of the anglophone Caribbean to secure more political power while the British state sought new administrative techniques to manage and control these territories.

New Day appears at the very moment when the relationship between national consciousness, a newly fabricated and heavily promoted "West Indian" regional identity, and the commonwealth was very much in flux. Reid's novel formulates one way to think through these emergent forms of political belonging. By recounting these experiences in the vernacular, Reid seizes the narrative authority to figure that relationship, to adjust the scale of this transition in global sovereignty with everyday life. *New Day* make us aware of the acts of figuration that construe relations between peoples, locales, and intertwined but competing desires. Ultimately, this novel knows that Jamaica's postcolonial future depends on how one sees the present.

New Day is a historical novel narrated entirely in a Jamaican vernacular. Readers will find this tale bookended by an author's note that provides some historical background to the Morant Bay rebellion as well as an outright declaration that he has not "by any means attempted a history of the period 1865 to 1944," and by a dictionary of Jamaican dialect.[28] In between this paratextual apparatus, Reid weaves a tale of emergent national consciousness focalized through John Campbell, who lived through the infamous Morant Bay uprising of 1865 as a young boy and, in his old age, will witness the unveiling of Jamaica's 1944 constitution. At certain points throughout the narrative we listen to the elder Campbell speak from his present moment in 1944, at others we witness the unfolding of events focalized through his younger self, and occasionally that narrative stops so that the elder Campbell can apologize for lapses in his memory. The most notable feature, though, is Reid's manipulation of vernacular to create, as Joshua Miller writes in a different context, a "narrative idiom by piecing together despised and stigmatized speech forms."[29]

Despite the dictionary appended to the back of the novel, Reid had little desire to faithfully transcribe any actual Jamaican vernacular. Maureen Warner-Lewis identifies Reid's language as a patchwork of different types of English: "The recipe he produced for his first novel, *New Day*, 1949, then, was to forge an artificial compromise: to blend Jamaican Creole structures, vocabulary, and imagery with elements of Burns's Scots English and Synge's Irish English and to add to this a Biblical phrasing that would suggest the dominant literary influence among the Jamaican folk."[30] Reid, she notes, flips "John Crow," a pejorative Jamaican noun, into an adjective. He does not hold throughout to the Jamaican continuous tense, and at other times he uses the perfect tense, which is absent in Creole. While Reid's deliberate combination of multiple Englishes suggests a highly inventive use of vernacular, Warner-Lewis sees Reid's language as a "stilted, ill-assorted amalgam."[31] She concludes that Reid either felt compelled to elevate vernacular from the low realm of everyday, peasant speech to something more literary or, for other reasons, he was hesitant to use actual vernacular in a literary work. Yet, if we recall the rich histories of vernacular modernism from North, Miller, Hart, and others, the aesthetic transformation of everyday speech does not have to mean that an author looks disdainfully upon indigenous speech forms; it does, however, change the ways we approach and judge vernacular fiction.

Stuart Hall's 1955 essay "Lamming, Selvon, and Some Trends in the West Indian Novel" preempts the dismissive charges launched at West Indian writers who manipulate vernacular speech.[32] Hall argues for a closer engagement with the use of language and style in Reid and Selvon, among other West Indian writers. "It is the style," Hall urgently claims, "that evaluates, that makes sense of the substance of life as it is used by the artist."[33] Although he finds problems with the design of Reid's *New Day*, Hall maintains that "dialect for Reid is not merely an authentic record of speech, but a whole manner of writing, and it is wrong to blame him for inaccurate representation of Jamaican speech patterns"; what is at stake in Reid's manipulation of vernacular is the relation between "manner to matter," or what we might call form and content.[34]

Following Hall, we might ask about the relationship between Reid's invented vernacular and Jamaica's movement from the Morant Bay uprising to the 1944 constitution. That is, how do we link the figural power of the vernacular in *New Day* to the emergent national consciousness charted in the novel's historical narrative? To undertake this sort of investigation means treating Reid's vernacular in aesthetic terms, as something that requires the same critical attention one would devote to the materiality and figural power of language in James Joyce, William Faulkner, or Jean Toomer. With Hall's arguments in mind, we can begin by asking how vernacular mediates the historical events and processes that structure *New Day*.

Unlike the novels of Woolf and Isherwood that I examined in chapter 2, *New Day* sticks with developmental plots and historical progress. The same period of systemic disorder that Woolf and Isherwood perceived as an existential crisis appears here as a moment of optimism and possibility. The novel begins at evening and ends in the morning with narrator John Campbell looking ahead to the first hours of Jamaica's new day. Spanning the decades between the 1860s and the 1940s, John Campbell's narrative recounts a series of intertwined developments: progress from revolutionary violence to gradual reform in the political sphere; economic development away from a mode of production recovering from, but still reproducing, the relation of master and slave to a more "modern" antagonism between capital and labor; the pending legal change in Jamaica's status from colony to a sovereign nation-state. The Campbell family's story follows a similar developmental plot. Prior to the uprising, the Campbells own a farm and enjoy the modest privileges reserved for lighter skinned Jamaicans. By the novel's close, the Campbell family owns a productive, large estate that rivals those of English absentee owners and wealthy white Creole families. This economic success coincides with the family's transition from revolutionary antagonists to labor union leaders and nonviolent reformers. Economic, political, and personal developments are all coded as processes of maturation: from small- to large-scale agriculture, from revolution to reform, from violence to reason, and, indeed, from youth to adulthood. Reid's developmental narrative, though, comes to us from the eyes of a native whose family fought their colonial masters and enhanced their social and economic standing in spite of imperial power. For the Campbell family, world-systemic disorder opens the way for progress and development.

John Campbell's first utterance in *New Day* is notably in the future tense, eagerly anticipating Jamaica's new constitution: "Tomorrow I will go with Garth to the city to hear King George's man proclaim from the square that now Jamaica-men will begin to govern themselves" (3). His anticipation is augmented by his deep pride in his grandson, Garth, and, indeed, multiple generations of the Campbell family who played a significant role in the new Jamaica. Reid's vernacular quickly establishes itself as the authoritative language of narration. The orthographical capture of his speech ("I can no' go," "I ha' put"), vernacular expressions ("eyes will make four"), and the names of indigenous plants (*ma raqui, peahba, cerosee*) invite the reader into Jamaican history as figured by John Campbell and, at least for the nonnative reader, draws attention to the act of narration, to the relation between how one speaks and what one sees.

This first of *New Day*'s three parts centers on the days surrounding the 1865 Morant Bay uprising. Because Reid ties the uprising to Jamaica's coming independence, it is worth recounting briefly the history of this event. Two years of drought ravaged Jamaica, further impoverishing and starving an already poor population. Making matters worse, a war-torn America was incapable of providing relief. In January 1865 Edward Underhill, secretary of the Baptist Missionary Society in England, sent a letter to the Colonial Office alerting them to the deteriorating conditions among Jamaica's peasantry. Underhill's letter caused a public stir in England. Governor John Eyre countered that Jamaica suffered from native lassitude. Six months later, Paul Bogle, the Jamaican Baptist deacon and leader of the uprising, began advocating for resistance to Eyre's government. Tensions increased in St. Thomas Parish over the next few months and Baron von Ketelholdt, rechristened Custos Baron Aldenburg in *New Day*, issued a warrant for Bogle's arrest. On October 11 Bogle and a few hundred men arrived at the Morant Bay courthouse. Von Ketelholdt read the Riot Act and the crowd responded defiantly, throwing stones at the magistrate and openly defying the imperial administration. Von Ketelholdt's militiamen fired on the crowd, leading Bogle's men to retaliate and eventually torch the courthouse. Von Ketelholdt and seventeen of his men were killed as they attempted to flee the burning building.

Governor Eyre declared martial law and over the next month 439 black Jamaicans were killed; over 600 more were brutally tortured and beaten. Rande W. Kostal summarizes Eyre's response as "a protracted and calculated reign of terror."[35] George Gordon, a mulatto landowner and politician who may or may not have been at the courthouse on October 11, was put before a military tribunal and publicly executed. Eyre's response prompted four years of debate over law and violence in the public sphere in England.[36] Morant Bay would come to symbolize the legal and ethical crises of imperial rule. Yet, in the long view of Reid's narrative of Jamaica's new day, the Morant Bay uprising stands as a signature moment in Jamaica's struggle for economic and political justice. Reid's vernacular restages the meaning of the uprising, recasting disorder as progress.

Reid's narrative contrasts multiple forms of English, and each designates the gradations of power extending from the Standard English of the queen to the vernacular of the peasants to the more flexible, conscious code-switching of Garth Campbell. Reid's reconstruction of the queen's response to the miseries of Jamaica's peasants is pitched in the crisp English of imperial administration: "THE MEANS OF SUPPORT OF THE LABOURING CLASSES DEPEND ON THEIR LABOUR. HER MAJESTY WILL REGARD WITH INTEREST AND SATISFACTION THEIR ADVANCEMENT THROUGH THEIR OWN EFFORTS AND MERITS" (11).

Bearing the influence of Governor Eyre's account of Jamaica's situation, "The Queen's Advice" figures the results of structural exploitation and environmental disaster as a problem of individual effort. The empire's way of seeing shifts the blame from a system of labor exploitation to the exploited, impoverished laborer. Paul Bogle replies only with a question: "Is war it, or peace, they want?" (11). The two types of English—the Standard English of the queen's reply and Bogle's vernacular—capture alternative, and mutually opposed, perceptions of Jamaica's situation. The empire sees native poverty as an individual problem while Bogle sees it as imperial and systemic. The queen's dismissal of the material and environmental degradation is not only misinformed and negligent; from Bogle's perspective, the Queen's Advice amounts to an act of war against the population.

These competing perspectives, articulated and brought alive in different speech forms, introduce the recurring preoccupation with speech and violence in the first part of *New Day*. In the scenes preceding the outbreak of violence on October 11, the language of imperial power keeps violence and suffering invisible. When Deacon Bogle and the Jamaican peasants arrive at the courthouse to address their grievances with the Vestry, they are met with Custos Aldenburg. Aldenburg's German-tinged English contrasts with Bogle's vernacular:

"Vat do you vant?"
Deacon Bogle put his hands under his coat and stands akimbo.

"We ha' come to seek justice for the poor. We desire speech with the Vestry."

"Vat do you mean, justice? Vat do you imply, my man?" (123)

The daily injustices of colonial exploitation are not recognized, perhaps cannot be recognized, in the language of imperial power. To recall Lamming's insight, how one speaks indicates what one sees.

Reid's narration of the violence outside of the courthouse further dramatizes the relation between seeing and speaking. Young John Campbell bears witness to the brutal killings of Jamaicans:

> I am no' the only one shrieking. How could it be me one a-shriek? You ha' not heard say that forty o' we people fell when militiamen muskets talked the first time? And say that seven o' the forty looked at the sun without winking? You must ha' heard that one o' the seven fell from atop Humphrey's new church head-most into a mound of wet mortar and found his death there with his heels a-kick at the sun. Ha' you heard o' the woman who hugged musket ball to her breast, then went slow to her knees, so that long afterwards thought, we thought she was a-pray? (126–27)

Campbell's list of questions records the horrors unleashed on Jamaica's poor, most of which were absent from initial reports in the British press that emphasized the death of whites at the hands of a savage, unruly population. Eventually word of Eyre's month of terror circulated more widely, spawning heated debate within the empire over the rule of law and the use of violence. Many would come to see Eyre's actions as immoral and illegal.[37] From the perspective of the British, the Morant Bay uprising presented a crisis of imperial governance. While questions of the legal and moral authority of empire bedeviled British intellectual and politicians, the slain bodies of the Jamaican peasants did not figure quite so prominently. Campbell's firsthand account brings the dead to the level of public visibility.

These narrative scenes suggest two things: first, the language of power, whether Standard English or Aldenburg's German-accented speech, operates in part by making invisible the sufferings of the Jamaican people. In Reid's narrative, official speech wields the power to determine what counts as justice and injustice. Second, Jamaican vernacular, in the speech of characters and in the language of narration, is singularly capable of figuring the violence of British rule, whether in the systematic exploitation of labor and resources or the terrorizing of the population. In the first part of *New Day*, the experiences wrought in Reid's vernacular convey what is left out. In the second and third parts of the book, Reid continues to stage confrontations between two forms of speech, two types of experience, but the mode of address metamorphoses from antagonism and violence to debate and deliberation.

In part 2 of *New Day*, Davie Campbell, John's older, revolutionary brother, stands before the Jamaica Royal Commission to deliver his account of the Morant Bay uprising. In their opening remarks, the commissioners simply cannot understand how a light-skinned son of a "fairly well-to-do man" was not "sympathetic to the—er—rulers of your country" (207). Davie's linguistic performance narrates the uprising and the longer history of colonial Jamaica from the perspective of the colonized. He tells the commissioners that "hunger came to my door and I was no' blind" (207). The political solidarity with Jamaicans exceeds the relatively comfortable social and economic position of his family: "Everybody around me were my people, and when they hungered, hungered me too" (207). The commissioners prove hopelessly puzzled: "But why should you, the son of a hard-working, thriving father, cast his lot with people of whom Her Majesty wrote as being unprofiting because of their own indolence?"(207). Davie claims to "speak for the dead ones" from across the island and across Jamaica's colonial history (207). His invocation of the dead draws a longer history of oppression and violence into the very space of law and order. Davie's vernacular figuration of colonial rule as unbridled violence instigates disorder within the courtroom, replaying the violence outside the courthouse in 1865 within its interiors: "People in the room are stirring again and the Usher is bawling for order again, and believe, I believe that he will burst into blood" (208). In the face of the commissioners, Davie ties the history of the colony to slavery and violence. He ends his historical narrative with a prophecy: representative government will come to Jamaica, fulfilling the hopes and yearnings of those who died for this future freedom.

The concluding third part of *New Day* marks another moment of progress for the Campbell family and for Jamaican sovereignty. As with the other sections, all turns on language. Reid moves ahead to 1925, and the Campbell family "ha' prospered" (255). The antagonism between capital and labor has replaced the old conflict between Jamaica and Britain. The asymmetry between the commission and Davie Campbell is replaced by the more symmetrical balance of power between the Campbell family and other white landowners. Much of the narrative centers on Garth Campbell, Davie's grandson, and his efforts to build a union movement within Jamaica, beginning first with the Campbell estate. Reid invites us to see the battle of capital and labor as a repetition and transformation of the nineteenth-century contest between Jamaicans and their imperial rulers. John Campbell repeatedly likens Garth to Davie, linking the political agency of an older generation with that of the present generation. Speech again figures as the site of competing ways of seeing. The Standard English of the white estate owners pushes for the suppression of organized labor. Garth, educated in England and capable of switching smoothly between vernacular and Standard English, makes an eloquent case for unions in Standard English. Garfield, a longtime landowner, dismisses his "lecture" and invokes Morant Bay as the proper way to settle native grievances: "After we put them in their places once and for all, there will be no further trouble. It was done here before, in this same parish. It can be done again, I say!" (335). In a repetition of the court scene, another Campbell, this time John Campbell, recalls Morant Bay as a moment of violence and dehumanization, not the restoration of law and order: "It can no' be done again. . . . We saw bloodshed, Mr. Reeves and me, and tell, we are telling you, Mr. Garfield, that it frightened we. It frightened us 'cause we saw how bloodshed can make men forget how they are made on the Image and the Likeness. . . . High and low, rich and poor, black and white, they who kill and they who die, none are men in that time" (336). For Reid, it is not just another perspective (Garth's) but the figuration of that perspective in the vernacular that enacts another way of seeing, one that in this scene has transformative power. The unions remain on the Campbell estate and, in a clear indication that ways of seeing are changing, John Campbell and Mr. Reeves, another longtime estate owner, "are making four across the room, and we are looking on things what they young ones ha' never seen" (337).

What is notable about this scene is the decisive role of John Campbell's vernacular. It is not Garth's eloquent Standard English pleas that secure the presence of labor unions. Like Davie's testimony before the commissioners, Campbell's vernacular summons the ghosts of Morant Bay and changes the tone and direction of debate. Even if he comes up short in the this scene, Garth's linguistic mastery and his considerable rhetorical performances exemplify national progress and continuity with Jamaica's rebellious past. John Campbell hears and sees Davie in Garth's words and actions. When Garth speaks for Jamaican liberty, Campbell states that "men hear the voice o' Davie's seed" (367); he has "quick eyes, like Davie's" (371). After enduring a beating by the police, Garth's near lifeless face "is like Davie's under the tree" (301). Garth is an extension of Davie's political restlessness. He helps realize Davie's prophecy that Jamaica will one day acquire representative government. Yet Garth's public speeches in Standard English fall short of full independence: "Give us a chance to shape our own destinies!—Let us stand beside you, Mother England, but free and self-respecting—not as whining children, but as adults, with full respect to the obligation we owe our parent!" (367). Reid metaphorizes political progress as human development and, ultimately, imagines Jamaica's destiny as equal and still bound to England: "Give us the right to walk hand in hand in the march of the new Commonwealth—not as subjects, but as citizens . . . give us liberty to walk as Jamaicans, and we will walk up the same road as you, England!" (368). Garth's mastery of Standard English, demonstrated by his impassioned public speaking, allegorizes Jamaica's political maturity and Reid's overall political vision. Morant Bay remains a proper event, a historical rupture that engenders Jamaica's long march to greater autonomy. That historical progression also means that ideas of political belonging morph from the violent conflicts of the nineteenth century into rational debates between equal partners. Still, the goal of representative government does not presume full independence. Garth yearns for greater autonomy within the commonwealth, one that understands Jamaica and England's values and fates as intertwined. The horizon of political belonging in *New Day* extends only as far as the commonwealth.

Hall rightly argues that *New Day* is part of "the genre of the "stream-of-social-consciousness.""[38] As I have shown, Reid's use of vernacular mediates the broader process of decolonization through everyday speech. John Campbell's vernacular narration claims full authority for telling the story of Jamaica's past, figuring a "sensational" moment of English history into a pivotal moment of national awakening and, eventually, greater autonomy. For Reid, everyday speech becomes the language of history; it is equally the language of narrative and political authority. For Reid and those antagonizing for national autonomy, the systemic disorder that metropolitan authors register as crisis and finality is figured here as progress and futurity.

MIGRATION AS SIEGE

Migration from the colonies to the imperial metropole inaugurated an altogether different set of dangers and possibilities for political belonging. While the arrival of the *Empire Windrush* from Jamaica in 1948 often designates the beginnings of multiethnic England, scholars such as C. L. Innes and Sukhdev Sandhu remind us that the presence of blacks and Africans in London goes back at least to the twelfth century.[39] According to Sandhu, "by the 1570s black people were being brought to England fairly regularly. They were employed as household servants, prostitutes, and court entertainers. Their visibility far exceeded their numerical presence."[40] Still, two events in 1948 make the year a "hot chronology."[41] The British Nationality Act of 1948 (BNA) extended the rights and obligations of citizenship to all imperial subjects, including the rights to work and reside within England. This legislation served several purposes for a weakened imperial power that was intent on maintaining its global influence. Recasting imperial citizenship was part of a larger effort to manage relationships with current and former colonies and project an image of Britain's global power. Despite its massive debt, its war-wrecked cities, and the accelerating pace of decolonization, "Britain as a political unit grew into a 'global institution,' whether it was called the British Empire, or the British Commonwealth, or just the Common-wealth, and its formal membership was granted to ethno-linguistically diverse peoples."[42] Kathleen Paul argues that the passage of the act was meant to signal British strength while also quieting "dominion nationalism by recognizing the right of territories to legislate their own citizenship laws."[43] Of equal importance, though, were Britain's labor needs. In January 1946 the British government predicted a labor shortfall in the area of 600,000–1.3 million. Newly codified citizenship rights and the promise of employment lured immigrants from the slow economies in the Caribbean, Africa, and Asia.

The second of these events occurred in June of 1948 when the *Empire Windrush* arrived in Tilbury with 492 passengers, mostly Jamaican and Trinidadian. The "global institution" of Britain arrived onto its shores, initiating a period of movement that poet Louise Bennett famously called "colonizin' in reverse."[44] Although the BNA and the optimism crystallized in Lord Kitchener's famous calypso "London Is the Place for Me" make 1948 appear as a victory for expanded citizenship and opportunity, Trevor Phillips and Mike Phillips see it as "the beginning of a trauma about citizenship, race and nationality."[45] The British state's treatment of different immigrant groups illustrates the asymmetry between the legal membership encoded in the BNA and actual political belonging. European volunteer workers, many of whom were refugees after the war, and Irish immigrants were offered English-language classes, housing assistance, and even facilities for games and sports. By contrast, the hundreds and then thousands of black migrants arriving on British shores were shuttled into former bomb shelters until they could find other housing. The search for accommodations normally meant finding signs declaring "Rooms to Let: No Coloured Men" attached to vacant properties. Employers introduced racial quotas into their hiring practices to keep black workers out or, at the very least, to minimize their presence. Black Britons, the only group of the three with the legal right to reside and work in Britain, were subjected to racial violence and the refusal of housing and work, and soon became the screen for all types of national anxieties. MacInnes characterized Britain's "criminally irresponsible" migration policy as "Come to the UK—what the hell are you doing here?"[46] Not only did black migrants not belong, their very presence was conceived as a violation.

Many of the texts of the West Indian literary renaissance, including migration tales such as George Lamming's *The Emigrants*, Sam Selvon's *The Lonely Londoners*, and, earlier, Una Marson's poem "Quashie Comes to London" oscillate between the glittering dreams of metropolitan life and the cruel realities of everyday life, often reproducing formally the disorientation of migrant experience. The modified Caribbean vernacular of Selvon's *The Lonely Londoners* guides us through the sights and sounds, the dreams and disenchantments, of England's rapidly growing Afro-Caribbean communities; in similar fashion, MacInnes's *Absolute Beginners*, focalized entirely through a proto-mod teenager, spins out stories of black migrants, and various youth cultures all precariously positioned between cultural integration and social revolt. Both Selvon and MacInnes create vernaculars that resemble but do not replicate everyday speech. Like *New Day*, these novels privilege linguistic innovation over ethnographic fidelity. Also like Reid's novel, these texts are active imaginings of the consequences and possibilities of emergent forms of political belonging. These novels use vernacular to make legible the figural procedures by which legal citizens become existential threats to the nation. In their attention to everyday life, their verbal structures, and multiple speech forms, *The Lonely Londoners* and *Absolute Beginners* enact reworkings of linguistic and figural processes that aligned migration with national siege and transformed citizens into hostile aliens. These texts do not ask us merely to see from another perspective but to witness the production of perspectives and the forms of systemic violence they enable and sustain.

Most historians of migration in postwar Britain acknowledge a wider, complex transnational context for national debates over political belonging. Trevor and Mike Phillips trace a network of associations spanning from Africa to North America:

> The news from abroad struck an urgent personal chord in a way that is now difficult to imagine: the independence of Ghana; the guerilla war against the Mau Mau in Kenya; the struggle against racial segregation in the American South. All these events were accompanied by fiercely contested debates and, increasingly, they revolved around the issue of race. Every public confrontation, however trivial, in which migrants were involved, was suddenly underscored by a deep current of racial resentment and hostility.[47]

Wendy Webster foregrounds the link between black migration to Britain and the violence of decolonization in Malaya and Kenya. Webster's analysis of British representations of the Mau Mau rebellion shows an emerging postwar consensus that English culture, identity, and perhaps national survival were all "threatened not only within empire, but at home."[48] War reporting from Kenya focused on the deaths of white settlers and conveniently skirted the detention, torture, and mass killings of Kenyan civilians.[49] Yet the harrowing tales of the invasion of white homes by savage, bloodthirsty Kenyans and a steady supply of imperial imagery molded the public imagination, aligning blackness with invasion, violence, and threat.

When migrants began arriving and settling in English cities after the Second World War, a similar sense of invasion and threat took hold. Webster reports that "a number of black people in Britain in the 1950s discovered that white British reactions to them were informed by imagery of colonial wars."[50] Beryl Gilroy, a native of British Guiana, recalls being asked if she was a "Mau Mau lady."[51] The

White Defence League made the link quite explicitly in their 1959 "Stop the Coloured Invasion" meeting in Trafalgar Square. The siege narrative amplified the problem of belonging; it figured the expanded rights of citizenship of the 1948 BNA into the language and imagery of existential threat. This becomes evident in a post–Notting Hill report entitled "The Habit of Violence" published in *Universities and Left Review.* The journal collected statements from white residents about their black neighbors in the aftermath of the violence. The siege mentality pervades these responses: the "coloured people are a load of savages"; they lack hygiene; they are lazy, yet somehow stealing jobs and housing from white Britons; they "take our white girls" and lure them into a life of prostitution and vice. The journal's editors saw "the unmistakable profile of Britain's colonial policy over the last century" underpinning this collective siege mentality. "Behind each irrational phrase," they write, "stand an impressive list of names—Kenya, Cyprus, Malaya, British Guiana, Southern Rhodesia."[52] Whatever comprehension the public may have of this inventory of colonial history, it is certain that all the horrors and anxieties generated over centuries of imperial administration are projected onto blackness. "The terrible tragedy of colonialism—not the past only but the present as well—has at last come 'home.'"[53]

One of the softer but most telling figurations of black men besieging the population appears in a spread from the 1954 issue of *Picture Post,* which leads with the probing question "Would You Let Your Daughter Marry a Negro?" The first photograph greeting the reader depicts a white woman holding her biracial son (figure 5.1). The faces of mother and child consume the space of the photograph, pointing negatively to the absent father. Readers immediately are prompted not only to think about interracial marriage but to ponder the possibility of miscegenation, which played directly to heightening racial anxieties. On the following page we see the entire family of three in their Brixton apartment (figure 5.2). The mother and father stand apart from one another, disengaged and gazing at something beyond the frame; the young boy looks attentively, perhaps playfully, out to the viewer. The final image moves out to the street where three young girls peer over their shoulders, curiously staring at the sight of a white woman with a black child.

Even if the written text of *Picture Post* concludes that "mixed marriages *can* succeed," the portraiture of this ordinary family suggests otherwise:[54] the images show a disconnected family suffering social and economic hardship. The article

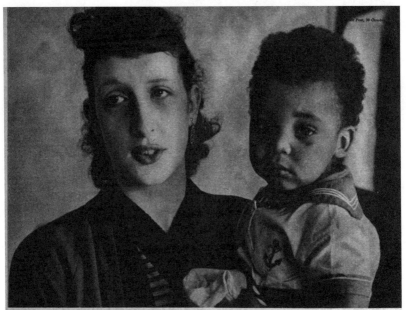

SOMETIMES THEY SAY IT LOUD ENOUGH FOR HER TO HEAR. "LOOK AT THAT, MAY. AIN'T IT A SHAME." *It's the middle-aged women that are the worst, although the working man can be cruel, too. Near here there used to be whitewash on the walls. "Keep Brixton white." This girl has been married nearly three years and has two children. Her husband is unemployed. He says that work is hard to find in Britain—especially for a Negro.*

WOULD YOU LET YOUR DAUGHTER

MARRY A NEGRO?

There are 100,000 Negroes in Britain today. Hundreds more are arriving every month. Thousands of them are already married to white girls. What do relatives and neighbours think about it? How do the children suffer? What is the price in insults, hardships and tears?

Written by TREVOR PHILPOTT

Photographed by SLIM HEWITT

THE man was sitting, in overalls, on a platform seat at Watford Junction. He looked like a good Union man, who probably voted Labour at the last election, and will vote Labour at the next.

The Negro serviceman came up the steps three at a time and he laughed loudly as the little blonde on his arm tried to keep up with him, her high heels clattering. "If she was my kid," muttered the man in overalls, "I'd tan the backside off her." Except that he didn't say backside.

Not so long ago, a West Indian stood on the doorstep of a house in Liverpool. Upstairs the girl that he'd 'got into trouble' was sobbing on the bed. The West Indian wanted to marry her, and she wanted to marry him. Her father shouted through the half-open door—"Rather than see her married to a nigger, I'd watch her die having the kid!"

This is the tough, unyielding core of the colour bar. Here, many a liberal-minded politician finds his politics peel raw. Here, many a sincere parson finds the logic of his Maker unbearable. "Love thy black neighbour, brethren and sisters. But in the name of decency, and the pure white race, don't marry him. And don't suffer your little sister to marry him either."

In the Union of South Africa, and some Southern States of America, mixed marriage is something you can be jailed for. People can even be imprisoned, for up to ten years, for contracting mixed marriages in the North of the U.S. and then going South to live.

In Britain, there is no law which bars blessed love between white and black. Here a man marries the woman he wants, and there's nothing to stop him. Nothing. Nothing, except the knowledge that seven British men out of ten feel their insides shrinking at the very thought of a coloured man fathering the children of a white girl.

The prejudice is stronger that way round. Soon, twenty-six British Guiana girls will be coming home as

the wives of British soldiers. They will probably get a sincere and warm-hearted welcome. But practically all mixed marriages in this country have been between Negro men and white women. The battle such couples must fight throughout their married lives is not one against reason. It is against ignorance, superstition and fear.

In the unstirred minds of many British mothers a black man is something out of the jungle. In taking a black man, her daughter is taking also black magic, black heartedness, and all kinds of black evil. Purity is white, sin is black. The association is so deep, that it cannot easily be shaken off. A friend of mine, who is small, tolerant and blonde described to me a few days ago the incredulous terror which swept through her as a Negro walked behind her up the stairs of a boarding house. The man was only going upstairs. She was terrified.

Among men, the suspicions are different, but no more reasonable. "Once a woman's had a nigger mate, *Continued overleaf*

21

FIGURE 5.1 "WOULD YOU LET YOUR DAUGHTER MARRY A NEGRO?"
PICTURE POST, OCTOBER 30, 1954, 21.

FIGURE 5.2 "WOULD YOU LET YOUR DAUGHTER MARRY A NEGRO?"
PICTURE POST, OCTOBER 30, 1954, 22–23.

itself tells of men racially excluded from skilled work, women exiled from families who will not accept black men, and children of interracial unions struggling with daily ridicule.

When Stuart Hall sorted through the contact sheets for these photographs, he discovered "a much wider range of shots, with alternative ways of representing the white mother and the black father: close, not distanced; together, or together with the child, doing things, in context—shopping, playing, walking about."[55] But the spread actually communicates the unintended but unavoidable consequences of black Britons, especially black men, invading the home and troubling the normal white family. Hall's findings not only suggest the existence of potential counternarratives, they cast into sharp relief the figural procedures by which the migration of citizens was transformed into national and cultural siege.

Wendy Webster reads these sorts of figurations as proof that the body of the white English woman became the new frontier for managing the separation between the English and the formerly colonized. "If black and Asian migration to Britain brought a fear of the collapse of boundaries between colonizers and colonized, black and white," she writes, "it was particularly through the breaching of this internal frontier [of sexuality] that such a collapse was managed."[56] This figuration of daily life in the *Picture Post* piece works in two ways. On one hand, the written text sympathizes with the struggles of loving couples suffering under social and economic hardships. On the other hand, the photographs amplify the anxieties over interracial unions, what Hall calls "the traumatic fantasy of miscengenation."[57] The signs of an absent, disengaged father, multiracial children, and a life of privation for white English women played to growing fears that black migration was a threat to the nation both culturally and biologically.

What I am suggesting here is that Selvon's and MacInnes's vernacular fictions engage this siege narrative in two distinct ways: first, both novels make legible the figural procedures that translate migration into siege; second, their use of vernacular reverses the trajectory of that figural procedure. I turn first to Selvon's 1956 novel *The Lonely Londoners*, which has remained one of the most highly canvassed texts for studies of race and migration in postimperial Britain since its publication.[58] Although *The Lonely Londoners* is narrated in the vernacular, Kenneth Ramchand notes that Selvon's novel employs vernacular less selectively than his earlier works, particularly *A Brighter Sun*; more specifically, and most noticeably, Selvon erases the division between "the language of narration and the language of the fictional character."[59] Selvon's narrative meanders in and out of the lives of Afro-Caribbean migrants making their way in a polite but largely inhospitable London. By Selvon's own account, he employed West Indian vernacular "to recapture a certain quality of West Indian everyday life."[60] To be sure, Selvon knew his audience would not be composed solely of Caribbean readers.[61] He wrote the first draft of *The Lonely Londoners* in Standard English, reserving dialect only for dialogue.[62] It was only after he converted the narrative voice into his own "modified version" that the novel took shape.[63] As mentioned previously, Selvon treated actual West Indian vernaculars as raw material for the narrative voice of his fictional narrative:

> I did not pick the Jamaican way of talking in London. I only tried to produce what I believed was thought of as a Caribbean dialect. The modified version in which I write my dialect may be a manner of extending the language. It may be called artificial or fabricated. . . . I only resorted to a modified Trinidadian dialect because, much more than Jamaican or Barbadian English, it is close to "correct" Standard English, and I thought it would be more recognizable to the European reader. . . . I only modified it so people outside the Caribbean would be able to identify it.[64]

By Selvon's own admission, his "intention was not primarily to be realistic and to differentiate between the several West Indian groups."[65] Freed from the demands of authenticity and ethnographic precision, Selvon's inventive use of vernacular in his London novel, in the words of Sandhu, makes "the quotidian vivid."[66]

In a scene that captures some of Selvon's anxieties about the legibility of vernacular, Daisy, a white English native, struggles to follow the pronunciation and slang of Galahad, a newly arrived Trinidadian: "You know it will take me some time to understand everything you say. The way you West Indians speak!"[67] Galahad responds with "Is English we speaking," highlighting his vernacular's proximity to and distance from Daisy's own English (93). Pitching the entire novel in Selvon's synthetic vernacular alerts readers to a broad range of linguistic differences between English natives and West Indians as well as within the West Indian community. Big City, another Trinidadian, mispronounces basic words: "fusic" instead of "music," "norphanage" instead of "orphanage." Familiar places also undergo slight transformations: Nottingham Gate, Kensington Mansion, and Claphand Common. When the boys try to correct Big City, he brashly asks, "You think I don't know English?" (94). Like other scenes in the book, these moments offer a little comic relief, offsetting the descriptions of grim living conditions and the existential malaise that permeates much of the novel. More than that, though, these two scenes establish the narrator's vernacular, not Standard English, as the novel's own standard. Readers measure and sort differences between the narrator's vernacular and other forms of English. In its displacement of Standard English as the authorized speech form, *The Lonely Londoners* ties a way of speaking to a way of seeing.

The novel opens with a scene of arrival and the figuration of that arrival by the British press. From the onset of the novel, Selvon articulates a specific relationship between speaking and seeing. Moses Aloetta, a Trinidadian who has resided in London for some time, arrives at Waterloo Station to meet a migrant from Trinidad, Henry Oliver, and help him get his bearings in his new city. Henry, soon to be rechristened Sir Galahad, sets foot on shore during a period of heightened racial anxiety. This is the era of the "colour bar," which Paul Gilroy characterizes as "the painful period in which Britain's blacks enjoyed extensive but empty rights of citizenship that could be easily overridden by informal patterns of exclusion in public and in private."[68] In the words of Selvon's narrator, Galahad enters London at the moment "English people starting to make rab about how too much West Indians coming to the country. . . . In fact, the boys all over London, it ain't have a place where you wouldn't find them, and big discussion going on in Parliament about the situation, though the old Brit'n too diplomatic to clamp down on the boys or to do anything drastic like stop them from coming to the Mother Country" (24). Yet the British press is far less diplomatic in its figuration of West Indian migration. Selvon's narrator likens the newspaper and radio to "the people Bible," lending those figurations theological force (24). Moses encounters an investigative reporter from *The Echo* searching the Waterloo platforms for stories and evidence of a migration problem. Armed with a notebook and pencil, the reporter assumes Moses has recently arrived from Jamaica. Moses is uniquely unqualified to answer the reporter's question, but, as a black man in Waterloo Station, he fits the type: "Now Moses don't know a damn thing about Jamaica—Moses come from Trinidad, which is a thousand miles from Jamaica, but the English people believe that everybody who come from the West Indies come from Jamaica" (28). Moses mimics the type until the reporter "feel that he get catch with Moses" (29).

Although it is tempting to see Moses as a trickster figure and to interpret his response as the playful subversion of a native informant, Moses quickly regrets what may have been a rare opportunity to "say his mind" (29). And yet Moses knows from past experience with "the people Bible" that such figurations of black migrant life only ever amplify racial tensions:

> It happen while he was working in a railway yard, and all the people in the place say they go strike unless the boss fire Moses. It was a big ballad in all the papers, they put it under a big headline, saying how the colour bar causing trouble again, and a fellar come with a camera and wanted to take Moses photo, but Moses say no. A few days after that the boss call Moses and tell him that he sorry, but as they cutting down the staff and he was new, he would have to go. (29)

Bringing to the fore the racial politics of labor and the workings of the "colour bar" does little to help Moses. In this account, black Britons either suffer silently from direct and indirect racism or reap the consequences of publicizing their grievances. Selvon's narrator indicates elliptically that Moses possesses little control over the relay of his own story. Although Moses refuses to let his photo be taken, the following sentence indicates that his place in the newspaper story has resulted in his firing. Has Moses been personally identified in the story, either by name or, against his own wishes, by photo? In any case, Moses exists only as the object, not the subject, of these figural procedures.

For Selvon's Afro-Caribbeans, representation and inclusion in the public sphere does not lead to greater freedom or understanding; the very act of representation works against their interests. This is perhaps what underlies Tolroy's distaste for the reporter from *The Echo*. He asks Tanty for a photo, and she calls out for her other family members. The reporter assures her that "one of you alone will be quite sufficient" (31). Tanty insists and the reporter eventually relents, taking a family photo instead. Yet racial typology proves flexible enough to accommodate a collective unit. When Tanty's family photo appears the next day in the newspaper, the caption reads: "Now, Jamaican Families Come to Britain" (32). Black migrants only ever figure as a problem, as an unwelcome, invasive species.

Selvon's tales of everyday immigrant life demonstrate how these figural procedures produce material effects. Galahad's early experiences with white Londoners convey the power of racial figuration. As with other characters in *The Lonely Londoners*, Galahad appropriates place names and urban spaces as part of what Rebecca Dyer calls "the creation of a new "immigrant" London."[69] In one way, Dyer is right. When Galahad tells Moses he has a date waiting for him at Charing Cross Station, for instance, the narrator alerts us to its electrifying power for Galahad: "Jesus Christ, when he say 'Charing Cross,' when he realise that is he, Sir Galahad, who going there, near that place that everybody in the world know about (it even have the name in the dictionary) he feel like a new man" (84). The novelty and charm of everyday life in London inspires other changes in Galahad: he takes to fashion and "stock up with clothes like stupidness, as if to make up for all the hard times when he didn't have nice things to wear" (85). Yet if places and clothes signal that Galahad is charting his own way of belonging in London and, as Dyer suggests, maps a new London altogether, Galahad's first London summer also displays the opposite: Galahad's black body impedes him from any sense of belonging, aligning him instead with those figurations of black migration as siege.

From the moment he arrives at Waterloo Station, Galahad's body seems out of sync with London. He is strangely hot in the cruel London winter and wears an overcoat in the summer to keep warm. Yet Galahad revels in London's urban ambience. Dressed in a tailored suit to meet Daisy, Galahad strolls through the city, and the narrative gives us a cut of free indirect discourse to record this moment of utter bliss: "This is London, this is life oh lord, to walk like a king with money in your pocket, not a worry in the world" (87). Selvon counters this scene with two instances of "polite" racism. A small child points at him and says "Mummy, look at that black man!" (87). "Putting on the old English accent," Galahad leans down to ask the child's name before the mother pulls the child away and gives him "a sickly sort of smile" (88). Galahad knows the routine well and adopts the language and manners to fit a certain way of seeing: "the old Galahad, knowing how it is, smile back and walk on" (88). The narrative juxtaposes this scene with an earlier one when Galahad overhears two white men in the lavatory "say how these black bastards have the lavatory dirty, and they didn't know he was there, and when he come out they say hello mate have a cigarette" (88). Under the pressure of everyday racism, Galahad separates himself from the blackness of his skin. He gazes at his hand and, "talking to the colour Black, as if is a person," assigns the cause of racism to blackness itself (88). Galahad relays his theory to Moses, suggesting "Is not we that the people don't like ... is the colour Black" (89).

In one way, Galahad is right. In Selvon's world, the reality of race, what Frantz Fanon called "the fact of blackness," demarcates who belongs and who does not. Echoing similar instances from Fanon's *Black Skin, White Masks*, the young child's acknowledgment of Galahad's race reduces him to a type, one bearing the history of imperial domination and its distorting tropes, imagery, and figurations of blackness as subhuman and uncivilized. Galahad's experiences testify to the "crushing objecthood" of blackness mediated by whiteness.[70] Any visual evidence of cultural fusion—a black citizen in "English" clothes, working "English" jobs, speaking with an "English" accent, and displaying "English" manners—registers not as assimilation but as an increased threat and amplifies the need to assert racial difference.

Galahad's encounters introduce a point of comparison for Harris, who appears to be the novel's quintessential postcolonial mimic man. Harris has mastered Standard English and, it seems, Englishness itself. His impeccable English bewilders other West Indians: "Man, when Harris start to spout English for you,

you realise that you don't really know the language" (111). At first blush, Harris's adaptation of English culture makes him more English than the English: his manners are textbook, even if he does things "them Englishmen don't do" (111). Similarly, his appearance carries all the signs of Englishness: "and when he dress you think is some Englishman going to work in the city, bowler and umbrella, and briefcase tuck under the arm, with *The Times* fold up in the pocket so the name would show" (111). Yet as Galahad painfully discovered, the narrator reminds us that for all of Harris's assumed Englishness, "Harris face black" (111).

Although it's tempting to read Harris as a tragic mimic man, his role in the text is far more complicated even than Galahad's. At first blush, Harris appears capable of gliding between two cultural worlds. He organizes fetes with steel bands geared for English consumption. John McLeod's sharp reading of this fraught scene frames it as an instance of "spatial creolization" where West Indian and English cultures cross with less friction.[71] I do not want to dismiss McLeod's interpretation because he is right that this space differs from other contact zones in the novel: as he points out, racial and sexual relations seem far less objectifying within St. Pancras Hall. Rather, I want to underscore the way Harris envisions his fete as a contact zone bereft of conflict and difference. Garbed in a suit and bow tie at the entrance of St. Pancras Hall, Harris greets his white English guests with English greetings and warns his West Indian friends to "behave yourselves like proper gentleman" (112); he monitors their drug use and their language. Harris's sanitized version of Caribbean dance hall culture repackages its exoticism, offering it up not only for family friendly English consumption but also to portray the fete and its participants as perfectly obedient English subjects.

When the fete closes with "God Save the Queen," Harris pleads with the boys to stand to attention and pay proper respect. This is also the moment when Harris, "forgetting to speak proper English for a minute" (122), slides back into West Indian vernacular: "Now it have decent people here tonight, and if you don't get on respectable it will be a bad reflection not only on me but on all the boys, and you know how things hard already in Brit'n. The English people will say we are still uncivilised and don't know how to behave properly" (122). Harris's favored words—"decent people," "respectable," and "behave properly"—repeat, but they circulate unmoored from the proper grammatical structure of his other lines.

Whether Harris forgets or consciously reverts back to the vernacular to per-suade his guests to exhibit proper English behavior, this moment of identification with the queen is an especially urgent one. "God Save the Queen" is rife with the language of a unified, collective nation: "*our* gracious Queen," "*our* noble Queen," "Long to reign over *us*." Harris's plea to the boys rhymes with the entire theme of his fete: assuming a visibly deferential posture to British traditions will combat the inevitable charges that Afro-Caribbeans are uncivilized and culturally incom-patible. Harris's Englishness as well as his staged fete are all efforts to blunt the force of the siege narrative, to suggest that all citizens of the empire belong equally because they are identifiably English.

The attempted fusions of cultural worlds we see with Galahad and Harris showcase the very fragile relationships that exist between Afro-Caribbeans and the English in even the most secure, least contentious of contact zones. As the survey from *University and Left Review* made clear, sexuality proved a far more threatening contact zone. Racism assumed a particularly violent form around any relation between Afro-Caribbean men and white women. As histories of midcen-tury migration bear out, one of the dominant myths concerned black men lur-ing white women into prostitution. As Ashley Dawson writes, "notions of sexual conduct helped blur the line between biological and cultural notions of differ-ence."[72] Perhaps more than blurring that line, sexual anxieties forced a reversion of racism from cultural incompatibility back into older arguments of genetic and biological purity.[73] Fear of miscegenation spread broadly enough to link up the far right's "Keep Britain White" campaigns with remarks from Labour Party leader John Steel, who worried that England would devolve into "a nation of half-castes. The result is that the nation will possess neither the rhythm of the coloured man, nor the scientific genius of the European. The only thing we will ever produce is riots, just as do the mixed races of the world."[74] As we saw with the spread in *Pic-ture Post*, nothing appeared so monstrous and threatening to the native English as miscegenation.

Several of the "ballads" in *The Lonely Londoners* explore sexual encounters between black men and white women, but the most remarkable scenes occur in the novel's stream of consciousness section. Here an unmistakably modernist style merges with West Indian vernacular to depict a series of sexual encounters that deconstruct the image of a predatory black male sexuality. The bookends to this section frame it as a tale of disappointment and dissatisfaction. Punctuation dissolves as London thaws, exposing the "legs and shapes that was hiding away from the cold blasts" (101). And yet this jolt of excitement and sexual awakening, at least for Moses, ends with "a long sigh like a man who lives life and see nothing at all in it and who frighten as the years go by wondering what it is all about" (110). From the dawning of summer until this episode's end, the accumulation of Moses's sexual encounters range from the comically naïve to crudely exploitative. The first encounter inverts the myth of predatory and primal black male sexuality. Moses brings a woman home and entirely misreads her orgasmic pleasure: "nearly dead with fright because the woman start to moan and gasp and wriggle and twist up she body like a piece of wire" (103). This naiveté contrasts markedly with the sexual type that white English women desire. "The cruder you are," the narrator tells us, "the more the girls like you . . . they want you to live up to the films and stories they hear about black people living primitive in the jungles of the world" (108). This desire seems most rampant among the intellectual class. The final sexual encounter depicts a white woman with "a smart flat with all sorts of surrealist painting on the walls and contemporary furniture in the G-plan" calling her Jamaican lover a "black bastard" (109). "She didn't mean it as an insult but as a compliment under the circumstances but the Jamaican fellar get vex and say why the hell you call me a black bastard and he thump the woman and went away" (109). In another scene a white woman carries Moses to an upper-class party in Knightsbridge and remunerates him for being the evening's exotic attraction. In this assemblage of scenes and their presentation in a disorienting stream of consciousness, Selvon gradually flips the script on predatory black male sexuality. In the end the West Indian men are the ones subjected to the wild desires and imaginings of the white English population.

Selvon's vernacular narration displaces Standard English as the primary mechanism for discussing migration; the novel aggressively negates the way of seeing that equates black migration with siege. Collectively, the stories of Moses, Galahad, Harris, Cap, and the others dramatize the material effects of figural procedures on everyday life. From *The Echo*'s typology of blackness to the fear of black sexuality, we see that it is Selvon's cast of migrants who are under siege. Selvon's novel seems to know that different levels of political belonging in postimperial

Britain will only exacerbate racial and social tensions. Exploring the same urban scene two years later, MacInnes's *Absolute Beginners* charts those heightened tensions and their violent eruption in 1958 when black Britons were quite literally besieged.

MacInnes's *Absolute Beginners* might appear an odd place to round out a discussion of vernacular, particularly when this chapter has dealt primarily with writers in or from the anglophone Caribbean.[75] MacInnes's 1959 novel is known primarily as a document of postwar youth culture, drawing comparisons since publication to J. D. Salinger's *Catcher in the Rye*. Yet contemporary writers Caryl Phillips and Helon Habila have recently paid homage to MacInnes for seeing the influx of black immigrants as a moment of Britain's "radical reinvention" that needed to be defended and, equally important, recorded.[76] In that regard, it is no accident that MacInnes's anonymous teenage narrator is also a photographer. The narrator guides us through the coffee bars, jazz clubs, record stores, and the in and outs of Napoli, a fictional Notting Hill inhabited by proto-mod teenagers, Teds, gay and lesbian youth, and black Britons. Like Selvon and Reid, MacInnes registers the daily doings of these emergent cultural worlds in a vernacular of his own making: "cloud-kissers" are buildings; "taxpayers" are average citizens, "absolute beginners" are fresh teenagers, and so on. Although the narrator's vernacular serves as the primary palette for this picture of postwar London, *Absolute Beginners* remains incredibly attentive to the power of different speech forms. The narrator somewhat ironically quotes phrases from "the women's weeklies" and "a certain evening paper," noting the way forms of language render, and potentially distort, experience.[77] He muses over the narcotic effect of television programs that marshal professors and experts and "their complicated language" to frame the public's knowledge of "art, and fashion, and archaeology, and long-haired music" (202). Yet, as a resident jazz aficionado and veteran teenager, he knows that the "complicated language" of experts makes the teenage phenomenon "simpler than it is"; "for anyone who knows the actual scene, they're crap" (202). The majority of the novel worries over the translation of subcultural lives into traditional forms; losing the power to figure and narrate these cultural worlds is tantamount to losing them altogether. And while this novel deserves far more attention than it has received, and far more than I have the space to devote to it here, the final chapter of *Absolute Beginners* becomes the necessary endpoint of my argument. MacInnes directs these meditations on language and power toward the Notting Hill riots of 1958.

The Notting Hill riots broke while MacInnes composed *Absolute Beginners*.[78] Racial violence had consumed Nottingham earlier that summer, forecasting what would arrive in London by summer's end. On a Friday evening in August, a white Swedish woman, Majbritt Morrison, and her West Indian husband, Raymond, were arguing outside of a Tube station and drew the attention of a gang of white youths. Believing they were protecting a white woman from an angry black man, the crowd approached the couple, hurling racial slurs at Raymond. Majbritt defended her husband and drew the ire of the crowd. When she was spotted the next evening, white youths attacked her with milk bottles and pieces of wood. Although she escaped relatively unharmed, the scene at her house was no less harrowing:

> Outside her house she was greeted by police cars and fire engines, their beacons flashing; smoke was pouring from her ground floor room where a petrol bomb had been thrown through the window. Police officers met her on the steps and told her to get inside but she refused, turning on the crowd which now surrounded her house. At first she tried pleading with them not to start anything, but when they responded with jeers and yet more abuse she exploded: "Is it blood you want? Go on then, KILL ME!" Someone took her at her word and she felt a piercing pain in her back."[79]

The crowd swelled to over two hundred and attacked a party at King Dick's house, breaking windows and shouting "Kill the niggers! Keep Britain White!" The four days of so-called rioting might better be perceived as an extended period of siege against London's West Indian community.

The riots overtook the writing of *Absolute Beginners*. In a letter to Reginald Davis-Poynter written in the immediate aftermath of Notting Hill, MacInnes believes the riots "will seem, with Suez, the key event of the post-war period."[80] The event, he believed, demanded a diary of the week similar to John Hersey's *Hiroshima* or *Ten Days that Shook the World*. Alan Sinfield contends that the event ruptures the actual structure of the novel: "Their appearance [the riots] in the book is organized with none of the tidy structural anticipation that is supposed to characterize the literary. They burst upon the reader as they do upon the boy."[81]

MacInnes and his young narrator know well that the figuration of the riots and how they are seen will reshape the entire debate over immigration and, quite possibly, the politics of race and citizenship in Britain.[82]

The "September" chapter of *Absolute Beginners* does not aspire to be an accurate report of the riots any more than MacInnes's vernacular strives to replicate actual speech. The novel is far more concerned with the figural procedures that allow events to attain visibility. Apart from recasting these sort of events, this final chapter also juxtaposes the Standard English account of a leading newspaper article on race riots by reporter Amberly Drove and the narrator's own vernacular. The narrator reads Drove's story, but his sentences are presented without quotes; the narrative voice sheds its typical slang and linguistic verve and more or less mimics Drove's language, which he calls "plain speaking" (236): "It said the chief thing was that we must be realistic, and keep a proper sense of due proportion. It said that many influential journals—including, of course, this Mrs. Dale production—had long been warning the government that unrestricted immigration, particularly of coloured persons, was most undesirable" (234). The demand for "realism" and "proportion" recycle the inveterate racism of the Mosleyites into journalistic "plain speak": black immigrants, who in their native countries "are no doubt admirable citizens" (234), are less civilized than the English; they prey upon white women and their mixed marriages will engender a "mongrel race" (236), and they are unskilled workers living mostly on the dole. By the end of his report, Drove's "realism" has figured a besieged immigrant population into the cause of violence.

The form and content of MacInnes's final chapter enact alternative figurations of the riots. MacInnes's biographer, Tony Gould, claims that many of the scenes in this final chapter were informed by reports from the *Guardian*. MacInnes does not graft actual information into his text so much as he rewrites it. He revisits the inaugural event that sparked the riots but replaces the assault of Majbritt Morrison with something far more trivial. The days of rioting and violence in *Absolute Beginners* follow from an accidental collision of two baby strollers, one being pushed by a black woman and the other pushed by a white woman. It would be tempting to say MacInnes has erred in removing the interracial couple and the racial anxieties that their mere existence provoked. In his nonfictional work and in this particular novel, MacInnes is alive to the volatile fusion of race and sexuality;

moreover, the narrator's love interest, Suze, is attacked by white youths who call her a "nigger's whore!" (273), echoing Morrison's incident. By swapping Morrison's encounter with angry white youths for a random accident, MacInnes suggests that rationales for racial violence, whether pitched in the racist sloganeering of the Mosleyites and the British Union of Fascists or the "plain speaking" of Amberly Drove, are entirely trivial. Quite simply, MacInnes wants to rob the racial violence of Notting Hill of any semblance of a justification, be it Drove's patronizing comments about cultural incompatibility or the biological fears of a mongrel nation.

In addition to his creative treatment of events, MacInnes also remakes the narrator's role during the riots: he passes from a veteran documentarian of subcultural London into a bewildered witness. After watching several assaults and attempted lynchings, the narrator likens his neighborhood to "a prison, or a concentration camp: inside, blue murder, outside, buses and evening papers and hurrying home to sausages and mash and tea" (266). Teenagers who moved in the same cultural worlds of the besieged West Indians join in the fray. Wiz, the narrator's crafty, drug-addled friend, chants "Keep Britain White!" at a rally for the White Protection League. Although MacInnes's London is susceptible to racial violence in even the most diverse of neighborhoods, it is never without its glimpses of other futures. On two occasions, at least one of them culled from actual reports, old white Londoners take direct action to protect black youths from the white mobs. In one instance, a "small old geezer" (250) escorts a young black boy to safety; another old woman locks a youth inside of her grocery store as the crowd shouts "Bring him out!" And "Lynch him" (248). The narrator, who has invested all his hopes for a classless, multiethnic Britain in youth culture, wonders "why it was the only two I'd seen who'd fought back had been old-timers?" (250). These figurations of Notting Hill see the riots less as the culmination of unbridgeable differences between black and white citizens, between English natives and Afro-Caribbean migrants; even within the most antagonistic conflicts, MacInnes asserts instances of sympathy if not solidarity that cut across the cultural and biological divisions cemented in Drove's report.

Like Selvon, MacInnes figures immigrants as a besieged population, as the subjects and victims of racial violence. Vernacular narration in *The Lonely Londoners* and *Absolute Beginners* has two primary effects: it casts into sharp relief the material effects of figural acts; second, these writers generate their own figurations, transforming everyday life into a scene where we witness other forms of belonging that have been erased or foreclosed in other Englishes. In this way we might see Selvon and MacInnes not merely as documentarians of marginal populations in postimperial England; these two novels actively conceptualize and explore political belonging, positioning it as a plastic concept that can be molded and remade.

POLITICS IN THE VERNACULAR

I want to close with the suggestion that these vernacular fictions participate in broader transformations in citizenship and political belonging at midcentury. The years following the Second World War were among the most fertile periods of legal, social, and political thinking on political belonging. It is from this period that we inherit some of the most important documents on human rights and citizenship theory. The Universal Declaration of Human Rights located rights within the very idea of the human, severing the legitimacy of rights from territorial boundaries or state sovereignty. Hannah Arendt's *The Origins of Totalitarianism* looked skeptically on the figure of the human at the heart of that doctrine, exposing the vulnerability of those who had nothing but their so-called human rights to guarantee their security. T. H. Marshall, Britain's foremost thinker of citizenship, tied the privileges of citizenship to economics, giving the proponents of the welfare state a theory of citizenship that supported social programs but left intact the capitalist mode of production.[83] Finally, the great thinkers and agents of decolonization, Léopold Senghor, Aimé Césaire, and Frantz Fanon among them, rethought the possibilities of decolonization and postcolonial nationhood within the emerging bipolar, Cold War world. The novels in this chapter belong on the same bookshelf as these works of theory and philosophy. I have argued throughout this book that artworks are conceptual acts; they think their moment in unique ways, disclosing the particulars of historical and social forces that could find no home in extant discursive models or conceptual abstractions. The cluster of works in this chapter marshal and flex vernaculars to think political belonging differently, and they do so through the attention they devote to everyday life. A barbershop scene, a train ride through a Trinidad city, a fete in London: these are the places where we witness lived experiences. They are also sites for reconceptualizing political belonging, for imagining alternative possibilities. For Reid, Selvon, and MacInnes, vernacular fictions expose ways of seeing and enact alternative ones. For this reason, these writers, too, are among the great thinkers of "de age of colonial concern."

EPILOGUE

"APPOINTMENTS TO KEEP IN THE PAST"

THIS STUDY BEGAN with a claim that late modernism's distinctive form of outwardness scrambles old literary historical models that conflate styles with periods. While there are certainly concentrations of realist or modernist aesthetic activity at different times, it makes little sense to speak of a "realist" or "modernist" period neatly bracketed by the beginning and endpoints of an aesthetic style's lifespan. In these pages, I historicize late modernism's outward turn as an aesthetic logic generated by the end of a world-system and uniquely capable of making that change appear; in this way, late modernism's preoccupation with everyday life serves primarily as a form of geopolitical description. By way of conclusion, I circle back now to the persistence, or perhaps lateness, of this distinct form of outwardness. In this brief epilogue, I speculate on how the outward turn might persist in contemporary literature that continues to think about the consequences of those midcentury years. How would we understand a contemporary form of outwardness, particularly one focused on remembering those years rather than charting them as they unfold? Several contemporary novels remain preoccupied with the period this book addresses, but this short epilogue will turn to W. G. Sebald's experimental and documentary work *Austerlitz*. Sebald's novel follows its eponymous amnesiac as he searches for his parents and his own forgotten history, which, we come to discover, is bound up with the Nazi incursion into Czechoslovakia. The novel, though, is not just concerned with the recovery of an individual's lost past; through the figure of Austerlitz, Sebald's novel maps out the links between distant times and places, embedding the afterlives of geopolitical tragedies in the shape of objects, the appearance of images and words, and even the movement of sentences. This novel, then, is not about Austerlitz's search to assemble a coherent identity or life narrative. Instead, we might treat it as a broader effort to see the history of the long twentieth century accumulated in the spaces, times, and affective zones of everyday life.

Sebald's works are known for their labyrinthine sentences and the visual images he grafts into his narrative; his novels, poems, and nonfiction all develop a unique documentary aesthetic. In his lecture "Air War and Literature," he specifically defends a descriptive, documentary aesthetic for what he calls "the serious study of material incommensurable with traditional aesthetics."[1] For Sebald, this documentary aesthetic was preferable also to avant-garde experimentation. In his analysis of postwar German literature, Sebald dismantles the nimble, technically advanced prose of Arno Schmidt's short novel *Scenes from the Life of a Faun*. Despite Schmidt's extraordinary use of language to depict an air raid, Sebald sees only "the author, eager and persistent, intent on his linguistic fretwork. . . . I do not think," he continues, "my dislike for the ostentatious avant-gardeist style of Schmidt's study of the moment of destruction derives from a fundamentally conservative attitude to form and language."[2] The experience of destruction, of a violence so excessive, requires something "concrete and documentary."[3]

Austerlitz is Sebald's experimental documentary aesthetic at its most mature. His novel combines hypotactic sentences with an odd assemblage of photographs, postcards, architectural plans, paintings, video stills, and other visual ephemera. The lengthy sentences mimic the style of eighteenth-century German naturalist writers, whose use of multiple subordinate clauses bolstered their observations with thick detail while outlining complex relationships within and among different phenomena.[4] In Sebald's narrative, however, hypotaxis decreases narrative reliability, casting into sharp relief the uncertainty of memory and the pressure of history. In an opening scene, the narrator compares the animals in the Antwerp Nocturama to the Antwerpen-Centraal Station. This signature Sebaldian sentence combines close attention to detail with a series of juxtapositions that establish indirect relationships among various phenomena:

Like the creatures in the Nocturama, which had included a strikingly large number of dwarf species—tiny fennec foxes, spring-hares, hamsters—the rail-way passengers seemed to me somehow miniaturized, whether by the unusual height of the ceiling or because of the gathering dusk, and it was this, I suppose, which prompted the passing thought, nonsensical in itself, that they were the last members of a diminutive race which had perished or had been expelled from its homeland, and that because they alone survived they wore the same sorrowful expression as the creatures in the zoo.[5]

Sebald's logic is associative, not causal; the relationships between phenomena are "prompted" and are "nonsensical." "Miniaturized" people, for instance, will connect later with ghosts who are "usually a little shorter than they had been in life" (54), and the Jews, the "tiny figures" (55) in an illustration of a camp in the desert of Sinai that Austerlitz sees in his Bible of Sinai; the Nocturama, with its collection of animals from across the globe, crystallizes the process of imprisonment and transport, recalling the horrific fate of Austerlitz's mother and scores of European Jews, Gypsies, leftists, and homosexuals. Throughout the novel, associations accumulate; the spaces and objects of everyday life harbor the spectral, violent histories of Europe's past.

Sebald's version of documentary writing spins out a ghostly philosophy of history, one that resembles that of Walter Benjamin, whom Sebald read. In both of their minds, the downtrodden and the vanquished of history have a claim on the present. For Sebald, acknowledging that claim entails a dramatic rethinking of historical time. In what is arguably the centerpiece of the novel, Austerlitz articulates his philosophy of time from an observation room at Greenwich.[6] Time, Austerlitz says, does not flow ahead as Newton thought; instead time is "nonconcurrent" (100). "And is not human life in many parts of the earth governed to this day less by time than by the weather, and thus by an unquantifiable dimension which disregards linear regularity, does not progress constantly forward but moves in eddies, is marked by episodes of congestion and irruption, recurs in ever-changing form, and evolves in no one knows what direction?" (101). Unmoored from the order of linear time, historical moments exist in a state of suspension and recurrence: "past events have not yet occurred but are waiting to do so at the moment when we think of them" (101). The recurrence of the past suggests two things: first, historical violence lingers into the present; second, we need alternate conceptualizations of time, alternate modes of perception, to see and respond to the claims of the past.

This is precisely where Sebald shares an affinity with late modernists in this study. The spaces, objects, and practices of everyday life are all signs of a historical past scarcely remembered. Sebald's novel suggests we need other forms of attention to bring the past into visibility, to construe concretely the relationship between historical events and daily life. Lucas van Valckenborch's sixteenth-century painting *View of Antwerp with the Frozen Schelde* discloses the extent of this problem for Austerlitz. Van Valckenborch's scene is a busy one: boats are stranded in the ice; people huddle around a fire to ward off the winter chill; city dwellers have playfully taken to the frozen river, some with better balance than others. But it is a lady in a yellow dress on the right side of the canvas that snares Austerlitz's attention:

> I feel as if the moment depicted by Lucas van Valckenborch had never come to an end, as if the canary-yellow lady had only just fallen over or swooned as if the black velvet hood had only this moment dropped away from her head, as if the little accident, which no doubt goes unnoticed by most viewers, were always happening over and over again, and nothing and no one could ever remedy it. (13–14)

Because the painting freezes the woman's fall, this moment is both suspended and yet always happening. What troubles Austerlitz more is the fact that this woman's accident, her ever-occurring yet never completed fall, passes unnoticed and, strangely, unremedied, recalling to mind the unnoticed disaster in Auden's "Musée des Beaux Artes." What would stir such a profound sense of obligation to this figure in the painting? That she is one of the "tiny figures" (13) in the painting slots her within an associative chain that includes the dead and the vanquished that litter the pages of history. Austerlitz's trouble is not with the woman per se but with a broader problem of how the past might attain legibility for us and, further, how we might then respond.

Over and over again Sebald's narrative will conjure the specter of historical traumas caught and recurring from within the most ordinary scenes and spaces of contemporary urban life. In the center of a bustling European metropolis with people moving about the city, Sebald directs our attention to a lingering colonial past that can neither be erased nor seen. Commenting on the history of Antwerpen-Centraal Station, Austerlitz links the grandeur of the building to the plunder and genocide of King Leopold's Congo. The plan of the elevated levels of the station mime the Roman Pantheon. Yet where "the gods looked down on visitors to the Roman Pantheon" (10) Louis Delacenserie, the station's designer, placed icons of capitalist modernity: "mining, industry, transport, trade, and capital" (11–12). The train station negates the brutal extraction of labor and resources that funded its construction while giving material expression to the population's identification with—even willful obedience to—the new gods of modern capitalism. The train station mediates between the sufferings of those in the Congo and the everyday comings and goings of those in the metropole. The actual existence of the train station, in Henri Lefebvre's words, "replaces a brutal reality with a materially realized appearance. . . . To the degree that there are traces of violence and death . . . the monumental work erases them and replaces them with a tranquil power."[7] Austerlitz's narrative makes legible those erased histories, tying the lethal processes of colonialism in the late nineteenth and early twentieth centuries to the structures and practices of everyday life in a contemporary European city. In Austerlitz's way of seeing, the architecture of the urban space suspends and repeats the historical violence that enabled it. This sort of networked spatial thinking suggests that life in one geographical locale enables life in another, and because Leopold's victims have a claim on us that goes unacknowledged, the past remains very much alive.

The form of attention Austerlitz develops through van Valckenborch's painting and Antwerpen-Centraal Station guides his investigations into his own lost past. An amnesiac for most of his life, Austerlitz has no recollection of his childhood before arriving in Wales. His parents, his Czech home, and what we come to find are many, many warm memories of his youth exist far beyond the reach of his memory. Upon hearing the word "Prague" mentioned in a bookshop, Austerlitz is convinced that somehow the city is part of his past. Like a detective, Austerlitz visits Prague, following the trail of clues and names, and gradually discovers that his mother perished in the camp at Terezin while he and his father we scattered across different parts of Europe. Yet the material Austerlitz collects, particularly the photos and documents inserted into the book, do not operate as evidence. A picture of Austerlitz as a young boy does little to consolidate his identity; instead, he senses the same obligation, the same demand put to him by the lady in the yellow dress in van Valckenborch's painting: "the piercing, inquiring gaze of the page boy who had come to demand his dues, who was waiting in the gray light of dawn on the empty field for me to accept the challenge and avert the misfortune lying ahead of him" (184). Austerlitz's walk through Terezin proves equally cryptic and equally demanding. The multiple images of abandoned buildings, shuttered windows, and closed doors appear back to back, inducing an almost claustrophobic effect. What is clear, though, is Austerlitz will never have complete access to the time or place of his mother's death.

Like the photo of himself as a young child, these discoveries of the past—his childhood home, his mother's whereabouts, his own youthful image—do not consolidate his identity. Instead, they prompt questions about the burdens of history. When Austerlitz later gazes at a random assortment of objects in the window of the Antikos Bazar in Terezin, he thinks yet again about the endless recurrence of the past in the present, but this time he understands his life, his own past, as somehow tied to those collective sufferings. Austerlitz looks curiously at a porcelain statue of a man on horseback reaching out to a woman "already bereft of her last hope": "They [the objects] were all as timeless as that moment of rescue, perpetuated but forever just occurring, these ornaments, utensils, and mementoes stranded in the Terezín bazaar objects that for reasons one could never know had outlived their former owners and survived the process of destruction, so that I could now see my own faint shadow image barely perceptible among them" (197).

His shadowy image, barely perceivable in the photo that accompanies this section of the narrative, aligns Austerlitz with the dispossessed and, very likely, the exterminated. Two things become clear at this juncture in the narrative: First, artworks, spaces, train stations, and ordinary objects bear the traces of history within them; however, we do not yet possess the forms of attention required to see those traces, much less to see or feel the demand they place upon us in the present. Second, Austerlitz's quest is not about filling in the missing details of his biography; rather, the suggestion is that Austerlitz's amnesia mirrors a collective forgetting. We do not yet know how to see the global historical processes sedimented into the spaces, objects, and habits of our daily lives. For Sebald, we cannot articulate our political and ethical obligations until we are able to see the everyday as a sign of history. This is what I take Austerlitz to mean when he poses what is very likely the novel's overarching question to its readers: "And might it not be, continued Austerlitz, that we also have appointments to keep in the past, in what has gone before and is for the most part extinguished, and must go there in search of places and people who have some connection with us on the far side of time, so to speak?" (258). Those people—the slaughtered natives in the Congo, those who perished in the deathscapes of Hitler's Europe, the dispossessed—and their sufferings continue and repeat unremedied until we acknowledge them, until we redeem them, as Benjamin might say.

Austerlitz scrutinizes the everyday so as to unlock the histories of those who suffered, to discern the connections between events in different geographical areas, and to chart the multidirectional lives of events in past and present. Those connections are never direct, but they bind individual experience and collective, transnational histories. I have maintained throughout this book that artworks are conceptual acts; I suggest here that part of the enduring claim of late modernism resides in its conviction, or perhaps obsession, that we might discern in everyday life those multidirectional histories that touch us and often disappear. *Austerlitz* tells us emphatically that everyday life is the scene where we can decipher historical processes during their unfolding and after their completion. Sebald's claim, though, is not identical to anything I have examined in this book. Sebald's text is largely retrospective, glancing backward at that period of world systemic disorder that these other late modernists tried to describe as it unfolded. In one way the claim of late modernism abides. *Austerlitz* suggests that the right form of attention can convert the everyday into a sign of history and reveal the obligations the recent past has on our present. And yet if the aesthetic appears to live on in Sebald's novel, the mood is decidedly different. This novel lacks the apocalyptic sense we saw in Woolf, Isherwood, Mass-Observation, and Bowen and there is surely none of the optimism, however skeptical, we saw in Vic Reid. If art can still transform the everyday into signs of history, Sebald's novel worries that we may have arrived too late to read them.

NOTES

INTRODUCTION: LATE MODERNISM
AND THE OUTWARD TURN

1. Elizabeth Bowen, *The Demon Lover and Other Stories* (London: Jonathan Cape, 1945), xii.
2. Ibid.
3. Elizabeth Bowen, "In the Square," in *The Collected Stories of Elizabeth Bowen* (New York: Knopf, 1981), 609; subsequent citations appear in the text.
4. For more on the periodization of imperial life cycles, see Giovanni Arrighi's *The Long Twentieth Century: Money, Power, and the Origins of Our Times* (New York: Verso, 1994); and see Immanuel Wallerstein's *The Modern World-System IV: Centrist Liberalism Triumphant, 1789–1914* (Berkeley: University of California Press, 2011) and his brief overview *World Systems Analysis: An Introduction* (Durham, NC: Duke University Press, 2004). Also see historian John Darwin's *The Empire Project: The Rise and Fall of the British World System, 1830–1970* (Cambridge: Cambridge University Press, 2011).
5. The Mass Observation archive is housed at the University of Sussex and is unimaginably large. The sheer size of it indicates that everyday life was first and foremost a problem for late modernist cultural producers.
6. John Grierson, Preface to *Documentary Film*, 3rd ed., by Paul Rotha (1952; repr. London: Faber and Faber, 1963), 16.
7. Virginia Woolf, *The Diary of Virginia Woolf*, 5 vols., ed. Anne Oliver Bell (New York: Harcourt Brace Jovanovich, 1978), vol. 4, December 19, 1932.
8. Stephen Spender, *The Destructive Element: A Study of Modern Writers and Beliefs* (London: Jonathan Cape, 1935), 205.
9. Fine studies on realism and the nineteenth century by Laurie Langbauer and Ruth Bernard Yeazell make strong, complex cases for realism's particular mode of rendering everyday life.

See Langbauer's *Novels of Everyday Life: The Series in English Fiction, 1850–1930* (Ithaca, NY: Cornell University Press, 1999) and Yeazell's *Art of the Everyday: Dutch Painting and the Realist Novel* (Princeton, NJ: Princeton University Press, 2008). Although it does not address everyday life as explicitly as these studies, Stuart Sherman's study of clocks and diurnal forms in the eighteenth century is equally impressive. See his *Telling Time: Clocks, Diaries, and English Diurnal Form, 1660–1785* (Chicago: University of Chicago Press, 1996).

10. See my "Late Modernism: British Literature at Midcentury" *Literature Compass* 9, no. 4 (2012): 326–37.

11. In *Everyday Life and Cultural Theory: An Introduction* (London: Routledge, 2002), Ben Highmore suggests cultural studies adopt avant-garde and modernist techniques in order to investigate everyday life.

12. Juan A. Suárez, *Pop Modernism: Noise and the Reinvention of Everyday Life* (Urbana: University of Illinois Press, 2007), 5.

13. Liesl Olson, *Modernism and the Ordinary* (Oxford: Oxford University Press, 2009), 4.

14. Lisi Schoenbach's work on habit also provides a thoughtful counter to traditional narratives of modernism as shock and rupture. See her provocative *Pragmatic Modernism* (Oxford: Oxford University Press, 2011).

15. For an overview of work on modernism and everyday life, see Liesl Olson's "Everyday Life Studies: A Review" Modernism/Modernity 18, no. 1 (January 2011): 175–80; also see Bryony Randall's excellent, comprehensive survey "Modernist Literature and the Everyday," *Literature Compass* 7, no. 9 (2010): 824–35.

16. John Grierson, *Grierson on Documentary*, ed. Forsyth Hardy (Berkeley: University of California Press, 1966), 121.

17. Christopher Isherwood, *Lions and Shadows: An Education in the Twenties* (Minneapolis: University of Minnesota Press, 2000), 113–14.

18. See Vincent Sherry, "Modernism Under Review: Edmund Wilson's Axel's *Castle: A Study in the Imaginative Literature of 1870–1930.*" *Modernist Cultures* 7 (2012): 145–59.

19. For a fine reading of the debates over modernism and socialist realism, see Peter Marks's excellent "Illusion and Reality: The Spectre of Socialist Realism in Thirties Literature" in *Rewriting the Thirties: Modernism and After*, ed. Steven Matthews and Keith Williams, 22–36 (London: Longman, 1997).

20. Michael North, *Henry Green and the Writing of His Generation* (Charlottesville: University of Virginia Press, 1988), 1.

21. See ibid.; and Rod Mengham, *The Idiom of the Time: The Writings of Henry Green* (Cambridge: Cambridge University Press, 1982).

22. Paul Saint-Amour, "Air War Prophecy and Interwar Modernism," *Comparative Literature Studies* 42, no. 2 (2005): 131.

23. Henry Green, *Loving; Living; Party Going* (1939; repr, New York: Penguin Classics, 1993), 395; subsequent citations appear in the text.

24. Marina MacKay, *Modernism and World War II* (New York: Cambridge University Press, 2007), 95.

25. For more on Green, crowds, and entrapment, see Marina MacKay's "'Is your journey really necessary?' Going Nowhere in Late Modernist London." *PMLA* 125, no. 5 (October 2009): 1600–1613; as well as chapter 4, "The Neutrality of Henry Green," in Marina MacKay, *Modernism and World War II* (Cambridge: Cambridge University Press, 2007): 91–117.

26. See Langbauer, *Novels of Everyday Life*.

27. For flexible and nuanced examinations of realism, see Stephen Arata, "Late-Victorian Realism," in *Cambridge Companion to the Fin de Siècle*, ed. Gail Marshall, 165–88 (Cambridge: Cambridge University Press, 2007); Nancy Armstrong, *Fiction in the Age of Photography: The Legacy of British Realism* (Cambridge: Harvard University Press, 1999); Peter Brooks, *Realist Vision* (New Haven, CT: Yale University Press, 2005); and Andrew H. Miller, *Novels Behind Plate-Glass: Commodity Culture and Victorian Narrative* (Cambridge: Cambridge University Press, 1995).

28. Gerald L. Bruns's characterization of modernism as nominalism poses a significant challenge to these schemas of literary history. On his reading, modernism is simply the incessant questioning of art or its negation of any set categorization of art. Although aesthetic negativity operates only within a particular historical context, it does suggest that modernism is not defined by a set of traits as much as by a conceptual challenge. Fittingly, his book has virtually nothing at all on postmodernism, even though it reaches into the late twentieth century. While it doesn't quite parallel my arguments here, I find his take refreshing. See his *On the Anarchy of Poetry and Philosophy: A Guide for the Unruly* (Bronx, NY: Fordham University Press, 2006). David James has recently called for a more thorough consideration of modernism's continuation into the present in his *Modernist Futures: Innovation and Inheritance in the Contemporary Novel* (Cambridge: Cambridge University Press, 2012). For a consideration of the conceptual and institutional logics governing the mania of periodization, see Eric Hayot's "Against Periodization; or, On Institutional Time." *New Literary History* 42, no. 4 (Autumn 2011): 739–56. Nathan K. Hensley offers an elaborate "model of discontinuous historicism able to compare aesthetic forms that emerge at the end of . . . imperial life-cycles." (Hensley, "Allegories of the Contemporary," *Novel: A Forum on Fiction* 45, no. 2 (2012): 276–300, doi:10.1215/00295132-1573976. This model allows us to isolate texts emerging at different moments of imperial life cycles—Robert Louis Stevenson's *Dr. Jekyll and Mr. Hyde*, Giorgio Agamben's *Homo Sacer: Sovereign Power and Bare Life*, Jonathan Franzen's *The Corrections*—and read them as mediations of the final, violent stages of a world-system.

29. While many of the key "statements" of the New Modernist Studies have emphasized its expanding temporal, spatial, and vertical boundaries, very few critics have targeted the value of the term "modernism." This increasing expansion has the celebratory overtones of an unwitting intellectual imperialism, whereby one colonizes all types of literary, artistic, and cultural phenomena by dubbing them "modernist." One wonders if the goals of such projects in twentieth-century literary criticism might benefit more from provincializing, not globalizing, "modernism." For a summary of the favored sites of expansion of New Modernist Studies, see Douglas Mao and Rebecca L. Walkowitz, "The New Modernist Studies,"

PMLA 123, no. 3 (2008): 737–48. The argument for pushing modernism into all geographies and across all temporal borders is probably best articulated by Melba Cuddy-Keane in "Modernism, Geopolitics, Globalization," *Modernism/Modernity* 10, no. 3 (September 2003): 539–58; and by Susan Stanford Friedman in a cluster of articles, which include "Definitional Excursions: The Meanings of Modern/Modernity/Modernism," *Modernism/Modernity* 8, no. 3 (September 2001): 498–513; "Periodizing Modernism: Postcolonial Modernities and the Space/Time Borders of Modernist Studies," *Modernism/Modernity* 12, no. 3 (September 2006): 425–44; and "Planetarity: Musing Modernist Studies," *Modernism/Modernity* 17, no. 3 (September 2010): 471–99. Max Brzezinski has taken issue with the depoliticization of the New Modernist Studies. See his "The New Modernist Studies: What's Left of Political Formalism?" *Minnesota Review* 76 (Summer 2011): 109–25.

30. Fredric Jameson, *A Singular Modernity: An Essay on the Ontology of the Present* (New York: Verso, 2002), 124.

31. Ibid.

32. Ibid.

33. Of course, Jameson does acknowledge the simultaneous existence of modernisms and realisms, and even the proliferation of new realisms at different historical moments. While I am sympathetic and in agreement with most of Jameson's charges against periodization and the ideology of modernism, my main departure from him here is on the key point of the categorical irreconcilability of aesthetics and epistemology. It strikes me as extraordinarily limiting to argue that either realism or modernism can be compartmentalized as primarily epistemological or primarily aesthetic. One feels that Jameson's polemic gets the best of his analysis on this point. He addresses the question of art and knowledge in truly provocative fashion in both *Marxism and Form: Twentieth Century Dialectical Theories of Literature* (Princeton, NJ: Princeton University Press, 1971); and *The Political Unconscious: Narrative as a Socially Symbolic Act* (Ithaca, NY: Cornell University Press, 1981), among other places.

34. Brooks, Realist Vision, 12, 210.

35. Yeazell, *Art of the Everyday*, 166.

36. Wallerstein, *World Systems Analysis*, 18.

37. Perhaps not surprisingly, many in the humanities have reacted to this brand of systemic thinking with what Bruce Robbins calls a "strange mixture of attraction and repulsion," with repulsion being the stronger of the two. Bruce Robbins, "Blaming the System," in *Immanuel Wallerstein and the Problem of the World: System, Scale, Culture,* ed. David Palumbo-Liu, Bruce Robbins, and Nirvana Tanoukhi, 41–63 (Durham, NC: Duke University Press, 2011), 43. Immanuel Wallerstein develops an idea of the "geoculture" or liberal consensus that emerged in the wake of the revolutions in the eighteenth and nineteenth centuries. See Wallerstein, *Modern World-System IV*.

38. Richard E. Lee, "The Modern World-System: Its Structures, Its Geoculture, Its Crisis and Transformation," in *Immanuel Wallerstein and the Problem of the World: System, Scale, Culture,* ed. David Palumbo-Liu, Bruce Robbins, and Nirvana Tanoukhi, 27–40. (Durham, NC: Duke University Press, 2011), 32.

39. Wallerstein defines culture in terms that would not be entirely alien to literary studies: "The culture, that is the idea-system, of this capitalist world-economy is the outcome of our collective historical attempts to come to terms with the contradictions, the ambiguities, the complexities of the socio-political realities of this particular system." Immanuel Wallerstein, *Geopolitics and Geoculture: Essays on the Changing World-System* (Cambridge: Cambridge University Press, 1991), 166.

40. See Pascale Casanova, *The World Republic of Letters* (Cambridge: Harvard University Press, 2004); Franco Moretti, *Graphs, Maps, Trees* (New York: Verso Books, 2005); and Nirvana Tanoukhi, "The Scale of World Literature," in *Immanuel Wallerstein and the Problem of the World*, ed. David Palumbo-Liu, Bruce Robbins, and Nirvana Tanoukhi, 78–98 (Durham, NC: Duke University Press, 2011).

41. W. H. Auden and Christopher Isherwood, *Journey to a War* (New York: Paragon House, 1990), 32.

42. Darwin, *Empire Project*, 419.

43. Ibid., 5.

44. In this regard I echo Heather Love's suggestion that criticism take more seriously the act of literary description. In recent articles, Love elaborates one way to think about descriptive reading and different interdisciplinary methods of treating description. My method and political commitments differ from most of what gathers itself under the banners of the "descriptive turn" or "surface reading," but I share the idea that literary description demands more attention and quite possibly demands dramatic shifts in our interpretive practices. For more, see Heather Love, "Close but not Deep: Literary Ethics and the Descriptive Turn," *New Literary History* 41, no. 2 (2010): 371–91; and Heather Love, "Close Reading and Thin Description," *Public Culture* 25, no. 3 (2013): 401–34.

45. See Jessica Berman's discussion of commitment and aesthetic form in her introduction to *Modernist Commitments: Ethics, Politics, and Transnational Modernism* (New York: Columbia University Press, 2011). In his famous takedown of committed art, Adorno demonstrates the way narrow conceptualizations of committed and autonomous art cancel out any possible relationship of art and reality. See his "Commitment," in *Aesthetics and Politics* (New York: Verso, 2007).

46. Matthew Hart, *Nations of Nothing but Poetry: Modernism, Transnationalism, and Synthetic Vernacular Writing* (Oxford: Oxford University Press, 2010), 5.

47. I would also add as exemplary articulations of modernist form and changing political and historical realities Marina MacKay's brilliant "'Is your journey really necessary?'"; Janice Ho's "The Spatial Imagination and Literary Form of Conrad's Colonial Fictions," *Journal of Modern Literature* 13, no. 4 (Summer 2007): 1–19; and Saint-Amour's "Air War Prophecy and Interwar Modernism."

48. Theodor W. Adorno, *Aesthetic Theory*, trans. Robert Hullot-Kentor (1970; repr. Minneapolis: University of Minnesota Press, 1998), 6.

49. For an Adornian-inspired rethinking of commitment and formalism, see W. J. T. Mitchell, "The Commitment to Form; or, Still Crazy After All These Years." *PMLA* 118, no. 2

(March 2003): 321–25. For a skeptical take on the turn to form as the erasure of the political in the New Modernist Studies, see Brzezinski, "New Modernist Studies."

50. Theodor W. Adorno, *Introduction to the Sociology of Music*, trans. E. B. Ashton (London: Continuum, 1988), 203–4.

51. This is what I take Fredric Jameson to mean when he suggests we reorient our historicizing impulses away from "forecasts of the past" and toward "archaeologies of the future." See his *A Singular Modernity*.

52. Ellen Rooney, "Form and Commitment," *Modern Language Quarterly* 61, no. 1 (2000), 34.

53. David Harvey is especially lucid on how Marx's investigations throughout *Capital* exemplify the dialectical method. See, for example, the introduction and chapter 1 ("Commodities and Exchange") in Harvey, *A Companion to Marx's Capital* (New York: Verso, 2010), 1–53.

54. Karl Marx, *Capital*, vol. 1, trans. Ben Fowkes (New York: Penguin, 1990), 129.

55. Rita Felski, "Suspicious Minds," *Poetics Today* 32, no. 2 (Summer 2011), 231. Also see Felski's "Modernist Studies and Cultural Studies: Reflections on Method," *Modernism/Modernity* 10, no. 3 (September 2003): 501–17.

56. James Hansen, "Formalism and Its Malcontents: Benjamin and De Man on the Function of Allegory," *New Literary History* 35, no. 4 (Autumn 2004), 680. In an astute reading of formalism via Paul de Man and Walter Benjamin, James Hansen tells us "formalism itself invariably becomes a way of thinking beyond form" (665).

57. Ian Baucom's stirring *Specters of the Atlantic: Finance Capital, Slavery, and the Philosophy of History* (Durham, NC: Duke University Press, 2005) undertakes close readings of archival and "non-aesthetic" documents to open previously foreclosed historical knowledges. Mary A. Favret's *War at a Distance: Romanticism and the Making of Modern Wartime* (Princeton, NJ: Princeton University Press, 2010) details the various ways war arrives in the language and textures of writing away from the war zone. Both of these works insist on the formal dimensions of texts but range over multiple genres of writing. There is no sense of any aesthetic hierarchy that Felski and others find intrinsic to formalist work.

58. Rooney, "Form and Commitment," 38.

59. Fredric Jameson, *Valences of the Dialectic* (New York: Verso, 2010), 555.

60. Wai Chee Dimock, *Through Other Continents: American Literature Across Deep Time* (Princeton, NJ: Princeton University Press, 2006), 73–74.

61. W. G. Sebald, *Austerlitz*, trans. Anthea Bell (New York: Modern Library, 2001), 258.

1. THE LAST SNAPSHOT OF THE BRITISH INTELLIGENTSIA

1. John Grierson, "Flaherty's Poetic Moana," *New York Sun*, February 8, 1926. The article is penned under the name "The Moviegoer." Many histories of documentary and much work on Grierson claim that he coined the word "documentary," wresting it from French and applying it to actuality films. This is not the case. Eric Barnouw's oft-used *Documentary: A History of Non-Fiction Film* (Oxford: Oxford University Press, 1983) cites Boleslaw Matuszewski's 1898 books *Une nouvelle source de l'histoire* and *La photographie animée, ce*

qu'elle est, ce qu'elle doit être as early arguments that film had the capacity to record history and was "of a documentary interest" (Barnouw, *Documentary*, 27). Brian Winston's *Claiming the Real II: Documentary: Grierson and Beyond* (New York: Palgrave, 2008) points to American Edward Sheriff Curtis, whose 1914 film *In the Land of the Headhunters* was likely known to both Robert Flaherty and John Grierson. See part 1 of his book for more on Flaherty and Curtis's meetings and the very real possibility that his ideas and his films found their way to Grierson via Vachel Lindsay's *The Art of the Moving Picture*.

2. Brian Winston notes that French critics used *documentaire* to distinguish "serious expedition films, from travelogues" (16). He contends that Grierson likely knew how this word was used in French, "although he referenced French usage as meaning simply travelogue at the outset of the 1932–4 manifesto" (16). For more on the history of the term documentary, see his sharply critical and invigoratingly polemical *Claiming the Real II*.

3. John Grierson, "The Documentary Producer," *Cinema Quarterly* 2, no. 1 (Autumn 1933): 8.

4. Storm Jameson, "Documents," FACT 4 (1937): 8, 19.

5. For a take on the broad reach of documentary, see Laura Marcus's "The Creative Treatment of Actuality," in *Intermodernism: Literary Culture in Mid-Twentieth Century Britain*, ed. Kristin Bluemel (Edinburgh: Edinburgh University Press, 2011).

6. Bill Nichols, "Documentary Film and the Modernist Avant-Garde," *Critical Inquiry* 27, no. 4 (Summer 2001): 581.

7. Ibid., 582.

8. Ibid., 603.

9. Ibid. Nichols has wrongly assumed much about Grierson's use of "significant form" and his relationship to Clive Bell and Bloomsbury. Grierson's articles from the mid-1920s routinely mock Bell and Fry and miss no opportunity to mock "significant form." I deal more closely with his remarks on Bell in the next section.

10. Many readers will recognize a similar dilemma in other areas of modernist culture, particularly in the theater of Bertolt Brecht and the arguments over art and its social function between Theodor W. Adorno, Walter Benjamin, Ernst Bloch, and Georg Lukács. The most accessible compilation of these debates remains *Aesthetics and Politics* (London: Verso, 2007).

11. I rely on Jacques Rancière to make this part of my argument, but I still find Peter Burger's *Theory of the Avant-Garde* (Minneapolis: University of Minnesota, 1984) enormously helpful. More recent considerations of art's social function, such as Krzysztof Ziarek's *The Force of Art* (Stanford, CA: Stanford University Press, 2004), also offer stimulating ways to rethink the politics of aesthetic autonomy.

12. Theodor W. Adorno, *Aesthetic Theory*, trans. Robert Hullot-Kentor (1970; repr. Minneapolis: University of Minnesota Press, 1998), 23.

13. Ibid., 4.

14. Jacques Rancière, *Aesthetics and Its Discontents*, trans. Steve Corcoron (Malden, MA: Polity, 2009), 40.

15. See Rancière's *Dissensus: On Politics and Aesthetics*, trans. Steve Corcoran. (London: Continuum, 2010).

16. Rancière, *Aesthetic and Its Discontents*, 122.

17. Walter Benjamin, "Surrealism: The Last Snapshot of the European Intelligentsia," in *Selected Writings*, Vol. 2, *Part 1: 1927–1930*, ed. Michael W. Jennings, Howard Eiland, and Gary Smith, 207–221 (Cambridge: Harvard University Press, 1999), 207.

18. Ibid.

19. Ibid.

20. Paul Rotha, *Documentary Film* (London: Faber and Faber, 1935), 32–33.

21. Tom Harrisson and Charles Madge, *Mass Observation* (London: Frederick Muller Ltd., 1937), 11.

22. John Grierson, Preface to *Documentary Film*, by Paul Rotha (London: Faber and Faber, 1935), 5.

23. Humphrey Jennings and Charles Madge, *May the Twelfth: Mass Observation Day Surveys* (London: Faber and Faber, 1937), 5.

24. John Grierson, *Grierson on Documentary*, ed. Forsyth Hardy (Berkeley: University of California Press, 1966), 207.

25. In addition to Barnouw and Winston, see also Jack C. Ellis and Betsy A. McLane's recent *A New History of Documentary Film* (New York: Continuum, 2005). Mark Wollaeger's excellent *Modernism, Media, and Propaganda: British Narrative from 1900 to 1945* (Princeton, NJ: Princeton University Press, 2006) takes up documentary, Alfred Hitchcock, and Orson Welles. See chapter 5 "From the Thirties to World War II: Negotiating Modernism and Propaganda in Hitchcock and Wells" (217–60).

26. In addition to those listed earlier, see Barnouw, *Documentary*; William Guynn, *A Cinema of Non-Fiction* (London: Associated University Presses); and Paul Swann, *The British Documentary Film Movement, 1926–1946* (Cambridge: Cambridge University Press, 1998).

27. Jack Ellis's *John Grierson: Life, Contributions, Influence* (Carbondale: Southern Illinois University Press, 2000) is particularly good in tracking all of Grierson's promotional activities. See especially his chapter on the General Post Office (GPO) Film Unit.

28. Although Rotha spent only a few months with Grierson's film unit at the GPO, he spoke in over twenty-five major cities and continued advocating for Grierson's aesthetic and political ideology of documentary cinema. For more on Rotha's passionate but brief spin through the Grierson's world, see Ian Aitken, *Film and Reform: John Grierson and the Documentary Film Movement* (New York: Routledge, 1990).

29. John Grierson, quoted in ibid., 11.

30. Aitken, *Film and Reform*, 49.

31. John Grierson, "Vorticism Brought to Serve Drama," *Chicago Evening Post*, February 17, 1925.

32. John Grierson, "Finding in Plato the Key to Modern Art," *Chicago Evening Post*, May 12, 1925.

33. Ibid.

34. John Grierson, "Vorticism Born with a Curse on Its Lips," *Chicago Evening Post*, June 16, 1925.

35. John Grierson, "The Personality Behind the Paint," *Chicago Evening Post*, June 30, 1925.

36. Grierson, quoted in Aitken, *Film and Reform*, 53.

37. Aitken, *Film and Reform*, 58.

38. Grierson, Preface to *Documentary Film*, 5.

39. Ibid., 13–14.

40. John Grierson, *Grierson on Documentary*, ed. Forsyth Hardy (Berkeley: University of California Press, 1966), 136.

41. Ibid., 148.

42. Ibid.

43. Ibid., 127.

44. Ibid., 131.

45. Ibid., 121.

46. Ibid., 165. Propaganda, of course, did not carry the same connotations as it does today. In *Modernism, Media, and Propaganda*, Mark Wollaeger writes that "during World War II, British officials still tended to use the words 'information,' 'propaganda,' and 'publicity' interchangeably among themselves" (7). This is the sense in which Grierson uses the word.

47. Grierson, *Grierson on Documentary*, 179.

48. Ibid., 180.

49. Ibid.

50. Ibid., 181.

51. See Sir Stephen Tallents, *The Projection of England* (London: Olen Press, 1932). Tallents's idea of national projection played an important role in the establishment and direction of the film units at both the EMB and the GPO.

52. *Song of Ceylon* was sponsored primarily by the Ceylon Tea Board, but Paul Rotha remembers it as being one of the films started at the EMB but completed at the GPO. See his *Documentary Diary* (New York: Hill and Wang, 1973), 123.

53. Ellis and McLane, *New History of Documentary Film*, 65.

54. Ibid.

55. William Guynn, "Art of National Projection," in *Documenting the Documentary: Close Readings of Documentary Film and Video*, ed. Barry K. Grant and Jeannette Sloniowski (Detroit: Wayne State University Press, 1998), 90.

56. These debates are endless, but the three classic ones are Chinua Achebe's "An Image of Africa: Racism in Conrad's Heart of Darkness," *Massachusetts Review* 18 (1977): 782–94; Patrick Brantlinger's *Rule of Darkness: British Literature and Imperialism, 1830–1914* (Ithaca, NY: Cornell University Press, 1988); and Edward Said's *Culture and Imperialism* (New York: Knopf, 1993), esp. 19–31. For a refreshing turn on these debates, see Janice Ho's very smart "The Spatial Imagination and Literary Form of Conrad's Colonial Fictions," *Journal of Modern Literature* 30, no. 4 (2007): 1–19.

57. Basil Wright, *Song of Ceylon* [Video, 1934]. Retrieved April 5, 2015, from www.colonialfilm .org.uk/node/486/.

58. Guynn, "Art of National Projection," 97.

59. Humphrey Jennings, "The Documentary Film: Transcript of a Discussion Between Humphrey Jennings and J. B. Holmes with Ian Dalrymple as Chair," Undated (circa 1940s) Humphrey Jennings Collection, Box 2, Item 16, British Film Institute National Library.

60. James Chapman, *The British at War: Cinema, State, and Propaganda, 1939–1945* (London: I. B. Tauris, 1998), 161.

61. See Malcom Smith's excellent reading "Narrative and Ideology in *Listen to Britain*," in *Narrative: From Malory to Motion Pictures* (Baltimore: Edward Arnold, 1985), 145–57.

62. Humphrey Jennings and Charles Madge, "Poetic Description and Mass Observation," New Verse 24 (1937): 3.

63. Harrisson and Madge, *Mass Observation*, 10.

64. Tom Harrisson, Humphrey Jennings, and Charles Madge, "Anthropology at Home," *New Statesman and Nation*, January 30, 1937, 155.

65. Kathleen Raine, *The Land Unknown* (New York: George Braziller, 1975), 81.

66. From his unpublished autobiographical manuscript, Madge recalls the problems with Mass-Observation that resulted in Jennings's departure:

> This was . . . , I think, because he was out of sympathy with the direction taken by Mass-Observation as a result of Tom's own initiatives or those which I took in an attempt to adapt my own initial approach to that of Tom. Collaboration of a sort between Tom and my-self, sometimes close and sometimes rather distant, continued for three years, until mid-1940. There was an underlying contradiction in this collaboration: Tom's version was that he was the scientist, concerned with the objective, while I was the poet concerned with the subjective. I did not see things that way—however inadequate my starting point, my aim throughout was to move towards a more objective, scientific methodology, and, much as I admitted Tom's enterprise in seeking to be observe, and where possible measure, the whole range of social behaviour in Bolton, I suspect his too sweeping claims for what he had done and was trying to do, as not really and truly scientific.

Madge moves on to work with Keynes on surveys of spending and saving after he quits M-O and then on to a professorship in Sociology; his recollection is refracted in such a way so as to fashion a teleology that begins with the poetic and scientific tensions in Mass-Observation's beginnings and ultimately ends with a conception of objectivity that exists nowhere in the initial phase of Mass-Observation.

67. Both James Buzard and Jeremy MacClancey synchronize Mass-Observation's eventual merger with the Ministry of Information with the decline of surrealist techniques. Laura Marcus's reading of *War Begins at Home* locates "echoes" (14) of surrealism, suggesting, as I do here, that Mass-Observation's incorporation into the Ministry of Information does not spell the end of its use and redeployment of avant-garde techniques.

68. Jed Esty, *A Shrinking Island: Modernism and National Culture in England* (Princeton, NJ: Princeton University Press, 2003), 45.

69. Extending Buzard's "Mass-Observation, Modernism, and Auto-Ethnography," *Modernism/Modernity* 4, no. 3 (1997): 93–122, Esty folds Mass-Observation's project within an expanded field of late modernist writing and cultural activity that participated in the re-

newal of English particularity. Our treatments of Mass-Observation make evident, I think, a different point of emphasis: Esty beautifully redraws the parameters of late modernism in cultural terms, but as I suggest in the introduction and through all of these chapters, aesthetic innovation also has political conditions of possibility. In this case, Mass-Observation's interest in the everyday has just as much, if not more, to do with multiple threats to the liberal democratic order as it does with a widespread sense of England as a shrinking island.

70. Harrisson and Madge, *Mass Observation*, 11.

71. Bronislaw Malinowski, "A Nation-Wide Intelligence Service," *First Year's Work*, by Mass Observation, ed. Tom Harrisson and Charles Madge (London: Lindsay Drummond, 1938), 121.

72. Harrisson and Madge, *First Year's Work* (London: Lindsay Drummond, 1938), 32.

73. Nick Hubble, *Mass Observation and Everyday Life: Culture, History, Theory* (New York: Palgrave, 2006), 14.

74. The Crystal Palace was built to house the Great Exhibition of 1851, which would showcase the cultural and technological achievements of the Industrial Revolution. It stood as an icon of Victorian achievement.

75. Valentine Cunningham, *British Writers of the Thirties* (Oxford: Oxford University Press, 1988), 42.

76. Charles Madge, The Charles Madge Archive, SxMs71, University of Sussex.

77. Jeremy MacClancey, "Brief Encounter: The Meeting, in Mass-Observation, of British Surrealism and Popular Anthropology," *Journal of the Royal Anthropological Institute* 1, no. 3 (1995): 501. See also James Clifford, *The Predicament of Culture: Twentieth Century Ethnography, Literature, and Art* (Cambridge, MA: Harvard University Press, 1988). Clifford footnotes Mass-Observation in his longer examination on the Collège de Sociologie.

78. Ben Highmore, *Everyday Life and Cultural Theory: An Introduction* (New York: Routledge, 2002), 111, 87, 107.

79. André Breton, *Nadja*, trans. Richard Howard (1928; repr. Grove Press, 1960), 64.

80. Paul C. Ray, *The Surrealist Movement in England* (Ithaca, NY: Cornell University Press), 1971; and Michel Remy, *Surrealism in Britain* (London: Ashgate, 2001).

81. Remy, *Surrealism in Britain*, 29.

82. See James Gifford, "Anarchist Transformations of English Surrealism: The Villa Seurat Network." *Journal of Modern Literature* 33, no. 4 (2010): 57–71.

83. Remy, *Surrealism in Britain*, 96.

84. Charles Madge, "Surrealism for the English," *New Verse* 6 (1933), 14.

85. Ibid.

86. Ibid., 18.

87. Charles Madge, "The Meaning of Surrealism," *New Verse* 10 (1934), 13.

88. Charles Madge, "Poetry and Politics," New Verse 3 (1933), 2.

89. Madge, "Meaning of Surrealism."

90. Charles Madge, "Review of *A Short Survey of Surrealism*," *New Verse* 18 (1935): 20–21.

91. Humphrey Jennings, "Surrealism," *Contemporary Poetry and Prose* 8 (December 1936), 167.

92. One can arguably divide the interpretation of surrealism for England along two lines: the first is from Hugh Sykes Davies and Herbert Read, who desperately wanted to make surrealism a part of the English tradition; the second line is that pursued by Madge and Jennings, who refused to reduce surrealism to easily packaged formulas and sought instead to stress its "scientific" aspect.

93. Hubble, *Mass Observation and Everyday Life*, 78.

94. Tom Jeffery, *Mass-Observation: A Short History*. Mass Observation Archive Occasional Paper Series, no. 10 (University of Sussex Library, 1999), 23.

95. Harrison and Madge, *First Year's Work*, 8.

96. Jennings and Madge, "Poetic Description," 3. Emphasis original.

97. Ibid., 2. It is worth nothing that this same passage was thought exemplary enough to be reprinted in the 1937 pamphlet.

98. Ibid., 3.

99. Humphrey Jennings and Charles Madge, "The Oxford Collective Poem," *New Verse* 25 (1937), 17. "The Oxford Collective Poem" might be seen as an indication of what Mass Observation would have been without Tom Harrisson.

100. Ibid.

101. Ibid., 18.

102. Jennings and Madge, *May the Twelfth*, iv.

103. Malinowski, "Nation-Wide Intelligence Service," 108.

104. Jennings and Madge, *May the Twelfth*, 89.

105. Ibid., 91.

106. Ibid., iv.

107. Ibid., 96.

108. Ibid., 100–101.

109. Ibid., 100.

110. Buzard, "Mass-Observation, Modernism, and Auto-Ethnography," 111.

111. Jennings and Madge, *May the Twelfth*, 138.

112. For a stimulating overview and close analysis of Mass-Observation, including a bit on *May the Twelfth* and narrative form, see Laura Marcus, "Introduction: The Project of Mass-Observation," *New Formations* 44 (Autumn 2011): 5–19.

113. Tom Harisson letter to Charles Madge (1940), qtd. in David Pocock, afterword to *May the Twelfth*, by Jennings and Madge, 418.

114. Tom Harrisson and Charles Madge, *Britain by Mass Observation* (Hammondsworth, UK: Penguin, 1939), 28.

115. Ibid., 9.

116. Ibid., 129.

117. Ibid., 234.

118. Chamberlain, qtd. in Tom Harrisson and Charles Madge, *War Begins at Home* (London: Chatto & Windus, 1940), 37.

119. For more on the population as a political problem, see the texts by Michel Foucault's *Society Must Be Defended! Lectures at the Collége de France 1975-1976* (New York: Picador, 2003) as

well as Giorgio Agamben's *Homo Sacer: Sovereign Power and Bare Life* (Stanford: Stanford University Press, 1998). Tony Bunyan's *The Political Police in Britain* (London: Quartet Books, 1977) traces the life of emergency powers in twentieth century Britain following the Great War. He begins with the passage of DORA (Defence of the Realm Act) in 1914, its use to quell labor riots in the 1920s, the reappearance of exceptional powers in the Emergency Powers Act in 1939, and its long, eventful afterlife in the 1970s even after it was repealed. He argues correctly that, far from being an exceptional circumstance, these acts provided the groundwork for a new paradigm and new technique of government. For a full discussion of law, emergency, and new paradigms of sovereignty, see Agamben's *State of Exception*, trans. Kevin Attell (Chicago: University of Chicago Press, 2005).

120. W. Ivor Jennings, "The Rule of Law in Total War," *Yale Law Journal* 50, no. 3 (1941): 376.

121. Ibid., 386.

122. Harrisson and Madge, *War Begins at Home*, 71.

123. Ibid., 11.

124. Angus Calder, *The People's War: Britain 1939–45* (New York: Pantheon Books, 1969), 63.

125. Sebastian Knowles, *A Purgatorial Flame: Seven British Writers in the Second World War* (Philadelphia: University of Pennsylvania Press, 1990), 12.

126. Harrisson and Madge, *War Begins at Home*, 131.

127. Ibid., 1.

128. Ibid.

129. Ibid., 43.

130. Ibid., 339.

131. Henri Lefebvre, *Critique of Everyday Life*, vol. 3: *From Modernity to Modernism (Towards a Metaphilosophy of Daily Life)*, trans. Gregory Elliott (New York: Verso, 2005), 123.

132. Ibid., 105.

2. THE HISTORICAL NOVEL AT HISTORY'S END

1. For a full survey on the political impulse behind the resurgence of the historical novel at midcentury, see John Connor, "Historical Turns in Twentieth-Century Fiction," in *A Companion to British Literature*, vol. 4, *Victorian and Twentieth Century Literature 1837–2000*, ed. Robert DeMaria Jr., Heesok Chang, and Samantha Zacher, 314–32 (London: John Wiley).

2. Virginia Woolf, *The Letters of Virginia Woolf*, ed. Nigel Nicholson and Joanna Trautman, 6 vols. (London: Hogarth Press, 1975–1980), 6:116.

3. Georg Lukács's *The Historical Novel*, trans. Hannah Mitchell and Stanley Mitchell (London: Merlin Press, 1962) remains a cornerstone for all theories of the historical novel. See also Avrom Fleishmann, *The English Historical Novel: Walter Scott to Virginia Woolf* (Baltimore: Johns Hopkins University Press, 1972); Diana Wallace, *The Women's Historical Novel: British Women Writers, 1900–2000* (New York: Palgrave Macmillan, 2005); and Jerome de Groot, *The Historical Novel* (New York: Routledge, 2010).

4. Tom Harrisson and Charles Madge, *Mass Observation* (London: Frederick Muller, 1937), 11.

5. For an encyclopedic treatment of the various manifestations of this crisis mentality throughout the decade, see Valentine Cunningham, *British Writers of the Thirties* (Oxford: Oxford University Press, 1988), ch. 3.

6. Maurice Blanchot, *The Infinite Conversation*, trans. Susan Hanson (1969; repr. Minneapolis: University of Minnesota Press, 1993), 272.

7. David Gascoyne, *Collected Journals 1936–1942* (London: Skoob Books, 1993), 25.

8. William Wordsworth, "Composed upon Westminster Bridge," in *Selected Poems* (New York: Penguin Classics, 2005), 170.

9. W. H. Auden, "September 1, 1939," in *Selected Poems* (New York: Vintage International, 1989), 86.

10. Two works, published about a decade apart from one another, account for the particular attraction of women writers to this genre. See chapter 5 of Janet Montefiore's *Men and Women Writers of the 1930s: The Dangerous Flood of History* (New York: Routledge, 1996); and Diana Wallace's extension of her investigations in chapter 3 of *Woman's Historical Novel*.

11. Montefiore, *Men and Women Writers of the 1930s*, 147.

12. John Connor notes that the publication history of Lukács's study makes it highly unlikely that any English writer referenced in this chapter had access to his ideas: "Lukacs' argument, though serialized in Russian in late 1937–1938, found publication in full only in 1955, when it appeared in the German edition that was then translated into English" ("Historical Turns in Twentieth-Century Fiction," 316). My point, and Connor's too, is that Lukács's attraction to the genre as a site of literary and political potentiality was widely shared across midcentury.

13. Lukács, *Historical Novel*, 29; subsequent citations appear in the text.

14. I take my cue here from Jacques Derrida's "The Law of Genre," trans. Avital Ronell, *Critical Inquiry* 7, no. 1, (Autumn 1980): 55–81.

15. Ibid., 6.

16. Walpole interestingly and provocatively asks, and then steps away from his own provocations, to what degree time determines a work's historical status: "Can Time make a difference? Is for instance James Joyce's *Ulysses* an historical novel *now* to the readers of 1932?" Hugh Walpole, "The Historical Novel in England Since Sir Walter Scott," in *Sir Walter Scott To-Day: Some Retrospective Essays and Studies*, ed. H. J. C. Grierson (London: Constable & Co., 1932), 162. Shifting the burden of historical fiction from its conception and execution to its changing status over time poses severe challenges which one would like to have seen Walpole attempt to tackle.

17. Ibid.

18. Lukács sees the transition from Sir Walter Scott to Balzac as a decisive moment in the trajectory of the historical novel. Balzac's endeavor to present bourgeois French society from the 1789 revolution to his contemporary moment marks the "formal aesthetic point at which Balzac passes from the portrayal of *past history* to the portrayal of the *present as history*" (*Historical Novel*, 83). Lukács concludes that "with Balzac the historical novel which in Scott grew out of the English social novel, returns to the presentation of contemporary society. The age of the classical historical novel is therewith closed" (ibid., 85).

19. Walpole, "Historical Novel," 162.

20. Virginia Woolf, *A Writer's Diary* (New York: Harcourt Brace Jovanovich, 1973), 277.

21. A handful of recent articles see *The Years* as a stylistically and politically complex work. See, for instance, David Bradshaw, "Hyams Place: *The Years*, the Jews and the British Union of Fascists" in *Women Writers of the 1930s: Gender, Politics, and History*, ed. Maroula Joannou, 179–91 (Edinburgh: Edinburgh University Press, 1999); Maren Linnett, "The Jew in the Bath: Imperiled Imagination in Woolf's *The Years*." *Modern Fiction Studies* 48 (2002): 341–61; and John Whittier-Ferguson, "Repetition, Remembering, Repetition: Virginia Woolf's Late Fiction and the Return of War." *Modern Fiction Studies* 57 (2011): 230–53. Also see Judy Suh's smart chapter "The Comedy of Outsiders in Virginia Woolf's *The Years*" in her *Fascism and Anti-Fascism in Twentieth-Century British Fiction* (New York: Palgrave Macmillan, 2009).

22. Woolf's novel figures scarcely in Valentine Cunningham's encyclopedic *British Writers of the Thirties* and is mentioned even less in Maria Dibattista's *Virginia Woolf's Major Novels: The Fable of Anon* (New Haven, CT: Yale University Press, 1980). More recently, Christine Froula's *Virginia Woolf and the Bloomsbury Avant-Garde: War, Civilization, Modernity* (New York: Columbia University Press, 2005) contains a chapter on *The Years* but focuses primarily on "a book that does not exist" (215); instead of a sustained analysis of *The Years*, Froula offers a remarkable set of readings of the diary entries, speeches, and manuscript versions surrounding the production of the novel. For an entertaining and incisive polemic on Woolf scholars' preference for *The Pargiters* over the finished novel, see Gloria G. Fromm's "Re-inscribing *The Years*: Virginia Woolf, Rose Macaulay, and the Critics" *Journal of Modern Literature* 13, no. 1 (1986): 288–306. Fromm's central point is that the desire to recover Woolf as a paragon of late twentieth and early twenty-first century progressive politics has skewed what we read from her and how we read it: hence the preference for the more openly feminist *The Pargiters* and the disdain for the less antagonistic and politically uncertain text that was published. That Fromm's essay appeared almost thirty years ago and still presents a formidable challenge to even the most recent readings of *The Years* attests to the veracity and force of her argument. Marina MacKay's chapter on Woolf in her recent *Modernism and World War II* (New York: Cambridge University Press, 2007) departs from the iconic presentation of Woolf "as a leftwing radical" (23) and historicizes Woolf's writing; her analysis locates a more complex and historically rooted relation of politics and aesthetics in the late works, particularly *Between the Acts*.

23. Virginia Woolf, "The New Biography," in Woolf, *Collected Essays*, vol. 4 (New York: Harcourt Brace Jovanovich, 1967), 235. Mark Hussey attributes the initial success of *The Years* to a "vogue for family chronicles" but also notes how quickly its star fell, especially among literary critics. Nonetheless, this is the novel that got Woolf on the cover of *Time*. Hussey, *Virginia Woolf A to Z: A Comprehensive Reference for Students, Teachers, and Common Readers to Her Life, Work, and Critical Reception* (Oxford: Oxford University Press, 1996), 391.

24. See chapter 4, "Remembering the War in the Years Between the Wars," in Karen Levenback, *Virginia Woolf and the Great War* (Syracuse, NY: Syracuse University Press, 1999);

Linnett, "Jew in the Bath; chapter 4, "Negotiating Genre: Re-visioning History in *The Pargiters*," in Anna Snaith, *Virginia Woolf: Public and Private Negotiations* (Hampshire, UK: Palgrave, 2000); and chapter 4, "The Comedy of Outsiders in Virginia Woolf's *The Years*," in Suh, *Fascism and Anti-Fascism*.

25. Whittier-Ferguson, "Repetition, Remembering, Repetition," 231.

26. Liesl Olson's *Modernism and the Ordinary* (Oxford: Oxford University Press, 2009) and Bryony Randall's *Modernism, Daily Time, and Everyday Life* (Cambridge: Cambridge University Press, 2011) offer the most thorough and sustained readings of Woolf's turn to everyday life.

27. See Emily Delgarno's "A British *War and Peace*? Virginia Woolf Reads Tolstoy," *Modern Fiction Studies* 50, no. 1 (Spring 2004): 129–50.

28. In both "Letter to a Young Poet" and "The Leaning Tower," Woolf reflects on the changing obligations of art after the 1920s.

29. Virginia Woolf, "The Novels of Turgenev," in *The Captain's Deathbed and Other Essays* (New York: Harcourt Brace Jovanovich, 1973), 249.

30. Peter Brooks, *Realist Vision* (New Haven, CT: Yale University Press, 2008), 3.

31. Ibid., 211.

32. Virginia Woolf, *Moments of Being* (New York: Harcourt Brace Jovanovich, 1985), 70.

33. The realignment of art and knowledge also entails an alternate way of examining gender relations. I deal with this only in part, as a full consideration requires much more space than I have here. In addition to Froula's smart analysis of gender politics in *The Years*, I have found Anna Snaith's comments in *Virginia Woolf: Public and Private Negotiations* to be among the most insightful and helpful. See also Jane Goldman, *The Feminist Aesthetics of Virginia Woolf: Modernism, Post-Impressionism, and the Politics of the Visual* (Cambridge: Cambridge University Press, 1998).

34. Virginia Woolf, *To the Lighthouse* (New York: Harcourt Brace, 1981), 29.

35. Jacques Rancière, *Dissensus: On Politics and Aesthetics*, trans. Steven Corcoran (London: Continuum, 2010), 167.

36. Virginia Woolf, *The Years* (1939; repr. New York: Harcourt Brace Jovanovich, 1965), 35; subsequent citations appear in the text.

37. Crosby's collection and random arrangement of objects she salvages from Abercorn Terrace after it is sold recalls John, the protagonist from Woolf's post–World War I short story "Solid Objects." To be sure, the repeated use of "solid objects" in *The Years* references this earlier story and the world-making power of objects. I can do no more here than gesture toward this connection; a sharp comparative analysis of these two texts still remains to be done.

38. Hayden White distinguishes between modernism and realism according to their treatment of the event. For him, modernism blurs the distinction between fact and fiction that was so important to nineteenth-century realism and its mode of treating and indexing historical events. Modernism, on the other hand, dissolves the reality of the event. This gives another layer to the modernist-realism of *The Years*. It certainly does not deny the reality of the event, but it understands the impact of an event as truly excessive of any narrative or his-

torical chronicle that would attempt to bracket it in a mere history of events. The vocation of the novel, or at least her novel, is to interrogate how these events impact our lives and how we go about living history, even if we do so unconsciously. See Hayden White, "The Modernist Event," in his *Figural Realism: Studies in the Mimesis Effect* (Baltimore: Johns Hopkins University Press, 1999), 67–86.

39. Levenback, *Virginia Woolf and the Great War*, 116.

40. Paul Saint-Amour convincingly shows how air war anxiety structures modernist form in key novels of the 1920s. See his "Air War Prophecy and Interwar Modernism" *Comparative Literature Studies* 42, no. 2 (2005): 130–61.

41. Sebastian Knowles reads much of the literature of the late 1930s as anticipatory and I rely on his readings here. See his *A Purgatorial Flame: Seven British Writers in the Second World War* (Philadelphia: University of Pennsylvania Press, 1990).

42. Arthur Marwick recounts many of the ways the British defended themselves against these early raids. Quoting the official figures from a 1919 edition of *The Observer*, Marwick states that "total civilian casualties were 5,611, including 1,570 fatalities, of whom 1,413 were killed in air attacks." Arthur Marwick, *Britain in the Century of Total War* (Boston: Little, Brown, 1968), 68.

43. Carl Schmitt, *The Concept of the Political*, trans. George Schwab (1932; repr. Chicago: University of Chicago Press, 1996), 34.

44. See Sigmund Freud, "Creative Writers and Day-Dreaming" (1908), in *Criticism: The Major Statements*, ed. Charles Kaplan, 419–28 (New York: St. Martin's, 1991); and Jean Laplanche and J. B. Pontalis, "Fantasy and the Origins of Sexuality," *International Journal of Psycho-Analysis* 49, no. 1 (1968): 1–18.

45. The figurations of Ireland in Woolf's texts have yet to be analyzed in any comprehensive way. We know Woolf visited Ireland in 1934 and even stayed at Elizabeth Bowen's house. She saw *The Man of Aran* that same year and had quite a bit to say about Irish politics. I have found Lisa Weihman's article to be especially provocative on this issue. Weihman, "Virginia Woolf's "Harum-Scarum Irish Wife": Gender and National Identity in *The Years*" *Comparative Critical Studies* 4, no. 1 (2007).

46. Weihman, "Virginia Woolf's 'Harum-Scarum' Irish Wife," 40.

47. Froula, *Virginia Woolf and the Bloomsbury Avant-Garde*, 238.

48. Barbara Green maps out the relationship between Woolf's use of feminist archives in her late work, especially *Three Guineas* (New York: Harcourt Brace Jovanovich, 1938). Yet, as Green importantly reminds us, "Woolf was anything but an activist, and had only a tangential relation to the suffrage struggles of Edwardian England" (144). Woolf's later affinities were with the nonmilitant sectors of the suffrage movement: "In tracing Woolf's connection to suffrage via the London Society for Women's Service, we should remember that those members of the LSWS who had been active in the suffrage campaign, for example Pippa Strachey, would have belonged to the constitutionalist NUWSS; thus in working with the Marsham Street Library, Woolf did not affiliate herself with the suffragettes" (144). Green goes on to analyze the way *Three Guineas* draws on the activities, ideas, and histories of both groups, militant and constitutionalist. See chapter 4 of her *Spectacular*

Confessions: Autobiography, Performative Activism, and the Sites of Suffrage 1905–1938 (London: Macmillan, 1997).

49. Women would not gain complete suffrage until 1928, leading some historians such as A. J. P. Taylor to ask, and rightly so, if one could consider England a proper democracy before that year.

50. One thinks here of Clarissa Dalloway: "What she loved was this, here, now, in front of her; the fat lady in the cab. Did it matter then, she asked herself, walking towards Bond Street, did it matter that she must inevitable cease completely; all this must go on without her." Virginia Woolf, *Mrs. Dalloway* (New York: Harcourt Brace Jovanovich, 1925), 9.

51. John Maynard Keynes, quoted in Alex Zwerdling, *Virginia Woolf and the Real World* (Berkeley: University of California Press, 1987), 295.

52. Virginia Woolf, *The Diary of Virginia Woolf*, 5 vols., ed. Anne Oliver Bell (New York: Harcourt Brace Jovanovich, 1978), 5:168.

53. James J. Berg and Chris Freeman, eds. *Conversations with Christopher Isherwood* (Jackson: University Press of Mississippi, 2001), 101.

54. Christopher Isherwood, *Isherwood on Writing*, ed. James J. Berg (Minneapolis: University of Minnesota Press, 2007), 162.

55. Christopher Isherwood, *Christopher and His Kind* (New York: Farrar, Straus Giroux, 1976), 49.

56. Eric Weitz divides the shaky economic history of the Weimar Republic into three phases: "The first phase, 1918–23, was the era of inflation; 1924–29, of rationalization; 1929–33, of depression" (131). See chapter 4, "Turbulent Economy, Anxious Society," of his fascinating and wide-ranging book *Weimar Germany: Promise and Tragedy* (Princeton, NJ: Princeton University Press, 2007).

57. Ibid., 163.

58. Giorgio Agamben calls the Third Reich a "state of exception that lasted twelve years." See his *State of Exception*, trans. Kevin Attell (Chicago: University of Chicago Press, 2005), 2.

59. Walpole, "Historical Novel in England," 162.

60. Although *The Last of Mr. Norris* was published first, Isherwood's recollection from *Christopher and His Kind* indicates that his early drafts were of "Sally Bowles" and "The Nowaks" chapters: "From the middle of August onward, Christopher had begun work on what was to be the very first draft of his fiction about Berlin. This was a short story or outline for a novel; its subject matter was Jean's adventures combined with Christopher's encounters with the Nowaks" (108).

61. Christopher Isherwood, *The Berlin Stories* (New York: New Directions, 1963), v.

62. Georg Lukács, *Studies in European Realism*, trans. Edith Bone (New York: Grosset and Dunlap, 1964), 145.

63. Isherwood, *Berlin Stories*, v; and Isherwood, *Isherwood on Writing*, 164.

64. Berg, *Conversations with Christopher Isherwood*, 77. Isherwood refers to the individual sections of *Goodbye to Berlin* in various ways, but all of them refer to visual media such as portraits and sketches. He tells David J. Geherin in a 1972 interview that ultimately *Goodbye to Berlin* proved to be "too plotty." See ibid., 77.

65. David Garrett Izzo, Christopher Isherwood: His Era, His Gang, and the Legacy of the Truly Strong Man. Columbia: University of South Carolina Press, 2001, 140.

66. Berg, Conversations with Christopher Isherwood, 6, 77.

67. Christopher Isherwood, quoted in Jamie M. Carr, Queer Times: Christopher Isherwood's Modernity (New York: Routledge, 2006), 96.

68. Christopher Isherwood, Goodbye to Berlin in The Berlin Stories, 1; subsequent citations appear in the text.

69. See, for instance, Brian Finney, Christopher Isherwood: A Critical Biography (New York: Oxford University Press, 1979); Samuel Hynes The Auden Generation: Literature and Politics in England in the 1930s (Princeton, NJ: Princeton University Press, 1982); Izzo, Christopher Isherwood; Antony Shuttleworth, "In a Populous City: Isherwood in the Thirties," in The Isherwood Century: Essays on the Life and Work of Christopher Isherwood, ed. James Berg and Christopher Freeman, 150–61 (Madison: University of Wisconsin Press, 2000); and Alan Wilde, Christopher Isherwood (New York: Twayne Publishers, 1971).

70. Joseph Frank, The Idea of Spatial Form (New Brunswick, NJ: Rutgers University Press, 1991), 63.

71. Hynes, Auden Generation, 354.

72. Fredric Jameson, Postmodernism, or the Cultural Logic of Late Capitalism (Durham, NC: Duke University Press, 1995), 156.

73. G. W. F. Hegel, The Philosophy of History, trans. J. Sibree (Mineola, NY: Dover, 2004), 47.

74. Alan Wilde, Horizons of Assent: Modernism, Postmodernism, and the Ironic Imagination (Philadelphia: University of Pennsylvania Press, 1987), 68.

75. Roland Barthes, Camera Lucida: Reflections on Photography, trans. Richard Howard (1980 New York: Farrar, Straus and Giroux, 1981), 93, 89.

76. Ibid., 9.

77. Ibid., 96. In Camera Lucida, Barthes distinguishes between two methods of receiving a photograph. The studium is "that very wide field of unconcerned desire, of various interest, of inconsequential taste" (27). This leads to a general interest in, perhaps, the technique used in a particular photograph, its cultural relevance, or the historical scene it reveals to us. On the other hand is a more affective reaction far removed from the order of cognition or contemplation. This is the punctum, "that accident which pricks me" (27); the punctum is a detail that is not always intentional, but a product of the photographer's "second sight" (47), a way of attesting to something "that he could not not photograph" (47) that nevertheless causes a sort of shock or inflicts a "wound" as Barthes is fond of saying. Barthes analysis, as unapologetically personal as it is, repeats in a way the old division of rational cognition and aesthetic experience and is not entirely unlike the "shock" effect of modern art that Adorno discusses in Aesthetic Theory.

78. Isherwood, Berlin Stories, v.

79. Isherwood, Isherwood on Writing, 164.

80. Isherwood recalls that he never lost track of the "real" Sally Bowles, Jean Ross. Her absolute disappearance is constructed for narrative purposes.

3. LATE MODERNISM'S GEOPOLITICAL IMAGINATION: EVERYDAY LIFE IN THE GLOBAL HOT ZONES

1. Among the many things written about global and transnational modernism, see Mark Wollaeger and Matt Eatough, eds., *The Oxford Handbook of Global Modernisms* (New York: Oxford University Press, 2011), as well as *English Language Notes* 49, no. 1 (Spring/Summer 2011), a special issue on "Transnational Exchange."

2. See Alexander M. Bain, "International Settlements: Ishiguro, Shanghai, Humanitarianism," *NOVEL: A Forum on Fiction* 40, no. 3 (2007): 240–64; Leo Ou-fan Lee, *Shanghai Modern: The Flowering of a New Urban Culture in Shanghai, 1930–1945* (Cambridge: Harvard University Press, 1999); Shu Mei-Shih, *The Lure of the Modern: Writing Modernism in Semicolonial China, 1917–1937* (Berkeley: University of California Press, 2001); Eric Hayot, *The Hypothetical Mandarin: Sympathy, Modernity, and Chinese Pain* (Oxford: Oxford University Press, 2009); and Patricia Laurence, *Lily Briscoe's Chinese Eyes: Bloomsbury, Modernism, and China* (Columbia: University of South Carolina Press, 2003).

3. Jessica Berman, *Modernist Commitments: Ethics, Politics, and Transnational Modernism* (New York: Columbia University Press, 2012); Matthew Hart, *Nations of Nothing but Poetry: Modernism, Transnationalism, and Synthetic Vernacular Writing* (Oxford: Oxford University Press, 2009); and Rebecca Walkowitz, *Cosmopolitan Style: Modernism Beyond the Nation* (New York: Columbia University Press, 2007).

4. Jessica Berman's *Modernist Commitments* argues against the separation of the ethical and the political generally but especially makes good on that argument in the discussion of "the continuity between experimental narrative and war writing" (187) in the novels, reportage, and visual culture of the Spanish Civil War. See chapter 3 "Commitment and the Scene of War: Max Aub and Spanish Civil War Writing," 184–236.

5. Melba Cuddy-Keane, "Modernism, Geopolitics, Globalization," Modernism/Modernity 10, no. 3 (2003): 539–58.

6. See Christopher GoGwilt, *The Fiction of Geopolitics: Afterimages of Culture, from Wilkie Collins to Alfred Hitchcock* (Stanford, CA: Stanford University Press, 2000); and Laura Winkiel and Laura Doyle, eds., *Geomodernism: Race, Modernism, Modernity* (Bloomington: Indiana University Press, 2005).

7. Cuddy-Keane, "Modernism, Geopolitics, Globalization," 545–46.

8. Paul Fussell, *Abroad: British Literary Travel Writing Between the Wars* (Oxford: Oxford University Press, 1980), 219.

9. Ibid.

10. It is also curious that Fussell praises very similar formal problems as part and parcel of all modern writing, including the interwar travel book. In "All These Frontiers" he focuses specifically on the changing geographies and frontiers of the postwar world and links that geospatial fragmentation to the formal fragmentation of modern writing and painting. The travel book, it would seem, could only ever internalize these same tensions and present them as formal problems.

11. The publication of *Nomos of the Earth* was greeted with a mix of praise and skepticism. See *South Atlantic Quarterly* 104, no. 2 (Spring 2005), a special issue devoted to *Nomos*, for a number of smart meditations on the potential and risks of Schmitt's text.

12. Carl Schmitt, *The Nomos of the Earth in the International Law of Jus Publicum Europaeum*, trans. G. L. Umen (1950; repr. New York: Telos Press Publishing, 2003), 141. The Napoleonic Wars certainly pose a challenge to Schmitt's historical claim that Europe bracketed all interstate wars during this lengthy period. Schmitt makes some allowance for this and suggests that the *jus publicum Europaeum* was restored at the Congress of Vienna.

13. Ibid., 150–51.

14. Ibid., 142.

15. Sven Lindqvist, *A History of Bombing*, trans. Linda Harvety Rugg (New York: New Press, 2000), 21.

16. Ibid.

17. Enzo Traverso, *The Origins of Nazi Violence*, trans. Janet Lloyd (New York: New Press, 2003), 70.

18. Adolf Hitler, quoted in ibid., 71.

19. Peter Hallward, "Beyond Salvage," *South Atlantic Quarterly* 104, no. 2 (2005): 238.

20. "The Hague Declaration (IV) of 1899 Concerning Expanding Bullets," in *Pamphlet Series of the Carnegie Endowment for International Peace, Division of International Law* (Washington DC: Carnegie Endowment for International Peace, 1915).

21. James Wilford Garner, *International Law and the World War* (London: Longmans, 1920), 452.

22. As Janet M. Manson remarks, Leonard Woolf issued no proposals for suprastate sovereignty and made no gestures toward disarmament. He did, however, retain the use of force for defensive measures. When the League of Nations finally emerged in 1919, war remained the centerpiece of international relations, but it was the prevention, not coordination, of military force that preoccupied the league. Despite the influence of Woolf's book on British policy, disarmament, along with collective security, deliberation, and proceduralism, formed a major component of a far-reaching plan to limit the conditions and resources that culminated in the First World War. Such measures enjoyed massive popular support across a war weary Europe and this buoyed the league early on. It appeared to embody all the utopian hopes for a pacifist, demilitarized world. See Janet M. Manson, "Leonard Woolf as an Architect of the League of Nations," *South Carolina Review* (2007): 1–13.

23. Leonard Woolf, *International Government* (Westminster: Fabian Society, 1916), 232.

24. Leonard Woolf, *Barbarians at the Gate* (London: Victor Gollancz, 1939), 188–89. Woolf gives us his own recollection of the emergence of the league and his participation in it in *Beginning Again: An Autobiography of the Years 1911–1918* (London: Hogarth Press, 1964).

25. Schmitt writes that *jus publicum Europaeum* effectively ended with the First World War and "it was replaced by an empty normativism of allegedly recognized rules, which for a few decades, obscured consciousness o the fact that a concrete order of previously recognized powers had been destroyed and that a new one had not yet been found" (*Nomos*, 227).

26. Article 10 of the covenant specifically states that a war against any member of the league is a war against every member. Articles 11, 12, and 13 set guidelines for arbitrating conflicts between states, supplanting open war with "judicial settlements."

27. See F. P. Walters's two-volume *A History of the League of Nations* (London: Oxford University Press, 1965), as well as George Scott's historical account *The Rise and Fall of the League of Nations* (New York: MacMillan, 1974); and Peter J. Yearwood's, *Guarantee of Peace: The League of Nations in British Policy 1914–1925* (Oxford: Oxford University Press, 2005).

28. Akira Iriye, *Cultural Internationalism and World Order* (Baltimore: Johns Hopkins University Press, 2000).

29. F. S. Northedge, *The League of Nations: Its Life and Times, 1920–1946* (Leicester, UK: Leicester University Press, 1986), 18.

30. Looking back on the ICIC in 1946, Murray remarked that even at Europe's most volatile, "one found that intercourse in music, painting, philosophy, science, and letters remained alive and acted as a force of goodwill" (*From the League*, 5). Murray also notes Britain's lack of interest in the ICIC and his inability to secure any support from Britain for the ICIC's work. "I am ashamed," he writes in 1946, "of my failure in Great Britain to convince either the people or the Government of the value of this work" (*From the League*, 5). In a letter from 1938 he would extol the committee's work but regret that "unfortunately, the British Empire still maintains its mistrust of all that is intellectual" (*Unfinished Autobiography*, 200). See Gilbert Murray, *From the League to the U.N.* (London: Oxford University Press, 1948); and Gilbert Murray, *An Unfinished Autobiography with Contributions by His Friends* (London: Allen and Unwind, 1960).

31. For more on the ICIC and its place within other contemporaneous efforts to internationalize intellectual activity, see Daniel Laqua, "Transnational Intellectual Cooperation, the League of Nations, and the Problem of Order," *Journal of Global History* 6 (2011): 223–47. Laqua also makes the argument that these efforts, progressive as they may seem in historical context, should not be thought of as cosmopolitan: "With civilization viewed as a building block of global order, it is evident why the term 'cosmopolitanism'—often understood as the embrace of diversity and difference—does not capture the nature of cultural internationalism in the interwar years. Its inherent boundaries were underlined by the ambiguous role of race in intellectual cooperation" (232).

32. Albert Einstein and Sigmund Freud, *Why War?* in *An International Series of Open Letters*, vol. 2 (Paris: International Institute of Intellectual Co-operation, League of Nations, 1933), 11–12; further references cited in the text.

33. In *Civilization and Its Discontents* (trans. James Strachey [New York: W. W. Norton, 1961]), Freud argues that before we speculate on the value of civilization, much less ways to secure it, we need a fundamental change in our understanding of human nature.

> The element of truth behind all this, which people are so ready to disavow, is that men are not gentle creatures who want to be loved, and who at the most can defend themselves if they are attacked; they are, on the contrary, creatures among whose instinctual endowments is to be reckoned a powerful share of aggressiveness. . . . Anyone who calls to mind the atrocities committed during the racial migrations or the invasions of the Huns, or

by the people known as Mongols under Jeghiz Khan and Tamerlane, or at the capture of Jerusalem by the pious Crusaders, or even, indeed, the horrors of the recent World War—anyone who calls these things to mind will have to bow humbly before the truth of this view (68–9).

34. Viscount Cecil, Foreword to *Challenge to Death*, ed. Storm Jameson (London: Constable & Co., 1934), vii.

35. Rebecca West, "The Necessity and Grandeur of the International Ideal," in *A Challenge to Death*, ed. Storm Jameson, 240–60 (London: Constable & Co., 1934), 240.

36. Ibid., 243.

37. Ibid., 242.

38. Ibid., 245, 80.

39. Ibid., 77.

40. Ibid.

41. Ibid.

42. Ibid., 78.

43. Ibid., 75.

44. I am expanding a basic claim from Carl Schmitt's *Political Theology: Four Chapters on the Concept of Sovereignty* (Chicago: University of Chicago Press, 1985). In chapter 3, "Political Theology," he states "all significant concepts of the modern theory of the state are secularized theological concepts" (36).

45. West, "The Necessity and Grandeur," 245.

46. Ibid., 249.

47. Ibid., 250.

48. Ibid.

49. Ibid., 253.

50. Ibid.

51. Peter Monteath calls *Homage to Catalonia* a *bildungsreportage* and maintains that Orwell moves from naiveté to a stronger, deeper political conviction. My reading of development departs significantly from his as does my consideration of *Homage to Catalonia* as a war travel book rather than just reportage. See Monteath, *Writing the Good Fight: Political Commitment in the International Literature of the Spanish Civil War* (Westport, CT: Greenwood Press, 1994), especially chapter 6, "Heresies of the Left." Bernard Schweizer's analysis also underlines the relationship between writing and political commitment in Homage to Catalonia. See Schweizer, *Radicals on the Road* (Charlottesville: University of Virginia Press, 2001). And, as a possible stamp of Orwell's commitment to truth and demystification, Margery Sabin's essay "The Truths of Experience: Orwell's Nonfiction of the 1930s," in *The Cambridge Companion to George Orwell*, ed. John Rodden, 43–58 (Cambridge: Cambridge University Press, 2007) on Orwell's 1930s nonfiction tells us that even when Orwell admits partiality or partisanship, it has "the effect of increasing more than they detract from Orwell's air of truthfulness" (45).

52. George Orwell, *The Collected Essays, Journalism, and Letters*, Book 1, *An Age Like This 1920–1940*, ed. Ian Angus and Sonia Orwell (Boston: David R. Godine, 2000), 267.

53. Ibid., 270.

54. See Raymond Carr, *The Spanish Tragedy: The Civil War in Perspective* (London: Weidenfeld and Nicolson, 1977); and Antony Beevor, *The Battle for Spain: The Spanish Civil War 1936–1939* (New York: Penguin, 2006). For a focused look at Britain's involvement and perception of the Spanish Civil War, see Tom Buchanan, *Britain and the Spanish Civil War* (Cambridge: Cambridge University Press, 1997).

55. Salvador de Madariaga, "Peace in Spain: An Anniversary Appeal." *Times*, July 19, 1937. Nonintervention did not necessarily equal neutrality. Steven Lobell remarks that even more than threatening to ignite a full European war, the "Spanish Civil War (1936) posed a threat to Britain's passage to its Far Eastern empire through the Straits of Gibraltar and the Strategic Balearic islands" (85). For more on Britain's geopolitical maneuverings during the wars of the 1930s, see chapter 4 of his *The Challenge of Hegemony: Grand Strategy, Trade, and Domestic Politics* (Ann Arbor: University of Michigan Press, 2003).

56. Madariaga, "Peace in Spain: An Anniversary Appeal."

57. When European states met at the Non-Intervention Committee met in September 1936, they were determined precisely to prevent any foreign intervention in Spain out of fear that a local conflict would spark a wider European war. Italy, Germany, and the Soviet Union flouted the voluntary agreement by arming the warring factions and the Spanish Civil War became an international civil war and those searing domestic issues took a back seat to a global ideological conflict.

58. Hannah Arendt, *The Origins of Totalitarianism* (New York: Harcourt, Brace, Jovanovich, 1973), 280.

59. In addition to Buchanan's book, see also Angela Jackson's *British Women and the Spanish Civil War* (New York: Routledge, 2002), which, in addition to filling an enormous gap in the history of the Spanish Civil War, contains remarkable observations on Sylvia Townsend Warner and Valentine Ackland. James K. Hopkins's *Into the Heart of the Fire: The British in the Spanish Civil War* (Stanford, CA: Stanford University Press, 1998) is arguably the best and most thorough history of Britain's involvement in the war. Hopkins casts his net a bit wider than the literary circles that receive so much attention in many cultural histories of the war; he attends equally closely to popular culture, the lower classes, and others who were captivated by Spain.

60. W. H. Auden, "Spain," in *Selected Poems* (New York: Vintage International, 1989), 71; and Louis MacNeice, Collected Poems, ed. Peter McDonald (London: Faber and Faber, 1979), 112. These sort of declarations are numerous. See Valentine Cunningham, ed. *The Spanish Front: Writers on the Civil War* (Oxford: Oxford University Press, 1986); Murray A. Sperber, ed. *And I Remember Spain: A Spanish Civil War Anthology* (New York: Collier Books, 1974); and Stephen Spender and John Lehmann, eds. *Poems for Spain* (London: Hogarth Press, 1939).

61. Nancy Cunard, *Authors Take Sides on the Spanish War* (London: Left Review, 1937). 3.

62. George Orwell, quoted in Jeffrey Meyers, *Orwell: Wintry Conscience of a Generation* (New York: Norton, 2000), 172. Orwell's response to Cunard did not appear in the famous *Authors Take Sides* pamphlet. Gayle Rogers demonstrates in precise detail the struggles among the British intelligentsia over who had the authority to speak for Spain. See his illuminating

account of Britain and Spain's cultural exchange in *Modernism and the New Spain: Britain, Cosmopolitan Europe, and Literary History* (Oxford: Oxford University Press, 2012), esp. 174–78.

63. Cunard, *Authors Take Sides*, 10.

64. Spender and Lehmann, *Poems for Spain*, 9. See also by Spender, chapter 4 of his *World Within World: An Autobiography of Stephen Spender* (London: Faber & Faber, 1977), which tracks his visits to Spain. Also see his "Heroes in Spain," in *The Thirties and After: Poetry, Politics, People 1933–1970* (New York: Random House, 1967), 46–50.

65. George Orwell, "Inside the Whale," in *Collected Essays*, Book 1, *An Age Like This*, 516.

66. Auden, "Spain," 54.

67. Edward Mendelson marks out two versions of necessity in his reading of the poem: there is necessity as in a "necessary evil," where something so morally deplorable is nevertheless required by circumstance; the other version is one that figures necessity "as in the necessary obedience of matter to the laws of physics" (322). For Mendelson, this latter version of necessity, one bound to the laws of History, is what Auden had in mind. Mendelson also reminds us that the poem couples necessity with choice. See Mendelson, *Early Auden* (Cambridge: Harvard University Press, 1983), esp. 315–24.

68. Auden, "Spain," 52.

69. Ibid., 53.

70. Orwell, "Inside the Whale," 516.

71. In a letter to Monroe K. Spears, Auden clarifies the necessary murder and remains skeptical about the possibility of a just war: "I was not excusing totalitarian crimes but only trying to say what, surely, every decent person thinks if he finds himself unable to adopt the absolute pacifist position. (1) To kill another human being is always murder and should never be called anything else. (2) In a war, the members of two rival groups try to murder their opponents. (3) If there is such thing as a just war, then murder can be necessary for the sake of justice" (quoted in Monroe K. Spears, *The Poetry of W. H. Auden: The Disenchanted Island* (Oxford: Oxford University Press, 1963), 157).

72. George Orwell, *Homage to Catalonia* (New York: Harcourt Brace Jovanovich, 1952), 48; further references cited in text.

73. See T. C. Worsley's eye-witness account, "Malaga Has Fallen," in Sperber's anthology *And I Remember Spain*.

74. Antony Shuttleworth suggests that Orwell's war is "comic, rather than heroic" (207). In many ways Shuttleworth is right: the scant combat, the fumbling, untrained militiamen, and the stagnation at the front are not the raw materials of war stories. See his "The Real George Orwell: Dis-Simulation in *Homage to Catalonia* and *Coming up for Air*," in *And in Our Time: Vision, Revision, and British Writing of the 1930s*, ed. Antony Shuttleworth, 204–20 (Lewisburg, PA: Bucknell University Press, 2003).

75. For more on intimacy and enmity, see Carl Schmitt, *The Concept of the Political* (Chicago: University of Chicago Press, 2007). One might also see Michel Foucault's *Society Must Be Defended! Lectures at the College de France 1975–1976* (New York: Picador, 2003). "We are all," he writes, "inevitably someone else's adversary" (51).

76. More recently, Achille Mbembe has made the point that, unlike the war in the form of Schmitt's golden era of the *jus publicum Europaeum*, the extralegal wars that raged in the colonies, and eventually returned to Europe, routinely denigrated enemies from *justi hostes* to "savages" and "uncivilized" peoples. See his "Necropolitics," *Public Culture* 15, no. 1 (Winter 2003): 11–40.

77. George Orwell, "Looking Back on the Spanish War," in *The Collected Essays, Journalism and Letters of George Orwell*, ed. Sonia Orwell and Ian Angus, vol. 2, *My Country Right or Left 1940–1943*, 249–266 (Boston: David R. Godine 2000), 254.

78. Ibid., 253.

79. Valentine Cunningham, *British Writers of the Thirties* (Oxford: Oxford University Press, 1988), 424.

80. To be clear, my analysis is concerned with the text, not with Orwell as a figure or with his broader biography. Certainly, Spain was not the only moment of disillusionment or disappointment Orwell would face. His politics after Spain would eventually come more or less into line with the welfare state capitalism that began emerging during the Second World War and took full shape thereafter.

81. W. H. Auden, quoted in Humphrey Carpenter, *W. H. Auden: A Biography* (New York: Houghton Mifflin, 1982), 225.

82. Auden, quoted in ibid., 239.

83. For a full explanation of the way Auden and Isherwood ironize their own preconceptions of China, see chapter 5 of Marsha Bryant, *Auden and Documentary in the 1930s* (Charlottesville: University of Virginia Press, 1997).

84. Douglas Kerr, "Disorientations: Auden and Isherwood's China," *Literature & History* 5, no. 2 (Autumn 1996): 55.

85. W. H. Auden and Christopher Isherwood, *Journey to a War* (New York: Paragon House, 1990), 59–60; further references cited in the text.

86. For a sustained reading of the photographs in *Journey to a War*, see chapter 5 in Marsha Bryant's Auden and Documentary in the 1930s, 128–70.

87. The publication history of the various essays, poems, and photographs is dutifully mapped out by Edward Mendelson in *The Complete Works of W. H. Auden: Prose and Travel Books in Prose and Verse*, vol. 1, *1926–1938* (Princeton, NJ: Princeton University Press, 1997), 822–31. Also see chapter 15, "From This Island," in his *Early Auden* as well as chapter 7, "Traveller," in Humphrey Carpenter's *W. H. Auden: A Biography*, both of which chart Auden's itineraries.

88. Humphrey Carpenter notes that "Hongkong" was composed in Brussels months after Auden and Isherwood concluded their journey. Carpenter, *W. H. Auden*, 234.

89. Bain, "International Settlements," 245.

90. Wen-hsin Yeh, "Prologue: Shanghai Besieged, 1937–45," in *Wartime Shanghai*, ed. Wen-hsin Yeh (New York: Routledge, 1998), 3.

91. See Alexander Nemerov, "The Flight of Form: Auden, Bruegel, and the Turn to Abstraction in the 1940s," *Critical Inquiry* 31, no. 4 (Summer 2005): 780–810. "Aerial machines, squinting upwards, innocent victims—these experiences so fresh in Auden's mind must have given the fate of Brueghel's falling boy a contemporary resonance" (785).

92. W. H. Auden, "Musée des Beaux Arts," in *Selected Poems*, 80.

93. Ibid.

94. Ibid.

95. Stanley Baldwin and his cohorts were thought to be admirers of Franco, as was Neville Chamberlain. Lady Ivy Chamberlain, wife and later widow of Sir Austen Chamberlain, frequently wore Fascist badges and scripted an essay lauding fascist Spanish painter Ignacio Zuloaga. Most historians of the Spanish Civil War believe that the conservative wing of the British government feared for the security of their commercial investments in Spain should the Republic win and "go red." For more on the geopolitical positioning of the British, French, and American governments with regard to Spain, see chapter 15 of Raymond Carr's *The Spanish Tragedy*, as well as chapter 13 of Anthony Beevor's *The Battle for Spain*.

96. See Gijs van Hensbergen, *Guernica: The Biography of a Twentieth-Century Icon* (New York: Bloomsbury, 2004). Also see the discussions about the value of the painting contained in Cunningham, *The Spanish Front*.

4. WAR GOTHIC

1. Louis MacNeice, *Collected Poems*, ed. Peter McDonald (London: Faber and Faber, 2007), 102.

2. Ibid, 101–2.

3. The Germans did conduct air raids in the First World War, first with slow Zeppelin bombers and then with Gotha. The civilian body count totaled 670, but the psychological toll was far greater. Aerial bombardment proved to be far more advanced than any defense.

4. MacNeice, *Collected Poems*, 109.

5. Vera Brittain, *England's Hour* (New York: Macmillan, 1941), 116.

6. Angus Calder's *The People's War* (New York: Pantheon Books, 1969) and *The Myth of the Blitz* (London: Jonathan Cape, 1991) are two of the most seminal works on the construction of the People's War mythos. A wave of recent work further complicates the story of a resilient, fearless population shouldering the burden of the war. See Amy Bell, "Landscapes of Fear: Wartime London, 1939–1945," *Journal of British Studies* 48, no. 1 (January 2009): 153–75; Sonya Rose, *Which People's War? National Identity and Citizenship in Britain 1939–1945* (Oxford: Oxford University Press, 2003); and Robert McKary, *Half the Battle: Civilian Morale in Britain During the Second World War* (Manchester: Manchester University Press, 2002).

7. Patrick Deer provides one of the most lucid and compelling accounts of the overlap of propaganda, documentary, and aesthetic experimentation during the Second World War. See *Culture in Camouflage: War, Empire, and Modern British Literature* (Oxford: Oxford University Press, 2009), esp. chap. 3, which includes his fantastic analysis of *London Can Take It!*

8. Ibid., 113.

9. Over the last several years, a welcome series of books has revisited the relationship between modernism and the Second World War, treating it as a key moment in the development

of modernist aesthetics. In addition to Deer's *Culture in Camouflage*, see Marina Mackay, *Modernism and World War II* (Cambridge: Cambridge University Press, 2007); Leo Mellor, *Reading the Ruins: Modernism, Bombsites and British Culture* (Cambridge: Cambridge University Press, 2011); and Lyndsey Stonebridge, *The Writing of Anxiety: Imagining Wartime in Mid-Century British Culture* (London: Palgrave, 2007).

10. See John Paul Riquelme, "Introduction: Toward a History of Gothic and Modernism: Dark Modernity from Bram Stoker to Samuel Beckett," *Modern Fiction Studies* 46, no.3 (Fall 2000): 585–605.

11. Maggie Kilgour locates the gothic's rise between Enlightenment and Romantic thought. On her reading, it internalizes a process where organic communities declined as the conception of the rational individual took hold in Western societies. See her *The Rise of the Gothic Novel* (New York: Routledge, 1995). Robert Miles and Nancy Armstrong both note the gothic's affinity for dislocated, fractured, and delegitimized forms of subjectivity. See Miles's *Gothic Writing, 1750–1820: A Genealogy* (Manchester: Manchester University Press, 2002), and Armstrong's *How Novels Think: The Limits of British Individualism from 1719–1900* (New York: Columbia University Press, 2005), esp. chap. 4, "The Polygenetic Imagination," and chap. 5, "The Necessary Gothic."

12. Fred Botting, *Gothic* (New York: Routledge, 1996), 12.

13. Kilgour, *The Rise of the Gothic Novel*, 32.

14. In addition to Armstrong's reading of *Dracula* in chapter 4 of *How Novels Think*, see Seamus Deane, *Strange Country: Modernity and Nationhood in Irish Writing Since 1790* (New York: Oxford University Press, 1997), and Joseph Valente, *Dracula's Crypt: Bram Stoker, Irishness, and the Question of Blood* (Urbana: University of Illinois Press, 2001), for strong, insightful readings of *Dracula* in relation to Ireland and empire.

15. Fredric Jameson, *The Political Unconscious: Narrative as a Socially Symbolic Act* (Ithaca, NY: Cornell University Press, 1983), 141.

16. See, for example, Sandra M. Gilbert, "'Rats' Alley': The Great War, Modernism, and the (Anti)Pastoral Elegy," *New Literary History* 30, no. 1 (Winter 1999): 179–201.

17. Margot Norris, *Writing War in the Twentieth Century* (Charlottesville: University of Virginia Press, 2000), 80.

18. Erich Maria Remarque, *All Quiet on the Western Front*, trans. A. W. Wheen (New York: Ballantine, 1982), 126.

19. Allyson Booth, *Postcards from the Trenches: Negotiating the Space Between Modernism and the First World War* (New York: Oxford University Press, 1996), 57.

20. Former vorticist C. R. W. Nevinson's 1917 painting *Paths of Glory* was banned from a 1918 exhibition of war art. Pulling away from the avant-garde stylings of his previous work, this canvas depicts two fallen soldiers tangled in barbed wire in some muddy, anonymous trench. When the War Office demanded that Nevinson remove his art from the exhibition, he covered it in brown paper and scribbled "CENSORED" over it.

21. Wilfred Owen, "Dulce et decorum est," in *The War Poems of Wilfred Owen*, ed. Jon Stallworthy, 29–30 (London: Chatto & Windus, 1994).

22. Lillian Browse, "Review of British War Artists," *Horizon* (September 1940): 139–51.

23. Ibid.

24. Herbert Read, Preface to *Britain at War*, ed. Monroe Wheeler (New York: Museum of Modern Art, 1941), 12.

25. Ibid.

26. Alan Wilkinson writes that "in 1941, 1942, and 1944 his wartime drawings were shown in three exhibitions under the title *War Pictures at the National Gallery*" (24). See Henry Moore, *Henry Moore: Writings and Conversations*, ed. Alan Wilkinson (Aldershot: Ashgate, 2002).

27. David Mellor, "'And Oh! The Stench': Spain, the Blitz, Abjection, and the Shelter Drawings," in *Henry Moore*, ed. Chris Stephens (London: Tate Publishing), 56.

28. Kenneth Clark, letter to the War Artists Advisory Council (WAAC), Kenneth Clark Correspondence, Tate Britain, TGA 8812/1/4/442a.

29. Mass Observation, Observer's report of the 1942 the Tate Gallery's Wartime Acquisitions, Mass Observation Archive, University of Sussex, SxMOA 1/2/33/3/C.

30. Moore, *Henry Moore*, 263.

31. See the account in chapter 4 of Julian Andrews, *London's War: The Shelter Drawings of Henry Moore* (Aldershot: Lund Humphries, 2002).

32. Mellor notes that Moore's sketch *Women and Children in the Tube* was given the precise date of September 12, 1940, the day after he first saw the shelters. It is this sketch that bears an undeniable resemblance to the photos in the October 12, 1940, *Picture Post*.

33. Elizabeth Bowen, Preface to *Ivy Gripped the Steps and Other Stories* (New York: Knopf, 1946), ix.

34. Henry Moore, quoted in Andrews, *London's War*, 38.

35. See John Gregg, *The Shelter of the Tubes: Tube Sheltering in Wartime London* (London: Capital Transport, 2001).

36. Ibid., 78.

37. Eve Kosofsky Sedgwick's classic *Coherence of Gothic Conventions* (New York: Metheun, 1986) gives considerable attention to live burial and its psychic and sexual connotations in gothic fiction.

38. Quoted in Andrews, *London's War*, 142n23.

39. H. D., *Trilogy* (New York: New Directions, 1998), 4.

40. Mark Rawlinson, *British Writing of the Second World War* (New York: Oxford University Press, 2000), 71.

41. Bell, "Landscapes of Fear," 154.

42. Bill Brandt, "A Photographer's London," in *Bill Brandt: Selected Texts and Bibliography*, ed. Nigel Warburton (New York: G. K. Hall, 1993), 92.

43. Rawlinson, *British Writing of the Second World War*, 69.

44. Elizabeth Bowen, "Oh Madam, . . . ," in *The Collected Stories of Elizabeth Bowen* (New York: Knopf, 1981), 579.

45. Ibid.

46. H. D., *Trilogy*, 45–51.

47. Basil Liddell Hart, *Paris; or, the Future of War* (New York: E. P. Dutton, 1925), 31.

48. J. F. C. Fuller, *The Reformation of War* (New York: Dutton, 1923), 141.

49. Hart, *Paris*, 29.

50. Stephen Spender, Introduction to *War Pictures by British Artists*, 2nd series, no. 4: *Air Raids* (London: Oxford University Press, 1943), 6.

51. Georges Bataille, "Architecture," in *Rethinking Architecture: A Reader in Cultural History*, ed. Neil Leach, 21–23 (New York: Routledge, 1997), 21.

52. Henri Lefebvre, *The Production of Space*, trans. Donald Nicholson-Smith (1974; repr. Malden, MA: Blackwell Publishers, 2000), 39.

53. Ibid., 41.

54. James Pope-Hennessy and Cecil Beaton, *History Under Fire: 52 Photographs of Air Raid Damage to London Buildings, 1940–41* (London: B. T. Batasford Ltd., 1941), vi. Subsequent citations appear in the text.

55. John Betjeman's take on the destruction of London's churches, "Domine Dirige Nos," in *The Listener* (January 9, 1941), also makes the comparison between the German bombing and the Great Fire of 1666.

56. Pope-Hennessy, *History Under Fire*, 113.

57. Herbert Read, "Art in an Electric Atmosphere," *Horizon* (January–June 1941), 309.

58. George Orwell, "My Country Left or Right," in *Collected Essays, Journalism and Letters of George Orwell*, eds. Sonia Orwell and Ian Angus, Book 1, *An Age Like This 1920–1940* (Boston: David R. Godine, 2000), 539.

59. Ritchie Calder, *The Lesson of London* (London: Secker & Warburg, 1941), 125.

60. Ibid., 128.

61. The Uthwatt Report stopped short of land nationalization, which the Labour Party abandoned altogether by the time of the 1945 election. For more on the evolution of land ownership and postwar reconstruction, see Michael Tichelar's excellent account in "The Labour Party, Agricultural Policy and the Retreat from Land Nationalisation During the Second World War," *Agricultural History Review* 51 (2003): 209–25; and "The Conflict Over Property Rights During the Second World War: The Labour Party's Abandonment of Land Nationalization," *Twentieth Century British History* 14, no. 2 (2003): 165–88.

62. Quoted in Arthur Marwick, *Britain in the Century of Total War* (Boston: Little, Brown, 1968), 311.

63. J. B. Priestley, *Out of the People* (London: Heinemann & Collins, 1941), 9.

64. Brittain, *England's Hour*, 190–91.

65. Again, I refer to John Darwin's *The Empire Project: The Rise and Fall of the British World-System, 1830–1970* (Cambridge: Cambridge University Press, 2011).

66. W. J. McCormack's *Dissolute Characters: Irish Literary History Through Balzac, Sheridan Le Fanu, Yeats, and Bowen* (Manchester: Manchester University Press, 1993) provides an essential and, at times, skeptical reading of the Anglo-Irish gothic. For particular arguments on Bowen's place in this tradition, see Margot Backus, *The Gothic Family Romance: Heterosexuality, Child Sacrifice, and the Anglo-Irish Colonial Order* (Durham, NC: Duke University Press, 1999); Neil Corcoran, *Elizabeth Bowen: The Enforced Return* (New York: Oxford

University Press, 2004); and Hermione Lee, *Elizabeth Bowen: An Estimation* (Totowa, NJ: Barnes & Noble Books, 1981).

67. There is a long and very smart tradition of reading Bowen as one of the preeminent and most experimental writers of the Second World War. See, for example, Deer, *Culture in Camouflage*, esp. chap. 4; Phyllis Lassner, *Elizabeth Bowen: A Study of the Short Fiction* (New York: Twayne Publishers, 1991); Kristine A. Miller, *British Literature of the Blitz: Fighting the People's War* (London: Palgrave, 2009); Michael North, "World War II: The City in Ruins," in *The Cambridge History of Twentieth-Century English Literature*, ed. Laura Marcus and Peter Nicholls, 436–51 (Cambridge: Cambridge University Press, 2004); Gill Plain, "Women Writers and the War," in *The Cambridge Companion to the Literature of World War II*, ed. Marina Mackay, 165–78 (Cambridge: Cambridge University Press, 2009); and Rawlinson, *British Writing of the Second World War*.

68. See Vera Kreilkamp, "The Ascendancy Modernist," in *Eibhear Walshe*, ed. Elizabeth Bowen, 12–26 (Dublin: Irish Academic Press, 2009).

69. Backus interprets "The Demon Lover," a war story with no direct or indirect references to Ireland, as mediating Irish historical conflicts through its "patterns of repetition and historical recurrence that are characteristic of Anglo-Irish narrative structure" (157).

70. Kreilkamp, "Ascendancy Modernist," 17–18.

71. W. J. McCormack, "Irish Gothic and After 1820–1945," in *The Field Day Anthology of Irish Writing*, ed. Seamus Deane, 832–54 (Derry: Field Day Press, 1991), 831. Riquelme and Nancy Armstrong also make strong cases for the gothic as a subversive force. See Riquelme's "Introduction: Toward a History of Gothic Modernism," and Armstrong's *How Novels Think*. For a broader overview of gothic subversion in the twentieth century, see the second volume of David Punter's *The Literature of Terror: A History of Gothic Fictions from 1765 to the Present Day*, vol. 2, *The Modern Gothic* (New York: Longman, 1996).

72. Bowen, Preface to Ivy Gripped the Steps, viii.

73. Ibid.

74. Ibid.

75. Ibid., ix.

76. Ibid.

77. Reinhart Koselleck, *Futures Past: On the Semantics of Historical Time*, trans. Keith Tribe (Cambridge, MA: MIT Press, 1985), 108–9.

78. Elizabeth Bowen, *The Demon Lover and Other Stories* (London: Jonathan Cape, 1945), 80. Subsequent citations are provided in the text.

79. North, "World War II," 448.

80. In *Anglo-Irish: The Literary Imagination in a Hyphenated Culture* (Princeton, NJ: Princeton University Press, 1995), Julian Moynahan argues that the tradition of Anglo-Irish literature is inaugurated with its own end in view. "The paradox of this literature . . . is that it flowers just when the social formation producing it enters a phase of contraction and decline. As Anglo-Irish literature "arises," the Anglo-Irish begin to go down in the world" (9).

81. Neil Corcoran, *Elizabeth Bowen: The Enforced Return* (New York: Oxford University Press, 2004), 149.

82. Matthew Eatough treats *Bowen's Court* less as a typical narrative of class decline and sees it more as a mediation of Ireland's, particularly Anglo-Ireland's, place in the world-system. His reading explains the tense relationship between the gothic and professional narratives that "rectify each other's deficiencies but cannot sublate the contradictions into a stable set of social structures." See his compelling analysis in "*Bowen's Court* and the Anglo-Irish World System." *Modern Language Quarterly* 73, no. 1 (March 2012): 69–94.

83. Elizabeth Bowen, *Bowen's Court* (New York: Knopf, 1942), 453.

84. Ibid., 125.

85. Jed Esty takes on the antidevelopmental logic of *The Last September* in *Unseasonable Youth: Modernism, Colonialism, and the Fiction of Development* (Oxford: Oxford University Press, 2011). See chapter 6, "Virgins of Empire: The Antidevelopmental Plot in Rhys and Bowen."

86. Walter Benjamin, *The Arcades Project*, trans. Howard Eiland and Kevin McLaughlin (Cambridge, MA: Harvard University Press, 1999), 463. There are surely significant problems with likening Bowen's lament for the defeat of the ruling classes with Benjamin's historical materialism, which seeks desperately to reclaim the stories, hopes, and yearnings of the vanquished and the oppressed. Still, this is also what I find most interesting. Like Benjamin, Bowen coordinates two historical moments that achieve recognition and become charged with meaning.

87. Bowen, *The Demon Lover*, 108.

88. Ibid., 100.

89. Ibid.

90. Ibid.

91. Lassner, *Elizabeth Bowen*.

92. Bowen, *The Demon Lover*, 108.

93. Ibid., 103.

94. Corcoran, *Elizabeth Bowen*, 149.

95. Eagleton, *Heathcliff and the Great Hunger*, 187.

96. Quoted in Calder, *The People's War*, 137.

97. Bowen, Preface to *Ivy Gripped the Steps*, xi; and Declan Kiberd, *Inventing Ireland* (London: Jonathan Cape, 1993), 370.

98. Maud Ellmann, *Elizabeth Bowen: The Shadow Across the Page* (Edinburgh: Edinburgh University Press, 2004), 42.

99. Bowen, *Bowen's Court*, 455.

100. Bowen, *The Demon Lover*, 17.

101. Ibid., 21.

102. Ibid., 22.

103. Ibid.

104. Ibid., 25.

105. Ellmann, *Elizabeth Bowen*, 169.

106. Bowen, *The Demon Lover*, 26.

107. Elizabeth Bowen, *The Mulberry Tree: Writings of Elizabeth Bowen* (London: Virago Press, 1986), 247, 249.

108. Bowen, *The Demon Lover*, 173.

109. Ibid., 174.

110. Ibid., 176.

111. Ibid., 186.

112. Louise Bennett, "Colonisation in Reverse" (1966). In *Writing Black Britain 1948–1998: An Interdisciplinary Anthology*, ed. James Procter, 16–17 (Manchester, UK: Manchester University Press, 2000).

5. "IT IS DE AGE OF COLONIAL CONCERN": VERNACULAR FICTIONS AND POLITICAL BELONGING

1. George Lamming, *The Emigrants* (1954; repr. Ann Arbor: University of Michigan Press, 1994), 132.

2. Giovanni Arrighi, *The Long Twentieth Century: Money, Power, and the Origins of Our Times* (New York: Verso, 1994), 17.

3. For more on postimperial sovereignty, see Spencer Mawby, *Ordering Independence: The End of Empire in the Anglophone Caribbean, 1947–69* (New York: Palgrave MacMillan, 2012); and Anne Spry Rush, *Bonds of Empire: West Indians and Britishness from Victoria to Decolonization* (New York: Oxford University Press, 2011).

4. Michael North, *The Dialect of Modernism: Race, Language, and Twentieth-Century Literature* (New York: Oxford University Press, 1998), 25–26.

5. Evelyn Nien-Ming Chi'en, *Weird English* (Cambridge: Harvard University Press, 2004), 11–12.

6. In addition to Chi'en and North, see Matthew Hart, *Nations of Nothing but Poetry: Modernism, Transnationalism, and Synthetic Vernacular Writing* (Oxford: Oxford University Press, 2010); see also Joshua L. Miller, *Accented America: The Cultural Politics of Multilingual Modernism* (Oxford: Oxford University Press, 2011).

7. Zora Neale Hurston, "At the Sound of the Conch Shell," *New York Herald Tribune Weekly Book Review*, March 20, 1949, 4.

8. Ibid.

9. See James Procter's comments on the reception of *The Lonely Londoners* in his *Dwelling Places: Postwar Black British Writing* (Manchester: Manchester University Press, 2003), 46–49.

10. Ibid., 48. Susheila Nasta sums up the early reception of West Indian fictions in the metropole: "Placed firmly, therefore, outside the protected boundaries of the established canon, many were only seen to be worth commenting on for the exotic novelty of their themes, their naturalist subject-matter, the naïve authenticity of their uses of vernacular forms of English, or their otherwise realistic sociological portraits of the UK's new immigrant communities" Susheila Nasta, "'Voyaging In': Colonialism and Migration," in *The Cambridge*

History of Twentieth-Century English Literature, ed. Laura Marcus and Peter Nicholls, 563–82 (Cambridge: Cambridge University Press, 2004), 571.

11. Both Caryl Phillips and Helon Habila have acknowledged MacInnes as one of the very few white writers to include black characters in their fiction. See Phillips, "Kingdom of the Blind," *Guardian*, July 16, 2004, http://www.guardian.co.uk/books/2004/jul/17/featuresreviews.guardianreview1; and Habila "Out of the Shadows," *Guardian*, March 16, 2007, http://www.guardian.co.uk/books/2007/mar/17/society1.

12. Stuart Hall, "Absolute Beginnings," *Universities and Left Review* 7 (Autumn 1959): 23.

13. Samuel Selvon, "Samuel Selvon: Interviews and Conversations," in *Critical Perspectives on Sam Selvon*, ed. Susheila Nasta, 64–76 (Washington, DC: Three Continents Press, 1988), 67.

14. Ibid.

15. Notebooks that MacInnes kept during the writing of *Absolute Beginners* contain lists of invented words and phrases that he dutifully checks off.

16. Dohra Ahmad, "Introduction: 'This is ma trooth,'" in *Rotten English: A Literary Anthology*, ed. Dohra Ahmad, 15–32 (New York: Norton, 2007), 25.

17. George Lamming, *The Pleasures of Exile* (1960; repr. Ann Arbor: University of Michigan Press, 1991), 56. Subsequent citations appear in the text.

18. It should also be said that Simon Gikandi's insight and Lamming's formulation of Prospero and Caliban rhyme with Paul Gilroy's rereading of Hegel's master/slave dialectic in *The Black Atlantic*. See especially chapter 2, "Masters, Mistresses, Slaves, and the Antinomies of Modernity" in Paul Gilroy, *The Black Atlanta: Modernity and Double Consciousness* (Cambridge, MA: Harvard University Press, 1993), 41–71. For a full account of Caliban and postcolonial writing, see Bill Ashcroft, *Caliban's Voice: The Transformation of English in Postcolonial Literature* (New York: Routledge, 2008).

19. See chapter 1, "The Negro and Language," of Frantz Fanon's *Black Skin, White Mask*, trans. Richard Philcox (New York: Grove Press, 1967), 17–40.

20. Mary Lou Emery, *Modernism, the Visual, and Caribbean Literature* (Cambridge: Cambridge University Press, 2007), 166.

21. Jacques Rancière has elaborated this theory in multiple places, but the most direct formulation comes in his *The Politics of Aesthetics*, trans. Gabriel Rockhill (New York: Continuum, 2004).

22. See Edward Pilkington, *Beyond the Mother Country: West Indians and the Notting Hill White Riots* (London: I. B. Tauris, 1988), 149–52. Mike Phillips and Trevor Phillips discuss Cochrane's funeral and draw on several personal narratives in *Windrush: The Irresistible Rise of Multi-Racial Britain* (London: HarperCollins, 1999), 181–88.

23. Pilkington, *Beyond the Mother Country*, 152.

24. Phillips and Phillips, *Windrush*, 182.

25. Lamming, *The Pleasures of Exile*, 45. I do not have the space to engage the peasant as a type here, but Lamming's praise of "the peasant" verges on condescension. Selvon's and Reid's novels both give a more detailed, differentiated sense of peasant life than Lamming allows. There are peasants with more financial and social power than others, for example.

See Partha Chatterjee, "The Nation and Its Peasants," in *Mapping Subaltern Studies and the Postcolonial*, ed. Vinayak Chaturvedi, 9–23 (New York: Verso, 2000).

26. Rush, *Bonds of Empire*, 167.

27. Mawby, *Ordering Independence*, 48.

28. Vic Reid, *New Day* (New York: Knopf, 1949), viii. Subsequent citations appear in the text.

29. Miller, *Accented America*, 20.

30. Maureen Warner-Lewis, "Language Use in West Indian Literature," in *A History of Literature in the Caribbean*, vol. 2, ed. Albert James Arnold, Julio Rodriguez-Luis, J. Michael Dash, 25–37 (Philadelphia: John Benjamins, 1994), 30.

31. Ibid.

32. This essay was first published in the Barbadian journal *BIM* 23 (1955): 172–78.

33. Stuart Hall, "Lamming, Selvon, and Some Trends in the West Indian Novel," *BIM* 23 (1955), 173.

34. Ibid., 174.

35. Rande W. Kostal, *A Jurisprudence of Power: Victorian Empire and the Rule of Law* (New York: Oxford University Press, 2008), 13.

36. The historiography of the Morant Bay uprising ranges from imperial apologists to sympathy for the Jamaican peasants. Kostal's *A Jurisprudence of Power: Victorian Empire and the Rule of Law* addresses the controversy over the uprising and the crisis it caused for British law and the administration of the empire.

37. In addition to Kostal, see Ian Baucom's exploration of the Morant Bay event and Victorian intellectuals in *Out of Place: Englishness, Empire, and the Locations of Identity* (Princeton: Princeton University Press, 1999), 41–74.

38. Hall, "Some Trends," 175.

39. See C. L. Innes, *A History of Black and Asian Writing in Britain 1700–2000* (Cambridge: Cambridge University Press, 2002); and Sukhdev Sandhu, *London Calling: How Black and Asian Writers Imagined a City* (London: HarperCollins, 2004).

40. Sandhu, *London Calling*, xiv.

41. I borrow this phrase from Claude Levi-Strauss's *The Savage Mind* (Chicago: University of Chicago Press, 1966), 259.

42. Rieko Karatani, *Defining British Citizenship: Empire, Commonwealth and Modern Britain* (New York: Routledge, 2002), 3.

43. Kathleen Paul, *Whitewashing Britain: Race and Citizenship in the Postwar Era* (Ithaca, NY: Cornell University Press, 1997), 16.

44. Louise Bennett, "Colonisation in Reverse" (1966), in *Writing Black Britain 1948–1998: An Interdisciplinary Anthology*, ed. by James Procter, 16–17. Manchester: Manchester University Press, 2000.

45. Phillips and Phillips, *Windrush*, 75.

46. Colin MacInnes Papers at the University of Rochester, CM D140/1.11.

47. Phillips and Phillips, *Windrush*, 163–64.

48. Wendy Webster, *Englishness and Empire 1939–1965* (New York: Oxford University Press, 2007), 119.

49. See Wendy Webster, *Imagining Home: Gender, Race, and National Identity, 1945–1964* (London: UCL Press, 1998); and Caroline Elkins, *Imperial Reckoning: The Untold Story of Britain's Gulag in Kenya* (New York: Henry Holt, 2005).

50. Webster, *Englishness and Empire*, 123.

51. Beryl Gilroy, quoted in ibid., 123.

52. "The Habit of Violence," *Universities and Left Review* 5 (Autumn 1958), 1.

53. Ibid.

54. Trevor Philpott, "Would You Let Your Daughter Marry a Negro?" *Picture Post*, October 30, 1954, 23.

55. Stuart Hall, "Images of Postwar Black Settlement," in *The Everyday Life Reader*, ed. Ben Highmore, 251–61 (New York: Routledge, 2002), 261.

56. Webster, *Englishness and Empire*, 152.

57. Hall, "Images of Postwar Black Settlement," 260.

58. In addition to Procter's *Dwelling Places*, see chapter 4, "Becoming Minor," of Jed Esty's *A Shrinking Island: Modernism and National Culture in England* (Princeton, NJ: Princeton University Press, 2004), 163–226; Peter Kalliney, *Cities of Affluence and Anger: A Literary Geography of Modern Englishness* (Charlottesville: University of Virginia Press, 2007), 75–111; Rebecca Dyer, "Immigration, Postwar London, and the Politics of Everyday Life in Sam Selvon's Fiction," *Cultural Critique* 52 (October 2002): 108–44; and Lisa Kabash, "Mapping Freedom, or Its Limits: The Politics of Movement in Sam Selvon's *The Lonely Londoners*," *Postcolonial Text* 6, no. 3 (2011): 1–17.

59. Kenneth Ramchand, *The West Indian Novel and Its Background* (London: Heinemann, 1983), 101–2.

60. Selvon, "Interviews and Conversations," 66.

61. Selvon's remarks on his attunement to audience vary across his interviews. Still, the vast majority of them suggest he aimed for a broad readership. In 1982 he expresses his own sense of audience and his disenchantment with being read as a "realist": "Some people accuse me of writing a kind of hybrid dialect which is not truly authentic. What they fail to see is that apart from Vic Reid's *New Day* I was the only other West Indian novelist to write a novel in which both narrative and dialogue were written in dialect, and that I had to consider being read by an audience outside of the Caribbean to whom a presentation of the pure dialect would have been obscure and difficult to understand." Kenneth Ramchand, "Sam Selvon Talking: A Conversation with Kenneth Ramchand," in *Critical Perspectives on Sam Selvon*, ed. Susheila Nasta, 95–103 (Washington, DC: Three Continents Press, 1988), 99.

62. A similar preoccupation with audience appears in the changes Selvon made to his short story "Calypso" when it was published as "London Calypso," refurbished with an English setting and vocabulary and phrases specific to West Indian migrants.

63. Selvon, "Interviews and Conversations," 67.

64. Ibid.

65. Ibid.

66. Sandhu, *London Calling*, 145.

67. Samuel Selvon, *The Lonely Londoners* (1956; repr. New York: Longman, 1989), 93. Subsequent citations appear in the text.

68. Paul Gilroy, *Black Britain: A Photographic History* (London: Saqi Books, 2008), 81.

69. Dyer, "Immigration, Postwar London," 112.

70. Fanon, *Black Skin, White Masks*, 109.

71. John McLeod, *Postcolonial London: Rewriting the Metropolis* (New York: Routledge, 2004), 38.

72. Ashley Dawson, *Mongrel Nation: Diasporic Culture and the Making of Postcolonial Britain* (Ann Arbor: University of Michigan Press, 2007), 29.

73. Wendy Webster argues that the white woman figured as "the 'inviolate centre' which defined the boundaries of England" (*Englishness and Empire 1939–1965*, 157). If migration pierced and weakened the spatial boundaries of empire, the preservation of white women served as the last designation between the English and the formerly colonized. See chapter 6 of her *Englishness and Empire 1939–1965*, 149–81.

74. John Steel, quoted in Dawson, *Mongrel Nation*, 28.

75. Jon McLeod's *Postcolonial London* juxtaposes MacInnes and Selvon, positioning both writers as visionaries of a utopic, multiethnic England.

76. Phillips, "Kingdom of the Blind"; and Habila, "Out of the Shadows."

77. Colin MacInnes, *Absolute Beginners* (1959; repr. London; Allison & Busby, 2011), 53, 63. Subsequent citations appear in the text.

78. See Edward Pilkington's full account of the Notting Hill events in *Beyond the Mother Country*.

79. Ibid., 5–6.

80. Colin MacInnes Papers at the University of Rochester, CM D140/1.13.

81. Alan Sinfield, *Literature, Politics and Culture in Postwar Britain* (New York: Continuum, 2004), 194.

82. Paul Gilroy examines the articulation of blackness with criminality during and after the Notting Hill riots. See *"There Ain't No Black in the Union Jack": The Cultural Politics of Race and Nation* (Chicago: University of Chicago Press, 1987), 72–113.

83. T. H. Marshall's "Citizenship and Social Class," in *Citizenship and Social Class and Other Essays*, 1–85 (London: Cambridge University Press, 1950), has recently come into vogue in contemporary political theory. Marshall has become a touchstone for thinkers of global citizenship in works such as Seyla Benhabib's *The Rights of Others: Aliens, Residents, and Citizens* (Cambridge: Cambridge University Press, 2004); Linda Bosniak's *The Citizen and the Alien: Dilemmas of Contemporary Membership* (Princeton, NJ: Princeton University Press, 2006); and Margaret Somers's *Genealogies of Citizenship: Markets, Statelessness, and the Right to Have Rights* (Cambridge: Cambridge University Press, 2008).

EPILOGUE: "APPOINTMENTS TO KEEP IN THE PAST"

1. W. G. Sebald, *On the Natural History of Destruction*, trans. Anthea Bell (New York: Modern Library, 2004), 59.

2. Ibid., 58.

3. Ibid.

4. Sebald acknowledges his affinity for German naturalist writing in a conversation with Michael Silverblatt. See W. G. Sebald, Interview with Michael Silverblatt, *Bookworm*, KCRW, December 6, 2001, http://www.kcrw.com/news-culture/shows/bookworm/w-g-sebald.

5. W. G. Sebald, *Austerlitz*, trans. Anthea Bell (New York: Modern Library, 2001), 6–7; subsequent citations appear in the text.

6. See Amir Eshel's reading of this scene in "Against the Power of Time: The Poetics of Suspension in W. G. Sebald's *Austerlitz*," *New German Critique* 88 (Winter 2003): 71–96. Jens Brockmeier offers a slightly different reading of this particular scene and, more generally, the novel's treatment of temporality and memory. See "Austerlitz's Memory," *Partial Answers: Journal of Literature and the History of Ideas* 6, no. 2 (June 2008): 347–67.

7. Henri Lefebvre, *The Production of Space*, trans. Donald Nicholson-Smith (1974; repr. Malden: Blackwell Publishers, 2000), 221.

BIBLIOGRAPHY

UNPUBLISHED SOURCES

THE COLIN MACINNES PAPERS, UNIVERSITY OF ROCHESTER, ROCHESTER, NEW YORK

CM 1.11 Indexed Correspondence: Elspeth Huxley
CM 1.13 Indexed Correspondence: Reginald Davis-Poynter
CM 4.2 Absolute Beginners Manuscript Notebook
CM 12.4 Sundry Printed Reviews and Letters
CM 13.13 *Spectator* 1957–1971
CM 14.8 *Manchester Guardian*, 1958–1959
CM 22.1 Correspondence, 1948–1978: Colin MacInnes to Francis and Violet Wyndham

HUMPHREY JENNINGS COLLECTION, BRITISH FILM INSTITUTE, LONDON

Box 1.7 Treatments Entitled *National Gallery* (1941) and *The Music of War*
Box 2.16 Talks, Lectures, Etc.
Box 2.17 Transcripts of Broadcast Talks by Jennings

KENNETH CLARK CORRESPONDENCE, TATE BRITAIN, LONDON

TGA 8812/1/4/442a Correspondence Regarding Henry Moore and WAAC

MASS OBSERVATION ARCHIVE, UNIVERSITY OF SUSSEX, BRIGHTON, UK

SxMOA 1/2/33/1/H
SxMOA 1/2/33/3/C

PUBLISHED SOURCES

Achebe, Chinua. "An Image of Africa: Racism in Conrad's Heart of Darkness." *Massachusetts Review* 18 (1977): 782–94.

Adorno, Theodor. *Aesthetic Theory.* Trans. Robert Hullot-Kentor. 1970. Reprint, Minneapolis: University of Minnesota Press, 1998.

——. *Aesthetics and Politics.* New York: Verso, 2007.

——. *Introduction to the Sociology of Music.* Trans. E. B. Ashton. London: Continuum, 1988.

Agamben, Giorgio. *Homo Sacer: Sovereign Power and Bare Life.* Trans. Daniel Heller-Roazen. Stanford, CA: Stanford University Press, 1998.

——. *State of Exception.* Trans. Kevin Attell. Chicago: University of Chicago Press, 2005.

Ahmad, Dohra. "Introduction: 'This is ma trooth.'" In *Rotten English: A Literary Anthology,* ed. Dohra Ahmad, 15–32. New York: Norton, 2007.

Aitken, Ian. *Film and Reform: John Grierson and the Documentary Film Movement.* London: Routledge, 1990.

Andrews, Julian. *London's War: The Shelter Drawings of Henry Moore.* Aldershot: Lund Humphries, 2002.

Arata, Stephen. "Late-Victorian Realism." In *Cambridge Companion to the Fin de Siècle,* ed. Gail Marshall, 165–88. Cambridge: Cambridge University Press, 2007.

Arendt, Hannah. *The Origins of Totalitarianism.* New York: Harcourt, Brace, Jovanovich, 1973.

Armstrong, Nancy. *Fiction in the Age of Photography: The Legacy of British Realism.* Cambridge: Harvard University Press, 1999).

——. *How Novels Think: The Limits of British Individualism from 1719–1900.* New York: Columbia University Press, 2005.

Arrighi, Giovanni. *The Long Twentieth Century: Money, Power, and the Origins of Our Times.* New York: Verso, 1994.

Ashcroft, Bill. *Caliban's Voice: The Transformation of English in Postcolonial Literature.* New York: Routledge, 2008.

Auden, W. H., and Christopher Isherwood. *Journey to a War.* New York: Paragon House. 1990.

——. *Selected Poems.* New York: Vintage International, 1989.

Backus, Margot. *The Gothic Family Romance: Heterosexuality, Child Sacrifice, and the Anglo-Irish Colonial Order.* Durham, NC: Duke University Press, 1999.

Bain, Alexander M. "International Settlements: Ishiguro, Shanghai, Humanitarianism." *NOVEL: A Forum on Fiction* 40, no. 3 (Summer 2007): 240–64.

Balibar, Étienne. *We, the People of Europe? Reflections on Transnational Citizenship.* Trans. James Swenson. Princeton, NJ: Princeton University Press, 2003.

Ball, John Clement. *Imagining London: Postcolonial Fiction and the Transnational Metropolis.* Toronto: University of Toronto Press, 2004.

Barnouw, Erik. *Documentary: A History of the Non-Fiction Film.* Oxford: Oxford University Press, 1983.

Barthes, Roland. *Camera Lucida: Reflections on Photography.* Trans. Richard Howard. New York: Farrar, Straus and Giroux, 1981.

Bataille, George. "Architecture." In *Rethinking Architecture: A Reader in Cultural History*, ed. Neil Leach, 21–23. New York: Routledge, 1997.

Baucom, Ian. *Out of Place: Englishness, Empire, and the Locations of Identity*. Princeton, NJ: Princeton University Press, 1999.

——. *Specters of the Atlantic: Finance Capital, Slavery, and the Philosophy of History*. Durham, NC: Duke University Press, 2005.

Baudelaire, Charles. *The Painter of Modern Life and Other Essays*. Trans. Jonathan Mayne. New York: Phaidon Press, 2010.

Beevor, Antony. *The Battle for Spain: The Spanish Civil War 1936–1939*. New York: Penguin, 2006.

Bell, Amy. "Landscapes of Fear: Wartime London, 1939–1945." *Journal of British Studies* 48, no. 1 (January 2009): 153–75.

Benhabib, Seyla. *Dignity in Adversity: Human Rights in Troubled Times*. Malden, MA: Polity, 2011.

——. *The Rights of Others: Aliens, Residents, and Citizens*. Cambridge: Cambridge University Press, 2004.

Benjamin, Walter. *The Arcades Project*. Trans. Howard Eiland and Kevin McLaughlin. Cambridge: Harvard University Press, 1999.

——. "On Some Motifs in Baudelaire." In *Selected Writings*, Vol. 4, *1938–1940*. Cambridge: Harvard University Press, 2003.

——. "Surrealism: The Last Snapshot of the European Intelligentsia." In *Selected Writings*, Volume 2, *Part 1: 1927–1930*, ed. Michael W. Jennings, Howard Eiland, and Gary Smith, 207–221. Cambridge: Harvard University Press, 1999.

Bennett, Louise. "Colonisation in Reverse" (1966). In *Writing Black Britain 1948–1998: An Interdisciplinary Anthology*, ed. James Procter, 16–17. Manchester, UK: Manchester University Press, 2000.

Berg, James J., and Chris Freeman, eds. *Conversations with Christopher Isherwood*. Jackson: University Press of Mississippi, 2001.

Berman, Jessica. *Modernist Commitments: Ethics, Politics, and Transnational Modernism*. New York: Columbia University Press, 2011.

Bernstein, J. *Against Voluptuous Bodies: Late Modernism and the Meaning of Painting*. Stanford, CA: Stanford University Press, 2006.

Bickers, Robert. *Settlers and Expatriates: Britons over the Seas*. Oxford: Oxford University Press, 2010.

Blanchot, Maurice. *The Infinite Conversation*. Trans. Susan Hanson. 1969. Reprint, Minneapolis: University of Minnesota Press, 1993.

Bloch, Ernst. *Heritage of Our Times*. Trans. Neville Plaice and Stephen Plaice. Berkeley: University of California Press, 1991.

Booth, Allyson. *Postcards from the Trenches: Negotiating the Space Between Modernism and the First World War*. New York: Oxford University Press, 1996.

Bosniak, Linda. *The Citizen and the Alien: Dilemmas of Contemporary Membership*. Princeton, NJ: Princeton University Press, 2006.

Botting, Fred. *Gothic*. New York: Routledge, 1996.

Bowen, Elizabeth. *Bowen's Court*. New York: Knopf, 1942.

——. *The Collected Stories of Elizabeth Bowen*. New York: Knopf, 1981.

——. *The Demon Lover and Other Stories*. London: Jonathan Cape, 1945.

——. *The Mulberry Tree: Writings of Elizabeth Bowen*. London: Virago Press, 1986.

——. *Pictures and Conversations*. London: Allen Lane, 1975.

——. Preface to *Ivy Gripped the Steps and Other Stories*. New York: Knopf, 1946.

Bradshaw, David. "Hyams Place: The Years, the Jews and the British Union of Fascists" in *Women Writers of the 1930s: Gender, Politics, and History*, ed. Maroula Joannou, 179–91. Edinburgh: Edinburgh University Press, 1999.

Brandt, Bill. "A Photographer's London." In *Bill Brandt: Selected Texts and Bibliography*, ed. Nigel Warburton. New York: G. K. Hall, 1993.

Brantlinger, Patrick. *Rule of Darkness: British Literature and Imperialism, 1830–1914*. Ithaca, NY: Cornell University Press, 1988.

Breton, André. *Nadja*. Trans. Richard Howard. 1928; Reprint, Grove Press, 1960.

Brittain, Vera. *England's Hour*. New York: Macmillan, 1941.

Brockmeier, Jens. "*Austerlitz*'s Memory." *Partial Answers: Journal of Literature and the History of Ideas* 6, no. 2 (June 2008): 347–67.

Brooks, Peter. *Realist Vision*. New Haven, CT: Yale University Press, 2008.

Brown, Nicholas. *Utopian Generations: The Political Horizon of Twentieth-Century Literature*. Princeton, NJ: Princeton University Press, 2005.

Browse, Lillian. "Review of British War Artists." *Horizon*, September 1940, 139–51.

Bruns, Gerald L. *On the Anarchy of Poetry and Philosophy: A Guide for the Unruly*. Bronx, NY: Fordham University Press, 2006.

Bryant, Marsha. *Auden and Documentary in the 1930s*. Charlottesville: University of Virginia Press, 1997.

Brzezinski, Max. "The New Modernist Studies: What's Left of Political Formalism?" *Minnesota Review* 76 (Summer 2011): 109–25.

Buchanan, Tom. *Britain and the Spanish Civil War*. Cambridge: Cambridge University Press, 1997.

Burger, Peter. *Theory of the Avant-Garde*. Minneapolis: University of Minnesota, 1984.

Burton, Antoinette. *After the Imperial Turn: Thinking With and Through the Nation*. Durham, NC: Duke University Press, 2003.

Buzard, James. "Mass-Observation, Modernism, and Auto-Ethnography." *Modernism/Modernity* 4, no. 3 (1997): 93–122.

Calder, Angus. *The Myth of the Blitz*. London: Jonathan Cape, 1991.

——. *The People's War: Britain 1939–45*. New York: Pantheon, 1969.

Calder, Ritchie. *The Lesson of London*. London: Secker & Warburg, 1941.

Carpenter, Humphrey. *W. H. Auden: A Biography*. New York: Houghton Mifflin, 1982.

Carr, Jamie M. *Queer Times: Christopher Isherwood's Modernity*. New York: Routledge, 2006.

Carr, Raymond. *The Spanish Tragedy: The Civil War in Perspective*. London: Weidenfeld and Nicolson, 1977.

Casanova, Pascale. *The World Republic of Letters*. Cambridge: Harvard University Press, 2004.

Cecil, Viscount. Foreword to *A Challenge to Death*. Ed. Storm Jameson. London: Constable & Co., 1934.

Chapman, James. *The British at War: Cinema, State and Propaganda, 1939–1945*. London: I. B. Tauris, 1998.

Chatterjee, Partha. "The Nation and Its Peasants." In *Mapping Subaltern Studies and the Postcolonial*, ed. Vinayak Chaturvedi, 9–23. New York: Verso, 2000.

Ch'ien, Evelyn Nien-Ming. *Weird English*. Cambridge: Harvard University Press, 2004.

Christopher, David. *British Culture: An Introduction*. New York: Routledge, 1999.

Clifford, James. *The Predicament of Culture: Twentieth Century Ethnography, Literature, and Art*. Cambridge: Harvard University Press, 1988.

Connor, John. "Historical Turns in Twentieth-Century Fiction," in *A Companion to British Literature*. Vol. 4, *Victorian and Twentieth Century Literature 1837–2000*, ed. Robert DeMaria Jr., Heesok Chang, and Samantha Zacher, 314–32. London: John Wiley.

Corcoran, Neil. *Elizabeth Bowen: The Enforced Return*. Oxford: Oxford University Press, 2008.

Cuddy-Keane, Melba. "Modernism, Geopolitics, Globalization." *Modernism/Modernity* 10, no. 3 (2003): 539–58.

Cunard, Nancy. *Authors Take Sides on the Spanish War*. London: Left Review, 1937.

Cunningham, Valentine. *British Writers of the Thirties*. Oxford: Oxford University Press, 1988.

——, ed. *The Spanish Front: Writers on the Civil War*. Oxford: Oxford University Press, 1986.

Darwin, John. *The Empire Project: The Rise and Fall of the British World-System, 1830–1970*. Cambridge: Cambridge University Press, 2011.

Davis, Thomas S. "Late Modernism: British Literature at Midcentury" *Literature Compass* 9, no. 4 (2012): 326–37.

Dawson, Ashley. *Mongrel Nation: Diasporic Culture and the Making of Postcolonial Britain*. Ann Arbor: University of Michigan Press, 2007.

Deane, Seamus. *Strange Country: Modernity and Nationhood in Irish Writing Since 1790*. New York: Oxford University Press, 1997.

Deer, Patrick. *Culture in Camouflage: War, Empire and Modern British Literature*. Oxford: Oxford University Press, 2009.

Delgarno, Emily. "A British War and Peace? Virginia Woolf Reads Tolstoy." *Modern Fiction Studies* 50, no. 1 (Spring 2004): 129–50.

Derrida, Jacques. "The Law of Genre." Trans. Avital Ronell. *Critical Inquiry* 7, no. 1 (Autumn 1980): 55–81.

Dibattista, Maria. *Virginia Woolf's Major Novels: The Fable of Anon*. New Haven, CT: Yale University Press, 1980.

Dimock, Wai Chee. *Through Other Continents: American Literature Across Deep Time*. Princeton, NJ: Princeton University Press, 2006.

Doyle, Laura. *Freedom's Empire: Race and the Rise of the Novel in Atlantic Modernity, 1640–1940*. Durham, NC: Duke University Press, 2007.

Dyer, Rebecca. "Immigration, Postwar London, and the Politics of Everyday Life in Sam Selvon's Fiction." *Cultural Critique* 52 (2002): 108–44.

Eagleton, Terry. *Heathcliff and the Great Hunger: Studies in Irish Culture*. New York: Verso, 1995.

Eatough, Matthew. "Bowen's Court and the Anglo-Irish World System." *Modern Language Quarterly* 73, no. 1 (March 2012): 69–94.

Einstein, Albert, and Sigmund Freud. *Why War?* In *An International Series of Open Letters*. Vol. 2. Paris: International Institute of Intellectual Co-Operation, League of Nations, 1933.

Elkins, Caroline. *Imperial Reckoning: The Untold Story of Britain's Gulag in Kenya*. New York: Henry Holt, 2005.

Ellis, Jack. *John Grierson: Life, Contributions, Influence*. Carbondale: Southern Illinois University Press, 2000.

Ellis, Jack C., and Betsy A. McLane. *A New History of Documentary Film*. New York: Continuum, 2005.

Ellmann, Maud. *Elizabeth Bowen: The Shadow Across the Page*. Edinburgh: Edinburgh University Press, 2004.

Emery, Mary Lou. *Modernism, the Visual, and Caribbean Literature*. Cambridge: Cambridge University Press, 2007.

Eshel, Amir. "Against the Power of Time: The Poetics of Suspension in W. G. Sebald's *Austerlitz*." *New German Critique* 88 (Winter 2003): 71–96.

Esty, Jed. *A Shrinking Island: Modernism and National Culture in England*. Princeton, NJ: Princeton University Press, 2003.

——. *Unseasonable Youth: Modernism, Colonialism, and the Fiction of Development*. Oxford: Oxford University Press, 2011.

Fanon, Frantz. *Black Skin, White Masks*. Trans. Richard Philcox. New York: Grove Press, 1967.

Farley, David. *Modernist Travel Writing: Intellectuals Abroad*. Columbia: University of Missouri Press, 2010.

Favret, Mary A. *War at a Distance: Romanticism and the Making of Modern Wartime*. Princeton, NJ: Princeton University Press, 2010.

Felski, Rita. "Modernist Studies and Cultural Studies: Reflections on Method." *Modernism/Modernity* 10, no. 3 (September 2003): 501–17.

——. "Suspicious Minds." *Poetics Today* 32, no. 2 (Summer 2011): 215–34.

Finney, Brian. *Christopher Isherwood: A Critical Biography*. New York: Oxford University Press, 1979.

Fleishman, Avrom. *The English Historical Novel: Walter Scott to Virginia Woolf*. Baltimore: Johns Hopkins University Press, 1972.

Forbes, Curdella. *From Nation to Diaspora: Samuel Selvon, George Lamming and the Cultural Performance of Gender*. Mona: University of the West Indies Press, 2005.

Foucault, Michel. *Society Must Be Defended! Lectures at the College de France 1975–1976*. Trans. David Macey. New York: Picador, 2003.

Frank, Joseph. *The Idea of Spatial Form*. New Brunswick, NJ: Rutgers University Press, 1991.

Freud, Sigmund. *Civilization and Its Discontents*. Trans. James Strachey. New York: W. W. Norton, 1961.

——. "Creative Writers and Day-Dreaming." In *Criticism: The Major Statements*, ed. Charles Kaplan, 419–28. New York: St. Martin's, 1991.

Friedman, Susan Stanford. "Definitional Excursions: The Meanings of Modern/Modernity/ Modernism." *Modernism/Modernity* 8, no. 3 (September 2001): 498–513.

——. "Periodizing Modernism: Postcolonial Modernities and the Space/Time Borders of Modernist Studies." *Modernism/Modernity* 12, no. 3 (September 2006): 425–44.

——. "Planetarity: Musing Modernist Studies." *Modernism/Modernity* 17, no. 3 (September 2010): 471–99.

Froula, Christine. *Virginia Woolf and the Bloomsbury Avant-Garde: War, Civilization, Modernity.* New York: Columbia University Press, 2005.

Fuller, J. F. C. *The Reformation of War.* New York: Dutton, 1923.

Fussell, Paul. *Abroad: British Literary Travel Writing Between the Wars.* Oxford: Oxford University Press, 1980.

Garner, James Wilford. *International Law and the World War.* London: Longmans, 1920.

Gascoyne, David. *Collected Journals 1936–1942.* London: Skoob Books, 1993.

Gasiorek, Andrzej. *Post-War British Fiction: Realism and After.* New York: St. Martin's Press, 1995.

Genter, Robert. *Late Modernism: Art, Culture, and Politics in Cold War America.* Philadelphia: University of Pennsylvania Press, 2010.

Gikandi, Simon. *Writing in Limbo: Modernism and Caribbean Literature.* Ithaca, NY: Cornell University Press, 1992.

Gifford, James. "Anarchist Transformations of English Surrealism: The Villa Seurat Network." *Journal of Modern Literature* 33, no. 4 (2010): 57–71.

Gilbert, Sandra M. "'Rats' Alley': The Great War, Modernism, and the (Anti)Pastoral Elegy." *New Literary History* 30, no. 1 (Winter 1999): 179–201.

Gilroy, Paul. *The Black Atlantic: Modernity and Double Consciousness.* Cambridge, MA: Harvard University Press, 1993.

——. *Black Britain: A Photographic History.* London: Saqi Books, 2008.

——. *"There Ain't No Black in the Union Jack": The Cultural Politics of Race and Nation.* London: Hutchingson, 1987.

Glass, Ruth. *Newcomers: The West Indians in London.* London: Centre for Urban Studies/Allen & Unwin, 1960.

GoGwilt, Christopher. *The Fiction of Geopolitics: Afterimages of Culture, from Wilkie Collins to Alfred Hitchcock.* Stanford, CA: Stanford University Press, 2000.

Goldman, Jane. *The Feminist Aesthetics of Virginia Woolf: Modernism, Post-Impressionism, and the Politics of the Visual.* Cambridge: Cambridge University Press, 1998.

Gould, Tony. *Inside Outsider: The Life and Times of Colin MacInnes.* London: Allison & Busby, 1993.

Green, Barbara. *Spectacular Confessions: Autobiography, Performative Activism, and the Sites of Suffrage 1905–1938.* London: Macmillan, 1997.

Green, Henry. *Loving; Living; Party Going.* 1939. Reprint, New York: Penguin Classics, 1993.

Gregg, John. *The Shelter of the Tubes.* London: Capital Transport Publishing, 2001.

Groot, Jerome de. *The Historical Novel.* New York: Routledge, 2010.

Grierson, John. "The Documentary Producer." *Cinema Quarterly* 2, no. 1 (Autumn 1933): 7–9.

——. "Finding in Plato the Key to Modern Art." *Chicago Evening Post*, May 12, 1925.

——. "Flaherty's Poetic Moana," *New York Sun*, February 8, 1926.

——. *Grierson on Documentary*. Ed. Forsyth Hardy. Berkeley: University of California Press, 1966.

——. *Grierson on the Movies*. Ed. Forsyth Hardy. London: Faber and Faber, 1981.

——. "The Personality Behind the Paint." *Chicago Evening Post*, June 30, 1925.

——. Preface to *Documentary Film*. By Paul Rotha. London: Faber and Faber, 1935.

——. Preface to *Documentary Film*, 3rd ed. By Paul Rotha. 1952. Reprint, London: Faber and Faber, 1963.

——. "Vorticism Born with a Curse on Its Lips." *Chicago Evening Post*, June 16, 1925.

——. "Vorticism Brought to Serve Drama." *Chicago Evening Post*, February 17, 1925.

Guynn, William. "Art of National Projection." In *Documenting the Documentary: Close Readings of Documentary Film and Video*, ed. Barry K. Grant and Jeannette Sloniwoski, 83–98. Detroit: Wayne State University Press, 1998.

——. *A Cinema of Non-Fiction*. Cranbury, NJ: Associated University Presses, 1990.

Habila, Helon. "Out of the Shadows." *Guardian*, March 16, 2007. http://www.guardian.co.uk/books/2007/mar/17/society1.

"The Habit of Violence." *Universities and Left Review* 5 (Autumn 1958): 4–5.

"The Hague Declaration (IV) of 1899 Concerning Expanding Bullets." *Pamphlet Series of the Carnegie Endowment for International Peace, Division of International Law*. Washington, DC: Carnegie Endowment for International Peace, 1915.

Hall, Stuart. "Absolute Beginnings." *Universities and Left Review* 7 (Autumn 1959): 17–25.

——. "Images of Postwar Black Settlement." In *The Everyday Life Reader*, ed. Ben Highmore, 251–61. New York: Routledge, 2002.

——. "Lamming, Selvon and Some Trends in the West Indian Novel." *BIM* 23 (1955): 172–78.

H. D. *Trilogy*. New York: New Directions, 1998.

Hallward, Peter. "Beyond Salvage." *South Atlantic Quarterly* 104, no. 2 (2005): 237–44.

Hansen, James. "Formalism and Its Malcontents: Benjamin and de Man on the Function of Allegory." *New Literary History* 35, no. 4 (2004): 663–83.

Hansen, Randall. *Citizenship and Immigration in Post-War Britain: The Institutional Origins of a Multicultural Nation*. Oxford: Oxford University Press, 2000.

Hansen, Thomas Blom, and Finn Stepputat. *Sovereign Bodies: Citizens, Migrants, and States in the Postcolonial World*. Princeton, NJ: Princeton University Press, 2005.

Harney, Stefano. *Nationalism and Identity: Culture and the Imagination in a Caribbean Diaspora*. Mona: University of the West Indies Press, 2006.

Harootunian, Harry. *History's Disquiet*. New York: Columbia University Press, 2002.

Harrisson, Tom, Humphrey Jennings, and Charles Madge. "Anthropology at Home." *New Statesman and Nation*, January 30, 1937, 155.

Harrisson, Tom, and Charles Madge. *Britain by Mass Observation*. Hammondsworth, UK: Penguin, 1939.

——. *First Year's Work*. London: Lindsay Drummond, 1938.

——. *Mass Observation*. London: Frederick Muller, 1937.

——. *War Begins at Home*. London: Chatto & Windus, 1940.

Hart, Basil Liddell. *Paris; or, the Future of War*. New York: E. P. Dutton, 1925.

Hart, Matthew. *Nations of Nothing but Poetry: Modernism, Transnationalism, and Synthetic Vernacular Writing*. Oxford: Oxford University Press, 2010.

Harvey, David. *A Companion to Marx's Capital*. New York: Verso, 2010.

Hayot, Eric. "Against Periodization; or, On Institutional Time." *New Literary History* 42, no. 4 (Autumn 2011): 739–56.

——. *The Hypothetical Mandarin: Sympathy, Modernity, and Chinese Pain*. Oxford: Oxford University Press, 2009.

Hegel, G. W. F. *The Philosophy of History*. Trans. J. Sibree. Mineola, NY: Dover, 2004.

Henriot, Christian, and Wen-hsin Yeh. *In the Shadow of the Rising Sun: Shanghai Under Japanese Occupation*. Cambridge: Cambridge University Press, 2004.

Hensley, Nathan. "Allegories of the Contemporary." *Novel: A Forum on Fiction* 45, no. 2 (2012): 276–300.

Highmore, Ben. *Everyday Life and Cultural Theory: An Introduction*. New York: Routledge, 2002.

Hirst, Paul. *Space and Power: Politics, War and Architecture*. London: Polity, 2005.

Ho, Janice. "The Spatial Imagination and Literary Form of Conrad's Colonial Fictions." *Journal of Modern Literature* 13, no. 4 (Summer 2007): 1–19.

Hooker, William. *Carl Schmitt's International Thought: Order and Orientation*. Cambridge: Cambridge University Press, 2009.

Hopkins, James K. *Into the Heart of the Fire: The British in the Spanish Civil War*. Stanford, CA: Stanford University Press, 1998.

Houlbrook, Matt. *Queer London: Perils and Pleasures in the Sexual Metropolis, 1918–1957*. Chicago: University of Chicago Press, 2006.

Hubble, Nick. *Mass Observation and Everyday Life: Culture, History, Theory*. New York: Palgrave, 2006.

Hurston, Zora Neale. "At the Sound of the Conch Shell." *New York Herald Tribune Weekly Book Review*, March 20, 1949.

Hussey, Mark. *Virginia Woolf A to Z: A Comprehensive Reference for Students, Teachers, and Common Readers to Her Life, Work, and Critical Reception*. Oxford: Oxford University Press, 1996.

Hynes, Samuel. *The Auden Generation: Literature and Politics in England in the 1930s*. Princeton, NJ: Princeton University Press, 1982.

Innes, C. L. *A History of Black and Asian Writing in Britain 1700–2000*. Cambridge: Cambridge University Press, 2002.

Irele, F. Abiola, and Simon Gikandi. *The Cambridge History of African and Caribbean Literature*, 2 vols. Cambridge: Cambridge University Press, 2004.

Iriye, Akira. *Cultural Internationalism and World Order*. Baltimore: Johns Hopkins University Press, 1997.

Isherwood, Christopher. *The Berlin Stories*. New York: New Directions, 1963.

——. *Christopher and His Kind*. New York: Farrar, Straus Giroux, 1976.

——. *Isherwood on Writing*. Ed. James J. Berg. Minneapolis: University of Minnesota Press, 2007.

——. *Lions and Shadows: An Education in the Twenties.* Minneapolis: University of Minnesota Press, 2000.

Izzo, David Garrett. *Christopher Isherwood: His Era, His Gang, and the Legacy of the Truly Strong Man.* Columbia: University of South Carolina Press, 2001.

Jackson, Angela. *British Women and the Spanish Civil War.* New York: Routledge, 2002.

James, David. *Modernist Futures: Innovation and Inheritance in the Contemporary Novel.* Cambridge: Cambridge University Press, 2012.

Jameson, Fredric. *Marxism and Form: Twentieth Century Dialectical Theories of Literature.* Princeton, NJ: Princeton University Press, 1971.

——. *The Political Unconscious: Narrative as a Socially Symbolic Act.* Ithaca, NY: Cornell University Press, 1983.

——. *Postmodernism, or the Cultural Logic of Late Capitalism.* Durham, NC: Duke University Press, 1995.

——. *A Singular Modernity: An Essay on the Ontology of the Present.* New York: Verso, 2002.

——. *Valences of the Dialectic.* New York: Verso, 2010.

Jameson, Storm, ed. *Challenge to Death.* London: Constable & Co., 1934.

——. "Documents." *FACT* 4 (1937): 9–18.

Jay, Paul. *Global Matters: The Transnational Turn in Literary Studies.* Ithaca, NY: Cornell University Press, 2010.

Jeffery, Tom. *Mass-Observation: A Short History.* Mass Observation Archive Occasional Paper Series, no. 10. University of Sussex Library, 1999.

Jennings, Humphrey. "From *The Poet and the Public.*" In *The Humphrey Jennings Film Reader.* Ed. Kevin Jackson. Manchester: Carcanet, 1993.

——. *Humphrey Jennings: Film-Maker, Painter, Poet.* Ed. Mary-Lou Jennings. London: British Film Institute, 1982.

——. "Surrealism." *Contemporary Poetry and Prose* 8 (December 1936): 167.

Jennings, Humphrey, and Charles Madge. *May the Twelfth: Mass Observation Day Surveys.* London: Faber and Faber, 1937.

——. "The Oxford Collective Poem." *New Verse* 25 (1937): 16–19.

——. "Poetic Description and Mass Observation." *New Verse* 24 (1937): 1–6.

Jennings, W. Ivor. "The Rule of Law in Total War." *Yale Law Journal* 50, no. 3 (1941): 365–86.

Kabash, Lisa. "Mapping Freedom, or Its Limits: The Politics of Movement in Sam Selvon's *The Lonely Londoners.*" *Postcolonial Text* 6, no. 3 (2011): 1–17.

Kalliney, Peter. *Cities of Affluence and Anger: A Literary Geography of Modern Englishness.* Charlottesville: University of Virginia Press, 2007.

Karatani, Rieko. *Defining British Citizenship: Empire, Commonwealth and Modern Britain.* New York: Routledge, 2002.

Kennedy, David. *Of War and Law.* Princeton, NJ: Princeton University Press, 2006.

Kerr, Douglas. "Disorientations: Auden and Isherwood's China," *Literature & History* 5, no. 2 (Autumn 1996): 53–67.

Kiberd, Declan. *Inventing Ireland.* London: Jonathan Cape, 1993.

Kilgour, Maggie. *The Rise of the Gothic Novel.* New York: Routledge, 1995.

Knowles, Sebastian. *A Purgatorial Flame: Seven British Writers in the Second World War*. Philadelphia: University of Pennsylvania Press, 1990.

Kosseleck, Reinhart. *Futures Past: On the Semantics of Historical Time*, trans. Keith Tribe. Cambridge, MA: MIT Press, 1985.

Kostal, Rande W. *A Jurisprudence of Power: Victorian Empire and the Rule of Law*. New York: Oxford University Press, 2008.

Kreilkamp, Vera. "'Bowen: Ascendancy Modernist.'" In *Elizabeth Bowen*, ed. Eibhear Walshe. Dublin: Irish Academic Press, 2009.

Laqua, Daniel. "Transnational Intellectual Cooperation, the League of Nations, and the Problem of Order." *Journal of Global History* 6 (2011): 223–47.

Lamming, George. *The Emigrants*. 1954. Reprint, Ann Arbor: University of Michigan Press, 1994.

——. *The Pleasures of Exile*. 1960. Reprint, Ann Arbor: University of Michigan Press, 1991.

Langbauer, Laurie. *Novels of Everyday Life: The Series in English Fiction, 1850–1930*. Ithaca, NY: Cornell University Press, 1999.

Laplanche, Jean, and J. B. Pontalis, "Fantasy and the Origins of Sexuality," *International Journal of Psycho-Analysis* 49, no. 1 (1968): 1–18.

Lassner, Phyllis. *Elizabeth Bowen: A Study of the Short Fiction*. New York: Twayne Publishers, 1991.

Laurence, Patricia. *Lily Briscoe's Chinese Eyes: Bloomsbury, Modernism, and China*. Columbia: University of South Carolina Press, 2003.

Lee, Bradford A. *Britain and the Sino-Japanese War, 1937–1939: A Study in the Dilemmas of British Decline*. Stanford, CA: Stanford University Press, 1973.

Lee, Hermione. *Elizabeth Bowen: An Estimation*. Totowa, NJ: Barnes & Noble Books, 1981.

Lee, Leo Ou-fan. *Shanghai Modern: The Flowering of a New Urban Culture in Shanghai, 1930–1945*. Cambridge: Harvard University Press, 1999.

Lee, Richard E. "The Modern World-System: Its Structures, Its Geoculture, Its Crisis and Transformation." In *Immanuel Wallerstein and the Problem of the World: System, Scale, Culture*, ed. David Palumbo-Liu, Bruce Robbins, and Nirvana Tanoukhi, 27–40. Durham, NC: Duke University Press, 2011.

Lefebvre, Henri. *Critique of Everyday Life*. Vol. 3, *From Modernity to Modernism (Towards a Metaphilosophy of Daily Life)*. Trans. Gregory Elliott. London: Verso, 2005.

——. *The Production of Space*. Trans. Donald Nicholson-Smith. 1974. Reprint, Malden, MA: Blackwell Publishers, 2000.

Levenback, Karen. *Virginia Woolf and the Great War*. Syracuse, NY: Syracuse University Press, 1999.

Levi-Strauss, Claude. *The Savage Mind*. Chicago: University of Chicago Press, 1966.

Lindqvist, Sven. *A History of Bombing*. Trans. Linda Haverty Rugg. New York: New Press, 2000.

Linnett, Maren. "The Jew in the Bath: Imperiled Imagination in Woolf's *The Years*." *Modern Fiction Studies* 48, no. 2 (2002): 341–61.

Lobell, Steven. *The Challenge of Hegemony: Grand Strategy, Trade, and Domestic Politics*. Ann Arbor: University of Michigan Press, 2003.

Louis, William. Roger. *Ends of British Imperialism: The Scramble for Empire, Suez, and Decolonization*. London: I. B. Tauris, 2007.

Love, Heather. "Close but not Deep: Literary Ethics and the Descriptive Turn." *New Literary History* 41, no. 2 (2010): 371–91.

——. "Close Reading and Thin Description." *Public Culture* 25, no. 3 (2013): 401–34.

Lukács, Georg. *Essays on Realism*. Ed. Rodney Livingston. Trans. David Fernbach. Cambridge, MA: MIT Press, 1980.

——. *The Historical Novel*. Trans. Hannah and Stanley Mitchell. London: Merlin Press, 1962.

——. *Studies in European Realism*. Trans. Edith Bone. New York: Grosset and Dunlap, 1964.

MacClancey, Jeremy. "Brief Encounter: The Meeting, in Mass-Observation, of British Surrealism and Popular Anthropology." *Journal of the Royal Anthropological Institute*. 1, no. 3 (1995): 495–512.

MacInnes, Colin. *Absolute Beginners*. 1959. Reprint, London: Allison & Busby, 2011.

——. *England, Half English*. New York: Random House, 1961.

MacKay, Marina. *Modernism and World War II*. New York: Cambridge University Press, 2007.

——. "'Is your journey really necessary?' Going Nowhere in Late Modernist London." *PMLA* 125, no. 5 (October 2009): 1600–1613.

MacNeice, Louis. *Collected Poems*. Ed. Peter McDonald. London: Faber and Faber, 2007.

Madge, Charles. "The Meaning of Surrealism." *New Verse* 10 (1934): 13–15.

——. "Poetic Description and Mass Observation." *New Verse* 24 (1937): 1–6.

——. "Poetry and Politics." *New Verse* 3 (1933): 1–4.

——. Review of *A Short Survey of Surrealism*. *New Verse* 18 (1935): 20–21.

——. "Surrealism for the English." *New Verse* 6 (1933): 14–18.

Malinowski Bronislaw. "A Nation-Wide Intelligence Service." In *First Year's Work: 1937–1938*. By Mass Observation. Ed. by Tom Harrisson and Charles Madge, 83–121. London: Lindsay Drummond, 1938.

Manson, Janet M. "Leonard Woolf as an Architect of the League of Nations." *South Carolina Review* (2007): 1–13.

Mao, Douglas, and Rebecca L. Walkowitz. "The New Modernist Studies." *PMLA* 123, no. 3 (2008): 737–48.

Marcus, Laura. "The Creative Treatment of Actuality." In *Intermodernism: Literary Culture in Mid-Twentieth Century Britain*, ed. Kristin Bluemel. Edinburgh: Edinburgh University Press, 2011.

——. "Introduction: The Project of Mass-Observation," *New Formations* 44 (Autumn 2011): 5–19.

Marks, Peter. "Illusion and Reality: The Spectre of Socialist Realism in Thirties Literature." In *Rewriting the Thirties: Modernism and After*, ed. Steven Matthews and Keith Williams, 22–36. London: Longman, 1997.

Marshall, Gail, ed. *The Cambridge Companion to the Fin De Siècle*. Cambridge: Cambridge University Press, 2007.

Marshall, T. H. "Citizenship and Social Class." In *Citizenship and Social Class and Other Essays*, 1–85. London: Cambridge University Press, 1950.

Marwick, Arthur. *Britain in the Century of Total War*. Boston: Little, Brown, 1968.

——. *A History of the Modern British Isles, 1914–1999: Circumstances, Events, and Outcomes*. Oxford: Wiley-Blackwell, 2000.

Marx, Karl. *Capital*, vol. 1. Trans. Ben Fowkes. New York: Penguin, 1990.

Mawby, Spencer. *Ordering Independence: The End of Empire in the Anglophone Caribbean, 1947–69*. New York: Palgrave Macmillan, 2012.

Mbembe, Achille. "Necropolitics." *Public Culture* 15, no. 1 (Winter 2003): 11–40.

McCormack, W. J. *Dissolute Characters: Irish Literary History Through Balzac, Sheridan Le Fanu, Yeats, and Bowen*. Manchester: Manchester University Press, 1993.

——. "Irish Gothic and After 1820–1945." In *The Field Day Anthology of Irish Writing*, ed. Seamus Deane, 832–54. Derry: Field Day Press, 1991.

McHale, Brian. *Postmodernist Fiction*. New York: Metheun, 1987.

McKary, Robert. *Half the Battle: Civilian Morale in Britain During the Second World War*. Manchester: Manchester University Press, 2002.

McLeod, John. *Postcolonial London: Rewriting the Metropolis*. New York: Routledge, 2004.

Mei-Shih, Shu. *The Lure of the Modern: Writing Modernism in Semicolonial China, 1917–1937*. Berkeley: University of California Press, 2001.

Mellor, David. "'And Oh! The Stench': Spain, the Blitz, Abjection, and the Shelter Drawings." In *Henry Moore*, ed. Chris Stephens, 52–65. London: Tate Publishing.

Mellor, Leo. *Reading the Ruins: Modernism, Bombsites, and British Culture*. Cambridge: Cambridge University Press, 2011.

Mendelson, Edward. *Early Auden*. Cambridge: Harvard University Press, 1983.

——. *The Complete Works of W. H. Auden: Prose and Travel Books in Prose and Verse*. Volume 1, *1926–1938*. Princeton, NJ: Princeton University Press, 1997.

Mengham, Rod. *The Idiom of the Time: The Writings of Henry Green*. Cambridge: Cambridge University Press, 1982.

Meyers, Jeffrey. *Orwell: Wintry Conscience of a Generation*. New York: Norton, 2000.

Miles, Robert. *Gothic Writing, 1750–1820: A Genealogy*. Manchester: Manchester University Press, 2002.

Miller, Andrew H. *Novels Behind Plate-Glass: Commodity Culture and Victorian Narrative*. Cambridge: Cambridge University Press, 1995.

Miller, Joshua L. *Accented America: The Cultural Politics of Multilingual Modernism*. Oxford: Oxford University Press, 2011.

Miller, Kristine A. *British Literature of the Blitz: Fighting the People's War*. London: Palgrave, 2009.

Miller, Tyrus. *Late Modernism: Politics, Fiction, and the Arts Between the World Wars*. Berkeley: University of California Press, 1999.

——. "Documentary/Modernism: Convergence and Complementarity in the 1930s." *Modernism/Modernity* 9, no. 2 (April 2002): 226–41.

Mitchell, W. J. T. "The Commitment to Form; or, Still Crazy After All These Years." *PMLA* 118, no. 2 (March 2003): 321–25.

Monteath, Peter. *Writing the Good Fight: Political Commitment in the International Literature of the Spanish Civil War*. Westport, CT: Greenwood Press, 1994.

Montefiore, Janet. *Men and Women Writers of the 1930s: The Dangerous Flood of History*. New York: Routledge, 1996.

Moore, Henry. *Henry Moore: Writings and Conversations*. Ed. Alan Wilkinson. Berkeley: University of California Press, 2002.

——. *A Shelter Sketchbook*. London: British Museum Publications, 1988.

Moretti, Franco. *Graphs, Maps, Trees*. New York: Verso Books, 2005.

Moynahan, Julian. *Anglo-Irish: The Literary Imagination in a Hyphenated Culture*. Princeton, NJ: Princeton University Press, 1995.

Murray, Gilbert. *From the League to UN*. London: Oxford University Press, 1948.

——. *An Unfinished Autobiography with Contributions by His Friends*. London: Allen and Unwind, 1960.

Neff, Stephen C. *War and the Law of Nations: A General History*. Cambridge: Cambridge University Press, 2005.

Nemerov, Alexander. "The Flight of Form: Auden, Bruegel, and the Turn to Abstraction in the 1940s." *Critical Inquiry* 31, no. 4 (Summer 2005): 780–810.

Nichols, Bill. "Documentary Film and the Modernist Avant-Garde." *Critical Inquiry* 27, no. 4 (Summer 2001): 580–610.

Nasta, Susheila. "'Voyaging In': Colonialism and Migration." In *The Cambridge History of Twentieth-Century English Literature*, ed. Laura Marcus and Peter Nicholls, 563–82. Cambridge: Cambridge University Press, 2004.

Norris, Margot. *Writing War in the Twentieth Century*. Charlottesville: University of Virginia Press, 2000.

North, Michael. *The Dialect of Modernism: Race, Language, and Twentieth-Century Literature*. New York: Oxford University Press, 1998.

——. *Henry Green and the Writing of His Generation*. Charlottesville: University of Virginia Press, 1988.

——. "World War II: The City in Ruins." In *The Cambridge History of Twentieth-Century English Literature*, eds. Laura Marcus and Peter Nicholls, 436–51 Cambridge: Cambridge University Press, 2004.

Northedge, F. S. *The League of Nations: Its Life and Times, 1920–1946*. Leicester: Leicester University Press, 1986.

Olson, Liesl. "Everyday Life Studies: A Review." *Modernism/Modernity* 18, no. 1 (January 2011): 175–80.

——. *Modernism and the Ordinary*. Oxford: Oxford University Press, 2009.

Ong, Aihwa. *Flexible Citizenship: The Cultural Logics of Transnationality*. Durham, NC: Duke University Press, 1999.

Orwell, George. *The Collected Essays, Journalism, and Letters of George Orwell*, ed. Sonia Orwell and Ian Angus. Book 1, *An Age Like This 1920–1940*. Boston: David R. Godine, 2000.

——. *The Collected Essays, Journalism and Letters of George Orwell*, ed. Sonia Orwell and Ian Angus. Book 2, *My Country Right or Left 1940–1943*. Boston: David R. Godine, 2000.

——. *Homage to Catalonia*. New York: Harcourt Brace Jovanovich, 1952.

Owen, Wilfred. "Dulce et decorum est." In *The War Poems of Wilfred Owen*, ed. Jon Stallworthy, 29–30. London: Chatto & Windus, 1994.

Page, Kezia. *Transnational Negotiations in Caribbean Diasporic Literature: Remitting the Text*. New York: Routledge, 2010.

Paul, Kathleen. *Whitewashing Britain: Race and Citizenship in the Postwar Era*. Ithaca, NY: Cornell University Press, 1997.

Phillips, Caryl. "Kingdom of the Blind." *Guardian*, July 16, 2004. Accessed July 2, 2012. http://www.theguardian.com/books/2004/jul/17/featuresreviews.guardianreview1.

Phillips, Mike, and Trevor Phillips. *Windrush: The Irresistible Rise of Multi-Racial Britain*. London: HarperCollins, 1999.

Philpott, Trevor. "Would You Let Your Daughter Marry a Negro?" *Picture Post*, October 30, 1954.

Pilkington, Edward. *Beyond the Mother Country: West Indians and the Notting Hill White Riots*. London: I. B. Tauris, 1990.

Pocock, David. Afterword to *May the Twelfth: Mass Observation Day Surveys*, by Humphrey Jennings and Charles Madge. London: Faber and Faber, 1987.

Plain, Gill. "Women Writers and the War," in *The Cambridge Companion to the Literature of World War II*, ed. Marina Mackay, 165–78. Cambridge: Cambridge University Press, 2009.

Pope-Hennessy, James, and Cecil Beaton. *History Under Fire: 52 Photographs of Air Raid Damage to London Buildings, 1940–41*. London: B. T. Batsford, 1941.

Priestley, J. B. *Out of the People*. London: Heinemann & Collins, 1941.

Procter, James. *Dwelling Places: Postwar Black British Writing*. Manchester: Manchester University Press, 2003.

Punter, David. *The Literature of Terror: A History of Gothic Fictions from 1765 to the Present Day*. Vol. 2, *The Modern Gothic*. New York: Longman, 1996.

Raine, Kathleen. *The Land Unknown*. New York: George Braziller, 1975.

Ramchand, Kenneth. "Sam Selvon Talking: A Conversation with Kenneth Ramchand." In *Critical Perspectives on Sam Selvon*, ed. Susheila Nasta, 95–103. Washington, DC: Three Continents Press, 1988.

——. *The West Indian Novel and Its Background*. London: Heinemann, 1983.

Rancière, Jacques. *Aesthetics and Its Discontents*. Trans. Steven Corcoran. Malden, MA: Polity, 2009.

——. *Dissensus: On Politics and Aesthetics*. Trans. Steven Corcoran. London: Continuum, 2010.

——. *The Politics of Aesthetics*. Trans. Gabriel Rockhill. New York: Continuum, 2006.

——. *Politics of Literature*. Trans. Julie Rose. Malden, MA: Polity, 2011.

Randall, Bryony. *Modernism, Daily Time and Everyday Life*. Cambridge: Cambridge University Press, 2011.

——. "Modernist Literature and the Everyday," *Literature Compass* 7, no. 9 (2010): 824–35.

Rawlinson, Mark. *British Writing of the Second World War*. New York: Oxford University Press, 2000.

Ray, Paul C. *The Surrealist Movement in England*. Ithaca, NY: Cornell University Press, 1971.

Read, Herbert. "Art in an Electric Atmosphere." *Horizon*, January–June 1941, 309.

——. *Britain at War*. Ed. Monroe Wheeler. New York: Museum of Modern Art, 1941.

Reid, Vic. *New Day*. New York: Knopf, 1949.

Remarque, Erich Maria. *All Quiet on the Western Front*. Trans. A. W. Wheen. New York: Ballantine, 1982.

Remy, Michel. *Surrealism in England*. London: Ashgate, 1999.

Rich, Paul B. *Race and Empire in British Politics*. Cambridge: Cambridge University Press, 1990.

Riquelme, John Paul. "Introduction: Toward a History of Gothic and Modernism: Dark Modernity from Bram Stoker to Samuel Beckett." *Modern Fiction Studies* 46, no. 3 (Fall 2000): 585–605.

Robbins, Bruce. "Blaming the System." In *Immanuel Wallerstein and the Problem of the World: System, Scale, Culture*, ed. David Palumbo-Liu, Bruce Robbins, and Nirvana Tanoukhi, 41–63. Durham, NC: Duke University Press, 2011.

Rogers, Gayle. *Modernism and the New Spain: Britain, Cosmopolitan Europe, and Literary History*. Oxford: Oxford University Press, 2012.

Rooney, Ellen. "Form and Contentment." *Modern Language Quarterly* 61, no. 1 (2000): 17–40.

Rose, Sonya. *Which People's War? National Identity and Citizenship in Britain, 1939–1945*. Oxford: Oxford University Press, 2003.

Rotha, Paul. *Documentary Diary*. New York: Hill and Wang, 1973.

——. *Documentary Film*. London: Faber and Faber, 1935.

——. *Documentary Film*, 3rd ed. 1952. Reprint, London: Faber and Faber, 1963.

Rush, Anne Spry. *Bonds of Empire: West Indians and Britishness from Victoria to Decolonization*. New York: Oxford University Press, 2011.

Sabin, Margery. "The Truths of Experience: Orwell's Nonfiction of the 1930s." In *The Cambridge Companion to George Orwell*, ed. John Rodden, 43–58. Cambridge: Cambridge University Press, 2007.

Said, Edward. *Culture and Imperialism*. New York: Knopf, 1993.

Saint-Amour, Paul. "Air War Prophecy and Interwar Modernism." *Comparative Literature Studies* 42, no. 2 (2005): 130–61.

Salkey, Andrew. *Escape to an Autumn Pavement*. Leeds: Peepal Tree Press, 2009.

Sandhu, Sukhdev. *London Calling: How Black and Asian Writers Imagined a City*. London: Harper Perennial, 2004.

Sassen, Saskia. *Guests and Aliens*. New York: New Press, 2000.

——. *Territory, Authority, Rights: From Medieval to Global Assemblages*. Princeton, NJ: Princeton University Press, 2008.

Schmitt, Carl. *The Concept of the Political*. Trans. George Schwab. Chicago: University of Chicago Press, 1996.

——. *The Nomos of the Earth in the International Law of Jus Publicum Europaeum*. Trans. G. L. Umen. New York: Telos Press Publishing, 2003.

——. *Political Theology: Four Chapters on the Concept of Sovereignty*. Trans. George Schwab. Chicago: University of Chicago Press, 1985.

Schoenbach, Lisi. *Pragmatic Modernism*. Oxford: Oxford University Press, 2011.

Schweizer, Bernard. *Radicals on the Road*. Charlottesville: University of Virginia Press, 2001.

Scott, George. *The Rise and Fall of the League of Nations*. New York: MacMillan, 1974.

Sebald, W. G. *Austerlitz*. Trans. Anthea Bell. New York: Modern Library, 2001.

——. *On the Natural History of Destruction*. Trans. Anthea Bell. New York: Modern Library, 2004.

Sedgwick, Eve Kosofsky. *Coherence of Gothic Conventions*. New York: Metheun, 1986.

Selvon, Samuel. *A Brighter Sun*. New York: Longman, 2006.

——. *The Lonely Londoners*. 1956. Reprint, New York: Longman, 1989.

——. "Samuel Selvon: Interviews and Conversations." In *Critical Perspectives on Sam Selvon*, ed. Susheila Nasta, 64–76. Washington, DC: Three Continents Press, 1988.

"Shelter Life." *Picture Post*, October 26, 1940.

Sheringham, Michael. *Everyday Life: Theories and Practices from Surrealism to the Present*. Oxford: Oxford University Press, 2009.

Sherman, Stuart. *Telling Time: Clocks, Diaries, and English Diurnal Form, 1660–1785*. Chicago: University of Chicago Press, 1996.

Sherry, Vincent. "Modernism Under Review: Edmund Wilson's *Axel's Castle: A Study in the Imaginative Literature of 1870–1930*." *Modernist Cultures* 7 (2012): 145–59.

Shuttleworth, Antony. "In a Populous City: Isherwood in the Thirties." In *The Isherwood Century: Essays on the Life and Work of Christopher Isherwood*, ed. James Berg and Christopher Freeman, 150–61. Madison: University of Wisconsin Press, 2000.

——. "The Real George Orwell: Dis-Simulation in *Homage to Catalonia* and *Coming up for Air*." In *And in Our Time: Vision, Revision, and British Writing of the 1930s*, ed. Antony Shuttleworth, 204–20. Lewisburg, PA: Bucknell University Press, 2003.

Sinfield, Alan. *Literature, Politics and Culture in Postwar Britain*. New York: Continuum, 2004.

Smith, Malcolm. "Narrative and Ideology in *Listen to Britain*." In *Narrative: From Malory to Motion Pictures*, ed. Jeremy Hawthord, 145–57. London: Edward Arnold, 1985.

Snaith, Anna. *Virginia Woolf: Public and Private Negotiations*. Hampshire, UK: Palgrave, 2000.

Somers, Margaret. *Genealogies of Citizenship: Markets, Statelessness, and the Right to Have Rights*. Cambridge: Cambridge University Press, 2008.

Spears, Monroe K. *The Poetry of W. H. Auden: The Disenchanted Island*. Oxford: Oxford University Press, 1963.

Spender, Stephen. *The Destructive Element: A Study of Modern Writers and Beliefs*. London: Jonathan Cape, 1935.

——. *The New Realism: A Discussion*. London: Hogarth Press, 1939.

——. *The Thirties and After: Poetry, Politics, People 1933–1970*. New York: Random House, 1967.

——. *War Pictures by British Artists*, 2nd series, no. 4: *Air Raids*. London: Oxford University Press, 1943.

——. *World Within World: An Autobiography of Stephen Spender*. London: Faber & Faber, 1977.

Spender, Stephen, and John Lehmann, eds. *Poems for Spain*. London: Hogarth Press, 1939.

Sperber, Murray A., ed. *And I Remember Spain: A Spanish Civil War Anthology*. New York: Collier Books, 1974.

Squier, Susan Merrill. *Communities of the Air: Radio Century, Radio Culture*. Durham, NC: Duke University Press, 2003.

Stollery, Martin. *Alternative Empires: European Modernist Cinemas and Cultures of Imperialism*. Exeter: University of Exeter Press, 2000.

Stonebridge, Lyndsey. *The Writing of Anxiety: Imagining Wartime in Mid-Century British Culture*. London: Palgrave, 2007.

Suárez, Juan A. *Pop Modernism: Noise and the Reinvention of the Everyday*. Urbana: University of Illinois Press, 2007.

Suh, Judy. *Fascism and Anti-fascism in Twentieth-Century British Fiction*. New York: Palgrave Macmillan, 2009.

Swann, Paul. *The British Documentary Film Movement, 1926–1946*. Cambridge: Cambridge University Press, 2008.

Tallents, Sir Stephen. *The Projection of England*. London: Olen Press, 1932.

Tanoukhi, Nirvana. "The Scale of World Literature." In *Immanuel Wallerstein and the Problem of the World*, ed. David Palumbo-Liu, Bruce Robbins, and Nirvana Tanoukhi, 78–98. Durham, NC: Duke University Press, 2011.

Tichelar, Michael. "The Conflict over Property Rights During the Second World War: The Labour Party's Abandonment of Land Nationalization." *Twentieth Century British History* 14, no. 2 (2003): 165–88.

——. "The Labour Party, Agricultural Policy and the Retreat from Land Nationalisation During the Second World War." *Agricultural History Review* 51 (2003): 209–25

Tilly, Charles. *Coercion, Capital, and European States, AD 990–1992*. Cambridge, MA: Blackwell, 1992.

Traverso, Enzo. *The Origins of Nazi Violence*. Trans. Janet Lloyd. New York: New Press, 2003.

Valente, Joseph. *Dracula's Crypt: Bram Stoker, Irishness, and the Question of Blood*. Urbana: University of Illinois Press, 2001.

van Hensbergen, Gijs. *Guernica: The Biography of a Twentieth-Century Icon*. New York: Bloomsbury, 2004.

Walkowitz, Rebecca. *Cosmopolitan Style: Modernism Beyond the Nation*. New York: Columbia University Press, 2007.

Wallace, Diana. *The Woman's Historical Novel: British Women Writers, 1900–2000*. New York: Palgrave Macmillan, 2008.

Wallerstein, Immanuel. *Geopolitics and Geoculture: Essays on the Changing World System*. Cambridge: Cambridge University Press, 1991.

——. *The Modern World System IV: Centrist Liberalism Triumphant, 1789–1914*. Berkeley: University of California Press, 2011.

——. *World Systems Analysis: An Introduction*. Durham, NC: Duke University Press, 2004.

Walpole, Hugh. "The Historical Novel in England Since Sir Walter Scott." In *Sir Walter Scott To-Day: Some Retrospective Essays and Studies*, ed. H. J. C. Grierson. London: Constable & Co., 1932.

Walters, F. P. *A History of the League of Nations*. London: Oxford University Press, 1965.

Warner-Lewis, Maureen. "Language Use in West Indian Literature." In *A History of Literature in the Caribbean*, vol. 2., ed. Albert James Arnold, Julio Rodríguez-Luis, and J. Michael Dash, 25–37. Philadelphia: John Benjamins, 1994.

Webster, Wendy. *Englishness and Empire 1939–1965*. New York: Oxford University Press, 2007

——. *Imagining Home: Gender, Race, and National Identity, 1945–1964*. London: UCL Press, 1998.

Weihman, Lisa. "Virginia Woolf's "Harum-Scarum" Irish Wife: Gender and National Identity in *The Years*." *Comparative Critical Studies* 4, no. 1 (2007): 37–50.

Weitz, Eric D. *Weimar Germany: Promise and Tragedy*. Princeton, NJ: Princeton University Press, 2007.

West, Rebecca. "The Necessity and Grandeur of the International Ideal," in *A Challenge to Death*, ed. Storm Jameson, 240–60. London: Constable & Co., 1934.

White, Hayden. *Figural Realism: Studies in the Mimesis Effect*. Baltimore: Johns Hopkins University Press, 1999.

Whittier-Ferguson, John. "Repetition, Remembering, Repetition: Virginia Woolf's Late Fiction and the Return of War." *Modern Fiction Studies* 57, no. 2 (2011): 230–53.

Wilde, Alan. *Christopher Isherwood*. New York: Twayne Publishers, 1971.

——. *Horizons of Assent: Modernism, Postmodernism, and the Ironic Imagination*. Philadelphia: University of Pennsylvania Press, 1987.

Winkiel, Laura, and Laura Doyle, eds. *Geomodernism: Race, Modernism, Modernity*. Bloomington: Indiana University Press, 2005.

Winston, Brian. *Claiming the Real II: Documentary: Grierson and Beyond*. New York: Palgrave, 2008.

Wolin, Richard. *Walter Benjamin: An Aesthetic of Redemption*. Berkeley: University of California Press, 1994.

Wollaeger, Mark. *Modernism, Media, and Propaganda: British Narrative from 1900 to 1945*. Princeton, NJ: Princeton University Press, 2006.

Wollaeger, Mark, and Matt Eatough, eds. *The Oxford Handbook of Global Modernisms*. New York: Oxford University Press, 2011.

Woolf, Leonard. *Barbarians at the Gate*. London: Victor Gollancz, 1939.

——. *Beginning Again: An Autobiography of the Years 1911–1918*. London: Hogarth Press, 1964.

——. *Collected Essays*, vol. 2. London: Hogarth Press, 1967.

——. *Collected Essays*, vol. 4. New York: Harcourt Brace Jovanovich, 1967.

——. *International Government*. London: Fabian Society, 1916.

Woolf, Virginia. *Between the Acts*. New York: Harcourt Brace Jovanovich, 1941.

——. *The Diary of Virginia Woolf*, 5 vols. Ed. Anne Oliver Bell. New York: Harcourt Brace Jovanovich, 1978.

——. *The Letters of Virginia Woolf*, 6 vols. Ed. Nigel Nicolson and Joanna Trautman. London: Hogarth Press, 1975–80.

——. *Moments of Being*. New York: Harcourt Brace Jovanovich, 1985.

——. *Mrs. Dalloway*. New York: Harcourt Brace Jovanovich, 1925.

——. "The Novels of Turgenev." In *The Captain's Deathbed and Other Essays*. New York: Harcourt Brace Jovanovich, 1973.

——. *The Pargiters*. Ed. Mitchell Leaska. New York: Harcourt Brace Jovanovich, 1977.

———. "Solid Objects." In *The Complete Shorter Fiction of Virginia Woolf*. Ed. Susan Dick. London: Hogarth Press, 1989.

———. *Three Guineas*. New York: Harcourt Brace Jovanovich, 1938.

———. *To the Lighthouse*. New York: Harcourt Brace, 1981.

———. *A Writer's Diary*. New York: Harcourt Brace Jovanovich, 1973.

———. *The Years*. New York: Harcourt Brace Jovanovich, 1939.

Wordsworth, William. *Selected Poems*. New York: Penguin Classics, 2005.

Wright, Basil. *Song of Ceylon* [Video, 1934]. Retrieved April 5, 2015, from www.colonialfilm.org .uk/node/486/.

Yearwood, Peter J. *Guarantee of Peace: The League of Nations in British Policy 1914–1925*. Oxford: Oxford University Press, 2005.

Yeazell, Ruth Bernard. *Art of the Everyday: Dutch Painting and the Realist Novel*. Princeton, NJ: Princeton University Press, 2009.

Yeh, Wen-hsin, ed. *Wartime Shanghai*. New York: Routledge, 1998.

Ziarek, Krzysztof. *The Force of Art*. Stanford, CA: Stanford University Press, 2004.

Ziegler, Philip. *London at War*. New York: Knopf, 1995.

Zwerdling, Alex. *Orwell and the Left*. New Haven, CT: Yale University Press, 1974.

———. *Virginia Woolf and the Real World*. Berkeley: University of California Press, 1987.

INDEX

Page numbers in *italics* indicate illustrations.

occupation of, 21, 75; "externality" and,
11; historical novel and, 22–23, 68, 72, 82;
Hogarth Press of, 93; New Burlington
Galleries exhibit and, 139; presented as
left-wing radical, 247n22; on progress and
repetition, 68; realism and, 13, 77; suffrage
movement and, 249n48; world-systemic
disorder and, 195, 198
Woolf, Virginia, works of: *Between the Acts*,
74; *Jacob's Room*, 74, 80; *Mrs. Dalloway*, 4, 6, 7, 8, 60, 74; "A Sketch of the
Past," 77; "Solid Objects," 248n37; *Three
Guineas*, 68, 74; *To the Lighthouse*, 74,
77–78, 82, 89; *The Waves*, 60, 74. See also
Years, The
Work in Progress (Joyce), 52
World Film News, 27, 28, 34
world-system, British, 2, 14, 18, 24, 108, 225;
Anglo-Ireland and, 264n82; balance of
power and, 106; empire as world-system,
4, 14, 16; form and, 20; liberal norms
of, 22; philosophies of progress and, 23;
poswar shift to American-centered system,
185, 186, 187; structural transformation in,
19; waning of, 91
world-systemic disorder, 17, 21, 135; everyday
life as mediated expression of, 4, 5–6, 105,
118; as opportunity for colonized people,
195, 198
World War, First (the Great War), 79–82,
92, 96, 245n119, 253n22; colonial wars as
anticipation of, 110; at end of geopolitical
golden era, 108, 253n25; gothic genre and,
145–46; international law and, 111–12; just

war doctrine and, 116–17; Second World
War as return of, 176–77, 178
World War, Second, 14, 16, 58, 173; Anglo-
Irish gothic as mediation of, 174; destruction of cities in, 50; documentary film
during, 39, 43–46; emergency powers
legislation and, 62–64; gothic genre
and, 144; literature of, 21; turning point
of, 46; war art exhibitions, 147–48. *See
also* People's War ideology; Sino-Japanese
war
Wright, Basil, 22, 40–43, 47; *Song of Ceylon*
(film), 22, 40–43, 45, 105, 241n52
Wright, Frank Lloyd, 35

Years, The (Woolf), 22–23, 67, 68, 173; dreams
and fantasies in, 82–91; early success of,
247n23; as eulogy for narrative of historical progress, 92; everyday objects in, 78,
248n37; gender politics in, 248n33; *Goodbye to Berlin* contrasted with, 92; history
and everyday life in, 74–82; as "picture
of society as a whole," 69; realism of, 72;
recursive historicism in, 103, 104; status as
historical novel, 73
Yeats, W. B., 7
Yeazell, Ruth Bernard, 13, 233n9; *Art of the
Everyday*, 13
Yeh, Wen-hsin, 136
Young, Edward, 53
Youngs, Tim, 131
youth culture, 190, 206, 219, 222

Zuloaga, Ignacio, 259n95